Affirmative Action in Malaysia and South Africa

Malaysia and South Africa implement the most extensive affirmative action programmes worldwide. This book explores why and how to effect preferential treatment which has been utilized in the pursuit of inter-ethnic parity, specifically in higher education, high-level occupations, enterprise development and wealth ownership. Through methodical and critical analyses of data on education, workforce and population, the book evaluates the primary objectives of increasing majority representation in education, employment, enterprise and ownership.

The book also critically considers questions of the attainments and limitations of ethnic preferential treatment in reducing disparity, the challenges of developing capability and reducing dependency and the scope for policy reforms.

Hwok-Aun Lee is Senior Fellow at the ISEAS-Yusof Ishak Institute, Singapore.

Routledge Research in Public Administration and Public Policy

Corruption Prevention and Governance in Hong Kong
Ian Scott and Ting Gong

Judicializing the Administrative State
The Rise of the Independent Regulatory Commissions in the United States, 1883–1937
Hiroshi Okayama

State Politics and the Affordable Care Act
Choices and Decisions
Edited by John Charles Morris, Martin K. Mayer, II, Robert C. Kenter and Luisa M. Lucero

The Transformative Potential of Participatory Budgeting
Creating an Ideal Democracy
George Robert Bateman Jr

City Sextons
Tales from Municipal Leaders
Staci M. Zavattaro

Multiorganizational Arrangements for Watershed Protection
Working Better Together
John Charles Morris and Madeleine Wright McNamara

Affirmative Action in Malaysia and South Africa
Preference for Parity
Hwok-Aun Lee

For more information about this series, please visit: www.routledge.com/ Routledge-Research-in-Public-Administration-and-Public-Policy/book-series/ RRPAPP

Affirmative Action in Malaysia and South Africa

Preference for Parity

Hwok-Aun Lee

LONDON AND NEW YORK

First published 2021
by Routledge
2 Park Square, Milton Park, Abingdon, Oxon OX14 4RN

and by Routledge
52 Vanderbilt Avenue, New York, NY 10017

Routledge is an imprint of the Taylor & Francis Group, an informa business

British Library Cataloguing-in-Publication Data
A catalogue record for this book is available from the British Library

Library of Congress Cataloging-in-Publication Data
A catalog record for this book has been requested

ISBN: 978-1-138-08007-2 (hbk)
ISBN: 978-1-315-11407-1 (ebk)

Typeset in Galliard
by Apex CoVantage, LLC

To Jacqui, Kieran, Naomi and Ezra, whose love, grace and zest sustained this endeavour

To the memory of my father and mother, who first got me thinking

Contents

Figures

Tables

Foreword

With this book Hwok-Aun Lee has filled a major gap in the literature on race-based affirmative action, which he correctly views as designed to promote capability acquisition and upward social and economic mobility among marginalized racial or ethnic groups – not to address poverty in general. He has provided the first rigorously researched and comprehensive comparative study of affirmative action in the two major countries that have adopted policies designed to benefit disadvantaged *majorities*. These are Malaysia and South Africa, whose governments have sought to improve the status of Bumiputeras and blacks, respectively.

Much work has already been done to compare the experiences of different countries adopting affirmative action policies designed to aid disadvantaged *minorities*; the most prominent of such countries are India, the United States and Brazil. Such policies were first adopted, albeit on a small scale, in India (still under British rule) in the early 20th century. After India's independence in 1947, affirmative action in favour of the highly disadvantaged "scheduled castes" and "scheduled tribes" was written into the Indian constitution. It was applied in a centralized fashion throughout India, in the spheres of education, employment as well as political representation. In the United States a much more decentralized form of affirmative action in favour of African-Americans, Hispanic-Americans and Native Americans was started in the 1960s, primarily by many universities and by some federal government agencies. In Brazil affirmative action policies in favour of disadvantaged Afro-Brazilians and indigenous natives of Brazil were introduced much later, in the early 21st century, and in a similarly decentralized fashion they have been adopted primarily by higher-educational institutions. This book presents the first systematic comparative study of the important and quite different cases of Malaysia, which adopted affirmative action in the 1970s, and South Africa, whose affirmative action policies were introduced when the democratic movement led by the African National Congress finally gained power in the 1990s.

Lee's comparative research is impressive in both its breadth and its depth. He addresses the available evidence on affirmative action policies in several important spheres in which they have been applied: in higher education, in high-level employment and in private enterprise development and ownership. He examines carefully the differing affirmative action policy instruments applied in the two countries, contrasting Malaysia's more centralized approach with the decentralized policies of South Africa. And he musters a great deal of empirical evidence on the outcomes of those policies, which have proven to be very mixed – in different ways – in the two countries. Yet he concludes that in both of these countries the quantitative achievements have been significantly greater than qualitative ones.

Particularly insightful is Lee's discussion of the historical origins of affirmative action in Malaysia and in South Africa, which are among the few countries where it is embedded in the nation's constitution. Affirmative action policies in the two countries differ significantly with respect to both the nature of their constitutional foundation and their timing. As he points out, when Malaysia introduced its affirmative action policies in the 1970s, the wider world environment was relatively favourable to government intervention to guide the economy. On the other hand, when South Africa initiated its affirmative action policies in the 1990s, the wider world environment displayed much scepticism about governmental action and favoured market solutions to economic problems. This helps to explain the more centralized approach of Malaysia as compared with the more decentralized approach of South Africa's affirmative action instruments.

Throughout his analysis Lee displays a very sensitive understanding that affirmative action policies are likely to have both adverse and favourable effects. He is keenly aware that these policies – even at their best – generate costs as well as benefits, and he evaluates thoroughly the multiple consequences of different affirmative action policies in each country. Among his carefully argued conclusions is that it is critically important for the success of affirmative action in achieving its goal of raising the social and economic status of disadvantaged communities to focus attention on improving both the quantity and the quality of their education.

Thomas E. Weisskopf
Professor Emeritus of Economics, University of Michigan

Acknowledgements

This book grows out of a doctoral dissertation completed at the University of Massachusetts, Amherst, in August 2010. Although it has been thoroughly restructured, revised, updated and rewritten, credit for this eventual product must start flowing from the origins. My dissertation committee, through their guidance and counsel, helped lay the bedrock for this book. I thank the chair, Bob Pollin, for his critical comments, challenging questions and generous encouragement, Jerry Epstein for sharpening the focus and clarity along the way and James Heintz for consistently offering incisive and helpful feedback.

Towards the latter stages of the dissertation's progress, I had the distinct privilege of meeting Professor Thomas Weisskopf on his visit to Amherst. His published work provided important references, but face-to-face conversation crystallized my conceptual grasp and empirical handling of affirmative action. I thank Tom for his formative impact. It is no coincidence that his principal work on affirmative action is also a two-country study of India and the United States, specifically on higher education. While our scope and approach differ significantly, I have taken comfort in the precedent of a robust, insightful and scholarly book that unpacks affirmative action across a range of objectives and empirical evidence. And I appreciate his kind and measured foreword.

This endeavour was blessed with support, big and small, and opportunities to witness the countries being studied. A PERI (Political Economy Research Institute) Dissertation Fellowship, PERI Travel Grant and a short-term research grant from the University of Malaya provided the means for doing fieldwork in Malaysia in May–August 2007 and in South Africa from October 2007 to January 2008. I appreciate Seeraj Mohamed and the Corporate Strategy and Industrial Development unit at the University of the Witwatersrand for letting me set up base on their premises. I thank Seeraj, along with Ganief Bardien, Lumkile Mondi and Ntombikanina Malinga for their hospitality, generosity and enlightening conversations during my stay in Johannesburg and recall the kindness of Michael and Nelleke Elston, my hosts in Cape Town, with deep gratitude.

Completing graduate school was, of course, another necessary step. I benefited immensely from the friendship and collective spirit of economics graduate-student comrades, their spouses and families, North Village neighbours and a wider sustaining community. Some must be named: Adam Hersh and Dawn Le,

Mohammed Moeini and Maryam Amjadi, Florian Kaufmann and Katrin Maurer, Anders Fremstad and Janessa Landeck, Hasan Comert, Noah Enelow, Ben Zipperer, Luis Rosero, Phil Mellizo, Heidi Peltier and Martin Rapetti.

The dissertation took a slow passage to book publication. My energies were channelled to journal articles, book chapters and other research projects. The original analyses, based on household surveys of 1995–2004 in Malaysia and 1998–2006 in South Africa, became increasingly outdated. The work had been confined to affirmative action in higher education and employment, two out of four main policy sectors. Omission of enterprise development and wealth ownership became increasingly conspicuous.

New policy dogmas and agendas also emerged. The New Economic Model (NEM) of 2010 rousingly questioned Malaysia's affirmative action policies but in the process put misguided and incoherent notions of "reform" in the mainstream. The launch of the Bumiputera Economic Transformation Programme in 2012 seemingly contradicted those promises of reform. My research would need to get immersed in this stew of flux and confusion. Around the same time, South Africa was engrossed in policy debates with resulting realignments in national development, industrial policy and, of course, affirmative action – embodied in the 2013 amendments to employment equity and black economic empowerment legislation. Affirmative action policy was increasingly emphasized but continually faced practical challenges and social pushback, amidst chronic high unemployment and sluggish economic conditions, compounded by malfeasance in high office. To remain relevant to the contemporary situation of both countries, I needed to address the policy shifts, broaden the research project to cover all four policy sectors and update the empirical analysis. The labour has been fulfilling, and I hope the product makes a meaningful contribution to the literature.

I am indebted to workplaces that have furnished the space for ideas to brew and research to make its way. I am grateful to have been based at the Department of Development Studies, Faculty of Economics and Administration, University Malaya, in 2001–2004 when my prospective doctoral research subject germinated, and again in 2010–2016 when the impetus for this book took root. The Nikkei Asian Scholarship to visit the Japan Center for Economic Research in June–September 2013 was brief but timely, intervening when I needed a cloister to revisit the work. The ISEAS-Yusof Ishak Institute, my vocational home since 2017, has provided a collegial and fertile setting for the final legs of this long trek.

Research may sprout in solitude, but it flourishes in community and camaraderie, through conversation and debate. This book has imbibed insights and disputes from fellow students and observers of Malaysia and South Africa.

Friends, colleagues and associates have informed and challenged my thinking on this subject, pointed out data sources, detected gaps and flaws and collaborated on projects (in alphabetical order): Abdul Rahman Embong, Ahmad Fuad Rahmat, Ahmad Yazid Othman, Andrew Aeria, Azlan Awang, Cassey Lee, Christopher Choong, Francis Hutchinson, Greg Lopez, Helen Ting, Johan Saravanamuttu, Jomo KS, Kai Ostwald, Kamal Salih, Khoo Boo Teik, the late Khoo Kay Jin, KJ John, Lee Hock Guan, Lee Wang Yen, Liew Chin Tong, Lorraine

Carlos Salazar, Maznah Mohammed, Meredith Weiss, Mohan Ambikaipaker, Muhammed Abdul Khalid, Nicholas Chan, Nizam Mahshar, Nungsari Ahmad Radhi, Nurhisham Hussein, Ong Kian Ming, Ooi Kok Hin, Ragayah Mat Zin, Rajah Rasiah, Rama Ramanathan, Serina Rahman, Shankaran Nambiar, Sharaad Kuttan, Sumit Mandal, Syed Husin Ali, Tee Meng Yew, Terence Gomez, Tey Nai Peng, R. Thillainathan, Tricia Yeoh, VGR Chandran Govindaraju, Wan Chang Da, Wan Saiful Wan Jan Wong Chin Huat, Yin Shao Loong and Zouhair Rosli. I thank them for the many ways they have enabled and enriched, wittingly or otherwise, my understanding of Malaysia, a land that still intrigues, bewilders and confounds.

Among informants and interlocutors that have guided my novice academic journey through South Africa, I gratefully acknowledge Avinash Govindjee, Colin Reddy, Duma Gqubule, Fiona Tregenna, Ganief Bardien, Gerhard Maré, Glen Robbins, Hein Marais, Imraan Valodia, Lumkile Mondi, Nimrod Zalk, Roger Southall and Seeraj Muhammed. As an outsider to South Africa, my trepidation at publishing this work is tangibly allayed by the ways they have helped me grapple with this kaleidoscopic, complex and fascinating country.

I thank Lam Yong Ling and the Routledge team for steering this work to its final product.

Above all, my gratitude flows to Jacqui, for lovingly and patiently partnering in this work, as in life, and to Kieran, Naomi and Ezra, for making home a place of radiance, delight and refuge.

Abbreviations and terms

AA	affirmative action
Alliance	Malaysia's ruling coalition (1957–1969)
ANC	African National Congress
ASB	*Amanah Saham Bumiputera* (Bumiputera share trust)
ASN	*Amanah Saham Nasional* (national share trust)
AsgiSA	Accelerated and Shared Growth Initiative – South Africa
B40	bottom 40% of households (based on income)
BBBEE	Broad-Based Black Economic Empowerment
BCIC	Bumiputera Commercial and Industrial Community
BEE	black economic empowerment
BEC	Bumiputera Economic Community
BETR	Bumiputera Economic Transformation
Black	Broad race category including African, Coloured, Indian
BMF	Black Management Forum
BN	*Barisan Nasional*, National Front, Malaysia's ruling coalition (1971–2018)
Bumiputera	"Sons of the soil": Malays and indigenous peoples of East Malaysia
CEE	Commission on Employment Equity
CHE	Commission on Higher Education
COSATU	Congress of South African Trade Unions
DTI	Department of Trade and Industry
EAP	economically active population
EEA	Employment Equity Act
EER	employment equity report
ETP	Economic Transformation Programme
GEAR	Growth, Employment and Redistribution
GLC	government-linked company
GNU	Government of National Unity
GTP	Government Transformation Programme
HBI	historically black institution
HDI	historically disadvantaged individual
HWI	historically white institution

IDC	Industrial Development Corporation
IPAP	Industrial Policy Action Plan
JSE	Johannesburg Stock Exchange
KLSE	Kuala Lumpur Stock Exchange
LFS	Labour Force Survey
M40	middle 40% of households (based on income)
MARA	*Majlis Amanah Rakyat* (Council of Trust for the People)
MCA	Malaysian Chinese Association
MIC	Malaysian Indian Congress
MRSM	*Maktab Rendah Sains MARA* (MARA Junior Science College)
MYR	Malaysian Ringgit
NDP	National Development Policy
NEF	National Empowerment Fund
NEM	New Economic Model
NEP	New Economic Policy
NP	National Party
Orang Asli	indigenous peoples of Peninsular Malaysia
PH	*Pakatan Harapan*, Malaysia's ruling coalition (2018–2020)
PIC	Public Investment Corporation
PNB	*Permodalan Nasional Berhad* (National Equity Limited)
RDP	Reconstruction and Development Programme
SACP	South African Communist Party
SAIRR	South African Institute of Race Relations
SASAS	South African Social Attitudes Survey
SEDC	State Economic Development Corporation
SET	science, engineering and technology
SOC	state-owned company
SOE	state-owned entity/state-owned enterprise
T20	top 20% of households (based on income)
UMNO	United Malays National Organisation
ZAR	South African Rand

1   Preference for parity
Purposes, contexts and instruments of affirmative action

Malaysia and South Africa maintain the largest affirmative action (AA) regimes worldwide. Colonial and apartheid rule passed on systemic disadvantages and structural inequalities, manifested in severe group disparities in upper socio-economic strata. Specifically, the under-representation of Bumiputeras in Malaysia and blacks in South Africa in higher education, high-level occupations, enterprise development, and wealth and property ownership have compelled state action to promote the entry and participation of these groups. The magnitude of socio-economic disadvantage of the majority group, coupled with political power, gave rise to AA regimes that are deep-seated and wide-ranging. Race preferential programs are institutionalized and intensively pursued in Malaysia and South Africa, with change and revision over time.

The quest for parity through preferential policies is also fiercely debated, the positions of both defenders and detractors often heightened by varying senses of justice and injustice. As sometimes quipped, with affirmative action, everyone claims to be a victim: the beneficiary, of discrimination and exclusion in the past; the non-beneficiary, of discrimination and exclusion in the present. Of course, these operate in opposing directions and for different reasons, and they cannot be equated both in form and magnitude. The underlying remedial purpose and salutary principles of AA markedly differ from the pernicious legacies of structural exclusion and inequality – and in the case of apartheid, its oppressive, malevolent, dehumanizing forces. However, the pushback against AA, and underlying issues and grievances, should be acknowledged. Candour and empathy on all sides can help facilitate honest and constructive discourse on a polarizing subject.

Alongside correcting historical circumstances, AA also rests on its positive capacity in the present, through promoting more equitable representation, fostering cross-racial interaction and diversity in prominent positions and decision-making roles and raising the esteem of groups previously absent in these strata. Nonetheless, given the finitude of the opportunities being distributed, preference granted to one group inevitably attenuates, to varying extents, the amount available to others. Ultimately, the project of AA must manage contending interests.

Countries the world over practice affirmative action of some form. While there is no universal template, the discernible fundamental thrust is to increase participation of designated population groups in areas where they are under-represented.

Warikoo and Utaukwa's (2019) cross-country synthesis of AA in higher education across 20 countries includes Malaysia and South Africa with a cluster of countries for whom post-colonial (or other transition) nation-building conditions catalyzed a specific goal of "national unity," distinguished from other clusters in which social mobilization and inequality alleviation are more salient conditions and objectives.

The spheres and extents of intervention vary across countries, but in view of the problem at hand, groups tend to be under-represented in upper socio-economic strata, where barriers to entry prevail: higher education, high-level occupations, enterprise and wealth ownership. About one quarter of all countries, across all the continents, employ AA to promote equitable group representation in higher education (Jenkins and Moses 2014). In some countries, affirmative action promotes political representation. In most instances the beneficiary groups, especially where designated by race or ethnicity, are in the minority. Affirmative action based on gender, promoting women's advancement, reaches out to half the population. A smaller group of countries promote the advancement of a majority group, and within this exceptional crowd, Malaysia and South Africa stand out further for these striking semblances: upper middle-income economies, sizable and urbanized populations, established universities and fairly advanced industrial and financial sectors.

Affirmative action in Malaysia and South Africa is driven by immense socio-political pressures, undergirded by constitutional authorization, bolstered by the imperative of redressing wide and persistent racial disparities and broadened by the range of educational and economic opportunity available for distribution. By today's count, the Bumiputera in Malaysia comprise the politically predominant Malays and other indigenous groups, constituting 67% of the population, while the "black" category in South Africa, conventionally referring to Africans, Coloureds and Indians, make up 92% of the country's citizens (Table 1.1). Malaysia registered Gross National Income per capita of $10,700 in 2016, while South Africa touched $7,300, and their urban populations constituted 75% and 65% of national populations, respectively. These profiles contrast with Namibia and Fiji, two other countries noted for majority-favouring affirmative action, where GNI per capita is less than US$6,000, the urban population below 55%.

This book investigates the foundations, policy instruments and outcomes of affirmative action regimes in these two countries. I adopt the term *regime* to denote the vast, diverse and inter-related web of race-preferential programs under the AA rubric. This inquiry – encompassing the full range of policy sectors and programs – is motivated by the breadth of the regimes and some gaps in the literature. For all the commonalities that cause Malaysia and South Africa to be frequently mentioned together in the context of AA, there is surprisingly little research that systematically considers the policy's precise basis, purpose and design across multiple sectors of intervention. Rigorous and coherent cross-country comparisons are even scarcer.

In Malaysia, AA is often equated with the New Economic Policy (NEP), despite the incongruence of the latter being an all-encompassing development

Table 1.1 Malaysia and South Africa: Population, demography and national income

Population, total and percentage urban (2016)	
Malaysia	South Africa
31.2 million, 75.4% urban	55.9 million, 65.3% urban

Ethnic composition (percent of total population)			
Malaysia (2012[1])		South Africa (2017)	
Bumiputera	67.4	Black	92.1
Malay	*54.8*	*African*	*80.8*
Non-Malay	*12.9*	*Coloured*	*8.8*
Chinese	24.1	*Indian*	*2.5*
Indian	7.2	White	8.0
Other	0.9		

Gross National Income per capita (2016)[2]	
Malaysia	South Africa
US$10,727	US$7,294

Sources: Malaysia: Department of Statistics (2013b); South Africa: Population Quick Info (http://pqi.stats.gov.my), Statistics South Africa, Mid-year Population Estimates 2017 (www.statssa.gov.za/publications/P0302/P03022017.pdf); World Bank (http://data.worldbank.org.).

Notes
1 Most recently available with Bumiputera disaggrated to Malay and non-Malay.
2 Constant 2010 US$.

vision with AA as one of its mainstays. The poverty alleviation pillar of the NEP is, in turn, frequently conflated with the affirmative action pillar. Thus, much of the literature, even while applying the term *affirmative action*, deals with broader problems of socio-economic development and income inequality, rather than focusing on the specific interventions to allocate Bumiputera opportunity through race-preferential treatment.

In South Africa, extensive research and publication on income inequality, employment equity and black economic empowerment (BEE) are germane to affirmative action but, similar to the literature on Malaysia, often deal with secondary outcomes of the policy or study each sector in isolation from the others. Redress in higher education, employment equity in labour markets and BEE in enterprise development, while threaded together by common policy objectives and instruments, are rarely viewed as a large, interwoven policy tapestry. Even terminologies vary across the different policy spheres – transformation, redress, affirmative action, empowerment – but all essentially refer to the same objective of increasing black representation.

The ongoing, worldwide ferment around inequality of opportunity, capability and prosperity, and persistence of such inequalities delineated by race, ethnicity and gender, affirm the timeliness of this study. The fertile state of AA research speaks to the subject's currency. Affirmative action also recurs in the media and public discourses; the highly prominent and influential *New York Times* and *The Economist* have on occasion shone the spotlight on South Africa and Malaysia.[1] Midway between academia and journalism, Brown and Langer's (2015) *Foreign Affairs* article provided a concise survey and synthesis of affirmative action spanning a few countries, including Malaysia and South Africa.

Cross-country comparative studies have been in a season of flourish, with numerous compilations of essays on different countries and an assortment of affirmative action subjects.

Edited volumes with chapters on Malaysia and South Africa are most pertinent to this book, notably Brown, Stewart and Langer (2012), Gomez and Premdas (2013) and Dupper and Sankaran (2014). Other countries in these works include Brazil, India, Nigeria, Fiji, the United States, France, Mexico, Northern Ireland, Sri Lanka and Israel. Besides geographic diversity of these country cases, the literature also differs widely in topic, academic discipline, concept and methodology. These studies and reports approach AA from numerous angles: legal and constitutional underpinnings, political representation, social relations, economic opportunity and outcome, upward mobility, or a combination of these subject areas. Some volumes focus on one aspect of affirmative action, notably higher education (Jenkins and Moses 2014) and employment equity (Jain, Sloane and Horwitz 2003). South Africa features in both these publications, and Malaysia appears in the latter. Affirmative action has also warranted inclusion as a public policy aspect of employment practices in the International Labour Organisation's reports on workplace equality (ILO 2003, 2007), within which Malaysia and South Africa appear.

Somewhat more germane to this book, various two-country comparative studies have delved deeper into policy contents and outcomes, utilizing the opportunity presented by the narrower geographic scope to construct and apply a common framework across both cases. Weisskopf's (2004) analysis of the United States and India is particularly helpful as a conceptual and methodological reference, for the ways he assembles interdisciplinary tools and integrates a cost-benefit framework for evaluating affirmative action in higher education – encompassing various direct and indirect policy objectives and outcomes. Featherman, Hall and Krislov (2010), comparing the United States and South Africa, collate a rich array of essays focused on the direct policy consequences in higher education.

While some attention was fixed on Malaysia from South Africa during the mid-1990s, to inform the transition from apartheid to democracy, the two have scarcely been studied comparatively. This book recognizes research gaps in the underpinnings, operations, outcomes and implications of affirmative action in Malaysia and South Africa. My enquiry aims to contribute insight on the specific institutional makeup and policy instruments of affirmative action in both countries, which bear remarkable semblances and differences, and empirical findings of policy outcomes across all sectors of intervention – higher education, high-level employment, enterprise development and ownership. Malaysia and South Africa are on contrasting trajectories in some spheres, particularly in higher education and employment, but they are drawing closer in the area of enterprise development.

This book will address five questions:

1   What is affirmative action, and why do it?
2   How did affirmative action come about?
3   How is affirmative action implemented?
4   To what extent has affirmative action achieved its goals? To what extent has it fallen short?
5   Where does affirmative action go from here?

The following chapters probe these questions, elaborating on the main points summarized here.

1   What is affirmative action, and why do it?

Part 1, comprising Chapters 2 and 3, covers theory and history. Chapter 2 launches the study by laying conceptual foundations, setting out the meaning and scope of affirmative action. I draw on literature particularly relevant and helpful to this inquiry, fundamentally rooted in a specific problem and a consequent set of policy instruments addressing the problem. Identifying and framing the particular problems and policies is instrumental for specifying the directly relevant policy outcomes to be empirically evaluated.

Affirmative action stems from the principal problem of a disadvantaged group's under-representation in esteemed and influential positions. The case for preferential interventions arises where the under-representation of a population group in the major policy sectors – higher education, high-level employment, management and enterprise, and wealth and property ownership – derives from past discrimination and continuing disadvantage and is compounded by barriers to entry – for instance, entry grades, professional qualifications, work experience, networks and connections. It is socially undesirable and politically unsustainable for a group, whether identified by race, ethnicity, religion, gender or other category, to be persistently absent or minimally present in these strata.[2] Moreover, lack of diversity and inter-group interaction arguably erodes decision-making bodies' credibility and national integrity.

Under affirmative action, varying forms of preferential selection and special measures may arise, but their operation and reach go beyond anti-discrimination and equal opportunity laws, particularly where socio-economic circumstances and political pressures call for these disparities to be redressed more speedily and robustly. In principal, the policy is also justified as a transitory solution that becomes less needed as it progresses. The imperative of redressing these forms of inequality is concomitant with the necessity of implementing the policy productively and cumulatively. Ultimately, the goal is to broadly imbue beneficiaries with capability, competitiveness and confidence, such that preferential treatment, particularly in overt forms, becomes redundant. Like any policy, affirmative action presents potentialities and perils, consequences intended and unintended.

This academic exercise is necessarily inter-disciplinary, in line with the multiple dimensions of affirmative action. I consider the legal constitutional basis, policy framework, and the socio-economic objectives and outcomes. AA can designate minority groups or majority groups as beneficiaries – in line with the structure of disadvantage. Undoubtedly, majority-favouring regimes will differ in form and magnitude, and AA premised on race and ethnicity is especially impassioned and contentious. The socio-economic imperatives are greater when the disadvantaged constitute a demographic majority. Where the majority also holds political power, the pressures and legal mandates for preferential treatment may translate into wide-ranging, deep-seated and seemingly permanently entrenched interventions. The long-term impacts on both majority and minority groups are significant and contentious, the debate often polarizing. This study will unpack these controversies, in general and with specific reference to the Malaysian and South African contexts.

Affirmative action is also interwoven with other policies; it is important to understand the relationships systematically. This book addresses two major veins of objection: first, that it does not help the poor; second, that it undermines meritocracy. I also engage with the further contention, recurrent in Malaysia and South Africa, that race-based affirmative action should be abolished and replaced with need-based, class-based, pro-poor or merit-based policies.

These critiques are rooted in concerns about equity and efficiency, but they inadequately define AA and specify the roles of other preferential selection processes. The predominance of Bumiputeras and blacks among the poor often prompts the contention that race preferential policies are unjustified and misdirected and that countries should instead focus on the poor, where Bumiputeras and blacks constitute disproportionately high shares. It must be emphasized that poverty alleviation and basic needs provision are paramount for society, and on moral and principled grounds they ought to take precedence in policy priority and the allocation of social assistance and public spending. Nonetheless, the specific problem that AA seeks to address is fundamentally different. To reiterate, the crux is racial under-representation in higher positions – not over-representation among the poor.

Efforts to promote development among the poor and marginalized are distinctly different in terms of policy objectives and instruments. Affirmative action principally seeks to promote upward mobility into higher socio-economic strata and to facilitate capability acquisition; its chief mission is not lifting the bottom out of poverty. Targeting assistance based on socio-economic need can be *a complement*, but *not a substitute*, for race-based affirmative action. Granting preference to the poor, needy or disadvantaged, can *reinforce* but *not replace* race-preferential AA. These inter-relationships must be clarified – in a systematic, sector-by-sector manner.

The different implications, based on policy spheres, must be recognized. Countries can effectively grant preference to the disadvantaged in higher education admissions and scholarships but will find it complicated, if at all possible, to apply the same to job promotions and enterprise development. "Merit" considerations vigorously enter the picture here, while vigilantly maintaining the context of promoting group representation. For affirmative action to be effective, transformative and temporary, the policy must cultivate capability, competitiveness and confidence. In short, merit comes into play in selection processes *within* the beneficiary group.

The need to systematically frame the inter-relationships between race-based affirmative action and need-based and merit-based considerations, to use terms familiar in Malaysia and South Africa, is acute in these countries, where the policies are embedded and extensive, and the debate highly polarizing. Admittedly, the notions of meritocracy, or need-based, class-based preferences, are also loaded and debatable terms, but I adopt them for simplicity, with need-based selection a shorthand for preferring disadvantaged and low-income candidates and merit-based connoting selection based on ability or potential. The discourses within these countries often do not define the particular purposes and instruments of different policies and do not locate the myriad programs within a broad regime, thereby failing to distinguish how group preferential programs can incorporate need-based and merit-based selection. I propose a framework and schematic to address this gap, with specific applications to the different spheres of intervention: higher education, high-level employment, enterprise development, and wealth and property ownership.

2 How did affirmative action come about?

From the conceptual underpinnings, Chapter 3 looks at policy regime formation. In line with affirmative action's operation in multiple sectors with multiple instruments, this book adopts a multidimensional approach. The exceptional scope and intensity of the AA regimes of Malaysia and South Africa derive from historical, legal, political and economic conditions at their inception. The parameters and constraints on racial preference, in which the countries show remarkable differences and similarities, were also shaped by various country-specific circumstances. My discussion is structured around four themes: (1) constitutional provisions; (2) dynamics of race and political transition; (3) magnitude of inter-racial disparity; (4) macroeconomic conditions.

First, each country's constitution lays the bedrock for affirmative action regimes, and Malaysia and South Africa are among the rare countries where the national founding document explicitly authorizes affirmative action. Article 153 of the Malaysian Constitution provides for government to take measures, "as may be necessary," to safeguard the "special position" of the Malays and native peoples of East Malaysia through reservation of positions in scholarships, university, civil service employment, training and licensing. This constitutional provision formed the basis for pro-Malay preferential treatment from Malaya's independence in 1957, with the status extended to indigenous non-Malay Bumiputeras of Sabah and Sarawak at Malaysia's formation in 1963. The promulgation of the New Economic Policy in 1971 massively expanded the pro-Bumiputera AA regime.

Affirmative action is continually buttressed by Article 153. However, selective readings or casual references, which have predominated the discourses, tend to overlook an underlying condition for racial preference. More overtly, Article 153 has also been distorted in popular parlance, with Malay "special *rights*" often invoked when the language stipulates "special *position*." This book grapples with these issues and the consequences of perpetuating partial readings of Article 153. I then propose an interpretation that provides latitude for Bumiputera preferential measures to be rolled back – that is, when they have achieved their intended purpose and hence are no longer necessary. Moreover, such a reading ties in with the South African constitution, where the basis for affirmative action is also codified in the constitution but in a very different manner.

The Republic of South Africa's constitution, negotiated during the nation's democratic transition and passed by parliament in 1996, authorizes measures to protect or advance persons disadvantaged by unfair discrimination. This provision is very prominent, being a component of the basic rights and guarantees of equality, and primarily references the apartheid legacy of racial and ethnic discrimination but not exclusively; indeed, women and the disabled are also designated beneficiaries of affirmative action in employment equity legislation enacted in 1998. Importantly, and in contrast to Malaysia's constitution, the beneficiary groups are not identified by race or ethnicity but by the structural factor underlying their disadvantage. Also unlike the Malaysian case, the particular spheres of intervention are not specified in South Africa's constitution, although it is readily apparent that the consequences of unfair discrimination are more pronounced in the upper socio-economic strata.

First, policy interventions under this constitutional purview correspond with the common affirmative action fields: most saliently, employment, university enrolment, public procurement and enterprise ownership. Other notable implications of the constitutional basis are the converse of Article 9's provision. Having stipulated that disadvantage derives from unfair discrimination, it follows that affirmative action constitutes fair discrimination. This opens some space for legal recourse and debate over the basis of affirmative action – that is, whether the disadvantage due to unfair discrimination remains a justification. While political forces may try to preclude inquisition of a high-stakes policy, the room for such debate at least unambiguously exists, in contrast to Malaysia.

Second, political transitions and racial relations also shaped affirmative action. Race preferential programs massively expanded in Malaysia from 1971 and became institutionalized in South Africa from 1994, amid reconfigurations of political systems and shifting balances of power, throughout which race and ethnicity weighed heavily. The contrasts are striking here. In Malaysia, the Malays continuously held political power and clear headship of the Alliance coalition of race-based parties, but Malay primacy was reasserted in the wake of the 13 May 1969 racial riots and national crisis and expansion of the Alliance into the UMNO-dominated Barisan Nasional. Pressures for increased scale and intensity of Bumiputera programmes had grown from the 1960s, but escalated in the early 1970s. Concomitantly, within government, the executive branch increased its dominance and effectively amplified the centralization of power in the federal government.

South Africa underwent a process of democratization, negotiating a shift from minority to majority rule, in which a new founding constitution was the cornerstone. The democratic thrust of these processes established checks and balances in law – reflected in Article 9 – and between the branches of government, which significantly constrained executive power. Race relations were tenuous, but commitments to reconciliation and a new order – articulated in the constitutional preamble's pledge to non-racialism and non-sexism – set a national tone for fostering relations and avoiding provocation, not only between blacks and whites but also within groups. The transition also faced challenges of pursuing personnel change in the public services while avoiding detrimental disruption of its competency and functionality. On top of all this, the country grappled with the merger of autonomous regions and fostering a more substantive federalism.

Third, the form and magnitude of inter-racial disparities elicited particular responses. The inequalities are greater than in most countries, but a few characteristics differentiate our cases. Malays and indigenous peoples in Malaysia were socio-economically disadvantaged and excluded in some ways from the mainstream, but they were not systemically discriminated against. In fact, Malays had not only held political power all along, as noted earlier, but also secured prominent positions in the public sector, while the Chinese were active in commerce and small- and medium-scale private enterprise – but not across all industries and scale of operations. Foreign-owned firms dominated in economy, especially in the powerhouse mining and plantation industries, and some were taken over by Malaysian government agencies. However, being overseas-based entities, targeting them averted conflict that would have escalated had the state taken similar action on domestic, especially Chinese-owned, businesses.

The dominance of the minority white population was colossal and comprehensive in South Africa. Blacks were disenfranchised, denied basic political and civil rights. Specific socio-economic consequences of the apartheid system are particularly pertinent to this book. Blacks were not only denied access to the same amount and quality of education but also subjected to schooling that institutionalized racism. In the labour market, opportunities were pre-determined by race. Engineering racial divisions of labour and masses of low-skilled black workers were veritable cornerstones of the regime. Over time, the colour bar moved up to supervisory and medium-skilled jobs, but blacks were continually precluded from upward mobility, as well as wealth and property accumulation. Minority dominance also spanned both private and public sectors. The democratically elected government would enter political office, but it held few bargaining levers in the bureaucratic and economic realms.

Fourth, some aspects of national and international macroeconomic conditions warrant our consideration, for the ways they shaped the relative roles of state and market and constrained policy options. The affirmative action regime that redefined Malaysia took shape in the 1970s, at a time that the global mainstream was more amenable to government intervention in general, while Northeast Asia was rapidly transforming through proactive industrial policy driven by developmental states. The template for a strong state was laid without much resistance, abetted by the fact that Malaysia was not dependent on foreign funding. Malaysia's pursuit of privatization and economic liberalization measures in the 1980s until the 1997–1998 Asian Financial Crisis are also instructive, in that the state maintained an orchestrating role, rather than relinquishing discretionary power to market forces. The re-emergence of state-owned enterprises, rebranded as government-linked companies, after the AFC, secured the state's continuing lead role in the economy in general, and in affirmative action in particular.

South Africa transitioned through a vastly different domestic and global milieu. Its economic system was moulded in the late apartheid years of the 1980s until the mid-1990s, while the country was needing to reintegrate with the world economy, amid the collapse of communism and the acme of neoliberalism. Although alternative policy visions were part of the discourses in the transition, the country faced tremendous pressures to conform to the global mainstream, and high-performing countries in the early 1990s were ones that appeared to embrace the Washington Consensus. That was the prevailing view. South Africa's economy was further characterized by immense concentration of power in a handful of sprawling conglomerates, who in turn threatened capital flight and seized the opportunity to secure international presence, while pre-emptively making concessions in terms of co-opting the black empowerment agenda. The dominance of conglomerates would persist. One area that South Africa did not concede to neoliberalism was in state-owned companies, which were maintained and arguably constitute most comparable policy sector vis-à-vis Malaysia's government-linked companies.

Arising from these conditions and dynamics, affirmative action regimes formed in strikingly contrasting ways. Broadly, Malaysia's affirmative action programs are characterized by discretionary executive power, centralized administration and application of Bumiputera exclusivity or racial quotas, while South Africa has pursued affirmative action more by instituting legislation, statutes and codes, in a more decentralized system, and by setting targets and less-direct preferential measures. These differences, and a few areas of similarity, are illustrated by the policy instruments in place.

3   How is affirmative action implemented?

Part 2 of this book systematically lays out affirmative action programs across the four principal policy sectors in Malaysia and South Africa, respectively, in Chapters 4 and 5. Since this portion of the book is denser with detail, I will keep to a more skeletal overview here and dive straight into a comparative summary. On the whole, there are more pronounced differences in higher education, employment, and wealth and property ownership and some notable similarities in enterprise development. The extensive scope of regimes is apparent, as well as the broad profile of both countries – that is, Malaysia's centralized, discretionary, quota-based system, juxtaposed against South Africa's decentralized, statutory, codes- and targets-based system.

First, in higher education, Malaysia's interventions are centralized and delineated by race. Centralized admissions and administration, coupled with racial quotas or Bumiputera exclusivity in admissions, scholarships and education sponsorship, vastly augment the group's access to education. Malaysia also had a *tabula rasa* of sorts: almost all universities were established after the advent of the NEP. South Africa preserved the autonomy of its numerous universities and higher education institutions inherited at the democratic transition. Each institution is mandated to pursue redress or transformation of its student body. Policy priority has also been placed on narrowing gaps between historically white institutions and historically black institutions.

Second, in high-level occupations, the overarching policy objective in Malaysia simply stipulates racial/ethnic proportionality at every level, but in practice, policies have applied predominantly to the public sector and, to some extent, in government-linked companies and through government contracting. In contrast, the employment sphere is a mainstay of South Africa's affirmative action regime, and it encompasses both public and private sectors. Employment equity legislation is intimately associated with affirmative action, and it arose out of and in response to the imperative of fostering redress and restitution for apartheid injustices, which were very pronounced in the labour market.

The third sector, enterprise development, is where cross-country similarities and differences are relatively more apparent. Malaysia went from a reliance on state-owned enterprises, nationalized foreign companies and heavy industries to one of the most massive national privatization exercises globally, only to suffer widespread collapse in the wake of the Asian Financial Crisis. Subsequently, privatized entities were renationalized and the Bumiputera enterprise development agenda was spearheaded by government-linked enterprises and large companies, with increasing contemporary focus on SMEs as well. Public procurement, contracting and licensing, and microcredit and development finance, have continuously been utilized for AA purposes, with modifications over time. South Africa's endeavour also passed through different phases and maintains multi-faceted operations. Large corporations exerted more influence over the process, including the promulgation of industry charters to racially transform ownership and participation. The public procurement system constitutes the main leverage for the Broad-Based Black Economic Empowerment (BBBEE) programme. State-owned companies, formerly known as public enterprises, have also undertaken a major role in promoting black business alongside credit agencies. The newly launched Black Industrialists Policy marks a distinct, state-led intervention.

Fourth, in wealth and property ownership, stark contrasts resurface. Malaysia demonstrates again an exceptional capacity to pursue overt race preferential programs, with a variety of (active and defunct) equity allocation requirements for investment and public listing, the creation of unit trust schemes exclusively for Bumiputera investors, which also became vehicles for state takeovers of foreign companies, as well as Bumiputera quotas and price discounts in housing purchases.

Interventions in promoting enterprises also involve wealth transfers; Malaysia's privatization project massively accumulated wealth in the hands of selected Bumiputera capitalists. South Africa has implemented a narrower range of programs for promoting black wealth ownership, although the emergent structure, centred on equity holdings, is complex and economy-wide in scope. Industry-based charters and the subsequent BBBEE legislation and codes, in which equity transfers have been emphasized, are the main vehicles for this agenda that involve race preferential treatment.

4 To what extent has affirmative action achieved its goals, and to what extent has it fallen short?

Part 3 turns to the empirical evidence of affirmative action outcomes. Chapter 6 surveys the empirical literature of affirmative action globally and specific works on Malaysia and South Africa. There is substantial literature to build upon, but also a paucity of extant research that has conceived affirmative action in a systematic fashion and multi-sectoral scope as adopted in this book. Few articles have assessed the direct policy outcomes, with most works touching on AA within broader studies of income inequality, and likewise, the literature scarcely differentiates quantitative from qualitative policy outcomes to provide a fuller-bodied evaluation of the immediate goal of increased group representation as well as the ultimate goal of developing of capability and competitiveness.

Affirmative action pursues parity in both quantitative and qualitative aspects. Quantitative outcomes are, by definition, more measurable and tangible, and hence the main substance of this empirical inquiry. I primarily examine patterns of racial/ethnic representation in higher education enrolment and certification, professional and management positions, the corporate and SME scene and wealth ownership. The qualitative outcomes are more difficult to research, but capability and competitiveness can be assessed by referencing supplementary data, such as student performance, worker mobility (both upward and laterally, across public and private sectors) and growth and dynamism of companies. Ultimately, continual dependency on preferential treatment and resistance to its removal also signals the extent to which capability, competitiveness and confidence have been broadly inculcated and expressed.

Chapter 7, evaluating Malaysia's affirmative action achievements and shortfalls, traces out the rapid gains in Bumiputera attainment of higher education and steady upward mobility into high-level positions, although momentum has apparently slowed in the past decades. Public institutions play key roles in both sectors, with Bumiputeras predominantly studying in public education institutions and significantly moving up the occupational ladder, especially in the public sector and GLCs. However, beyond acquiring qualifications, in which Bumiputeras, especially Malays, have steadily advanced, the community persistently lags in terms of educational achievement and labour market mobility. Increased attention to disadvantaged students in recent years signals a progressive shift and holds out some scope for a more progressive distribution within Bumiputeras of opportunity, perhaps even a shift toward incorporating more non-race-based targeting, although this poses operational challenges in Malaysia's highly centralized education system. The continuation of programs offering alternative and easier entry routes to university, which inadequately equip students for higher learning, fails to narrow achievement gaps – and may indeed perpetuate them.

Malaysia has made markedly less progress in creating a broad-based managerial class and dynamic, competitive private enterprises. GLCs remain flagbearers of affirmative action in business; Bumiputera SMEs continue to be concentrated at micro and small scales and are largely dependent on public procurement and state support. Recent rhetoric and policy initiatives have placed more emphasis on developing capability and weeding out rent-seeking and corruption. The intent is timely and vital, although moving forward requires methodical policy formulation, room for experimentation and modification, and assiduous implementation. On the wealth ownership front, Bumiputeras have also made sizable gains, including meeting individual ownership targets, albeit without reaching the institutional ownership milestones – according to the official accounts. This policy sector remains fraught with empirical controversy, but focusing on the achievements, while clearly committing to caution and restraint in further pursuit of wealth redistribution, arguably presents a more constructive path forward.

South Africa's affirmative action achievements and shortfalls display considerably different patterns, as discussed in Chapter 8. Its educational challenges are much steeper; chronic deficiencies in basic schooling have constricted the supply of university entrants. However, blacks have increasingly entered public universities and graduated into the labour market – although quality disparities between historically white/advantaged institutions and others continually influence enrolment patterns and stratify job prospects of graduates. These structures basically persist, despite institutional mergers and reconfigurations and adoption of a new classification scheme. Higher education institutions, which operate autonomously, have recently expanded the application of disadvantage in admissions policies. However, high costs persist as a barrier to university, and black participation in certain fields of study remains low, and in general African and Coloured participation in higher education considerably lags behind Indian and White populations. On the employment front, black representation in managerial, professional and technical positions has progressed vigorously in the public sector and state-owned companies, gradually in the private sector. Employment equity is deeply embedded and constitutionally upheld, but continuously embroiled in polarizing debate. It has accelerated black mobility into work positions for potentially gaining experience and capability but has also been utilized for political patronage. Thus, South Africa will foreseeably need to rigorously and judiciously balance productive gain and fair process.

Efforts to raise black ownership and management control, and enterprise development, have progressed relatively less steadily. The slower and more volatile pace of change is expected; these policy objectives are more complicated, with higher structural barriers to entry and practical constraints to sustaining success. The development of a black managerial corps and black-controlled enterprise, indirectly through the BBBEE codified points system leveraging on public procurement, and directly through the state-owned companies, has considerably fallen short of expectations. The complexity of barriers and profound challenges to these endeavours, however, urge caution and patience. As in Malaysia, the measurement of ownership has been saddled with contentions, with some sources reporting that BBBEE targets have not been met and others asserting the opposite. This empirical debate notwithstanding, the gaps in effective control and enterprise development are more widely agreed upon, leading to more emphasis on these aspects of the BBBEE codes and direct interventions to groom black industrialists. The barrier to breakthrough is arguably less in policy design than implementation, as well as conducive macroeconomic conditions.

5 Where does affirmative action go from here?

What do the findings hold for the policy in the present and future? Having analyzed the achievements and shortfalls of affirmative action in Malaysia and South Africa, this book concludes in Chapter 9 with a condensed comparison of policy outcomes and a discussion of lessons learned, individually and mutually. On philosophical and moral grounds, affirmative action comes with an attendant proviso that the special measures under its aegis are to be transitory, subjected to revision as the interventions progress and conditions change. The specific constitutional provisions for affirmative action in both countries are also premised on socio-economic conditions providing underlying justification.

An overarching theme of my findings is that the quantitative achievements are substantial, but progress on qualitative aspects is lagging. Of course, distributing opportunity and increasing participation in some ways precede the attainment of parity higher up the socio-economic strata. Nevertheless, there is a particular importance in delivering the results when it comes to affirmative action. As with many interventions that confer a degree of preferential treatment and protection, the ultimate objective of removing protection is very challenging and often elusive. However, the scope of affirmative action is greater and pertains to opportunities more widespread and basic than infant industry protection and other selective interventions, and hence the implications are also more immense. The regime must effectively and broadly cultivate capability, competitiveness and confidence, utilizing need-based and merit-based selection to enhance existing programs while devising graduation or exit strategies.

Each country encounters specific policy implications. Malaysia's AA discourses need to surmount an incoherence that currently prevails, which conflates poverty alleviation with affirmative action and consequently precludes systematic and sector-specific policy reformulation. Its affirmative action regime, in which exclusively Bumiputera programs and racial quotas feature more prominently than perhaps any other country, must respond to the evidence that the system has fallen short of the ultimate goals of capability development, while also considering the long-term impacts of perpetual preferences on its multiracial fabric. Higher education presents openings for incorporating more preferential selection based on socio-economic disadvantage, alongside efforts to enhance academic achievement and promote diversity. In employment and enterprise development, greater emphasis on merit-based selection can bolster the desired objective of Bumiputeras gaining competitiveness and confidence in these sectors, in tandem with introduction of graduation plans or exit/sunset clauses. In wealth ownership, schemes targeting the poor can clearly shift from a race to need as the basis for operation, while exercising restraint in programs that distribute wealth among middle- and high-income households and seeking out specific ways, especially among the elite, to demonstrate graduation out of preferential treatment.

For South Africa, the conceptual challenge similarly requires differentiating affirmative action from poverty alleviation and mass employment, but it also involves the adoption of a more integrated perspective on affirmative action encompassing the four main policy sectors.

South Africa has set itself on certain trajectories, particularly in prioritizing high-level employment and ownership, which is understandable given the intense pressures to transform the labour market and the highest echelons of economic power – two major arenas of the apartheid-era prevailing conditions at the time of the democratic transition. However, it has been a bumpy and miry passage. The stakes and vested interests are high, but the capacity of beneficiaries to deliver is contingent on complex factors and has often been undermined by patronage and clientelism. Persisting shortages in high-skilled workers and entrepreneurial experience have inclined public policy to return to more bottom-up emphasis on education and training and SME development, but the means for enforcing employment equity and BEE have also been magnified. Of course, the room for discretion remains quite wide, and in this context, South Africa will need to strike a judicious balance. Public policy must exercise restraint in setting expectations and pursuing transformation, while resolutely ensuring broad delivery of quality schooling and cultivating skills, knowledge and resourcefulness. As with Malaysia, South Africa also must focus on higher education as the preeminent sector for capacity building and inter-generational upward mobility and for sustaining the supply of highly-skilled professional and technical workers.

Of course, policies can be designed and refined, but the socio-political milieu and economic conditions also influence and constrain the scope, direction and efficacy of implementation. A complex of historical factors conceived affirmative action in the Malaysian and South African national journey; their contemporary experience sees many of those factors endure and new ones emerge. The world's two largest affirmative action regimes are the heaviest to steer and assuredly the most difficult to change. The quest for parity between groups continues to be elusive, and potentially perilous in some spheres, especially wealth ownership. Race-preferential programs remain, but in the current global milieu of mass discontent with economic systems failing to benefit the masses, it is all the more fitting and productive for the focus to be shifted to the policy sectors that spur learning, work experience and hands-on leadership, which also hold greater potential to reach a broad swathe of society and uplift the next generation. Other forms and approaches to affirmative action besides the direct preferential treatment mode in both countries, including outreach and diversity-promoting measures, present constructive alternatives. Affirmative action must succeed, especially in broadly and effectively building capability, competitiveness and confidence. Parity in these areas matters most of all.

Notes on terminology

Before we proceed, a discussion of terms and concepts might be helpful to clarify this book's approach, orientation and scope. First, while *affirmative action* is a familiar name and a seemingly obvious choice, the reasons for using this heading over others warrant a brief note. I apply affirmative action in view of its common usage and broad scope, the sufficient consistency of its meaning in the scholarly literature and the dispassionate tone of its wording. The terms *positive action* or *corrective action* mildly differ in connotation but are rarely used. *Positive discrimination* is arguably more precise in denoting the policy's constructive thrust and the preferential treatment involved. But it is also less widely applied, and the central appearance of the word *discrimination* risks triggering reactions and detracting from the empirical and critical engagement I hope to foster here.

Affirmative action should also be clarified in both countries' contexts. There is no official articulation of the term in Malaysia, but it recurs in popular parlance and academic literature. The crux of this matter is simpler in Malaysia and has been noted earlier, but bears reinforcing: affirmative action is one component of, but must not be equated with, the NEP. Affirmative action conforms to the NEP's second prong, and to reiterate a point made earlier, it must not be conflated with the NEP's first prong, which specifically sets out the objective of poverty eradication irrespective of race.

In South Africa, by contrast, a multiplicity of terms and concepts has proliferated, revolving around the same theme. Early- and mid-1990s discourses on affirmative action were heavily focused on past discrimination in labour market relations (Nzimande and Sikhosana 1996). The Employment Equity Act (1998) distinguishes two stages to the process of attaining equity: legislation of non-discrimination and official provision for affirmative action to correct historical unfair discrimination. Chapter 3 of the Employment Equity Act, which carries the heading "Affirmative Action," outlines the hiring regulations designed to increase access of historically disadvantaged persons to positions in which they are under-represented. Employment equity is indisputably an affirmative action programme, but the articulations in the EEA are probably the reason affirmative action is conventionally *equated* with employment equity. However, affirmative action as conceptualized in this study is not confined to employment equity.

Black economic empowerment, as a programme for redressing systemic disadvantage, also fits within our rubric of affirmative action. However, BEE is often differentiated from affirmative action and employment equity, whether due to varying ideological connotations of the terms or efforts to either dissociate BEE from affirmative action as practiced in other countries and to distinguish BEE as a larger programme than employment equity. These distinctions are mainly valid, but a systematic definition of affirmative action clearly subsumes BEE, recognizing its primary application in ownership, managerial control and enterprise development. In this regard we are in agreement with former Constitutional Court justice Albie Sachs (2007), who maintains BEE as a subset of affirmative action.

Transformation and *redress* are broader terms denoting the processes of correcting inequalities and injustices of the past, including but not limited to measures to attain racial and gender proportionality in education, employment, management and ownership. To the extent that redress or transformation programs aim to increase the representation of disadvantaged groups, they will fall under our umbrella of affirmative action. This point is most pertinent to the education sector, where affirmative action is conspicuously absent in policy discourse, although the mandate to diversify historically white institutions and uplift historically black institutions has been made clear. Absence of the term, of course, implies neither absence of positive discrimination nor its presence by another name. Indeed, the point is precisely that we must examine policies with affirmative action intent and that involve some form of preferential selection premised on historical disadvantage, even if South African convention applies different classifications.

Second, clarification of some country references may be helpful. This study, being focused on majority-favouring affirmative action, covers the post-apartheid, democratic era in South Africa. I therefore omit the rather redundant use of the term *post-apartheid* and specify apartheid South Africa where relevant. Wherever South Africa is mentioned in general, it is in the post-1994 context. Some historical discussions of Malaysia will use the national names befitting the context. Specifically, *Malaya* and *Peninsular Malaysia* refer to the same place but at different times. *Malaya* designates the period prior to 1963 and *Peninsular Malaysia* the period after.

Third, on race, ethnicity and other terms for identifying population groups, the choice can be complicated, sometimes polarizing. *Ethnicity* denotes common historical and cultural characteristics; *race* hinges on physical appearance, intertwined with genetic lineage. An amalgam of both, such as the term *ethno-racial identity*, perhaps most completely encapsulates the underlying complexities (Ambikaipaker 2013). But it also complicates our diction. I have elected to keep the language simpler.

This book uses *race* as the operative term for identifying population groups and categorizing policy beneficiaries, while referring to ethnicity when making reference to literature in which that term appears. This choice is undeniably contentious and reached with pragmatism and a tinge of reluctance. Racial categorization of people groups stems from invidious colonial origins and tendentious methodology, and the association of race with physical appearance has been exploited for vile and cruel ends (Hirschman 1986; Alexander 2007). Nonetheless, addressing race speaks to such historical legacies and their persisting impact today, which in some ways needs to be tackled head-on, including by deploying the language of race. There is no corollary within an ethnicity-defined framework for *racism*, no word that can match its visceral tone and pernicious thrust. The sweeping categories that have emerged as conventions in Malaysia and South Africa – in both countries, the population is sorted into three to four main classifications – grossly aggregate and dilute the rich cultural, linguistic and ancestral heritage of subgroups (Nagaraj *et al.* 2009; Maré 2011). The broad categories are used in this book with due acknowledgment of their limitations and a firm caveat that group heterogeneity permeates the backdrop.

Race and *ethnicity* tend to be used interchangeably in Malaysia, with a gravitation to the latter in recent decades. In South Africa, *race* remains an operative reference, and the political project of redressing apartheid expressly seeks to bridge racial inequality and past racial discrimination. The problem of artificial, and politically-shaped, group categorization affects ethnicity as well as race. This cannot be avoided; any categories must be applied with due caution. For simplicity, I also adopt the official norms of *Bumiputera* as subsuming Malays and non-Malay indigenous peoples, and *blacks* as comprised of Africans, Coloureds and Indians. I refer to the Bumiputeras and blacks as the beneficiary group or designated group. These terms are used interchangeably.

Our preliminaries conclude with a final note on a peculiar occurrence in the South African discourse, regarding the appearance of some in general and specific contexts. The terms *black* and *white* carry a generic connotation, but they also appear in a more formal sense, particularly with reference to Broad-Based Black Economic Empowerment and the fourfold categorization of African, Coloured, Indian and White. I thus apply capitalization of these terms according to these contexts. *BEE* also appears in a more general sense, while *Broad-Based BEE* (BBBEE) refers specifically to formal regulations and policies. As much as possible, I adhere to this general and specific differentiation in referencing BEE vs BBBEE, although at times the distinction can be arbitrary.

Notes

1 "Race-based Affirmative Action is Failing Poor Malaysians", *The Economist*, 18 May 2017; "Deformative Action: Malaysia's System of Racial Preferences Should be Scrapped", *The Economist*, 18 May 2017; "A Never Ending Policy", *The Economist*, 27 April 2013; "University of Cape Town Sees Affirmative Action Rift", *New York Times*, 22 November 2010; "Affirmative Action in South Africa", *New York Times*, 23 November 2010.

2 Affirmative action in political representation is practiced in some countries, but not in Malaysia and South Africa, where the majority group's electoral strength assuredly translates into political power.

Part 1

Theoretical and historical underpinnings

2 Concepts, complexities, contentions

This chapter addresses the rationales, objectives and mechanisms of affirmative action and discusses the complex and contentious implications of the policy. I unpack underlying concepts and theories, focusing on the particular forms of disparity and disadvantage that affirmative action aims to redress. Drawing on a broad range of multidisciplinary literature and country studies, and taking into account the circumstances of Malaysia and South Africa, I formulate a definition of *affirmative action* to guide the analysis: preferential measures to promote the representation of a disadvantaged group in socially esteemed and economically influential positions.

I also discuss the complexities of the specific problems being addressed – under-representation of disadvantaged groups in higher education, high-level occupations, enterprise development and wealth ownership – where entry barriers, discrimination and other systemic factors can perpetuate disparity between groups. The exercise of preferential selection, while inherent to affirmative action, is also contentious. Like any policy involving group preference, the potentialities and pitfalls are both immense, although the vested interests and resistance to reform can be magnified when the preference is based on race and ethnicity, particularly in societies where race and ethnicity are integral to political mobilization and contestation. This chapter will also discuss the debates and controversies that permeate this policy, stemming from three specific critiques: AA is unwarranted and market processes are adequate; the policy should be structured by need or class instead of race; such interventions undermine merit-based selection and perpetuate dependency.

It is imperative to adhere to the objectives and instruments of AA in our analysis and to situate critiques in proper context. To inform current policies, as this book intends, my research addresses how countries can implement AA in an effective – and transitory – manner, rather than whether countries should have implemented it in the first place. I venture forth a systematic approach to chart pathways out of the current regime of overt racial preferences. This is especially germane in the contexts of Malaysia and South Africa, where AA is constitutionally authorized, institutionally embedded and practically ingrained. Rather than posing counterfactuals of scenarios in the absence of AA, this book focuses on policy practices and outcomes, critically examining the initial objective of increasing representation as well as the ultimate goal of developing capability, competitiveness and self-reliance. Beyond the more quantitative issue of the beneficiary group's participation in higher education, high-level occupations, enterprise and wealth ownership, various qualitative aspects must also be incorporated, conceptually and empirically, with a view to constructing a framework that addresses how AA can work more systematically and effectively.

Much of the debate surrounds the implications of race-based targeting on class or socio-economic disadvantage and the impacts of preferential selection on merit. The efficacy of AA is augmented with more progressive distribution and more meritocratic selection *within* the beneficiary group. The greater the extension of benefits to the poor and for inter-generational upward mobility, and to those with greater ability or potential, the greater the likelihood that AA broadly cultivates capability and facilitates rollback of preferential treatment. With particular reference to Malaysia and South Africa, where opposition to AA tends to be framed in terms of need and class, respectively, I provide a framework for conceptualizing the primacy of race-based preferences while incorporating need-, class- and merit-based considerations as means to complement and reinforce the policy. Differences across policy sectors stand out: need-based considerations eminently apply in higher education, and merit-based considerations importantly complement AA in high-level employment and enterprise development. Need can be integrated into AA wealth ownership programmes that target low-income households, but allocation of assets that involve productive output – large or small – must place more emphasis on proven or potential ability.

Defining affirmative action

Affirmative action is a multifaceted subject approached from various angles. However, surveying the scholarly literature and publications by international bodies, we find a broad commonality in that affirmative action, explicitly or implicitly, incorporates some element of the application of preference to members of a designated population group in specific areas. Different definitions, however, tend to emphasize one or more aspects of AA, related to the basis, scope and duration of group preference. A substantial portion of the conceptual debate, drawing on the United States experience, engages with legal and philosophical aspects of AA that lie beyond our scope (Beckwith and Jones 1997; Cahn 2002; Curry 1996).

Before proposing a working definition for this book, I survey some definitions of AA, focusing on literature that draws on economics traditions most pertinent to the empirical work to follow. I then locate the subject in the context of Malaysia and South Africa and account for specific historical and institutional considerations that shape my approach to AA. It is instructive to contemplate the definitions of AA as articulated in these sources:

> [the] practice of preferential selection of members of under-represented groups to widely esteemed positions.
>
> (Weisskopf 2004)

any measure that allocates goods . . . – such as admission into selective universities or professional schools, jobs, promotions, public contracts, business loans, and rights to buy, sell, or use land and other natural resources – through a process that takes into account individual membership in designated groups, for the purpose of increasing the proportion of members of those groups in the relevant labor force, entrepreneurial class, or student population, where they are currently underrepresented as a result of past oppression by state authorities and/or present societal discrimination.

(Sabbagh 2012)

[regulation of] the allocation of scarce positions in education, employment or business contracting so as to increase the representation in those positions of persons belonging to certain population subgroups.

(Fryer and Loury 2005)

any policy which seeks to explicitly address horizontal inequalities between ethnically, culturally or religiously-defined groups.

(Brown, Stewart and Langer 2012)

[a] coherent packet of measures, of a temporary character, aimed specifically at correcting the position of members of a target group in one or more aspects of their social life, in order to obtain effective equality.

(ILO 2003)

special temporary measures . . . to accelerate the pace of improvement of the situation of groups that are at a serious disadvantage because of past or present discrimination.

(ILO 2007)

measures to raise the participation of members of an economically disadvantaged group in the areas of education, employment and business, where they had been historically excluded or under-represented.

(Lee 2005)

[a] form of state-sponsored social mobility [and a] remedial strategy which seeks to address the legal, historical exclusion of a majority.

(Adam 2000)

strategic racial favoritism that favors previously disadvantaged groups.

(Matambo and Ani 2015)

Three perspectives stand out as justifications for affirmative action: discrimination, disadvantage and under-representation. Discrimination and disadvantage tend to be inter-linked, resulting in under-representation, especially in higher education institutions and high-level occupations, and ownership of wealth and capital. However, different approaches to affirmative action emphasize one or two aspects over the other.

A host of other sources refer to fundamental, underlying causes of disparity. Sabbagh (2012) stipulates past – and institutionalized – oppression, or present discrimination, as a premise for AA. The ILO definitions, likewise, make the case for AA on the grounds of disadvantage due to past discrimination (ILO 2007), which call for measures to accelerate positive change or take corrective action in pursuit of "effective equality" (ILO 2003). For Fryer and Loury (2005) and Weisskopf (2004), the chief purpose of AA is to increase the representation of under-represented groups. Notably, Lee (2005), Adam (2000) and Matambo and Ani (2015), writing respectively about South Africa and Malaysia, premise AA on historical exclusion. These positions echo Maphai (1989, 17) who, writing in the late apartheid years, expounded how affirmative action is justified by the "need for the advancement of the oppressed." For Brown, Stewart and Langer (2012), the purpose of AA is to address horizontal inequalities, which have structural and historical roots. Time-bound considerations may also come to bear on AA, not in mutually exclusive but complementary ways that draw attention to the pervading dynamics of restitution and integration. In this vein, Tierney (1997) and Dupper (2005) usefully distinguish between AA that is primarily concerned with compensation for past discrimination (backward looking), correction of ongoing discrimination (present looking) or diversification and multiculturalism (future looking).

The scope of affirmative action is specified in some approaches, encompassing education, employment and business (Fryer and Loury 2005; Lee 2005). Weisskopf (2004) emphasizes the importance of redressing under-representation in "widely esteemed positions" – especially upper-tier universities and professional and managerial ranks. Barriers to entry are especially acute in these areas, but more importantly, these positions confer a significant level of social standing and economic influence. Perennial under-representation of disadvantaged groups can reinforce perceptions within the group that the upper rungs of educational and occupational ladders are inaccessible or perpetuate social stigmas towards the capabilities of the group as a whole.

The duration of AA is usually not explicitly incorporated as a definitive criterion. However, most conceptions of AA implicitly justify interventions based on conditions (to overcome discrimination or disadvantage) and objectives (to increase representation and participation) that are impermanent and variable. The grounds for AA diminish as under-represented or disadvantaged groups progressively become more represented and less disadvantaged. At time same time, expiration timelines (dismantling AA after a period of time or after targets are reached) or milestones and sunset clauses (disqualifying members of the designated group who have received benefits from further preferential treatment) are crucial long-term considerations that warrant acknowledgement from the onset of AA. We return to this debate in the following section. It suffices to note here that the ILO definitions, which assuredly draw on extensive cross-country perspective, stress the temporariness of AA. This emphasis, as part of the definition of AA, is evidently a response to potential adverse effects of prolonged preferential policies that solidify into new forms of protectionism and exclusion.[1]

In Malaysia and South Africa, affirmative action operates with official authorization and terms of reference. In the next chapter, I will unpack the distinctive features of the constitutional mandates for AA in both countries. Nonetheless, at this juncture it is worthwhile to lay out the key articulations on the matter, to get a flavour of the overarching framework, which bear some semblance to the elements of AA discussed earlier:

> [t]he Yang di-Pertuan Agong shall exercise his functions under this Constitution and federal law in such manner as may be necessary to safeguard the special position of the Malays and natives of any of the States of Sabah and Sarawak and to ensure the reservation for Malays and natives of any of the States of Sabah and Sarawak of such proportion as he may deem reasonable of positions in the public service (other than the public service of a State) and of scholarships, [permits and licenses]
> (Article 153, Federal Constitution of Malaysia)

> accelerating the process of restructuring Malaysian society to correct economic imbalance, so as to reduce and eventually eliminate the identification of race with economic function
> (New Economic Policy, Malaysia 1971)

> [t]o promote the achievement of equality, legislative and other measures designed to protect or advance persons, or categories of persons, disadvantaged by unfair discrimination may be taken
> (Article 9, Constitution of the Republic of South Africa)

> Affirmative action can be defined as the laws, programmes or activities designed to redress past imbalances and to ameliorate the conditions of individuals and groups who have been disadvantaged on the grounds of race, gender and disability.
> (White Paper on the Transformation of the Public Service, South Africa 1995)

Malaysia arguably stands out most of all internationally. The Malaysian federal constitution implies increased group representation as the overriding objective and specifies some areas of intervention, akin to the scope of AA in many countries, but it articulates a premise for race-preferential treatment in a singular manner – the beneficiary group's special status. South Africa's constitution articulates a clearer premise for AA – disadvantage based on unfair discrimination – but more general terms of reference regarding the areas of intervention. Sabbagh (2012, 1140), in concluding his multi-country comparative overview, writes:

> AA is an instrument designed to achieve a more or less explicitly acknowledged goal of structural transformation. In all – with the possible exception of Malaysia – that transformation is geared towards an ideal of societal integration, to be realized by equalizing the distribution of a set of status-conferring goods among ascriptive groups so as to reduce the salience of the boundaries between them.

The array of definitions and conceptualizations surveyed, and their underlying values and normative biases, underscore the importance of clarity – and, to an extent, country specificity – in outlining the justification and scope of affirmative action. Four issues warrant our consideration in composing a definition. First, this study predicates AA in Malaysia and South Africa on the prevalence of systemic disadvantage faced by racial groups, deriving from historical discrimination, exclusion and structural inequalities particular to each country. Preferential policies towards a majority group entail interventions of greater magnitude. The scale and scope of programmes in Malaysia and South Africa substantially exceed those conventionally associated with affirmative action in social science literature (Jain, Sloane and Horwitz 2003; Weisskopf 2004). Preferential treatment of the beneficiary group in these two countries are also arguably more overt; thus, it is appropriate and prudent to incorporate this core feature of the selection process into the conceptualization and definition of AA.

Second, historical exclusion of the Bumiputera in Malaysia and blacks in South Africa from full educational opportunity and economic participation is undeniable, but the impediments have shifted over time, due to affirmative action, as well as economic development more broadly. Hence, the premise for affirmative action should accommodate such changes, specifically, by viewing disadvantage from a systemic rather than an historical perspective. This is judicious also for the purpose of assessing mechanisms or timelines for scaling down affirmative action.

Third, affirmative action invariably negotiates a tension between designating preference to some and preserving equitable opportunities to others. Malaysia and South Africa face such dilemmas, with two distinctive features: the designated group comprises a majority race group that is economically disadvantaged but politically dominant, and each country's constitution lays the foundations for affirmative action along with guarantees of equal rights to citizens. These inscriptions of grounds for preferential policies embody the sense of economic insecurity of the majority group and apprehension over the capacity of self-regulating markets to redress their severe under-representation in key areas, while demonstrating their political dominance and setting out the terms for discourse.

The question whether or not to institute AA is effectively precluded in Malaysia and South Africa; the politically possible debate through past decades and into the foreseeable future concerns the design and conduct of policies. The question of AA's duration arises occasionally, but rarely within a systematic consideration of graduation and exit strategies. Historical circumstances undoubtedly demanded extensive and intensive affirmative action. However, receiving preferential treatment can induce exceeding pressures for such programmes to be perpetuated, which can in turn entrench a system of entitlement, patronage and dependency. These detrimental and undermining outcomes reinforce the case for grounding AA in group disadvantage, and for balancing the cause of group preference against the principle of equality.

Fourth, the areas where affirmative action is implemented need to be specified. Obviously, the disadvantaged group will be under-represented in the upper rungs of educational and occupational ladders and in ownership and control of business. The spaces for preferential policies may be delineated according to these sectors. However, we also want to encapsulate an overarching purpose of affirmative action, which is to increase the presence of individuals from a disadvantaged group in positions that elevate the group's position and influence as a whole and concomitantly develop capability and self-reliance. Following from the earlier discussion, and drawing on portions of the definitions cited, this study conceptualizes affirmative action in Malaysia and South Africa as:

> preferential measures to promote the representation of a disadvantaged group in socially esteemed and economically influential positions.

Debates and contentions

Affirmative action is always contentious and often polarizing. At the extremes, it is unqualifiedly opposed as a violation of neoclassical market axioms or uncritically endorsed as a socio-political imperative. In between, more considered and nuanced positions may support AA by recognizing its justification and purpose while acknowledging limitations and contradictions, or they may maintain predilection for alternatives to race-based AA that arguably can attain the same objectives. This section synthesizes the debates, outlining and discussing salient criticisms against affirmative action and proposed policy alternatives that claim to pursue the same objective but with different means.

Market mechanisms and anti-discrimination versus state intervention and positive discrimination

One area of contention pits the position that markets render discrimination untenable over time against the position that state intervention is necessary to counter past discrimination with proactive, positive discrimination. Neoclassical economic assumptions – chiefly, no structural barriers to human capital acquisition and long-run unprofitability of discrimination in competitive labour markets – drive the conclusion that competitive labour markets over time will facilitate the attrition of negative discrimination and the diminishment of unequal pay for equal human capital.

Becker's theory of discrimination deserves mention, in view of its considerable influence on economic thought. He defines discrimination as a departure from objective behaviour, related to "non-pecuniary, psychic costs of interaction." People prefer to work with others of the same race or culture and may lack adequate information about such persons to make proper assessments of their capabilities (Becker 1971).[2] This argument for the existence of discrimination rests on the starting point that black and white workers are equally productive. Attaching competitive market assumptions, the returns to human capital would in the absence of discrimination equalize between blacks and whites. In sum, the explanation for disparity reduces to a "taste for discrimination." Moreover, the theory predicts that in the long run, discrimination will be eliminated by competitive forces in the labour market, since companies that restrict hiring to one group will eventually pay wage premiums or employ less productive workers at the expense of more productive workers from the discriminated group, and thus become less profitable.

This conceptualization of discrimination assumes that workers of different groups have attained equivalent levels of human capital and that there are no persistent between-group disparities in access to education that characterize many societies, especially those with ethno-racial divisions. This approach omits structural inequalities that prevail disproportionately on certain groups *before* they participate in labour markets, thereby precluding the systemic disadvantages that affirmative action seeks to address. The Becker model assumptions, being difficult to sustain, have been amended, chiefly with the introduction of imperfect competition. These amendments posit that some firms have a monopoly in product markets and those firms prefer to hire white workers, or white workers prevent black workers from competing with them in some labour markets, or racial disparities prevail in access to financial capital (Darity 1982, 72–73). The diagnoses and solutions, however, remain ensconced in a neoclassical, ahistorical, market-centric framework. Addressing the deficiencies more forthrightly, Loury (2002) draws an instructive distinction between "reward bias" (post-labour market entry) and "development bias" (pre-labour market entry) and asserts that neoclassical economics pays inadequate attention to latter.

The confinement of discrimination to solely post-labour market entry phenomenon is emphatically deficient in the Malaysia and South Africa context, where the historical problem is that a majority group has received a systemically lesser education and economic opportunity and has suffered poorer living environments. However, I refrain from the term *discrimination*, since varying – indeed opposing – forms of discrimination have prevailed since the administration of majority-favouring affirmative action. Framing persistent inequalities preceding labour market entry as systemic disadvantages allows for the diminishment of historical and current disadvantage alongside the establishment of positive discrimination.

However, within the neoclassical framework, one could still argue that alleviating inequalities in access to and quality of education suffices to equip previously disadvantaged groups to participate in higher educational and occupational strata, thereby equalizing opportunity for self-advancement in competitive markets. This indirect and incremental route to redressing under-representation in employment, nonetheless, is clouded by two major issues that cast doubt on its adequacy.

First, the assumption of competitive markets is exceedingly questionable in the context of labour markets, where barriers are endemic, such as the role of networks and referrals, the practice of employers targeting graduates of elite institutions, or tendencies to sustain norms and avert risks, real or presumed (Bergmann 1996). Formally removing labour market entry barriers and increasing educational access may create more conducive conditions for firms to hire and promote on the basis of capability and merit, increasingly overlooking race and gender, but there is no cogent motive facilitating this outcome. Overt or subliminal discrimination may be influenced by racism, ignorance, inertia or stigma towards a particular group, which in turn can be fuelled by lack of visibility of persons from that group in prominent and influential positions. This condition poses a coordination problem, particularly if there is continually no shortage of qualified labour market entrants from advantaged groups. Individual, profit-driven firms will likely be disinclined to venture on their own to hire or promote persons from under-represented groups, due to perceived risks, real needs for further training or mentorship or other factors.

Do free markets necessarily and always employ the "best person for the job?" Bergmann (1996) points out, with reference to labour market research, that employers may discriminate against persons from under-represented groups or be inclined towards persons from groups that have established a presence. The effects are acute where on-the-job experience matters heavily, in which case under-represented persons may be continually overlooked by employers who are risk-averse or unwilling to invest in further training and mentorship. Breaking out of vicious cycles of discrimination or exclusion then requires a coordinated, external push. State intervention fills the coordination gap and engenders institutional change, not just behavioural change. But it must also endeavour to ensure that racial preference proceeds at a reasonable pace, with adequate attention to the supply and suitability of participants and to avert indefinite entrenchment.

Second, even if formal entry barriers dissipate, the pace of change may not be as fast as is socially desirable or politically imperative. Affirmative action responds to socio-political pressures, usually converging at momentous transition periods, which generate expectations and perhaps set specific targets of substantial, robust and visible change. The case for affirmative action rides not just on the existence of inter-racial disparities but also on the premise that race-preferential selection is necessary to accelerate change, to provide an extra and direct push. Uplifting the poor, who are predominantly Bumiputera in Malaysia and black in South Africa, and prohibiting unfair discrimination to seemingly "level the playing field," will to some extent and in indirect manner facilitate the community's entry to university and subsequently professional positions, and eventually into management and ownership. However, these processes would make gradual, incremental gains. The time required to bridge widespread and complex disparities in educational access and quality may eventually, but too slowly, translate into more equitable economic participation.

Anti-discrimination legislation may compel employers to be more circumspect about overt or subliminal prejudice in hiring and remuneration practices, but it still does little to compel or induce employers to seek out a representative workforce. Moreover, even if legislation prohibits discrimination, the monitoring mechanism relies heavily on individuals initiating legal proceedings against alleged unfair discrimination, which are costly and intimidating to the persons confronting institutions or employers and more reactive and dispersed in their occurrence. In contrast, affirmative action by definition operates more proactively and in a coordinated manner, being executed by the state, which is in a position to balance the objectives of equitable representation and opportunity.

Historical experience demonstrates the limitations of relying on anti-discriminatory legislation, even when buttressed by the principle of equal opportunity. AA in the United States initially revolved around prohibiting discriminatory practices, but those efforts turned out to be insufficient for increasing representation of the black minority in tertiary education. Over time, AA came to be associated with the notion and practice of positive discrimination (Weisskopf 2004). Also referencing real world experience, ILO (2007, 10) takes "recognition of the fact that the mere act of ending discrimination will never level the playing field once deep-seated and long-standing deprivation has occurred."

In sum, equal opportunity and anti-discrimination law enforcement are sometimes proposed as systemic alternatives to AA, but the proposition lacks theoretical and empirical cogency. Solutions deriving from belief in the self-demise of discrimination in competitive markets hinge on key underlying assumptions, especially regarding equal access to development and zero barriers to entry. Historical experience of racially divided societies demonstrates these to be false (disparities in development between population groups persist) or partial (informal barriers to entry can prevail, even if formal or legal discrimination is prohibited). A system of class-based AA would benefit the disadvantaged group since they are over-represented among the socio-economically needy. However, the notion that class-based AA provides a systemic alternative obfuscates its objective – to redress under-representation in high-level positions – and is viable in some spheres, notably higher education, but largely inapplicable in other areas, particularly high-level occupations and enterprise development.

Anti-discrimination legislation and class-based redistribution are most coherently conceived as complementary, not adversarial, to race-based affirmative action, and in concert all should pursue the most effective and opportune means of redressing systemic disadvantage over a bounded time horizon. Race-based AA offers direct and more effective means for facilitating the progress of a disadvantaged group into socially esteemed and economically influential positions. Where possible, this endeavour should jointly pursue increased representation with inter-generational social mobility by incorporating socio-economic criteria into selection processes. However, the project's success rides on selecting those who are well positioned to acquire and advance capabilities and hence must allow for selection of candidates who may not be considered under-privileged, even those originating from middle-class and upper-class households.

Affirmative action is by no means the only policy intervention that comes with perils and pitfalls, that should be transitory and ultimately require that beneficiaries exit and graduate out of special assistance. A parallel logic applies to infant industry protection. Undeniably, the challenges are greater in affirmative action, due to the steeper obstacles arising from historical discrimination and exclusion of population groups, but the notion of temporary special treatment is in principle less contentious.

Some affirmative action programmes involve wealth ownership in various forms, including equity, contracts, licenses or property, of which a further point should be registered. This policy sphere is among the most impactful and complicated. Wealth corresponds with places of residence, financial security, capacity to invest in higher education, access to networks and a complex of factors. The case for reducing wealth inequality rests substantially on the durable effects and potential virtuous cycles of raising wealth ownership, especially of the lower-middle and low socio-economic strata. At the same time, however, wealth redistribution can be undermined by profiteering; degrees and jobs cannot be sold off for quick gains, property, equity and financial holdings can. The political demands for redistribution are immense. Emphatically, the need for policy to proceed with caution, restraint and vigilance is even greater.

Race-based versus need-based/class-based affirmative action

Beneath AA debates often lies a disquiet over designating a population group as beneficiary, whether by race, ethnicity or gender, instead of a socio-economic category. Designating beneficiaries by race, the argument maintains, commits injustice and inefficiency by not explicitly targeting the neediest in society, i.e. the poor and economically disadvantaged. Moreover, granting preference to a formerly disadvantaged group denies opportunities to other groups, negating the purpose of fostering integration and, some would assert, committing "reverse discrimination." In addition, AA based on race, ethnicity, gender or other group identity accentuates inter-group differences, contrary to its objective of attenuating the role of these identity markers in economic interactions. Class-based or means-tested AA are commonly posed alternatives to race-based AA (Jain 2006; CPPS 2006b).

A policy framework that designates beneficiaries in terms of class or means is structured such that the neediest in society, regardless of identity, will be accorded preference. Among those qualifying for state assistance, members of disadvantaged racial or gender or other groups will disproportionately gain by virtue of their predominance in low-income brackets. Additionally, this attenuates the scope for abuse and allocative inefficiency within the designated group, by curbing *rentier* behaviour of elites and staunching the flow of benefits to the middle class, who can afford tertiary education and qualify on merit. These criticisms raise some valid and important concerns, outlining fundamental philosophical and practical dilemmas.

Framing this debate as a binary choice between two schemes of affirmative action, however, falters on two main fronts: imprecision and inconsistency on the purpose of AA and neglect of historical context and practical constraints. The argument against race-based AA generally claims that the same objective of uplifting a race group will be attained by designating beneficiaries according to other criteria, particularly socio-economic status. However, the structure and form of this uplifting must be specified, and as we do so, it becomes clear that presenting pro-poor assistance conflates helping the poor with the objectives of AA defined earlier. Can helping the poor be a coherent, operable and effective strategy for facilitating upward mobility or developing competitive enterprise? Disadvantaged persons will benefit disproportionately more from assistance targeted at low-income households, but such assistance is distinctly and fundamentally different from the underpinnings and premises of AA.

The case for need-based or class-based AA also conflates the problem of group under-representation with the manifestations of group over-representation. These systemic alternatives place policy pre-eminence on areas where disadvantaged groups are *over*-represented – i.e. among the poor and socio-economically excluded – rather than the problem of *under*-representation, which is manifest in distinctly separate areas. Thus, the arguments are not so much proposing alternative solutions as framing an altogether different set of problems. If the question of *under*-representation is accepted as the problem at hand, the focus accordingly falls on the precise target group and effective measures to increase their proportions in spheres where they are under-represented. The barriers to entry underlying this under-representation – academic grades, higher education qualifications, work experience – are minimally, if at all, addressed by instituting preferences for the poor.

Two other inconsistencies are worth noting. First, the critique of affirmative action on the grounds of neglect of the poor generally implies that AA fails, in absolute terms, as long as some benefits accrue to the middle or upper classes, when the outcome is one of relative magnitude. Surely, whether AA excludes all or some of the poor bears importance in assessing the efficacy of specific policies. Second, the case against race-based AA on the grounds that it accentuates inter-group differences finds corollaries in other dimensions of inequality that are generally not considered problematic. Conferring preferential status on poor, rural or inner-city persons may drive wedges between rich and poor, urban and rural or suburban and inner-city, but such measures are generally approved due to the benefits of bridging these gaps. In the same way that university campuses should not be the preserve of the rich in a stratified society, student bodies should not be racially homogenous in a heterogeneous society. The justification for providing special means for the poor to gain access, in principle, does not differ from the rationale for race-based AA.

The premise of equitable group representation is repudiated by some on stronger grounds – that it is neither desirable nor achievable. One attempt at pointing out the innocuous existence of non-representative workforces is to refer to the concentration of ethnic groups in particular sectors or occupations in societies that are fairly cohesive: e.g. in the US, Korean corner stores and West African taxi drivers (Hermann 2007; Sowell 2004). While such niches and business networks thrive and are not necessarily deleterious to social relations, they are characterized by spatial differentiation (concentration of some groups in the operation of certain activities), which is much less fractious and potentially destabilizing than hierarchical patterns (predominance of one group at the top of the economic hierarchy). This critique of AA conflates two different problems and on the whole provides a weak case against redressing under-representation of disadvantaged groups in positions conferring social status and economic influence.

Preferential treatment of one group unavoidably comes at some expense of other groups. However, characterizing positive discrimination as reverse discrimination commits a false equivalency, most gravely in cases where past discrimination took the form of slavery, denial of basic rights and systemic exclusion, such as in South Africa. The argument also generally precludes the potential gains from positive discrimination, even while it espouses non-interventionism on the basis of the potential for dismantling negative discrimination, which in turn hinges on assumed propensities of market behaviour outlined and critiqued previously.

Emphatically, transformative national agendas such as affirmative action emerge at historical watersheds and in country-specific conditions that give momentum to the designation of beneficiaries by race or ethnicity. The trajectories and entrenchment of AA programmes receive the bulk of deprecatory attention, but a judicious assessment must be mindful of the initial conditions and appreciate historical context and practical constraints. The notion that race can be overlooked or proxied by socio-economic variables in racially fractured societies, while attractive, superimposes a future ideal on a present reality in which racial identity, disparity and perhaps stereotypes are deeply embedded and sharply experienced. In most cases, the vast majority of the disadvantaged group is ill-equipped for tertiary education and economically influential positions. Practical constraints thus require policies to factor in the availability of persons who possess at least partial qualifications or experience to enter the upper echelons of the education system or labour market, regardless of socio-economic status.

One notable example of non-race-based mechanisms for facilitating representation of disadvantaged groups concerns public university entry in some states of the US. The practice, which grants admission of a certain proportion of top students of all high schools, was initiated to counteract ballot propositions banning preferential admissions policies. This regionally egalitarian mechanism engenders diversity of student representation, to the extent that ethnic groups are concentrated in particularly districts. However, disparities across schools in quality of teaching and facilities may propel some under-prepared minority-group students into distinguished tertiary institutions. Students of low-income families may also have less funds to defray education costs, entailing larger commitments of public finance (Weisskopf 2004; Fryer and Loury 2005). Of course, the issues do not translate directly to more centralized education systems where national, university entrance examinations are administered, such as Malaysia and South Africa, but the general implication holds, i.e. proportionate regional representation or need-based admission can adversely affect the average level of student preparedness for tertiary education.

In employment and enterprise development spheres, need-based or class-based AA becomes considerably less operable. While education institutes are in a position to factor in family income in admissions and financial aid decisions, it is much less clear how employers can be induced or obligated to hire or promote persons based on family socio-economic background or how contracts and business opportunities can be awarded preferentially to poorer – and likely under-performing – firms. Adam (2000), while advocating such systemic alternatives in place of race-based employment equity programmes in South Africa, scarcely furnishes details on how class-based AA will be implemented. In terms of ownership and control over capital, class-based AA is the most problematic and prone to abuse, even while dominance of one race group at the commanding heights of the economy is a dimension of disparity with immense political consequence. Any endeavours in this sphere must be managed with utmost circumspection, to check against profligacy and to leverage on asset allocation as a means to gain productive learning and working opportunity. At the bottom end, another application of need-based selection is worth exploring; wealth distribution to low-income households can possibly operate on means-tested basis instead of racial identity.

Historical conditions and practical constraints under which AA is instituted provide important context for understanding the designation of beneficiaries by race or other population group. While the policy discourses and political dynamics surely vary by country, the prospect of redressing disadvantage and under-representation without preferential schemes generally falls short of societal or political expectations and relies on agents, especially employers, taking risks on their own volition that they are predisposed against. AA fills a coordination gap, which is all the more required for an intervention that disrupts norms or biases. Policies follow trajectories and acquire inertia, producing outcomes that can be scrutinized retrospectively. No amount of hindsight, however, changes the fact that race-based AA has become institutionalized. Critics of race-based AA highlight negative outcomes and unintended consequences; advocates draw out positives and raise possibilities that outcomes could be worse without AA. Simulating counterfactuals of what might transpire in the absence of race-based AA may be an interesting academic exercise, but focusing on the practical matters and empirical evidence presents a more productive and constructive direction for AA research to take. Arguments over the existence of race-based AA are less germane and helpful than arguments over its design and duration.

It must be recognized that race-based and class-based AA are not mutually exclusive (Darity 2013) and that they operate as complements rather than substitutes. Class considerations can be integrated into selection procedures within the designated race group to reinforce the process of redress. On the paramount issue of access, completion and quality of basic schooling, reducing disparities is a precondition for both race-based affirmative action and alternate schemes to be effective. Expansion and improvement of basic schooling alleviates tensions that arise from preferential selection into tertiary education.

High expectations of change, we have noted, inevitably infuse the inception of any AA programme, compounded by informational deficits and fundamental uncertainty. Amid uncertainty, the most direct route for correcting racial disparities is by designating beneficiaries by race. The constraints must be acknowledged. However, they do not necessarily nullify the state's capacity to manage expectations and set prudent, incremental goals, e.g. targeting the increase in representation in select occupations in correspondence with the designated group's proportion of the tertiary educated labour force or registered professionals, instead of the national labour force or economically active population. There are advantages to race-based affirmative action programmes, particularly in education and employment, as well as pitfalls. The alternatives often present solutions inconsistent with the problem (specifically, class-based selection to redress race-based inequality) or solutions that are impracticable (class-based criteria for selection into employment or equity ownership). Ultimately, however, the goal of "deracialization" demands critical attention toward cultivating self-reliance of the designated group and rolling back preferential selection in due course.

Another criticism of AA – that it omits intra-group inequality or exacerbates the problem – warrants a brief note. A further assertion typically accompanies this view: AA benefits are reaped or captured by political and corporate elites, and therefore the system fails to help the poor, whom it was meant to help.[3] Privileged households and well-connected elites can certainly reap the gains of AA, but the ramifications are less clear-cut than often presented. These critiques tend to zoom in on the more conspicuously acquisitive, venal and profligate cases of AA. Undoubtedly, profiteering and corruption undermine the policy. But to evaluate whether these represent the entire system and the aggregate, multifaceted outcomes, we must undertake a broader, more complex and nuanced investigation. In many countries AA promotes higher education attainment, upward job mobility and business opportunities, which enlarge middle classes.

Inequalities of opportunity, while undeniably prevalent in society, are not readily traceable to AA policies. Indeed, income and wealth concentration and rich-poor gaps derive from various structural and institutional factors besides AA, including systemic patronage, poor governance and weak labour market institutions. In Malaysia and South Africa, evidence points to widening gaps between the extremities of the distribution – with increasing Bumiputera and black wealth and income concentration at the top and lagging gains for the bottom segments – while middle classes have expanded, especially when we observe AA's primary objectives of increasing entry to higher education, high-level employment and public procurement.

Furthermore, to reiterate the arguments laid out earlier, the notion that AA is meant to help "the poor" is also misguided. AA can be inclined to help the poor in certain areas where need-based preferences are applicable, but its principle objective and operations involve capability development, in which targeting the poor cannot uniformly work as an alternative. Financial support for university students bolsters access, but it is also crucial that recipients succeed academically. A government contract practically cannot be reallocated from a large Bumiputera or black contractor to a poor Bumiputera or black household or community; again, the prime goal is for beneficiaries to demonstrably deliver on the job. In these and other AA interventions, the persons with capacity to learn and excel will likely be the more advantaged households or more established firms who, besides being more equipped, also possess greater financial means, which may reduce the burdens on public funding and logistical support. The more pressing concern for Bumiputera and black empowerment is to induce or compel the beneficiary, whether a small, medium or large company, to use the preferential opportunity received to deliver on the project and acquire skill and experience and to set visible examples of achievement. On the whole, the more pressing questions concern the extent to which opportunities are being equitably and progressively distributed and how effectively the instrument is spurring beneficiaries to be productive, dynamic and increasingly self-reliant.

Merit and effort, efficiency and dependency

Arguments against affirmative action – in general, and not specifically race-based programmes – commonly assert that interference with competitive markets vitiates the fairness and efficiency of "meritocracy" and "equal opportunity." AA also devalues accomplishments of members of the designated group who could have advanced without preferential treatment, stigmatizes beneficiaries as a group, creates dependence on the state and alienates members of non-designated groups. These stances raise considerable questions regarding AA formulation and implementation.

Ascribing preference to disadvantaged groups may curtail the effort exerted by beneficiaries and entrench dependency on state assistance. Although these problems are not confined to race-based AA, they are plausibly more severe due to the capacity of ethno-racial political entities to kindle sentiments and galvanize popular support. Even more severe is the issue of elite "capture" – the manipulation of policy, especially regarding wealth ownership, for the express enrichment of a politically connected class. We should note that inequality and corruption could conceivably increase, and middle classes and elites consolidate their position, in the absence of affirmative action. Nevertheless, these pitfalls of AA underscore the need for judiciously formulated and vigorously implemented affirmative action that, like infant industry programmes, avert *rentier* behaviour and decisively transition away from protracted protectionist and preferential elements.

One response is to probe the supposed objectivity and adequacy of the notions of merit and opportunity. The meaning and parameters of merit arise out of a particular social context, and thus are not neutral, and indeed tend to perpetuate a status quo. Tierney (2007, 389–390) points out that merit fits with a capitalist conception of justice, with its valorization of survival of the ostensibly ablest and repudiation of government intervention in general as a threat to capitalism.[4]

Assessment of merit is presumed to be a measure of intelligence and individual effort, confirmed by one's peers through unbiased and objective criteria, e.g. standardized tests or national examinations. In reality, however, privileges disproportionately enjoyed by particular population groups, such as private schooling or extra-tuition classes, can set children on trajectories towards reputed tertiary institutions, cementing their access to networks and opportunities for accelerated career advancement.[5] Merit-based appraisal, furthermore, is typically individual-centred, omitting the person's social context, and present-looking, being based on past-to-present attainments, not future capacities. The dynamic social objective of equitable representation, however, necessitates some consideration of potential for learning.

Another response maintains that *a priori* postulates about how AA affects incentives are unfounded, thus the subject is ultimately a "subtle and context-dependent empirical question" (Fryer and Loury 2005, 154). Holzer and Neumark's (2000, 514) expansive literature survey concludes that evidence of discrimination in racial, gender or other spheres is sufficient to "rule out a facile conclusion that affirmative action must reduce efficiency or performance." The assessment of how affirmative action impacts on beneficiaries' performance is also in an important sense a subjective matter of attitudes and perceptions. Some empirical approaches directly ask persons benefiting from AA to self-evaluate their experience. Adam (2000) finds, among a sample of preferentially selected black business trainees in South Africa, no sentiment that their advancements were devalued and as much motivation to put in effort as qualified participants.[6]

The aggregate efficiency effects of affirmative action are, likewise, theoretically indeterminate. On the one hand, as it is more often argued, discrimination reduces efficiency by admitting or promoting lesser-qualified candidates to meet distributional targets or quotas. On the other hand, and less often recognized, negative discrimination and systemic disadvantage also curtail efficiency by, respectively, denying capable candidates opportunities and persistently inhibiting the human development of certain groups (Holzer and Neumark 2000). To reiterate a point made in the previous section, policy-making at the inception of AA grapples with steep constraints and risks. Another aspect of the process involves balancing the efficiency losses of not accelerating redress through AA against the losses due to overly aggressive implementation of programmes. The ultimate effect hinges on this balancing act.

The meritocracy critique must be placed in the context of alternatives to race-based AA, where causal relations are not straightforward. First, complete absence of AA may stimulate individual effort and bring about material gains for some in the disadvantaged group. But disadvantaged and marginalized youth may also perceive tertiary education and upward mobility as inaccessible and be discouraged from participating. Second, it is unclear how class-based AA will be more effective in motivating excellence. This framework may well create disincentives against raising income to remain below eligibility thresholds, since one's class can be changed, whereas one's race cannot. On the other hand, race-based AA might generate competition within the designated group (Weisskopf 2004).

AA may become associated with stigmas and negative stereotypes towards the competency of beneficiaries. The perils of such perceptions and enmities are undeniable, hence AA must be conducted in line with the ultimate objective of developing capability to moderate such ramifications. As a cautionary note, the critique is pertinent. However, as an argument against the institution of AA, it rests on a tenuous assumption that those stereotypes did not exist in the first place, when in most contexts stereotypes are likely to already be prevalent, even pervasive (Tierney 1997; Brown, Stewart and Langer 2012). A less vigorous critique may maintain that AA reinforces pre-existing stigmas or stereotypes. Still, there is no guarantee that the absence of AA will enhance perceptions toward the group, and lack of pace and visibility in the disadvantaged group's upward mobility may well reinforce pre-existing stereotypes. These are also, ultimately, empirical questions in societies already implementing AA, where the more consequential policy question is how implementation can mitigate adverse side effects.

While avoiding absolutist positions for or against race-based affirmative action, we must acknowledge that perennial dependence on state-sponsored intervention can impede, even imperil, its fruition. Maintaining preferential treatment in perpetuity negates the goal of attaining self-reliance and economic independence. Dependence on state intervention and a sense of entitlement may become entrenched among the beneficiary group. We should note that this problem is not confined to racial preference, but it can also beset other development programmes offering some form of protection, which can be broadly subsumed under the infant industry rubric.

Nonetheless, pressure to retain preferential policies can conceivably be more intense where race is the basis of preference, deriving from the strength and resilience of collective political identity, and mobilization on the grounds of group interest, nationalism or discrimination. The likelihood that AA turns into a permanent institution and the lack of a precedent of a country removing AA (except perhaps white-favouring Apartheid South Africa) reinforce the case for total opposition to the policy. The necessity of eventually removing racial preference also serves a sharp caveat to advocates and to countries that are implementing the policy for whom complete and instant elimination of AA are fraught with political peril and potential electoral backlash. Relevant and productive discourse, therefore, should focus on systematic and workable transitions away from racial preference.

The complex ramifications of AA on social cohesion and inter-group sentiments must be also be noted here (although these phenomena are manifested less tangibly, and their scope is multi-dimensional and much broader than this book's focus). Critics often impugn race-based AA for alienating members of the non-designated group, especially those who are denied entry or promotion to positions offered to less formally qualified persons of the designated group. The contentions of the non-designated group arguably derive from more complex factors than economic opportunity, such as cultural and democratic freedom, lack of political representation, personal safety or governance and corruption perceived as related to AA. Nonetheless, this antipathy stemming from a sense of personal injustice is palpable, and if protracted and accumulated may generate social discord.

A few perspectives can be briefly outlined. First, the extent to which opportunities become limited significantly depends on economic variables outside AA jurisdiction. Sluggish economic and employment growth compound the difficulties faced by members of non-designated groups; as much or more fault may lie with economic policies or fortuitous circumstances. Second, instituting strict meritocracy, typically presented as the solution for both instituting fairness and alleviating the alienation of non-designated groups, bears the risk of perpetuating group disadvantage, potentially resulting in continual lagging development of AA beneficiary group. In consonance with the earlier discussion on the issue of feelings of grievance among the non-designated group, the trade-off is also not as straightforward as justice and cohesion under meritocracy versus diametric opposites under affirmative action. Societies shaped by complex disparities have to grapple with elements of both preferential treatment and meritocracy.

Third, advocacy of need-based or pro-poor programmes are often presented as a substitute for race-based AA based on one commonly expressed objection – that the latter provides opportunity to lesser qualified policy beneficiaries at the expense of more qualified non-beneficiaries. However, similar scenarios of non-beneficiaries "losing out" would also prevail to some extent under the alternate policy regime, except that those granted preferential access would be persons of poor, disadvantaged backgrounds. This may be a more morally palatable scenario; however, the reality remains that the alternative of need-based AA does not fully alleviate these grievances of non-beneficiaries.

Other ramifications of affirmative action, specifically the stigmatization of beneficiaries and alienation of non-beneficiaries are real and present. However, once countries have embarked on AA, the pressing question becomes how to implement it in a manner that mitigates these adverse effects. Posing counterfactuals of national trajectories in the absence of AA remains an engaging intellectual exercise, but it needs to acknowledge that stigmas, stereotypes and schisms typically pre-exist the policy, and that can endure or even deepen with persisting inter-group disparities. Disadvantaged groups may be stigmatized for receiving preferential treatment or if their presence in esteemed and empowered positions is continually low. Alienation of non-beneficiaries correlates partly with the efficacy and duration of preferential policies that disfavour them, but this must be weighed against the possible sense of deprivation that a disadvantaged group may experience without specific programmes that compel and coordinate its upward mobility. The more important task of academic and policy inquiry is empirical.

All in all, then, it is more pertinent to ask how race-based affirmative action can be made more effective rather than whether it should exist; and it is more productive to consider incremental instead of instantaneous elimination of policies, especially in Malaysia and South Africa, where the political imperative is overwhelming. Avoiding the polemics and absolutist positions on merit versus preference, the important inquiry revolves around safeguards that benefits are distributed equitably within the designated group, with a balance of allocation based on present qualification and on potential learning. It is prudent to limit the scope and duration of AA, placing more emphasis on education and employment and less on procurement and wealth, and to apply timelines, graduation clauses or exit conditions suited to each policy sector.

Building from the debate

It is worth reminding ourselves that affirmative action intervenes in societies riven by historical injustices, systemic disparities and socio-political schisms between racial groups. The policy objectives are as difficult and seemingly intractable as the conditions they seek to redress. Contradictions cannot be denied, nor avoided: applying positive discrimination to eliminate past discrimination, designating beneficiaries by race towards the goal of attenuating the role of race in economic advancement, instituting preferential treatment to augment equal opportunity. These conditions are also highly country-specific; policy solutions must take into account the distinctive structures and dynamics of each country, even while synthesizing general trends and applying ideas across countries.

What can we take from the polarized, and often polemical, debate in our effort to construct frameworks for thinking about AA and empirically researching policy outcomes and implications? The purpose, targeting and practical design of AA frame the policy instruments and outcomes to be investigated. The ultimate objective of developing capability, and the ultimate fruition in terms of phasing out preferential treatment, are also vital aspects to be incorporated into conceptual frameworks, empirical inquiry and policy discourse. Insights based on the critiques of AA, or caution and circumspection toward its possible adverse consequences, can contribute in this regard.

It is imperative that implementing countries make AA more effective and less prone to abuses and that they integrate graduation and exit plans (Brown, Stewart and Langer 2012). The scope of interventions is also broader than quotas and overt preferences; AA encompasses direct and indirect modes and can take the form of outreach and signalling to boost the prospects of the beneficiary group by encouraging participation and enlarging its share of candidate pools (Sabbagh 2012). A few conditions that enhance the efficacy of AA warrant consideration. More progressive and pro-poor distribution of AA opportunities facilitates inter-generational upward mobility and enhances and broadens the beneficiary group's capability development, while curtailing the risk of policy derailment through rent-seeking behaviour and elite enrichment. In Brown and Langer's (2015, 6) broad cross-country assessment, AA policies "work best when they target the poor." This in turn bolsters the capacity to phase out preferential treatment. More competitive selection *within* the beneficiary group also consolidates capability development, and it potentially demonstrates success and spurs effort in the broader community, while also being a precursor to facilitating graduation out of preferential treatment.

A few further principles and guidelines enter the frame, in terms of the moral underpinnings, economic consequences and pragmatic considerations of endeavouring to make AA more effective. First, higher education deserves a higher policy priority for a few reasons. The moral justification for granting preference to a disadvantaged group is reinforced when the disadvantage is due to circumstances beyond the person's control or choice. In the case of AA in higher education – whether scholarships, admissions or other forms of support – the beneficiaries are predominantly late adolescents who are still dependents, emerging from schooling, family and neighbourhood situations primarily not of their choosing. The basis for intervening through preferential treatment is also underscored when compared to the employment or business spheres, where beneficiaries are full adults who bear greater personal owner-ship and responsibility over their socio-economic circumstances. Disparity in opportunity and wealth, and exclusion from networks, may persist well beyond young adulthood. Nonetheless, it is fair to maintain that, as people progress beyond higher education and move up in employment and economic advance-ment, family background and socio-economic disadvantages due to conditions outside of one's choice substantially diminish as grounds for receiving prefer-ential treatment.

Other socio-economic perspectives factor into the case for higher education taking higher precedence among AA spheres. Weisskopf (2006) maintains that the effects of disadvantage are less compounded at this stage because socio-economic disadvantage of young beneficiaries is relatively less compared to working adults or business owners, for whom the cumulative effects are greater. Furthermore, possible adverse ramifications are less potent. The consequences of AA are largely confined to the individual rather than groups, where poor perfor-mance can hurt other parties. The consequences of effort in academic learning are quite confined to the individual, whereas occupying a high-level position or being awarded a construction contract entails organizational performance and product delivery, even public safety. Additionally, AA in the educational sphere, by engendering more diverse environments and social interactions at a formative stage of young adulthood, holds out potential to foster relationships that can extend into the future, yielding long-term benefits.

Reinforcing affirmative action with need, class and merit considerations

Affirmative action, in principle, serves as a transitory, special intervention that makes itself redundant. The prospects for rolling back preferential treatment depend significantly on the extent to which it distributes benefits equitably and productively. AA must also address the common presumptions – vigorously raised in Malaysia and South Africa – that it does not help the poor who need help the most, or that it *only* helps an undeserving, tiny Malay or Black elite.[7] These con-ceptual and policy debates were discussed earlier, recognizing valid points they raise while underscoring that AA maintains coherence as a race-based regime which cannot be *systemically* replaced with "need-based affirmative action," "class-based affirmative action," or "merit-based affirmative action."

A slight digression to both countries is pertinent in order to locate this somewhat contrarian discussion in a particular historical context. The rhetoric of replacing race-based AA with need-based AA became mainstreamed in Malaysia's popular consciousness from 2010, with the publication of the New Economic Model (NEM). The NEM omitted any definition or conceptualization of affirmative action but strongly implied that race-based policies were at the crux. While the report suitably highlighted rent-seeking, profiteering and fronting that had undermined Bumiputera advancement specifically in enterprise development, it failed to specify that these problems were particular to this policy sphere and not endemic to the entire preferential regime. It also pronounced various reforms to make affirmative action based on need and merit, to be executed in "market-based" and "market-friendly" fashion, again without clarifying the meaning of these concepts nor demonstrating any grasp of the conflations and contradictions in these proposals. However, the rhetoric of shifting away from race-based policies toward need-based assistance that helps the bottom 40% of households was irresistibly appealing to many Malaysians who have heartily embraced this prospect of "reform" despite there being no specific explanations of how need-based and merit-based programmes would actually function.[8]

This "reform" agenda was basically built on sentiment. The absence of attention to what would be retained and changed of the vast system of Bumiputera created conditions that could easily be exploited by playing up real, and in some ways legitimate, fears on the ground. The policy failed to allay concerns, particularly in the Peninsula Malay population, of diminishing preferential access to public procurement and licensing, public sector employment, higher education and wealth ownership – spectres they were not yet prepared to contemplate. The NEM seemingly relied on the palatable notion that helping the poor and those who need help the most – the bottom 40% (B40), according to a new shorthand – would serve as a catch-all that all parties could sign up to. However, political backlash and popular protest on Malay nationalist impulses proved fiercer and more forceful; the government retracted the NEM, even if it was not officially renounced. Many look back on the NEM as an opportunity foregone, but in fact it was a non-starter.

In South Africa, extreme magnitudes of disparity, stratification and marginalization and convergences of class and race, especially in the Apartheid era, posed stark realities saliently addressed in public discourses and academic literature. The severity of black disenfranchised underclasses and dispossessed masses heightened attention to these problems in the democratic transition. Undoubtedly, problems surrounding basic rights and basic needs were of utmost priority. However, as in Malaysia, affirmative action became conflated with different, and much broader, policy objectives and instruments – and it was erroneously faulted for shortcomings that are beyond its scope of increasing representation in specific spheres or for ostensibly not benefiting the poor or unemployed masses as intended. Policy rhetoric has, perhaps unintentionally, undermined itself. Lofty, sweeping articulation of BEE objectives, encompassing mass unemployment, also contributes to a muddled perspective and exposes the policy to accusations that it has failed on those grounds.

A coherent and systematic approach is built on the imperatives of integrating selection based on socio-economic disadvantage and merit into AA, to make it more effective and to chart reform paths. Emphatically, AA does not operate in isolation from other interventions. Indeed, various programmes and selection mechanisms can coalesce with the overarching mantle of promoting a beneficiary group's upward mobility, to augment and complement AA, enhancing the breadth and progressiveness of the distribution of benefits and facilitating conditions that enhance the possibility of graduating out of overt preferential treatment.

In essence, AA can and should be *reinforced* with need-based considerations that take into account socio-economic disadvantage and with merit-based considerations that strive to select the more capable within the beneficiary group. These reinforcements operate principally within the race-based framework – that is, selecting Bumiputeras and blacks who are relatively disadvantaged over relatively advantaged Bumiputeras and blacks and more capable and competitive Bumiputeras and blacks over less capable Bumiputeras and blacks. Importantly, these supplementary and complementary measures underpin policy transitions, and they do so in ways that are specific to each policy sector.

In some but not all policy sectors, race-based preferences can be phased out and need-based selection – granting preference to the socio-economically disadvantaged – phased in. For merit-based preference to play its transitory role, it must adhere to an overriding purpose of selecting capable and dynamic beneficiaries while also grooming and compelling them to operate and compete independently. All in all, graduating out of preferential treatment and rolling back overt racial preference is contingent on the beneficiaries having capability and confidence to stand on their own feet.

This chapter concludes by presenting a systematic framework for thinking about race, need and merit. Table 2.1 schematizes how need and merit considerations can be factored into selection processes to enhance race-based AA and generate conditions for policy reform and rollback. More extensive and well-targeted assistance to the disadvantaged selection facilitates inter-generational upward mobility, a crucial element of AA's efficacy. These considerations pertain primarily to higher education, where students of disadvantaged backgrounds can be granted preferential treatment, regardless of race or ethnicity, in university admissions and for award of bursaries.

Granting preferential access based on socio-economic disadvantage also rests on the principle that persons should not be penalized for circumstances not of their choosing, as noted previously. This is eminently applicable to school graduates seeking university admission, who are beginning to transition away from being dependents and for whom family background and schooling quality were basically beyond their control. The case for granting preference based on socio-economic disadvantage is more constrained in the employment sphere, where it is applicable predominantly at initial entry or on first job applications but scarcely

Table 2.1 Enhancement of race-based affirmative action through need-based and merit-based selection

Policy sector	*Need-enhanced selection* – *two distinct ramifications:*		*Merit-enhanced selection:*
	Preference for economically disadvantaged	*Limits or sunset clauses for repeat beneficiaries or economically empowered*	*Preference with respect to capability and competitiveness*
Higher education	• High potential for cultivating capability and inter-generational upward mobility, including through need-based financial aid • Family background (disadvantage due to circumstances beyond control): logical and practical selection criteria, can be applied regardless of race		• Promoting academic achievement and competitiveness are vital, besides increasing access for the disadvantaged • Scholarships can reward and promote achievement – not necessarily fully funded; amount of sponsorship can correspond with financial need
High-level employment	• Possible application to fresh graduates, at recruitment stage		• Important to demonstrate competency and capable leadership, especially in public sector and GLCs/ SOCs, and to promote diversity
Enterprise development	• Applicable to microfinance	• Maximum quantum/ repetition of benefits, or requirements to upscale or graduate	• Imperative that beneficiaries are capable and competitive, and that they graduate out of preferential treatment
Wealth and property ownership	• Broad-based distribution/ priority for low-income households should be prioritized – can be extended to all races	• Case for rolling back preferential treatment for high-income households	• Beneficiaries of wealth/asset transfers must be productive, process should prioritize new, innovative ventures

Source: Adapted from Lee (2017a).

for promotion decisions. Compared to students, labour market participants can be conferred much less preference based on background circumstances beyond their control, and they are also independent adults who should compete on their own merit. In addition, it is practically unreasonable and infeasible for employers to collect and evaluate information on applicants' socio-economic background in promoting employees. Attempts to foster a more racially representative workforce can scarcely rely on preference for the disadvantaged; to achieve that objective, race must substantially factor into selection processes.

Need-based selection holds vastly different ramifications when it comes to enterprise development. The objectives here are to provide opportunity for companies to grow and demonstrate success; there is a heavy onus on beneficiaries to be productive and to increase capacity and independence. Need-based preferences on a pro-poor basis, therefore, are improper – and possibly detrimental because favouring lower-earning companies may allocate opportunities to less capable recipients, although there is scope to give preference to young entrepreneurs. Microfinance, which principally constitutes a form of assistance to the socio-economically disadvantaged, can in the context of seeking alternatives to race-based AA coherently and effectively operate on the basis of need. However, in other sectors the need principle can apply conversely – i.e. limiting assistance for those who do not "need" it or who have benefited enough. Along these lines, there is scope to devise limits on repeatedly receiving rewards – e.g. by setting a maximum number of times contractors can win preferentially receive contracts at a scale level, beyond which they must move up to a higher category.

Merit-based selection can reinforce AA broadly, but we must remain circumspect and precise about the policy implications. In higher education, it is important to provide opportunity and reward for students based on achievement or potential. However, this project may sit in tension with the pursuit of equitable distribution because higher academic attainment is highly correlated with higher income and general socio-economic privilege. Compromise, noted in Table 2.1, can take the form of scholarships with competitive selection but with funding proportionate to financial need. In the employment sphere, particularly in appointment to important administrative and leadership positions, merit clearly enhances racial group empowerment. Selecting the more capable Bumiputeras and blacks increases the chances for successful occupation of high-level positions. The further objective is to demonstrate capability and build confidence in the community, which are prerequisite conditions for rolling back race-based preference.

The imperatives of selecting qualified and capable beneficiaries, and monitoring progress, are perhaps greatest in enterprise development compared to the other policy sectors in our consideration. Allocation of opportunities and rents here entail delivery of goods and services and development of managerial capability; thus, the social implications and the requisite experience or learning proficiency are exceedingly high. Disbursement of contracts, licenses, credit and financial assistance can be effective instruments for cultivating enterprise, capability and resourcefulness, or they can gravitate toward rent-seeking and dependency. Beneficiaries of preferential access to opportunities and rents should all the more be induced or compelled to graduate out of such special treatment.

In wealth and property ownership, need-based preference can enter the frame and even substitute for race-based preference in programmes aiming to increase low-income households' asset ownership or savings. In the other portions of the income distribution, it is reasonable, on moral and logical grounds, to append a self-expiring element or sunset clause to programmes that benefit middle- or high-income households – i.e. that race-based preferences should be rolled back for repeat beneficiaries. Wealth distribution may also involve ownership that entails participation in commerce and entrepreneurship. In these cases, similar to the enterprise development discussion earlier, emphasis must be placed on merit-based selection and productive outcomes, with further priority on start-ups and innovation. Ultimately, the objective is to visibly demonstrate success and facilitate graduation to more self-reliance.

Notes

1 The ILO has maintained a fairly consistent position on temporariness of redistributive programmes in the labour market. Its Convention 111, passed in 1958, stipulated that government measures to ameliorate the position of particular groups in society – as a precursor to implementing non-discrimination legislation – should be reviewed every ten years.

2 Becker maintains that a differential between marginal revenue product and marginal cost indicates discrimination and that non-pecuniary costs can be quantified in a "discrimination coefficient" representing the value of these costs. If an employer derives disutility from an interaction, this translates into a negative discrimination coefficient – hence, lower wages.

3 "Race-based Affirmative Action is Failing Poor Malaysians", *The Economist*, 18 May 2017; James Chin, "The Costs of Malay Supremacy", *New York Times*, 27 August 2015; Anthea Jeffery, "BEE: The Extortion Needs to Stop", *Politicsweb*, 27 July 2015.

4 Irving Kristol, 1978. "A Capitalist Conception of Justice", In R. T. DeGeorge and J. Pichler (eds.), *Ethics, Free Enterprise and Public Policy*, 57–79. Oxford University Press.

5 In the US context, Tierney (1997) points out "legacy" enrolment, which improves the prospects for children of alumni but defies meritocracy and disproportionately benefits whites to the exclusion of other groups lacking such multi-generational privilege. He also notes the discrepancy of the general approving tenor towards legacy enrolment against the widespread criticism of AA.

6 Adam's (2000) finding is based on a survey of black aspiring business executives of a project enabling under-qualified managerial students from educationally deprived backgrounds to compete for entry into an elite training programme at the University of Cape Town. On questions of perception of being an AA beneficiary, the vast majority did not consider themselves as passive recipients but as having rightly earned a place in the programme and, contrary to conventional wisdom, did not display different approaches to work compared to participants accepted based on formal qualification.

7 In addition to the articles in note 3 above, Peter T. C. Chang, "Mahathir's new Malay Dilemma: Tackle Poverty among the Majority Without Excluding Others, Particularly the Chinese", *South China Morning Post*, 1 August 2018; Preeti Jha, "Can New Malaysia Move Beyond Old Race Divides?", *The Diplomat*, 14 August 2019; Anthea Jeffrey, "BEE: The Extortion needs to Stop", *Politicsweb*, 27 July 2015; Linda van Tilburg, "Are the Calls for BEE Revision Growing? – An

Alternative Plan", *Biz News*, 3 December 2019. "Poverty won't be Solved by BEE: Moeletsi Mbeki", *IOL*, 24 June 2008.

8 The muddled and incoherent perspective of the NEM's reform perspective is encapsulated in its summary statement, replete with ambiguous notions of need and merit, and baffling specification of discrimination committed by "dominant groups": "Affirmative action programmes and institutions will continue in the NEM but, in line with the views of the main stakeholders, will be revamped to remove the rent seeking and market distorting features which have blemished the effectiveness of the programme. Affirmative action will consider all ethnic groups fairly and equally as long as they are in the low-income 40% of households. Affirmative action programmes would be based on market-friendly and market-based criteria together taking into consideration the needs and merits of the applicants. An Equal Opportunities Commission will be established to ensure fairness and address undue discrimination when occasional abuses by dominant groups are encountered" (NEAC 2010, 117).

3 Policy regimes
A study in contrasts

This chapter outlines and discusses the formation of affirmative action regimes in Malaysia and South Africa. I delve into historical dynamics and structures of racial inequality that the countries were compelled to redress, as well as multiple political, economic, social and legal factors that bolstered or constrained the mandate for affirmative action and the means for implementing the agenda. Beyond the broad commonality of a politically dominant but socio-economically disadvantaged majority race, these two countries depart significantly in terms of the political bedrock that shaped institutions, laws and policies; the structures and dynamics of race relations; the character and magnitude of socio-economic disparity and the prevailing macroeconomic conditions at policy inception and watershed moments. I survey both countries separately, then synthesize their similarities and especially their contrasts. Since the focus is on the policy formation, I pay particular attention to the 1960s and 1970s in Malaysia, and the 1980s and 1990s in South Africa.

Comparisons of affirmative action policies in Malaysia and South Africa and their political economic contexts are sparse and have faded in and out across time. In the early- to mid-1990s, when South Africa sought out other countries' experiences in devising its economic policies, Malaysia stood out as a model of majority-favouring affirmative action in a diversified economy. Much of this attention, it seems, was not substantively informed, prompting Emsley (1996) and Hart (1994) to caution against overestimating the commonalities between Malaysia and South Africa. The fact that South Africa initially adopted little of Malaysia's policies – saliently, in drawing on inputs from Canada and the US for employment equity legislation – may have been influenced by intellectual realization of some fundamental differences with Malaysia but was equally – if not more likely – compelled by the constraints of negotiating multiple transitions (democratization, governmental restructuring, counterbalancing white dominance in every sector) outlined in this chapter.

A quarter century after the democratic transition, similarities and differences between Malaysia and South Africa have remained but have also shown some new characteristics, providing valuable material for comparative analysis. This chapter will discuss notable comparative elements of affirmative action programmes in

Malaysia and South Africa and the political economic context out of which the policies emerged.

The contrasts stand out and are worth previewing here. First, the constitutions of both countries provide authorization for affirmative action, but on different grounds: special position of the Bumiputera in Malaysia, disadvantage due to unfair discrimination in South Africa. Quotas and reservations are also specified in Malaysia's constitution, while South Africa employs a system of codes and statutory requirements. Second, the political transition during the formation of affirmative action regimes differed, with implications on the expansion or introduction of racial preferences. In the 1970s, Malaysia consolidated Malay political dominance and gravitated toward authoritarian and centralized governance, while 1990s South Africa shifted from white minority to black majority rule, democratized and decentralized its political structure to a much greater extent.

Third, the magnitude of disparity varied across both countries. In Malaysia, Malays continuously held top positions and influence in the public sector, while in the private sector, foreign capital dominated the towering heights, and Chinese business had a foothold on commerce and small-to-medium operations. In contrast, South Africa's white hegemony and black repression extended across both public and private sectors and in all industries. Fourth, the macroeconomic conditions at AA's inception varied, with Malaysia in the 1970s enjoying steady growth and a relatively accommodating milieu toward state intervention, while South Africa in the 1990s faced severe economic constraints and ideological pressures.

These conditions gave rise to country-specific AA regimes. This chapter concludes with a discussion of key contrasting features. Malaysia's executive dominant, discretionary and centralized regime stands in marked contrast to South Africa's legislative, statutory, codified and decentralized regime.

Malaysia

Systemic disadvantage and affirmative action imperatives

Legal foundations for preferential measures were embedded in the federal constitution, which enshrines both the principle of equality and provisions for the special position of Malays/Bumiputeras. Malays were the majority group in Malaya (Peninsular Malaysia) since independence in 1957. *Bumiputera*, or "sons of the soil," includes indigenous groups from Sabah and Sarawak, which joined with the peninsula to form Malaysia in 1963. Individual equality and prohibition of discrimination is set out in Article 8, with a proviso: "[e]xcept as expressly authorized by this Constitution." The crafting of Article 153 was a laborious, deliberative process responding to contending interests, and it drew on the constitutions of Pakistan, the United States and India (Fernando 2015; Fernando and Rajagopal 2017).[1] This momentous statute granted specific departures from Article 8 and vested such authority in the *Yang Di-Pertuan Agong* (the national king), who could "exercise his functions . . . in such manner as may be necessary to safeguard the special position of the Malays and natives of any of the States of Sabah and Sarawak [i.e. non-Malay Bumiputera] and the legitimate interests of other communities," through reserving places for the designated group in public sector employment, scholarships, training programmes and licenses.

A slight digression on Article 153 is worth our while. Bumiputera special position has become deeply entrenched in Malaysia, often in ways that are imprecise, misplaced, distorted and expedient. Political rhetoric and popular discourses, departing from the constitution's original and unambiguous stipulation, have transmuted into "special rights," which wrongly impute a permanent and limitless quality. This is a polemical, and typically protracted, debate. It suffices, at this juncture and in the context of affirmative action's underpinnings and ultimate goals, to register three paramount points.

First, Article 153 contains a proviso that racial quotas are to be implemented "in such manner as may be necessary," which implies they are conditional on the need for such intervention. Ongoing discourses should take into consideration socio-economic fractures and dimensions of systemic disadvantage out of which it was negotiated and progress in overcoming these circumstances, which may render quotas unnecessary. Second, the specified areas of intervention – public sector employment, scholarships and enrolment, training programmes and licenses – principally involve learning and capacity-building, not wealth acquisition. These principles and policy ideals should continually be the focus of affirmative action. Third, the specific provisions for safeguarding the "legitimate interests of other communities," although popularly invoked as a minority-protecting counterbalance to racial quotas and pro-Bumiputera preferences, are anachronistic. The provision specifically pertains to rights and opportunities already in possession at the time of Malayan independence – jobs, land or contracts that could not be arbitrarily confiscated, revoked or dismissed. It secured continuity of possessions for the transition, but post-independence, provides no constitutional safeguard for distribution of new opportunities in education, employment, contracts and socio-economic opportunity in general. The transitory protections for minorities may have been articulated with an implicit outlook that Article 153 would be reviewed after fifteen years after independence, as the Reid Commission had initially proposed (Fernando 2015). Whatever the underlying issues, the inked wording endures – with all the explicit limits. Consequently, Article 153 cannot internally resolve the tensions between majority and minority stakes.

Nevertheless, a conciliatory and constructive path can be forged by focusing on the prerequisite of the Bumiputeras' need for preferential treatment and the principal purpose of capability building. This approach presages the argument that such measures should be impermanent, and it potentially transcends the stalemated debate over the constitutionality of majority special position versus minority legitimate interests. Affirmative action is warranted so long as it is socio-economically necessary, and it becomes less necessary when the beneficiaries are adequately enabled and empowered.

When Malaya's independent era commenced in 1957, its constituent race groups did not enter on equal footing. Fractures had formed through British colonial rule and migration processes in which foreign interests dominated the ownership of resources and capital, while Malays, Chinese and Indians, by and large, lived and worked in separate geographic and economic spheres. European, particularly British, interests held a massive portion of Malaya's rich primary commodity production, which centred on rubber plantations and tin resources.[2] Across the peninsula, the vast majority of the Malay population lived in rural settings, engaged in rice cultivation – generally at subsistence levels. They also constituted a large portion of the bureaucracy, police and security services. The Malay community was mostly stratified by its traditional hierarchical structure, comprising an aristocratic elite above an expanding administrative corps, followed by a vast agrarian peasantry mostly detached from wage labour markets and private capital. The Chinese population was highly urbanized, supplying a large share of labour and establishing enterprises in tin mines, plantations and factories and gaining a foothold in distribution and retail of goods. The community consisted of a substantial working class and a nascent capitalist class, with clan-based networks providing financial resources. The Indian population was most conspicuous in two areas: laborers on rubber plantations and lower-rung administrators in government services. They would be distributed more evenly between rural and urban economies, but in both spheres had not managed to advance beyond wage labour (Andaya and Andaya 2001; Gomez and Jomo 1999).

This social structure, outlined in Table 3.1, is aptly described as an ethnic division of labour, in which groups were preponderantly and persistently confined to particular occupations and industries (Khoo 2005). This hierarchy, and parallel rural-urban gaps, were reinforced by disparities in educational opportunities and access to credit. Educational institutions were fragmented, again, by race and socio-political factors and were not integrated into a broader system for facilitating social interaction and coordinating curricular content. The common standards of formal education were low, which magnified the advantage to

Table 3.1 Peninsular Malaysia: Racial distribution of labour force within industries, 1957

	Malay	Chinese	Indian	Others
Rice cultivation	95.8	2.4	0.0	1.2
Rubber cultivation	42.4	32.6	24.5	0.5
Mining and quarrying	17.7	68.3	11.6	2.4
Manufacturing	19.7	72.2	7.4	0.7
Commerce	16.4	65.1	16.8	1.7
Government services	52.4	15.4	26.3	5.9
Police, home guard and prisons	83.2	9.6	4.4	2.8
Armed forces	76.8	8.8	8.4	6.0

Source: Khoo 2005.

those attending one institution among the few offering superior instruction and reputation. More urbanized states demonstrated higher literacy rates, reflecting the educational advantages available to residents of towns and cities, which were largely Chinese populated, although they were also more racially mixed than rural communities (Leete 2007, 178–179).[3] The Malay masses were overwhelmingly excluded from these developments, except for the privileged or exceptional few who enjoyed access to elite schools, scholarships and civil service appointments. Indians on plantations were excluded on the grounds that plantations were classified as private property; hence, the educational and health needs of its workers fell outside of the state's jurisdiction.

The Alliance coalition of UMNO, MCA and MIC – respectively, Malay, Chinese and Indian race-based parties – recognized the problem of racial fragmentation by location and economic activity, but settled on a compromise that did little to fundamentally alter the configuration. Political power was vested in the aristocracy-led Malay majority while Chinese business was granted freedom to operate without distributive obligations, and cultural institutions were sustained (Jesudason 1989; Gomez and Jomo 1999; Leete 2007). In short, economic policy from 1957 to 1969 was characterized by a *laissez faire* dispensation.

Programmes and expenditures were put in place to alleviate rural poverty, reduce urban-rural disparities and bridge inter-racial inequalities, but no broad strategy for overcoming systemic disadvantages was laid out and no specific targets were set (Thillainathan 1976, 72). The regime did little to address the continuing dominance of foreign interests or to foster Chinese-Malay economic cooperation (Jesudason 1989). Schooling continued to be fragmented, as it was under colonial rule. The British provided a tiered system to Malays, while Chinese and Indians were permitted to establish vernacular schools and missionary organizations ran schools with instruction in English. The English-medium schools equipped graduates for formal employment operating in English, but few Malays enjoyed the attendant advantages, since few enrolled in such institutions, for locational or cultural reasons (Pong 1993, 246).

Some preferential policies were implemented in public sector employment and post-secondary education, notably scholarships. It could be said that the early set of interventions more closely and literally adhered to Article 153. The racial composition of federal and state governments in 1969 was 64.5% Malay, 18.4% Chinese, 15.7% Indian, 1.5% other categories. At the top rung (Division 1), the estimated proportion of Malays rose from 14.1% in 1957 to 39.3% in 1970. However, in the elite Malayan civil service, the proportion of Malays rose from 34.6% in 1957 to 86.6% in 1970. The number of public enterprises increased from 22 in 1960 to 109 in 1970 (Khoo 2005, 18 and 30). However, on a national scale, the impact of affirmative action was limited. The public sector comprised 11.9% of the working population in 1970 and exerted a modest impact on the overall racial employment profile, although it bolstered the proportion of Malays among professionals and technicians.

The lack of progress in redressing racial disparities and systemic disadvantages, and in raising incomes on the whole, is reflected in urbanization and poverty rates. Table 3.2 shows that between 1957 and 1970 small gains in poverty reduction

Table 3.2 Peninsular Malaysia: Composition of population and poverty, by race and area, 1957 and 1970

		1957	1970
Racial composition of total population			
	Malay	49.8	53.1
	Chinese	37.2	35.4
	Indian	11.3	10.5
Racial composition of urban population			
	Malay	22.6	27.6
	Chinese	63.9	60.0
	Indian	10.7	11.3
Poverty rate			
	Malay	70.5	64.8
	Chinese	27.4	26.0
	Indian	35.7	39.2
	All races	51.2	49.3

Sources: Khoo 2005; Leete 2007.

Table 3.3 Malaysia: Racial composition of occupation groups, 1970

	Malay	*Chinese*	*Indian*
Administrative and managerial	22.4	65.7	7.5
Professional and technical	47.2	37.7	12.7
Clerical	33.4	51.0	14.3
Sales	23.9	64.7	11.0
Services	42.9	42.5	13.4
Agriculture	68.7	20.8	9.6
Machine operation and elementary	31.3	59.9	8.6
Overall	*51.4*	*37.0*	*10.7*

Source: Malaysia 1976.

Note: Rows do not sum to 100 due to exclusion of other groups.

for all groups – even an increase in absolute poverty among Indians – and only slight changes in the vastly different constitution of urban and rural populations. In sum, as Khoo (2005, 24) puts it, "*laissez faire* capitalism could not resolve the destabilizing contradictions of an ethnic division of labor," which remained markedly drawn in 1970 (Table 3.3). Occupationally, Malays were under-represented among managers and professionals, and within these categories of high-level, decision-making and estimable positions, they were concentrated in tertiary and primary sectors – predominantly services and agriculture, respectively – while participating considerably less in the secondary, manufacturing sector (Table 3.4).

Most crucially, development policies had done little to facilitate entry of the vast majority of Malays into the modern, urban economy. However, while it

Table 3.4 Malay representation in administrative/managerial and professional/technical positions, by sector, 1970

	Primary	*Secondary*	*Tertiary*
Administrative and managerial	19.8	14.7	34.5
Professional and technical	55.9	26.0	48.7

Source: Malaysia 1976.

is generally accepted that distributive issues were insufficiently addressed, the Malaysian government faced some major constraints. Among the many issues the government had to confront was a communist insurgency and confrontation with Indonesia, with which British forces aided. Thus, it was hard to intervene with British commercial interest (Jesudason 1989, 52–53). In the education system, immense policy emphasis had to be placed on the more basic issues of unifying a disjointed schooling system, providing rudimentary schooling and reducing drop-out rates (Leete 2007, 188). Narrowing disparities in access to and quality of secondary schooling were in these contexts less urgent.

Disaffection had grown in the 1960s within the Malay community towards the lack of material progress, continued small landholdings and indebtedness and abuse of programmes for the poor to enrich wealthy Malays (Gomez and Jomo 1999; Andaya and Andaya 2001). Inter-racial conflict was more manifest in urban areas, where Malays saw gaps between themselves and Chinese that fuelled a sense of exclusion. Pressures for state support and proactive measures to develop a Malay business class grew in the 1960s. Administrative elites had cultivated close ties between government and a nascent capitalist class, as many moved from one sphere to the other or secured a footing in both spheres (Jesudason 1989, 51–52 and 65–68).

Momentum grew from the mid-1960s. The first Bumiputera Economic Congress, convened in 1965, advocated various policy measures, including the establishment of Bank Bumiputera that same year, and the reconfiguration of the Rural Industrial Development Authority (RIDA) to MARA (*Majlis Amanah Rakyat,* or the Council of Trust for the People) in 1966, with a broadened mandate, particularly in enterprise development and training, although rural populations remained the designated beneficiaries. In practice, however, MARA's programmes have been exclusive to Malays and Bumiputeras. The *First Malaysia Plan* (1965–1970), succeeding the 1960–1965 Five-Year Plan, allocated the inaugural budget for Malay business development. Thus, on the whole, affirmative action measures expanded from the mid-1960s. The formation of Malaysia in 1963 through the merger of Malaya, Sabah and Sarawak, enlarged the indigenous populations of the new nation. The Bumiputera category of beneficiaries was widened to encompass Malays and indigenous groups of Sabah and Sarawak.

However, income-diverging trends persisted through the decade. Inequality increased on a national scale, between and within racial groups, and deepening sentiments toward the failures of economic and social policies to uplift Malays made for a volatile political setting. Indeed, a political cataclysm compelled a shift of the policy regime onto a drastically different path. The 1969 general elections, in which the ruling coalition suffered losses and the opposition made gains – largely on the back of Chinese votes – created conditions for a combustible stand-off between ascendant Chinese political power and a backlash from the Malay establishment. On both sides, a sense of trespass escalated, with Malays wary of increased penetration of non-Malay opposition into the political domain, while non-Malays, especially Chinese, reacted against measures perceived to constrict their cultural and commercial space.

The May 13th riots momentously shook, then reinforced, coalition government and overhauled the policy regime. Galvanized by the tragedy, a top-down approach and centralized executive control set a precedent for Malaysia's mode of governance (Ho 1992; Ooi 2013). The Alliance co-opted more parties into its fold, forming a super coalition of Peninsula, Sarawak and Sabah components, formally reconstituted as the Barisan Nasional (BN) in 1973 – with UMNO increasingly hegemonic within. Politics and policy were infused with a reassertion of Malay dominance and pro-Malay policies, galvanized around a doctrine, somewhat legitimated by the ongoing crisis, that extensive and intensive state intervention would be necessary. Policy discourses were embroiled in a contestation over a new framework, broadly between a pro-market and growth-focused strategy and an intensive state-led expansionist and distributive agenda, of which the latter prevailed (Faaland, Parkinson and Saniman 1990).

Consolidation and expansion

Malaysia's affirmative action programme burgeoned in scale and scope with the promulgation of the New Economic Policy (NEP) from 1971. The NEP itself, especially at its initial, and seminal, presentation in the introduction to the *Second Malaysia Plan* (Malaysia 1971), was more of a political vision statement than a comprehensive set of policies. Arising from national crisis and social schisms, it proclaimed the loftiest of ultimate goals for Malaysia: national unity.[4] It outlined general ideas and objectives towards alleviating poverty and generating growth and increasing Bumiputera education, labour market participation and owner-ship, but more specific interventions would unfold over the subsequent years through specific programmes, executive decisions and legislations. The NEP term has come to designate and connote various things. A very brief overview of its basic tenets is therefore germane at this juncture, followed by discussion of specific affirmative action programmes within its rubric.

The NEP judiciously projected two overriding objectives: first, the eradication of poverty irrespective of race; second, acceleration of the restructuring of society to reduce and eventually eliminate the identification of race with economic func-tion (Tables 3.3 and 3.4).

The *Second Malaysia Plan* boldly launched "The New Development Strategy," the title of Chapter 1, laying out priorities as follows:

> The Plan outlines policies and programmes to modernize rural life, encourage a rapid and balanced growth of urban activities, provide improved education and training programmes at all levels, and above all, ensure the creation of a Malay commercial and industrial community in all categories and at all levels of operation, in order that within one generation Malays and other indigenous people can be full partners in the economic life of the nation.
>
> (Malaysia 1971, 6)

This summation, together with the 1971–1990 timeline, is probably the main reason that the NEP is sometimes interpreted as originally setting 1990 as an expiry date. This is a misreading; there was no express commitment to dismantle AA, nor even an explicit determination to evaluate whether Malaysia might be ready to do so. At most the document hinted that the attainment of Bumiputera full economic partnership within one generation would entail that the NEP could be decommissioned. Any dismantling of the policy would also be contingent on some assessment of Malay "full partnership," which was never broached. Moreover, the *Second Malaysia Plan* also acknowledged that satisfactory progress in some areas, particularly the Malay commercial and industrial community, "may require a generation or more for their full accomplishment" (Malaysia 1971, 9). Considering the tentativeness, it is no surprise that the NEP made no attempt to consider possible directions of future reforms, to differentiate sector-based timelines for policy rollout, or to outline a sequencing of reforms. To be fair, the NEP was formulated amid scarcity of time, data, and cross-country experiences to draw on. Nevertheless, the ambiguity of how it would conclude gave rise to two extreme expectations: the entire NEP edifice would be dismantled in 1990, or nothing needed to change over time.

The NEP was commissioned to tackle various dimensions of poverty and disparity, much of which lies beyond the scope of affirmative action. In 1976, the *Third Malaysia Plan* articulated a fuller bodied long-term plan, the Outline Perspective Plan 1971–1990 within which the NEP objectives would be pursued (Malaysia 1976). Interestingly, the ambition for Bumiputeras to be full partners was replaced by ownership and participation targets; the "within one generation" phrase was applied specifically to 30% ownership of commercial and industrial activities. This added further ambiguity to the issue of policy rollback in 1990. The Outline Perspective Plan, however, clarified and reinforced how AA would expand – along with comprehensive policies to promote economic growth, structural change, industrialization, basic education, skills and productivity. It is worth reiterating the importance of recognizing that the NEP supplied the mandate and outline for race-based redistribution but not equating the NEP with affirmative action.

Political economic context

Malay hegemony and executive dominance

Affirmative action under the NEP was formulated in the wake of a political crisis, to which Malay nationalism responded with vigour and force. The political watershed was characterized by consolidation of Malay political hegemony and enlargement of a Malay dominant ruling coalition. Accordingly, affirmative action policies expanded and intensified a framework that was partly in place, deploying many government agencies that were set up in the 1960s. Pressures for more proactive and extensive interventions to groom Malay business had mounted in the decade. Notwithstanding some continuities, the 1970s marked a clear break from the past in that state institutions involved in economic policy were infused with a more assertive pro-Bumiputera, and especially pro-Malay, agenda. Notably, the Sedition Act 1948 was amended in 1970 to make questioning Article 153, among other things, a punishable "seditious tendency."

Lacking policy models to emulate, Malaysia adopted a practical and experimental approach.[5] This combination of a strong state and pragmatist disposition concurs with the emergence of a state-centric regime often making discretionary decisions and policy shifts, oriented more around executive power than statutes or formalized procedures. Malaysia's centralized and executive dominant mode of policy-making and implementation has effected change that would otherwise involve more negotiation and formalization, and that would probably transpire less rapidly. Exclusive Bumiputera programmes, such as education institutions, scholarships and licensing, were politically possible and numerically feasible. Quotas in education, employment and ownership were also implemented with greater speed and latitude than would be conceivable in most countries. The drive to promote ownership and participation in business, articulated as the creation of a Malay Commercial and Industrial Community, featured in the NEP from its inception, and this agenda would gain momentum steadily, then accelerate from the 1980s.

Dynamics of race relations

The Malay-dominant state notwithstanding, policy-making has been shaped by race relations in Malaysia. While economic issues have been important to the Chinese and Indian communities, they have generally been more steadfast and voluble in advocacy of cultural preservation and access to mother tongue schooling and tertiary education than in opposition to state regulation in principle. The quota system for university enrolment and for scholarships, in particular, has been a source of friction, especially for non-Bumiputera families who cannot afford to send their children abroad. Chinese- and Tamil-medium schools provide avenues for linguistic and cultural expression, while proliferation of private higher education and increased non-Bumiputera quotas in government scholarships has alleviated to some extent grievances arising from restricted entry to university due to quotas.

Domestic-foreign interactions have also shaped development and affirmative action policies. It is important to note that, at the inception of the NEP, the Chinese did not control all sectors – indeed, foreign interests dominated ownership and control, especially in key commodities. The government, in service of the Malay/Bumiputera interest, had established banks and development funds and taken over hitherto foreign-owned entities. The existence of a non-domestic target for transfer of equity ownership significantly insulated Malaysia from an internal conflict over assets, particularly in primary commodities. At the same time, new foreign capital has been seen as a counterweight to Chinese capital, and has thus been courted, especially in manufacturing, as part of Malaysia's export-oriented industrialization programme.

Some ramifications of the dynamics of race relations on affirmative action may be noted. Malaysia has engaged more in implicit "bargaining" over safeguarding special domains for each race group instead of broad efforts to make all socio-economic spheres multiracial. Policies for attaining equitable representation within organizations, especially to foster Bumiputera-non-Bumiputera cooperation, were not pursued in a systematic manner in the private sector. The public sector, state-owned enterprises, privatized entities, and regulations on foreign capital were the main vehicles for increasing Bumiputera participation in management and highly skilled occupations, largely to the exclusion of meaningful engagement with non-Bumiputera. These inter-racial and cross-national dynamics are interwoven with the process of developing independent Bumiputera enterprises, which is one area where achievements have conspicuously fallen short of expectations. Bumiputera involvement in SMEs, particularly in manufacturing, is lacking, and largely dependent on subsidies.[6] Additionally, lack of cooperation between government and predominantly Chinese SMEs has arguably stunted skills training, research and development and technological upgrading (Ritchie 2005; Henderson and Philips 2007; Jomo 2007).

Economic growth and public expenditures

The Malaysian economy has enjoyed steady economic growth over the past 50 years, including some bursts of rapid expansion. Average annual real GDP growth registered 5.8% (1957–1970), 6.7% (1970–1987), 9.3% (1987–1997) and in the post-Asian financial crisis years: 4.3% (1997–2008) and 4.7% (2008–2017).[7] Economic growth provided ample means for Malaysia to undertake its extensive and intensive AA programmes. Additionally, discovery of oil reserves in the 1970s coincided with the OPEC price hikes and availed a windfall injection into public coffers. While the overall allocation of such funds is unknown – since Petronas, the government agency mandated to claim oil royalties, is exempted from financial disclosure – it is believed that substantial amounts were spent in social development, especially in the latter 1970s and the 1980s. The robust state of public resources is reflected in the annual growth in real government expenditures over the same intervals: 7.2% (1970–1987), 6.2% (1987–1997), 8.4% (1997–2008) and 5.3% (2008–2016).[8]

Malaysia also augmented public expenditure at a time when international convention was more accommodating towards expansionary macroeconomic policies than has subsequently been the case.[9] The accumulation of fiscal debt, partly in foreign denomination, forced cutbacks in public spending and hiring in the mid-1980s and accelerated the shift to privatization. Nonetheless, a relatively large public sector, in terms of employment and expenditure, has continued as a mainstay of the AA programme. AA-based distribution of education and employment opportunities has been facilitated by the opportunities availed and national policy autonomy, resulting in Malaysia's relatively large and continuously expanding public sector, including public colleges and universities, as well as the many government-linked companies mandated to support the policy. Of course, economic growth cannot be guaranteed ahead of redistributive interventions; policy decisions cannot be entirely contingent on some minimal level of economic performance. Nonetheless, analysis of AA must locate Malaysia's experience in the context of robust economic growth and considerable policy autonomy.

South Africa

Any consideration of post-Apartheid South Africa's problems must be framed within the comprehensive structures of disenfranchisement, oppression and discrimination that prevailed under colonialism and Apartheid. Non-whites were systemically disempowered in terms of citizenship and political voice, socially excluded from urban centres, legally prohibited from upward mobility and ownership – except in the Bantustans – and forced into inferior education, health services and employment.[10] This book cannot proceed without an attempt to survey the breadth and depth of Apartheid's legacy, even though some errors of over-simplification and omission will unavoidably be committed. However, the error of decoupling post-Apartheid policy formulation and outcomes from inherited conditions would be greater. Indeed, Terreblanche (2002, 29), in his seminal *History of Inequality in South Africa, 1652–2002*, acknowledges that, "[w]ith the wisdom of hindsight we now know that the legacy of colonialism, segregation and Apartheid was much worse, and the pauperizing momentum inherent in it much stronger, than was realized in 1994." The following brief overview will focus on aspects of Apartheid that most directly impacted on the transition to democracy, the transformations of South Africa's political, social and economic order and the formulation of affirmative action policies.

Apartheid legacy and affirmative action imperatives

The transition out of Apartheid applied pressures and constraints on affirmative action. Black South Africans for many generations were denied equal rights to vote, to own property and to organize labour or work on fair terms and were deprived of equal access to education, employment and self-determination. These various and enormous inequities of the Apartheid state and its racial division of labour – arguably more systematized than in any other country – had to be redressed, while negotiating a precarious rebalance of power. South Africa is distinctive for transferring political dominance from a domestic minority racial group with entrenched influence and generally well-developed human capabilities to a majority group characterized by an ascendant political elite and incipient capitalist class, economic disadvantage and mass poverty. The situation differs from countries that have introduced affirmative action, such as Malaysia, while largely preserving the political order.

Affirmative action in South Africa, aiming to redress multitudinous socio-economic disparities, rested on a political transformation. Inevitably, political and economic transitions were necessary; the question was whether they would take shape simultaneously or sequentially. It turned out more toward the latter. Political transformation – a thoroughly new constitution negotiated between old and new political blocs – preceded, and in many ways superseded, socio-economic transformation. Discourses over the post-Apartheid economic order no doubt took place concurrently with the political transition, but they were spread over a diversity of forums between delegations and unfolded in more disparate and opaque processes. This important element of the South African transition will be discussed later in this section.

Apartheid reinforced disparities through all-encompassing and institutionalized exclusion and repression, while effectively implementing affirmative action in favour of the white, specifically Afrikaner, population. Blacks were compelled to join the ranks of low-wage and unskilled labour on farms, mines or factories where they had no rights, or to reside – millions by force – in the ostensibly self-governing but resource-deprived and economically dependent Bantustans, or "independent homelands," while over 80% of South Africa's land was in the hands of the white population. Township populations at the periphery of cities and towns burgeoned, as blacks flocked to seek menial work under heavily policed conditions. South Africa's government and service delivery system was splintered into central government and homeland administrations.[11] The employment profile of these departments reflected Apartheid policy and enforcement. The public sector and parastatals constituted an important channel of employment, skill acquisition and upward mobility for whites. More generally, whites were disproportionately employed in senior positions and in security services, while blacks were predominantly laborers, or educators and nurses in the homelands (Naidoo 2008, 102–103).

The education system was further segregated and stratified under Apartheid from the mid-1950s. Schools were reordered to enforce racial homogeneity, while universities were explicitly segregated by law, and education departments were segmented by race or in alignment with Bantustan borders. Curricula were designed to prevent Africans from aspiring to positions beyond subservient functions of production or Apartheid administration, and black-populated schools were systemically deprived of funds. Schools in the Bantustans and tertiary institutions in general operated with a degree of autonomy; some universities enrolled blacks from the 1970s. On the whole, the education system was segmented and stratified by race, and academic learning was disrupted by political ferment and anti-Apartheid struggle that pervaded many schools. A glance at education statistics is revealing: in 1986, the passing rates for standard 10 examinations were 51.6% for Africans, 67.6% for Coloureds, 87.1% for Indians and 93.1% for Whites. In 1990, the passing rate for Africans had declined to 36.7%, while for other race groups it continued to increase (MERG 1993; Motala *et al.* 2007).[12]

Repression, segregation and discrimination in the Apartheid labour market are widely documented. Racial conflict and systematic discrimination were more direct and blatant in capitalist-worker relations than in other arenas. Terreblanche (2002) describes the persistent structural feature of the South African labour market as black labour repression, which has taken on various forms over three-and-a-half centuries. The Apartheid regime from 1948 reinforced discriminatory measures in various ways, whether through law or arbitrary exercise of power. A few directly relevant to labour markets are worth mentioning here. Amendments to the Industrial Conciliation Act in 1953 reserved certain classes of work for specified racial categories to "safeguard against inter-racial competition;" further amendments in 1956 prohibited registration of "mixed" unions. Black trade unions were not recognized until 1979. The Apartheid system militated especially aggressively against black skills acquisition, promotion, and advancement into management. White unions prevented training of African artisans, resulting in the absence of any African apprenticeship outside the Bantustans before 1975 (Seekings and Nattrass 2005, 138). Until 1977, it was illegal to employ African managers in urban areas (Nzimande 1996, 190).

The mid-1970s signalled new directions for South Africa. The 1973 Durban strikes forcefully marked a shift in worker activism from the relative quiescence of the 1960s. More momentously, the 1976 Soweto uprisings and the nationwide protest that it spawned were triggered by the imposition of Afrikaans instruction in black schools outside the Bantustans and other contributory factors. By then, township communities had settled beyond being migrant, transient populations, which in turn yielded township-born generations of schooled youths who were inflamed against their abject living conditions. The Apartheid government strategy of concentrating development for blacks in the Bantustans, to the neglect of urban townships, had laid conditions for such a backlash (Seekings and Nattrass 2005, 108).

The state and big business responded, notably through the Wiehahn, Riekert and de Lange Commissions, the Human Sciences Research Council and the Urban Foundation, which made recommendations for reforms in housing, industrial relations and social policy. Black trade unions were formally recognized from 1979. This strategy partly aimed at deflecting public protest away from black working class mobilization against the racist Apartheid state, towards conflict within formal industrial relations – and achieved this to some extent.[13] Black higher education also expanded in the aftermath of the 1976 uprisings as part of a strategy of fostering a black middle class that would "seek accommodation with the state and the predominantly white corporate business sector and also as a buffer against rising black, especially worker, political militancy" (Badat 2012, 124). Black student enrolment increased from 25,100 in 1977 to 140,600 by 1990 – although only 12% were enrolled at HWIs.

Indeed, the reforms were selective and amounted to an upward shift of the colour bar – barriers to black advancement were raised but were far from removed. Standing, Sender and Weeks (1996, 386–388) point out, for instance, that none of the Commissions made substantive recommendations towards the deracialization of training schemes. Racial segregation persisted in skill formation. Africans comprised about ten percent of qualified artisans by 1990 but were concentrated in six relatively low-skill trades, including welding, boiler-making, fitting and sheet metal working, while whites continued to predominate in higher skill trades in the metal, engineering, electrical and motor sectors. There was a steady relaxation of restrictions on African trade and business in urban areas, yet black business development remained severely inhibited (Southall 2004, 316).

Nevertheless, legal amendments to labour relations and policy attention to urban social and housing development from the late 1970s would set in motion two important developments in the distributional dynamics of South Africa. First, superficially altering Apartheid and perforating some barriers to black upward mobility became accepted as strategic objectives within the corporate world and the state. The business sector became more politicized in the 1970s, while at the same time more autonomous from the Apartheid state machinery and pro-active in advocating reforms. As Southall (2016, 67) notes, "throughout the 1980s, the large corporations and government became increasingly eager to promote support for capitalism by the encouragement of black entry into business." Consequently, Black professionals and managers became increasingly upwardly mobile, but many remained stuck as perpetual "trainees." Towards the end of the 1980s, more opportunities for blacks in management opened up, notably in sales and communication, and also in NGOs, and black managers grew more confident in confronting "corporate subversion of their career prospects" (Southall 2016, 133–134).

Second, the changes accentuated class differentiation in the African population – an important precursor to the process of social stratification and the demands for upward occupational mobility in the post-Apartheid era (Marais 2001; Seekings and Nattrass 2005; Terreblanche 2002). The reforms of "petty Apartheid," however, coincided with intensification of political repression and manipulations to maintain power, which fuelled resistance and mass mobilization through the 1980s. Thus, the Apartheid system faced demands for removal – in highly volatile circumstances.

At the democratic transition, racial hierarchies prevailed in the labour market; the higher up the occupational ladder, the greater the disparity. In 1990, Africans, while constituting three-quarters of the population, occupied a mere 3% of managerial positions and 11% of professionals. Disaggregating semi-professional/white-collar occupations and skilled trades, Table 3.5 shows racial demarcations corresponding with skill and rank: Whites predominated in jobs requiring higher qualifications, such as pharmacists and technologists, journalists and artisans, or

Table 3.5 South Africa: Racial distribution of semi-professional, routine white-collar occupations, skilled trades, 1990

	Whites	Coloureds	Indians	Africans	Unspecified
Semi-professionals					
Pharmacists	91	1	6	1	0
Technicians	40	2	54	2	1
Technologists	90	3	4	3	0
Head nurse/matron	69	5	1	25	1
Nurse	38	13	4	43	0
Journalists/editors/writers	86	3	1	8	0
School principal/inspector	22	13	3	62	0
School teacher	26	15	6	54	0
Routine white-collar					
Secretary/receptionist/typist	81	8	5	5	1
Sales representative and agent	76	7	6	11	1
Bookkeeper and financial clerk	70	11	9	8	1
General clerk	51	13	8	25	3
Bus and train conductor	65	6	2	27	0
Messenger	5	16	1	76	1
Skilled trades					
Electrical and electronic					
Artisans	82	7	4	6	1
Apprentices	76	7	3	12	2
Motor vehicle					
Artisans	72	9	5	11	3
Apprentices	71	8	7	14	0
Building					
Artisans	28	38	6	28	0
Apprentices	7	31	1	61	0

Source: Author's compilations from Crankshaw (1996).

in frontline service positions like receptionists and sales representatives. The hierarchy of opportunity to Indians, followed by Coloureds and Africans, is also strikingly obvious.

This brief overview of systemic disadvantage in South Africa raises a few themes that are taken up later. First, Apartheid was comprehensive. Consequently, redress measures – affirmative action and broad reforms – needed to be comprehensive. It is too farfetched to expect enforcement of equality and prohibition of discrimination to redress the breadth and depth of Apartheid's socio-economic legacy. Active measures for South Africa had to chart a path through multiple transitions perhaps unlike any other country in the late 20th century, and progress had to be substantial and expeditious given the social pressures and expectations of tangible change. The post-Apartheid state was constrained to respond urgently to a plethora of basic and deep-seated problems, notably, fragmented government and service delivery systems and grossly inadequate basic education and health and housing provision.

Second, features of the political and economic transitions impacted on the formation of affirmative action policies. South Africa faced huge challenges but enjoyed wide political legitimacy to redress systemic disadvantage and inequality. At the same time, the imperative of dismantling Apartheid demanded a new constitution and negotiations among top leadership, amid a volatile political climate. These circumstances subordinated economic policy formulation to a less centralized, transparent and coordinated process than the concurrent political reconstitution, effectively pre-empting broader economic bargains that could have bolstered the economic transformation, such as transitory wealth taxes.[14] In addition, historical and ideological factors, especially the end of the Cold War, South Africa's re-emergence from isolation and global pressures for financial liberalization, weighed in on an ANC leadership inexperienced in economic matters.

The Freedom Charter of 1955, de facto manifesto of the anti-Apartheid struggle, expressed intentions to return the nation's wealth to the people and to guarantee freedom of economic engagement. The Charter did not spell out economic programmes for redistribution and black empowerment; its most resonant policy was a hallowed reference to nationalization. Economic negotiations from the 1980s, however, had reached an elite pact that laid the groundwork for conservative policies. With reconciliation forming the basis of political transformation, the ANC, leading the Government of National Unity, initially adopted an accommodative stance towards white capital, but it grew more assertive over time towards cultivating a black capitalist class (Southall 2004).

Thus, the vision of a non-racial and non-sexist democracy, conceived in the liberation struggle and sustained as a bargaining position, became embedded in the Constitution, as were provisions for affirmative action. The South African Constitution also establishes equality with qualifications and distinct terms of reference (South Africa 1996). Article 9, while stipulating equality as a basic right, added that "[t]o promote the achievement of equality, legislative and other measures designed to protect or advance persons, or categories of persons, disadvantaged by unfair discrimination may be taken." In the spheres of education, employment and contracting, the Constitution provides for selection criteria that take into account redress of past discrimination or broad group representation. The fact that specific legislation and policy on affirmative action was promulgated after the enactment of a new constitution derives from the urgency of fostering political stability and a power-sharing deal, while formal AA legislation was introduced from the late 1990s.

Third, structural aspects of the Apartheid political economy further complicated the transition and introduction of affirmative action programmes: entrenchment of a developed capitalist class and marked class boundaries, reservation of upper-rung jobs in the formal economy for the white minority, presence of nascent black professional and middle classes and rise of political elites seeking reward for past discrimination. Apartheid's cultivation of Afrikaner capital and appeasement of English-speaking capital perpetuated monopolistic and oligopolistic markets. Hence, the challenge of overcoming racial inequality would inevitably be fraught with the complications of a multi-dimensionally divided society and economy.

Political economic context

Complex transitions

Negotiating a political settlement took primacy in South Africa's transition out of Apartheid, for fundamental and strategic reasons. Fundamentally, a comprehensively new and democratized political order provided the bedrock for facilitating concurrent transformations – and incorporating tensions – in economic and social realms. Of particular relevance to this book are the political and constitutional provisions to balance majority rule and minority rights, black political dominance and white economic security, fair discrimination and equal opportunity. Strategically, the ANC had for decades emphasized Apartheid's political dimension over socio-economic modes of oppression, encapsulated in the Freedom Charter, its "only official statement of economic intent" (Sparks 2003, 176). The liberation movement, under ANC leadership, accordingly pressed first and foremost for political democratization, having also mobilized masses to undermine the Apartheid government and economy. Strategies for the late Apartheid state and white capital to preserve rights and interests and resolve a decades-long accumulation crisis also converged on a negotiated political transition (Marais 2001).

A maelstrom of circumstances in the late 1980s and early 1990s that could not be fully predicted or controlled, including mass social instability, potential civil war, anxieties over the military's allegiance and uncertainties over homeland administrations, further compelled the centralized, summit-level level political bargaining and constitution-building that took place (Sparks 2003; Terreblanche 2002). The means for resolving the clash of political and ideological agendas across the spectrum of issues, and for unifying a fractured nation and fostering continuity in public administration, came in the form of a negotiated settlement transferring political power and guaranteeing socio-economic rights. Even equal suffrage was contested. Up to 1992, the National Party (NP) and de Klerk assured white constituencies of a commitment to uphold a "statutory entrenched minority [i.e. white] vote." However, in September 1992 the NP accepted "sunset clauses" under the auspices of the Government of National Unity (GNU), with the important guarantee of continuity of employment of white bureaucrats, which elicited agreement to a "one person one vote" system and the five-year power-sharing arrangement in the GNU (Terreblanche 2002, 80).

The transition to a post-Apartheid economic order, however, stands in marked contrast to the negotiated political settlement. While the political transition was a high-level bargaining process, dialogue and deal-making over economic spheres were conducted by various delegated groups or agenda proponents in a dispersed, non-consultative and somewhat opaque and tentative manner. Economic policy and development of post-Apartheid economic institutions unfolded through more gradual and contested processes that reflect conflicting ideology, lop-sided power and experience and lack of coordination. The following discussion touches on only a few out of many proposals and documents and their respective proponents.

From the mid-1980s, ANC economists met outside South Africa with various groups, including NP government delegates. Between 1955 and 1990, the ANC had published no new statement on economic policy issues except to reaffirm a commitment to the Freedom Charter in its 1988 constitutional guidelines. Marais (2001) points out that the lack of specific outlines of economic policy in the Freedom Charter also afforded the ANC room to manoeuvre in negotiations. From the late 1980s, various "economic scenarios" were promulgated, most prominently by corporate conglomerates (e.g. Anglo American, Old Mutual), parastatals (e.g. Sanlam) or business organizations (e.g. the South African Chamber of Commerce). These overtures reflect the strength and autonomy of the corporate sector, as well as the conservative milieu of the NP administration, which had initiated privatization from the 1980s and shifted towards deflationary macroeconomic policy in the early 1990s. Big business went out of its way to warn the democratic movement of ostensible dangers in pursuing a comprehensive redistributive programme and maintained a position on Apartheid that not only denied profiting from the system but also asserted that economic crisis resulted from an over-regulated system – and therefore supply-side policies and trickle-down effects would restore growth and prosperity to a stuttering economy (Bond 2000; Terreblanche 2002).

In contrast to the constant message emanating from the NP and business sector, ANC stances wavered. The organization was also shaped by internal politics and coalitional dynamics that transformed itself to be a "predominantly middle-class, rather than multiclass, organization" (Southall 2016, 40). By the late 1980s, the ANC had gravitated away from Freedom Charter pronouncements toward social democratic visions. Shifting positions on nationalization reflected the uncertainties and ambiguities in economic policy formulation and its weaker hand in the debate. At Nelson Mandela's release in 1990, nationalization retained salience on the ANC's agenda. Over the following two years, however, the ANC altered its position on nationalization and an expansive redistribution agenda. The 1992 World Economic Forum marked a watershed event, where Mandela decisively turned against nationalization and towards a system centred on the private sector with limited roles for the public sector in social and welfare services (Sparks 2003, 174–176). This ideological conversion was augmented by the collapse of the Soviet Union and the portent of a triumphal global capitalist order.

Amid the plethora of policy groups and policy documents, a few stand out as landmarks on South Africa's winding path to a new economic order. In terms of overall programmes of action, the ANC's Department of Economic Policy (DEP) initially called for an active role of the state. However, its 1992 report, *Ready to Govern*, which had become a de facto draft electoral platform, excised mention of growth through redistribution and scaled down its envisioned role of the state. The Reconstruction and Development Programme (RDP), the ANC's 1994 election manifesto, articulated a broad outline for reform, but it never translated into actual policy priorities or allocation of resources. The RDP was substantially curtailed and diluted in the 1994 White Paper on the RDP. The RDP Minister was not a designated government department with clear jurisdictions, rendering the programme practically inoperative (Sparks 2003).

More rigid foundations were laid in the specific quest for a macroeconomic paradigm. In 1993, the NP government's Department of Finance promulgated its *Normative Economic Model* (NEM), a document propagating economic orthodoxy that would cement state dispositions on economic matters beyond the transition (Bond 2000; Marais 2001; Terreblanche 2002). South Africa's macroeconomic framework was consolidated with the adoption in June 1996 of the Growth, Employment and Redistribution (GEAR) programme. South Africa adopted GEAR under some duress from the corporate and finance sectors,[15] but its conception and behind-the-scenes formulation, from late 1995, as an enhancement of the NEM suggest that the policies would have become regimented, regardless of public debate (Hirsch 2006, 99–101).[16] In the first decade from its launch, GEAR was broadly criticized on its theoretical underpinnings, and in light of the South African economy's falling short of all major growth, employment and investment targets except deficit reduction (Michie and Padayachee 1998; Habib and Padayachee 2000; Weeks 1999; Gqubule 2006; Pollin *et al.* 2006; Terreblanche 2002). Publicly articulated positive opinion of GEAR points to the decline in fiscal deficit and generally lower inflation rates as stabilizing outcomes and preconditions to the upswing in growth and employment after 2001 (Hirsch 2006).

GEAR would subsequently fade as a policy platform, but its macroeconomic mainstays and policy instruments were well entrenched, particularly with the official adoption of inflation-targeting in 2000. Nonetheless, while keeping inflation within its designated 3–6% band dictates monetary policy, the government's position on public spending became more expansionary. This shift responded to societal pressures, skills shortages and BEE demands, as well as more effective tax revenue collection. The Accelerated and Shared Growth Initiative for South Africa (AsgiSA), launched in 2006, gave a new mandate for harnessing public investment towards growth and distributive goals, focusing on infrastructure and skills development. Subsequent to AsgiSA, in 2007, the Department of Trade and Industry formulated the National Industrial Policy Framework and the Industrial Policy Action Plan (IPAP).

As with many aspects of South Africa's multiple transitions, affirmative action appeared with a spread of meanings in a range of forums. We focus on documents most closely associated with the ANC-led transitional bodies. Affirmative action first appeared in ANC lexicon its 1988 Constitutional guidelines (Mandaza 1996, 31). The ANC's 1992 *Ready to Govern* document delineated an expansive approach to AA, stating that, "[w]hile taking on a variety of forms, affirmative action means special measures to enable persons discriminated against on grounds of colour, gender and disability to break into fields from which they have been excluded by past discrimination."[17] In terms of specific proposals, in the short to medium term, "the ANC is committed to the active implementation of affirmative action strategies as part of a code of employment practice, to redress historically disadvantaged groups and regions." *Ready to Govern* also expressed a commitment to "vigorous affirmative action and restructuring programme for the public service to reflect the national composition of our population in order to meet the needs of all South Africans." The Reconstruction and Development Programme (RDP), prepared soon before the April 1994 elections and carried as a manifesto, referred to affirmative action in rather sweeping and nebulous terms, subsuming all measures in education and employment for redressing racial, gender and regional discrimination.[18] However, the *White Paper on Reconstruction and Development* of November 1994, ostensibly translating the RDP into a government programme of action, circumscribed affirmative action to the public service, which would be "broadly representative of the South African community."

The negotiated transition broadly traded off political and economic demands and concessions but omitted alternative visions and some potential trade-offs within the economic terrain. The enfranchised black majority was able to bring moral and electoral weight to bear on political negotiations. But it conceded much of the economic agenda to supply-side and trickle-down dispositions, persuaded by pro-market ideas and efficiency arguments and apparently believing that the economy would benefit from a structural break from the past and a jolt into a new economic order. Of course, it is difficult to present counterfactuals and inconclusive how growth and distribution would have turned out under a different ideological orientation.

However, the marginalization of varying proposals, such as from the Macro Economic Research Group (MERG), and dismissal of alternatives in general precluded some potential bargains. For instance, the black population's demands for transformation could have been moderated in return for predominantly white capital's acceptance of bearing a higher share of transformation costs, e.g. infusion of education funding. In the face of mounting fiscal debt on the one hand and growing prospects for private finance, South Africa could have widened revenue collection through wealth-related sources such as the capital gains tax (which was subsequently introduced in 2001). Also, the momentum towards trade and financial liberalization swung rapidly, arguably providing insufficient time to develop industrial policy and adapt capital controls to new modes of global finance. Reintroducing or amending regulations may have raised concerns about non-cooperation or abuse by business and fears of capital flight, but it is also perceivable that the clout and resistance of domestic capital, and expectations of capital inflows, were over-estimated.[19]

The political and economic transitions were also important to the temporal unfolding of AA policies. Following the 1994 elections, much effort was invested in industrial relations and regulation of basic work conditions, areas of gross injustices and focal points of the liberation struggle, which accordingly became urgent areas of tri-partite engagement. Policies for racial redress and transformation of education and public sector employment (1995–1997) preceded the Employment Equity and Skills Development Act, all of which were passed in 1998. Preferential public procurement and BEE were formalized soon after, with the formation of the BEE Commission in 1998 and BBBEE Act in 2003 as official markers.

The point in sketching out the contestation for South Africa's macroeconomic regime and the unfolding of AA-related legislation is not so much to deduce a logic to how AA transpired, but to locate AA programmes in politico-economic and temporal context and to be cognizant of manifold constraints. South Africa's multiple transitions were characterized by varying degrees of coordination and reaction, while facing resource constraints and striving to accommodate complex, contending interests. While criticism abounds on the lack of policy efficacy and particular policy designs, the profound difficulty in charting a coherent and systematic process of transformation must be appreciated.[20]

Notwithstanding the gargantuan task of resetting South Africa's foundations and directions, affirmative action could certainly be framed in more systematic and comprehensive ways, especially as the policy regime has become more settled over time. The multiple, intertwined measures to promote black advancement – in higher education, employment, enterprise development and ownership – were conventionally treated in a rather disparate manner, rather than as a corpus of integrated and co-dependent programmes. No defining plan was formulated for black advancement encompassing all these spheres. Again, the incremental approach can be traced to South Africa's transition, in which labour market interventions took precedence and safeguarding provincial and institutional autonomy was imperative. However, policy discourses remain somewhat disconnected. Affirmative action *per se* is often equated with employment equity but not identified with the redress or transformation measures in universities that seek the same basic goal of increasing black participation. Concomitantly, negative appraisals of affirmative action in employment are taken to represent affirmative action as a whole, without substantive consideration of concurrent and interdependent policy outcomes in higher education.

Big business and business-state nexus

Various features of the South African capitalist class mentioned earlier are worth reiterating. By the 1980s, white capital was politicized and organized, and concentrated in ownership, yet significantly autonomous from government. The English-speaking section of the capitalist class, dominant in privately-built business, had acquired considerable experience and tact in cultivating personal ties and reaching accommodations with the Afrikaner-dominant state.[21] Afrikaner capital, significantly grown out of Apartheid affirmative action programmes, was more entwined in institutional relationship with the state, but it had been shifting ideologically, perhaps expediently as well, towards privatization and looser ties with government. It is hard to discern an organized black capitalist class poised in the early-1990s with a clear agenda for pursuing its interest. Although organizations such as the African Federated Chamber of Commerce (NAFCOC) and Black Management Forum (BMF), lacking liberation struggle credentials, strove to exert policy influence, the rise of a nationally powerful black business elite was a later development. Practical constraints were also difficult to surmount. Southall (2005) notes the problems to black capital formation posed by industrial concentration, but assesses that lack of experience and skill, and constricted access to capital were greater obstacles. Other aspects of the complex of political motivations prevailed upon black economic empowerment in the corporate sphere. Marais (2011, 140–141) perceptively argues:

> During the 1980s, the Apartheid regime had sought to cultivate a "moderate" black middle class . . . [corporate leaders] harboured larger ambitions . . . that their "magnanimity" would help bring the ANC around to endorsing the kinds of corporate restructuring (and divestment) they desired. Here an odd meeting of minds occurred. If large South African corporations shifted parts of their operations abroad in the context of a BEE drive, some in the ANC reasoned, a black capitalist class could be assembled more rapidly in the abandoned spaces.

What are the implications on affirmative action? First, the redistribution programme on the whole was eroded, as the post-Apartheid state embraced a macroeconomic regime preserving capitalist levers of power. The state's capacity to formulate and execute policy is circumscribed by the structural power of capital and the favourable macroeconomic framework in place. While it will perhaps be an overstatement to describe the state as captured by capital, it was beholden to the primacy of sustaining "investor confidence."

Second, while big business most volubly advocated neoliberal, market fundamentalist policies, it also possessed most resources to engage in affirmative action and BEE, having more employment positions and assets to redistribute, as well as economic power. The upper strata of society are among the most racially integrated.[22] The basic structure of BEE that emerged out of interactive processes between the ANC government, BEE Commission and industry charters, also shifted the process "(possibly unintendedly) partly away from political debate and towards technical and system performance discussions" (Ponte, Roberts and van Sittert 2007, 941–942). The BEE codes do correspond with less state intervention in selection processes, although the determination of development projects remains in state hands. Policies to cultivate black ownership and enterprise run the risk of departing from original socio-economic and developmental objectives towards passive market-based solutions.

Third, there appears to have been little penetration into main sectors or growth in scale of black business established during the Apartheid era. Those who have prospered in big business in the first post-Apartheid decade were largely composed of a new generation of black capitalists (Southall 2004; Randall 1996; Iheduru 2004). Inevitable limits to ownership transfer were reached in areas and firms dominated by white capital, which underscores the importance of creating of new, politically independent black enterprises. Blacks held virtually zero equity. Furthermore, South Africa's white-owned conglomerates amassed gargantuan shares of wealth. In 1992, six conglomerates controlled companies accounting for 85.7% of market capitalization of the Johannesburg Stock Exchange (Hirsch 2006). The GNU administration expressed a priority for developing small, medium and micro enterprises (SMMEs) and passed the Small Business Act in 1996, but the programme struggled to take off.

Fourth, the entry of blacks into an entrenched capitalist structure posed some dilemmas for the transformation project. BEE projected the notion of "patriotic" African *bourgeoisie* to engender change within firms and trickle-down benefits to wider society, as a furtherance of the "national democratic revolution" (Marais 2001; Southall 2004). This endeavour has not been pursued much beyond a code of conduct for black capitalists or a form of moral suasion with voluntary participation. The *nouveau riche*, are generally observed to behave in no substantially different manner than general wealth owners towards the community – although their obligations to extended families are likely to be more extensive. Nonetheless, the potential remains for positive impacts of black capitalist class development in terms of general psychological confidence-boosting effects of breaching historical barriers and visibly succeeding. Emphatically, the onus is on black businesses, public enterprises and government departments to demonstrate capacities to compete, innovate and govern.

Economic growth and public expenditures

The South African economy entered its democratic era characterized by a contradictory mix of slow growth, high unemployment and mass poverty, alongside deindustrialization, relatively high capital-intensity and skills shortages.[23] The long view is instructive. Annual GDP growth averaged 4.5% in 1960–1980 and 1.2% in 1980–1994. Low growth in the 1980s had crippled training and apprenticeship programmes, administered mostly by parastatals.[24] These conditions posed major limitations on the priority accorded to and resources available for affirmative action. The years just prior to the democratic era were especially turbulent, resulting in an anaemic 0.3% annual growth from 1990 to 1994. This was followed, in the democratic era, by a few phases in overall economic performance. Real GDP recorded annual growth of 2.6% (1994–1999), 4.2% (1999–2008), and 1.6% (2008–2017). South Africa's government expenditures, in real terms, grew annually by 5.5% (1970–1980), 2.9% (1980–1994), -0.4% (1994–1999), 4.6% (1999–2008) and 2.6% (2008–2016).[25]

The patterns of public expenditure impact on the resources available for public sector employment and affirmative action programmes involving procurement. Fiscal tightening resulted in employment losses in the public sector in the late 1990s.[26] However, public administration also shifted organizationally, in its adoption of "managerialism" and market-oriented initiatives, namely "new public management" (Chipkin 2008). The public sector was reoriented around an expanded and managerial role for officials, in contrast to conventional hierarchies and bureaucratic operations. As a result, the proportion of public service employees classified as managers has risen, which also increases the openings for blacks at those occupational and salary levels. Accordingly, the number of public service workers of management rank increased from 24,000 in 1995 to over 70,000 in 2001, while total employment declined by 125,000 between 1994 and 2001

(Naidoo 2008, 108–109). In addition, as Chipkin (2008) argues, the new system has promoted under-qualified personnel to posts, sometimes newly created and poorly defined, who are unable to perform the functions, and it has induced rivalry between departments for staff, potentially inflating mobility and vacancy rates and hampering service delivery.

Malaysia and South Africa in comparative perspective

Affirmative action in Malaysia and South Africa emphatically derive from singular histories and trajectories, with striking contrasts and semblances. With the characteristics of the policy regimes and the circumstances of their formation in the background, we now place both countries side by side. In venturing to systematically account for differences and similarities in the underpinnings, impetus, constraints and mechanisms of racial preferences, I have found that the constitutional provisions, political transition and pattern and magnitude of inter-racial inequality crystallize the key underlying characteristics. These translate into fundamental institutional features of the policy regimes. Table 3.1 compacts the key points, which I proceed to unpack.

Constitutional provisions

The constitutions of Malaysia and South Africa both authorize affirmative action but differ markedly in the justification and scope provided for the policy. Malaysia's 1957 Constitution stipulates safeguarding Bumiputera "special position;" South Africa's 1996 Constitution premises its provision for AA on being disadvantaged due to unfair discrimination. This segment draws extensively on Lee (2016).

How do these constitutional provisions shape affirmative action? Three implications stand out. First, the legal mandate vests a substantial degree of legitimacy in AA, but it also increases the latitude for the policy to be politically captured or co-opted and for group preference to be perpetuated. The designation of a politically dominant majority group as policy beneficiary permits the promotion of Bumiputera and black interest to be taken to much greater lengths than in other countries and largely precludes direct debate and contestation over the policy's extensive scope and further expansion of its domain over time. As noted by Sabbagh (2004, 5), in reference to these two countries, "the constitutionalization of affirmative action has probably facilitated its radicalization."

Ambiguity and specificity of the legal wording also matter – or, more consequentially, the ways constitutional provisions for group preferences have been interpreted, utilized and sometimes distorted, in popular discourses, political agendas and policy debates. The stipulation in Malaysia's Article 153 that reservations and quotas can be implemented, if necessary, to safeguard the "special position" of the Bumiputera has transmuted in political and popular discourses – even in school syllabuses – into an unbounded and permanent basis for "special privileges" or "special rights" (Brown 2007). South Africa, where Article

Table 3.6 Malaysia and South Africa: Political economy context of affirmative action regimes

	Malaysia	*South Africa*
Constitutional provisions	• Basis for AA: special position of Bumiputera • Areas of intervention specified: education, public sector employment, licensing	• Basis for AA: disadvantage due to unfair discrimination; equitable representation • General mandate, specific reference to government procurement, public sector employment
Political transition	• Continuous Malay/Bumiputera political power and dominance in the bureaucracy	• Democratization; shift in electoral power base from white minority to black majority
Inter-group disparity	• High foreign ownership, Chinese presence not dominant in all sectors	• Dominant white ownership across all sectors
Economic conditions (at inception, until 2010s)	• Robust growth and fiscal expansion, except for mid-1980s and late 1990s recession • Global mainstream relatively accommodating state intervention	• Sluggish economic growth and fiscal contraction (1990s), steadier growth and fiscal expansion (2000s) slowdown again (2010s) • Global neoliberal, market fundamentalist pressures
Institutional framework	• Discretionary executive authority • Intensive, direct interventions in tertiary education, equity ownership, public sector employment; minimal intervention in private sector employment • Quota-oriented, relatively centralised administration	• Statutory and codified system • Intensive, direct interventions in public and private sector employment; less intensive, indirect interventions in tertiary education, equity ownership • Target-oriented, less centralised administration

Sources: Lee (2010), Lee (2016).

9 designates beneficiaries of affirmative action on the grounds of disadvantage due to unfair discrimination, does not explicitly identify a race group and does provide some measure of restraint toward permanent entitlements. It also allows for gender- and disability-based preferences to redress under-representation. In practice, preferential treatment has been afforded predominantly to blacks, in line with the defining factor of past unfair discrimination. However, while race constitutes the primary basis for preferences, a fundamental difference manifests across the countries, in that, whereas Malaysian law designates Bumiputera as recipients of preference and implies they face disadvantages, South African law designates persons disadvantaged through unfair discrimination, with the connotation of primacy to racial discrimination as the basis for redress.

Second, Malaysia and South Africa negotiate in distinctive ways the tensions between preference and equality, between majority and minority interest. In Malaysia, constitutionally authorized race-based preferences translate into an overtly race-based framing of both the identification of beneficiaries and the contentions of other groups. Article 153 appears to counterbalance pro-Bumiputera preferences by articulating a proviso that the legitimate interests of non-Bumiputera groups are to be safeguarded (Faruqi 2008). However, the protection of specific legitimate interests of minorities is specific – and anachronistic. The safeguards explicitly pertain to contracts, assets and jobs *already in possession* – which the constitution would protect from arbitrary non-renewal, confiscation or termination.[27] Therefore, minority protections in Article 153 were relevant to the transition to independence, but they are ineffectual and otiose in the post-Independence context because they do not apply to the award or allocation of *new* contracts, assets and jobs.

By precedent and convention, the administration of affirmative action has mainly taken the form of bargains between discriminatory practices in some spheres, most saliently the public sector, for relative non-intervention in other spheres, particularly small- and medium-scale business. The peculiar configurations of Malaysia's communal accommodations also involve trade-offs in social and political domains – concerning cultural and religious issues, and especially government support for Chinese- and Tamil-medium schools – which have moderated grievances against various unequal opportunities arising from affirmative action.

South Africa's legislation more substantively accounts for tensions between equality and affirmative action. The constitution establishes non-racialism and non-sexism as founding principles and provides some room for persons who contend they have received unfair treatment to seek legal recourse, including some cases against universities for giving preference to African applicants (February 2010). The Employment Equity Act (EEA) stipulates that preference be accorded on "suitably qualified" candidates of the disadvantaged groups and in doing so opens the way for legal challenge. Employers, especially public service departments, have faced lawsuits brought on the grounds that whites are unfairly discriminated against when less-qualified blacks are appointed ahead of them, or when positions are not filled even while qualified candidates are available, or when AA continues to be applied after targets are met. However, the Constitutional Court has upheld affirmative action, adjudicating that the law defers to the need for redress of past injustices, while adhering to principles of reasonableness (Dupper 2014).

Third, the constitutions set a template that orients the operational modes and mechanisms of AA programmes. Malaysia pursues AA mainly by setting Bumiputera quotas and reservations; South Africa utilizes targets and goals (Sabbagh 2004). Quotas and targets are not mutually exclusive. Indeed, targets lack meaning unless they are integrated with specific allocations, which are akin to quotas (Fryer and Loury 2005). Nonetheless, quotas and targets are distinguishable in the degree to which the designated portion is fixed and mandatory. South Africa's employment equity is instructive, for the way it imposes a mandate on employers, in consultation with workers, to achieve a workforce composition, especially in the upper echelons, proportionate to the economically active population, without reserving fixed allocations for particular groups. Indeed, the EEA explicitly states that affirmative action measures "include preferential treatment and numerical goals, but exclude quotas" (South Africa 1998a).

Political transition

Affirmative action formed amid political transitions. Malays took precedence in Malaysia's political establishment and bureaucracy throughout the post-Independence era from 1957, then asserted dominance from 1971, while executive powers were concomitantly augmented, and AA policies expanded and intensified. Malaya's 1957 Independence Constitution emerged from an "elite pact" among the three racially constituted parties of the Alliance government, entailing a set of compromises and concessions. In socio-economic spheres, non-Malays accommodated Malay preferential treatment, which was concentrated in the public sector, as a trade-off for a largely hands-off relationship between the state and private enterprise.

The New Economic Policy (NEP) marked a turning point. Post-1971, under the aegis of the NEP and its sweeping developmental vision, affirmative action proliferated, propelled by a reassertion of Malay primacy and promotion of more overtly pro-Malay policies. A new political order expanded and centralized discretionary executive power, capitalizing on the political uncertainties in the aftermath of the May 13th upheavals (Khoo 2005). Important to our interest in public policy, economic planning and information became more tightly controlled by the prime minister's department, and a range of legislative changes constricted dissent and broadened executive power, including the Sedition Act amendment, which proscribes the questioning of Article 153. This socio-political milieu accounts for the magnitude of racial preference – notably, in establishing racially exclusive education, microfinance and SME loans and support, and in quotas and discounts for public procurement and private equity and property purchases – which greatly exceeds the interventions of most AA regimes worldwide.

Structures of inter-group relations also shaped Malaysia's AA regime. Malays and non-Malays were not historically locked in head-to-head confrontational, hierarchical, or repressive relationships. Therefore, interventions morally premised on reparation for past unfair discrimination, such as requirements for employers to preferentially recruit Malays, did not materialize, since non-Malays were not executioners of any systematic exclusion of Malays. The magnitude of minority economic power was also lesser in Malaysia relative to South Africa, as discussed in the next point. Hence, in some spheres, particularly the labour market, the scope for redress and restitution in Malaysia was narrower. Furthermore, boundaries for AA have largely been demarcated by compromises, drawing on the constitution's specification of public education, public sector employment and government licensing and government contracting, while limiting interventions in private business.

On the whole, then, Malaysia's AA was massive and intensive, with marked concentration of interventions in the public sector and state-owed enterprise, while the private sector – except when involved in public procurement and public listing – was substantially exempted from racial representation requirements. The Industrial Coordination Act (ICA), requiring manufacturing firms to allocate 30% of equity to Bumiputeras, met stiff resistance from Chinese business at its introduction in 1975 due to the stakeholder diluting effects as well as the law's coercive encroachment into the ownership sphere where regulation had been minimal. Mounting protests led to the exemption of most firms from ICA conditions and a steady fadeout of the act.

In pronounced contrast, affirmative action took root in South Africa in extraordinarily different circumstances. It transitioned from Apartheid minority rule to democratic majority rule through a negotiated process, culminating in the 1994 elections and an all-encompassing transformation of polity, society and economy (Marais 2001; Terreblanche 2002). Introducing black preferential treatment faced prospective alienation or backlash from the white population that comprehensively dominated commerce, finance, industry and bureaucracy. South Africa's constitution established non-racialism and non-sexism as national founding principles and built in a framework for democratic governance and limits on executive power. Existing power structures – notably, autonomy of provincial government and public institutions, including universities – precluded political and administrative centralization of federal government powers.

Despite being a vast demographic majority, blacks in South Africa negotiated from a weak position, their leverage severely undermined by previous exclusion from executive, decision-making and ownership positions in government, the bureaucracy and the private sector. The "sunset clause" was forged to facilitate government functionality and retain experienced senior officials in the five years following the 1994 elections. Underlying this bargaining tactic was an acknowledgment of the paucity of qualified and experienced non-whites to fill key positions in the event of a rapid exodus of whites, which could be triggered by overzealous reappointments. Additionally, affirmative action was one of various political economic negotiations South Africa was embroiled in; indeed, transition authorities were pre-occupied with higher priority crises and threats to national integrity, public order and basic services. The need to quell social unrest and violence, integrate fragmented public services, coalesce separate education systems and ameliorate workers' grievances and basic demands took precedence over direct redistributive interventions to promote black upward mobility. The milieu compelled the government to assume a more conciliatory posture and temper executive power.

At the same time, the South African state could pursue redress initiatives vis-à-vis white capital and the public sector on the moral grounds of correcting past discrimination, unlike in Malaysia where Malay and non-Malay establishments were not historically interlocked in exploitative relationships. Hence, while South Africa adopted a more legislative and statutory mechanisms rather than Malaysia-style executive mandate, the scope of some interventions, chiefly employment equity, are wider.

A form of "racial bargain" also attended South Africa's democratic transition, but with contrasting elements to Malaysia's forthright negotiation between race-based political parties and its formalization through the constitution's framing of Bumiputera special position. South Africa's bargain was implicit and rather informal. As Southall (2007, 83) puts it, an accommodation coalesced in the 1990s, in which "whites/the NP/large-scale capital conceded formal political power, while blacks/the ANC/the incoming political elite agreed to the continuance of white domination of the economy." Exceedingly high inequality, compounded by mass unemployment and poverty, coupled with the leftist ideological thrust of the liberation movement and presence of COSATU in the liberation movement, provided some check against policies promoting black capital accumulation, compared to the broader latitude of the Malaysian state in pursuing Bumiputera capitalist development.

Nonetheless, from the late 1990s, slow progress in advancing black ownership induced pressures for more direct and effective interventions, out of which black economic empowerment (BEE) became mainstreamed and formalized. The pressures gave rise to the formation of the BEE Commission, while corporate South Africa initiated business-led and industry-specific charters. The Broad-Based BEE Act of 2003 sought to harmonize the terms across industries and to incentivize BEE among private, predominantly white, capital.

The political transitions traversed in Malaysia and South Africa shaped affirmative action in two key respects. First, in the mode of governance, Malaysia's federal government exercised discretionary, top-down policy making, whereas South Africa's relative constraints on executive power mapped out a more legislative route of statutes and codes. Second, regarding the general mechanism of AA, the intensification of Malaysia's racial politics and policy discourses post-13 May 1969, drawing on constitutional safeguards and pre-existing preferential treatment, set the stage for expansion of Bumiputera quotas or exclusive access and direct state intervention to groom a Bumiputera capitalist class. The founding principle of non-racialism in South Africa, in tandem with apprehension toward alienating the minority white population, inclined the AA regime to pursue racial representativeness and diversity through targets and incentives.

Inter-racial socio-economic disparity and minority economic strength

Malaysia and South Africa demonstrate the formative impact of the magnitude of inequality, even in situations of majority disadvantage and majority-favouring preferences. The wealth, achievement and power gulf between the majority blacks and minority whites in South Africa was considerably greater than that between majority Bumiputeras and minority Chinese and Indians in Malaysia.

South Africa's white population monopolized capital, mining rights and productive land, predominated in senior positions both in government and industry, and enjoyed exclusive access to the best schools and universities, whereas Malaysia's Chinese and Indians maintained a substantial but not entirely overpowering presence in education, employment and ownership.

A few compatible indicators of the late-1960s to early-1970s Malaysia, and the early- to mid-1990s South Africa, strikingly illustrate the differences. In Peninsular Malaysia in 1967, the Chinese-to-Malay household income ratio was recorded at 2.47 and the Indian-to-Malay household income ratio at 1.95 (Anand 1981). In South Africa, household income ratios in 1991 were 11.1 for White-African, 5.7 for White-Coloured, 3.0 for White-Indian (Whiteford and Van Seventer 2000). Access to education reveals a similar pattern of worse racial disparity in South Africa. In 1970, the composition of the University of Malaya – the only higher education institute to have graduated students at that point – broadly mirrored the national population, although Malay representation in some disciplines was exceptionally low. In South Africa, between 1986 and 1993, the number of African students at universities and *teknikons*[28] increased by 14% per year, against 0.4% for whites. Despite those relative gains, however, disparities prevailed in 1993, at the cusp of the democratic transition. The higher education participation rate – the enrolment rate of 20–24 year olds – for Africans stood at 12%, staggeringly dwarfed by that of whites, among whom 70% of young adults attended university (Department of Education 1997). Black students were also concentrated in the systemically inferior historically black/disadvantaged institutes, while white students progressed academically to historically white/advantaged institutes.

Under-representation of the disadvantaged group in top management and ownership in the private sector has perhaps been the highest hurdle to clear, and a most politically consequential policy sphere that also varies in its manifestations and magnitudes across these countries. In 1970, Malays occupied 22.4% of management and administration positions on the whole, and 39.3% in the upper echelons of the civil service, considerably below their 52.7% share of the Malaysian population (Malaysia 1976; Khoo 2005). Blacks comprised 76% of South Africa's population in 1996, but only 40% of managers in public service departments. Africans, comprising 76% of the population, accounted for a miniscule 3% among senior management in the private sector (Adam 2000; Naidoo 2008). In the distribution of wealth, equity holdings are one available data source. Bumiputera interests held 2.4% of total share capital, with non-Bumiputera Malaysians owned 28.3% and foreigners 63.4%. Blacks held a derisory share of equity; moreover, South Africa's wealth was concentrated in white-owned corporate behemoths.

The state's latitude and efficacy in reallocating opportunity and imposing new conditions in education, employment and ownership policies, differed across countries. In 1970, at the onset of AA's rapid expansion, Malaysia had just one university, which facilitated conducive conditions for creation of new universities and for administration of entry quotas or Bumiputera-exclusive access from their inception. South Africa encountered contrasting objectives: to increase black representation in the various established, autonomous historically white institutions, as well as to close the quality gap of lagging historically black institutions. Consequently, AA interventions had to deal with existing institutions and deliver on guarantees that their autonomy would be preserved, leading to a decentralized AA agenda and devolution of policy formulation and implementation to individual universities. Malaysia's public sector had consistently conferred Bumiputera preferences, with increased intensity from the 1970s, solidifying the public sector and public institutions as pathways for Bumiputera advancement. Prompted by the black population's systemic repression toward upward mobility in both government and businesses, South Africa promulgated legislation encompassing public and private sectors.

In the wealth-distribution sphere, minority economic strength was pivotal. Minority-owned, especially Chinese-owned, business in Malaysia had secured footholds in some sectors, but not comprehensive leverage. Therefore, the state was in a strong enough bargaining position to extract concessions, and moreover, the preponderance of foreign holdings provided opportunity to target an external source to appropriate into Bumiputera hands, thereby to some extent defusing domestic conflict that could have erupted had the government forcefully taken over Chinese businesses. South Africa's white-owned big business, with its dominance of the commanding heights of the economy, secured its interests and exercised leverage over economic policy from the 1980s.

The neoliberal, market fundamentalist template was laid before the political transition, sponsored by corporate South Africa, with the participation of government and the liberation movement. The threat of capital flight, coupled with pressures to draw South Africa out of global economic isolation, engendered guarantees for capital mobility. Thus, the incipient democratic South African state bargained with domestic capital from a relatively weak position, allowing capital to set the agenda (Sparks 2003; Gqubule 2006). However, from the mid-1990s, fears of more aggressive state-sanctioned redistribution spurred industry-based initiatives and charters to promote black economic opportunity and participation, which later evolved into the Broad-Based Black Economic Empowerment (BBBEE) scorecard, albeit in a continually market-centric framework (Southall 2004; Ponte, Roberts and van Sittert 2007).

A final brief note on macroeconomic conditions is also warranted. Malaysia's steadier and higher growth, and expansionary macroeconomic policies, availed more resources for public sector employment and various AA-related expenditures, including scholarships, business financing and creation of state-owned enterprises and numerous institutions. South Africa's slower and uneven economic growth, and serious constraints in public finance, affected the pace and scope of AA interventions.

The broad institutional features outlined in this chapter translate into policy formulations, programmes and instruments, which we turn to in the Part 2.

Notes

1 The Pakistan, United States and India constitutions provided preferential treatment to certain groups with regard to educational and business opportunities (Fernando and Rajagopal 2017).
2 Khoo (2005, 11) conveys Puthucheary's (1960) finding that Europeans controlled over 84% of large rubber estates and 60% of tin output, and accounted for about 70% of exports and 60% of imports.
3 In 1957, literacy rates in Northern Peninsular, Malay-dominant states and East Malaysia (Kelantan, Terengganu, Kedah, Perlis, Sabah, Sarawak) fell below the national average of 50%, while the West coast and central Peninsula states recorded significantly higher literacy rates (Leete 2007, 199).
4 Author's interview with Khoo Boo Teik, 15 August 2007.
5 Author's interviews with former Economic Planning Unit officials.
6 Authors interview with Suresh Narayanan, 14 August 2007.
7 Author's calculations from World Bank data (data.worldbank.org).
8 Author's calculations from World Bank data (data.worldbank.org).
9 Public expenditure per GDP registered 29.0% in 1970, 39.9% in 1979, and 58.4% in 1981.
10 The author is grateful to Gerhard Maré for highlighting major differences between the Bantustans and townships.
11 In 1993, there were 172 departments in the central government and homeland administrations (Naidoo 2008, 101).
12 In 1990, the standard 10 passing rate was 79.4% for Coloureds, 95.0% for Indians and 95.8% for Whites. Per capita educational expenditure in 1988 registered ZAR276 for Africans, ZAR1,358 for Coloreds, ZAR2,225 for Indians and ZAR3,080 for Whites, while the proportion of teachers with professional qualification in 1990 also showed disparities within the black population, with 87% for Africans; 96% for Coloureds and 98.5% for Indians (MERG 1993, 129–134). Other sources yield different estimates for disparity in education spending, e.g. Motala *et al.* (2007, 3 and 12) report ratios of average spending on whites to blacks of 3.2 in 1993, and as high as 15 in 1990.
13 Author's interview with Professor Eddie Webster, 29 October 2007.
14 Author's interview with Sampie Terreblanche, 21 January 2008.
15 The South Africa Foundation published *Growth for All* with the support of the fifty largest corporations, asserting that the government had no credible and comprehensive economic policy framework. The appointment of Trevor Manuel as finance minister in February 1996 was received negatively by business. The South African economy was also performing poorly in early 1996, saddled with high unemployment and stagnant growth, and the Rand was sliding, to which Manuel responded by announcing initiatives to placate the corporate and financial sectors (Terreblanche 2002).
16 GEAR was written and pushed aggressively, and obtained approval from the ANC's National Executive Committee, despite opposition from alliance partners COSATU and SACP, with Thabo Mbeki and Trevor Manuel closing the matter as "non-negotiable," while Mandela acknowledged: "I confess even the ANC learnt of GEAR far too late – when it was almost complete" (Marais 2001, 162).
17 The document continues: "The ANC proposes affirmative action with a view to establishing a law-governed, progressive and equitable way of ensuring advancement without on the one hand freezing present privileges or on the other going over to arbitrary compulsion. The issue has to be handled with both firmness and sensitivity." It underscored that "unless special interventions are made, the patterns of structured advantage and disadvantage created by Apartheid and

patriarchy replicate themselves from generation to generation" (ANC Department of Economic Planning 1992).

18 The RDP was in substance and tenor more a manifesto than policy blueprint. Marais (2001, 239) writes: "In the context of the transition, the RDP has become a form of shorthand for the values and principles that animated the anti-Apartheid struggle, thereby signifying continuity. The fact that government references to it have grown rarer and more selective only highlights this function." Nevertheless, its orientation and vision are reflective of political priorities, not unlike Malaysia's NEP.

19 I am grateful to Seeraj Muhamed for this insight.

20 Author's interview with Steven Friedman, 22 November 2007.

21 Indeed, until 1997–1998, white business remained hostile towards the ANC and still placed faith in the NP within the GNU. It was only after the passage of GEAR that white business began to see ANC as a friendly to them, a factor in the subsequent rapid demise of the NP (Author's interview with Stephen Gelb, 1 November 2007).

22 Author's interview with Adam Habib, 20 November 2007.

23 The proportion of industry in GDP declined continuously from 45.7% in 1981 to 40.1% in 1990, 34.8% in 1995, 31.8% in 2000 and 30.7% in 2005 (World Bank World Development Indicators).

24 The number of new apprenticeships fell from 14,497 in 1982 to 9,660 in 1986 (Standing, Sender and Weeks 1996, 386–388). The numbers of workers involved in industrial training and total apprenticeships plummeted, respectively, from 736,581 and 29,826 in 1986 to 152,870 and 16,577 in 1998 (Hirsch 2006, 185).

25 Author's calculations from World Bank data (data.worldbank.org).

26 A "leaner government" strategy was endorsed by Mandela in February 1998 in a state of union address, stressing the need to shed some of 1.2 million public sector jobs to prevent over-spending (Hirsch 2006, 164).

27 Directly quoting Article 153 is instructive. Clause (8) and (8) (a) read:

> Notwithstanding anything in this Constitution, where by any federal law any permit or licence is required for the operation of any trade or business, that law may provide for the reservation of a proportion of such permits or licences for Malays and natives of any of the States of Sabah and Sarawak; but no such law shall for the purpose of ensuring such a reservation –
>
> *(a)* deprive or authorize the deprivation of any person of any right, privilege, permit or licence *accrued to or enjoyed or held by him.*" (Malaysia 2010a, emphasis added)

28 *Teknikons* were technical colleges, renamed *universities of technology* in 2005.

Part 2

Affirmative action in practice

Quotas, codes and preferences

The next two chapters lay out affirmative action pillars and policies in Malaysia and South Africa. I briefly provide a critical survey of policy frameworks that have provided impetus for and placed constraints on affirmative action in practice. In view of Malaysia's executive dominance and centralized federalism, its planning documents have played a more consistent role as policy drivers and anchors. South Africa undertook a more responsive and incremental approach, but the overall orientation of laws and policies can be traced to a broader set of objectives and constraints. I also touch on turning points that have influenced the direction and tone of affirmative action.

The chapters then present comprehensive and chronological surveys of affirmative action programmes, in the four chief policy sectors: higher education, high-level employment, enterprise development and wealth ownership. Aligned with the character of the regimes discussed in the previous chapter, Malaysia's programmes predominantly apply discretionary executive power in a centralized system, while South Africa's deploy legislation, statutes and codes to a greater extent, operating in a more decentralized manner. I also present data on socio-economic conditions that help situate policy formulation or policy continuation in context. Where pertinent, I report indicators of how affirmative action progressed in the early years – or in the case of Malaysia, the first decades – to set the stage for the analysis which focuses on the early 1990s and onwards for Malaysia, and the period after the late 1990s for South Africa.

A preview and summary of key elements and cross-country comparison may be useful before launching into the specifics of each country. Table 4.1 summarizes the major policies.

Table 4.1 Malaysia and South Africa: Current affirmative action programmes and key features

	Malaysia	South Africa
Higher education	• Quotas in pre-university programmes, preferential treatment in public institutions • Centralized administration, including university admissions • Bumiputera-exclusive institutions and scholarships, some designated for disadvantaged Bumiputeras	• Redress programs within and between institutions • Institutional autonomy, university-level redress/transformation • Financial assistance based on need and disadvantage
High-level occupations	• Public sector: employment quotas/racial preference • State-owned enterprises/government-linked companies: de facto preferential treatment	• Employment equity legislation: • Applies to public sector and medium- to large-scale private companies • Involves consultation, planning and target-setting toward equitable representation
Enterprise development	• Different phases based on primary vehicle for promoting Bumiputera managerial and capitalist class: • State-owned enterprises (1970s) • Takeover of foreign companies (mid-1970s to early-1980s) • Heavy industries (early- to mid-1980s) • Privatization of state entities (late-1980s – late-1990s) • Government-linked companies (late-1990s –) • Quotas and price handicaps in licensing and public procurement • Loans and support schemes for SMEs • Bumiputera Economic Transformation Programme/Bumiputera Economic Community • Re-emphasis on independent, competitive Bumiputera enterprise • Range of experimental measures • Microfinance; training and advisory services for small/micro enterprise	• Broad-Based Black Economic Empowerment (BBBEE) codifies award system for public procurement, licensing and concessions, sale of state assets, and public-private partnerships, according to a "scorecard" with multiple criteria (launched 2007, amended 2013): ownership, management control, employment equity, skills development, preferential procurement, enterprise development, socio-economic development • State-owned companies: direct management, procurement • BEE codes applied especially in public procurement • SME financial support through the DTI and NEF • Black Industrialists Programme • Initiative to groom black enterprise, particularly in manufacturing
Wealth and property ownership	• Industrial Coordination Act (1975) equity requirements • Unit trust funds quotas • IPO quotas and discounts • Property quotas and discounts	• Equity transfers under BBBEE • NEF support to purchase equity

Source: Adapted and expanded from Lee (2016).

4 Affirmative action pillars and programmes
Malaysia

Policy visions and frameworks

The New Economic Policy transformed Malaysia by laying the bedrock for affirmative action to be expanded and intensified. Pro-Malay policies, riding on Malay political primacy, grew from the NEP's general imprimatur for programmes conferring preferential treatment or exclusive access to Malays and Bumiputeras and from specific articulations of policy priorities, such as university admissions and the creation of a Malay Commercial and Industrial Community.

The NEP, technically termed the *First Outline Perspective Plan* (1971–1990), was promulgated in the *Second Malaysia Plan* (1971–1975) and reinforced in the *Third Malaysia Plan* (1976–1980). Two outstanding elements warrant our consideration. First, it set out two fundamental national objectives, including affirmative action. The "two prongs" beneath the overarching aim of national unity resolved (Malaysia 1971, 1):

1 To "reduce and eventually eradicate poverty, . . . regardless of race;"
2 To "accelerate social restructuring to correct economic imbalance," so as to "remove and eventually eliminate the identification of race with economic function."

The NEP's lucid and judicious distinction of poverty alleviation and social restructuring is often under-appreciated. The NEP clearly maintained that pro-poor policies – which principally involve providing basic social services, especially primary and secondary education and health care, connecting households with infrastructure and helping them generate subsistence income – can clearly operate without consideration of race, whereas policy targeting based on racial identity was integral to social restructuring, or affirmative action. The NEP authors grasped that policies of the two prongs are "interdependent and mutually reinforcing" (Malaysia 1971, 3), but cannot serve as systemic substitutes: need-based assistance cannot replace race-based empowerment.

The second prong emphatically empowered affirmative action. Social restructuring conventionally came to mean increasing the participation of Bumiputeras in places where they are under-represented: higher education, employment, commerce and industry, and ownership. However, less reiterated within the NEP – which perhaps itself did not realize the importance of this articulation – is the proviso that interventions were necessary to *accelerate* the process. This added emphasis underscored the need for preferential selection. Social restructuring could have, and assuredly would have, taken place if Malaysia merely focused on economic growth and stability and assisted the poor: Bumiputeras would gradually increase incomes, improve schooling achievement and enter university, then rise up the occupational ladder and even start or acquire businesses.

However, *accelerating* the process called for preferential selection. Had the NEP been more grounded in the underlying justification that special measures served to accelerate change, consequent policy designs possibly might have paid more attention to the pace and sequencing of transformation, the capacity of different policy sectors to execute the change and the perils of pushing too fast. The fundamental feature of programmes empowered by the second prong – the application of race preferences – might have also become more clearly and consistently understood and articulated. The NEP scarcely considered whether social restructuring could be attained through other means besides overt race preference. Although there was internal government debate between a growth-centric national development strategy versus one focused on redistribution, detailed accounts of the process suggest that policy spheres were not decisively differentiated in terms of modes of preferential treatment, operations and constraints (Faaland, Parkinson and Saniman 1990). To be fair, there was less international literature and policy discourse to draw on then. Nonetheless, the NEP established a conventional mode of thinking that did not systematically consider whether and how equitable racial representation could be achieved through methods besides racial quotas and reservations.

The second important precedent of the NEP concerns the clear timeline laid out – 1971 to 1990 – and, more distinctively, intimations to the effect that the policy was to be unwound when it had achieved its objective. An evocative aspiration presented in the *Second Malaysia Plan* was for Malays to be uplifted "within one generation" to be "full partners in the economic life of the nation" (Malaysia 1971, 6). This time window, however, was not accompanied with coterminous exit or graduation conditions. When targets were set – notably, 30% Bumiputera equity ownership and proportionate representation in all occupations and industries – there was no clear articulation of policy measures when those thresholds were reached. The 30%, in turn, comprised two sub-targets: 7.4% held by Malay individuals;[1] 22.6% held by "Malay interests" – meaning shares held in trust agencies such as MARA, PERNAS, SEDCs, and Bank Bumiputera (Malaysia 1976, 86). And, as noted in Chapter 3, the fuller articulation of the NEP in the *Third Malaysia Plan*, by limiting the goal to be accomplished by one generation to equity ownership, effectively backtracked on the *Second Plan*'s general commitment to Malay full partnership in 1990.

From the mid-1980s, toward the conclusion of the NEP in 1990, public discourses flourished over policy succession – including, of course, the future of affirmative action. The investment climate had shifted by then, as Malaysia widely opened to foreign investment and privatization of state assets. Various appeals were made for racial preferences to be rolled back – often citing the over-representation of Malays in the civil service as an indication that the country was ready to remove preferential treatment. Recurrently, policy documents called for reduced emphasis on redistribution and more on poverty alleviation, particularly in urban areas where non-Bumiputera communities were affected (Gerakan 1984). Salih and Yusof (1989) called for emphasis on employment, entrepreneurship and productivity, rather than ownership, noting that Bumiputera mobility in modern sectors did not see productivity of Bumiputera enterprises rising in tandem.

Affirmative action was not dismantled in 1990. This is sometimes viewed with regret, as a missed opportunity or a failure of political will. Such stances are based on misreadings of the NEP. In hindsight, it is also fair to say the twenty-year timeline was unrealistic, even in the public sector – the policy sphere that experienced the most marked increase in Bumiputera participation. Increased Bumiputera, especially Malay, shares of public sector employment would signal quantitative progress but would not cogently address the question of the preparedness for preferential treatment to be rolled back. Malay over-representation in the civil service, while an undeniable outcome, decidedly does *not* signal a readiness and capacity to undertake systemic reforms.

Even with maximum "political will" mustered, it surely takes much longer than "one generation" to achieve inter-group parity, considering the paucity at the NEP's inception in 1971 of Bumiputera university-educated adults, professionals and managers, which was compounded by the entrenched positions of existing Chinese- and foreign-owned business due to experience, accumulated wealth, networks and inter-generational handovers. A more reasonable duration and long-term outlook, perhaps encompassing three generations undertaking systematic and sequenced reforms, extended beyond the scope and resources of the NEP. Although the NEP did set a precedent of a time boundary to race-preferential policies, it did not delve into the specifics of how Malaysia might exit or graduate from the policy, and it did not articulate possibilities for different timelines for different policy spheres – except for a passing remark that enterprise development could take an especially long time. NEP programmes endured beyond 1990, and discourses over timelines grew muted.

Other visionary plans rolled out, but none captured the public imagination nor acquired major clout. The National Development Policy (NDP), the NEP's immediate successor spanning 1991–2000, is noteworthy for the overarching emphasis on economic growth, investment liberalization and privatization, which impacted on affirmative action. The NEP remained the policy anchor for justifying affirmative action and for deeming that Malaysia still has unfinished business, but the NDP was a reference point for sustaining the momentum in attracting foreign direct investment – in which relaxation of hitherto Bumiputera equity ownership requirements played a key role – and in massive privatization, which would be the chief vehicle for carrying Bumiputera enterprise development. Relative to the NEP, the NDP did tone down the more overt policy rhetoric of social restructuring, and in the equity ownership sphere policies were scaled back, but concurrently – and with less official emphasis and scant critical scrutiny – numerous race-preferential programmes in education, employment, microfinance and property ownership continued expanding. The long-term objective of rolling back affirmative action was less explicitly articulated.

The next declaration to seize the public imagination came in the form of a speech. Prime Minister Mahathir Mohamed's Vision 2020, addressed to the Malaysian Business Council in 1991, reverberated far beyond that event. Mahathir projected nine lofty challenges, consonant with Malaysia attaining "fully developed" status and taking its place on the global stage. With regard to affirmative action, he envisaged "the creation of an economically resilient and fully competitive Bumiputera community so as to be at par with the non-Bumiputera community," implying that preferential treatment would be redundant – though not necessarily committing to unwind the system. Vision 2020 was not an official document, but like iconic orations, it galvanized popular sentiments. It gave greater impetus to the rapid creation of a Bumiputera capitalist class, under the auspices of the Bumiputera Commercial and Industrial Community in the early- to mid-1990s. The overarching Bumiputera development agenda placed less emphasis on capability development through education and showed a bias toward ownership and control of big corporations. This patron-client network facilitating massive distribution of rents was also enmeshed with political funding (Gomez and Jomo 1999). The 1997–1998 crisis-triggered collapse of Malay corporate titans spurred further efforts to pursue this agenda, but no longer under the aegis of the grand – and discredited – privatization plan that had speedily created them.

The influence of long-term visions continually declined. While the NEP transformed Malaysia and endured as a nation-building template, and the NDP served as a reference point, the National Vision Policy (2001–2010) never gained traction. It is no exaggeration to say the NVP has been collectively forgotten, almost never mentioned even while the NEP remains indelible and the NDP is occasionally mentioned in specialist circles. With regard to affirmative action, its irrelevance further retired considerations of dismantling preferential treatment on the far horizon.

In the early 2000s, Malaysia's development policies basically maintained Bumiputera preferential treatment, with some modifications – notably, the introduction of 10% non-Bumiputera quotas in previously Bumiputera-exclusive education programmes – but clearer policy directions were mapped out in sector-specific programmes. Policy shifts under the Abdullah Badawi administration (2003–2008) had some implication on affirmative action, especially a new emphasis on SMEs. The Government-Linked Companies (GLC) Transformation Programme launched in 2005 was significant. The programme marked out some clear and specific applications of pro-Bumiputera policies and indicated willingness to engage in challenging reforms. Of course, its confinement to GLCs, with extension to their vendors, requires us to contextualize the policy scope, while recognizing its substantial coherence and applicability. In marked contrast, the New Economic Model of 2010 features prominently, being enthusiastically embraced for its reform rhetoric. The NEM's incoherence has been discussed in Chapter 2. On that basis, coupled with the government's renunciation, the NEM is omitted here.

Post-2010, however, saw the emergence of a new corpus of Bumiputera programmes and agencies. The Bumiputera Economic Transformation (BETR) Programme, launched in 2012, comprised a range of new interventions and agencies, primarily focused on grooming medium-scale enterprises with true capability and competitiveness. The agenda sought to reach beyond the orbit of GLCs and their affiliates or subsidiaries, which had reaped the bulk of affirmative action support in the 2000s. Recent policies give more attention to the quality of vendors and contractors, more competitive selection and stringent monitoring. In the education sphere, the BETR has given some attention to facilitating advancement of Bumiputera students from challenging backgrounds in technical and vocational programmes.

On the whole, the current agenda, under the banner of the Bumiputera Economic Community, is significant in its reemphasis on providing assistance for disadvantaged Bumiputera students and its measures to catalyze entrepreneurship and build capability, competitiveness and independence in medium-scale companies, but the approach remains more piecemeal than systemic. Malaysia has yet to articulate a long-term, comprehensive and systematic framework for policy reform and rollback, although recent policies have mentioned the application of exit conditions for vendors (Teraju 2017; Malaysia 2018).

Affirmative action programmes

Higher education

Under the NEP, the agenda of educational reform was substantially carried by newly created institutions and backed by generous increases in public expenditure. Annual per capita public education expenditure, which had increased from MYR30 in 1961 to MYR50 in 1970, burgeoned to MYR206 in 1980 and MYR356 in 1990 (Leete 2007, 181). A significant portion of these expenditures did not operate on a race-preferential basis but designated children of rural and poor households as the principal beneficiaries. However, Bumiputeras witnessed the highest gains in schooling attainment after 1971. By comparing successive cohorts spanning pre-NEP and post-NEP periods, Pong (1993) found that secondary school completion was increasingly associated with race, after controlling for other socio-economic characteristics.[2]

Direct affirmative action policies in education created new school-level institutions for Bumiputeras and quota systems and scholarships for university enrolment. Article 153, hitherto providing specifically for Bumiputera reservation of scholarships, exhibitions and training, was amended to expand its educational scope, through the inclusion of Clause 8A which authorizes Bumiputera reservation in post-secondary education enrolment (Malaysia 2010a). The *Universiti Teknologi*

MARA Act 1976 stipulates that the institution is "established pursuant to and in accordance with the provisions of Article 153 of the Federal Constitution" (Malaysia 2006b). It is worth noting that Malaysia had progressed in increasing university student diversity in the first decade of independence. Malays students constituted a mere 20% of total enrolment in 1963–1964, but their share had risen to slightly above 40% by 1970 (Santhiram and Sua 2017, 39). In degree programmes of three public universities – University of Malaya, Science University (USM) and National University (UKM) – the student body in 1970 consisted of 40.2% Bumiputera, 48.9% Chinese, 7.3% Indian, and 3.7% others (Malaysia 1981).

However, although enrolment in university was not far off the racial make-up of the country as a whole, the under-representation of Malays in the sciences and technical subjects was acute, and dearth of Malay graduates in these fields exacerbated deficiencies in rural schools. In 1970, the University of Malaya was the only comprehensive university in Malaysia. In science subjects, Malay graduates numbered 22 out of a total 493 in science, 4 out of 67 in medicine, 1 per 71 in engineering, 15 per 49 in agriculture (Selvaratnam 1988, 180). Noting that only 12% of Bumiputera university enrolment was in science and technology, the *Mid-Term Review of the Second Malaysia Plan* asserted that "the Government will continue its efforts to increase Malay enrolments in science and technology in the universities" (Malaysia 1973, 191–197). High priority was ascribed to promotion of science and technical education among the Malays, including the rural Malays who would primarily benefit from upper secondary residential science colleges.

These shortfalls were compounded by the labour requirements of industrialization. From the mid-1970s, "manpower planning" – in particular, cultivation of science and engineering graduates – began to be prioritized in education policy (Lee 1994). To fill the gap, the Ministry of Education established exclusively Bumiputera residential science colleges. MARA also set up junior residential colleges primarily for students in rural and underprivileged areas. These institutes, which youth entered after six or nine years of schooling, enjoyed higher standards of teaching and facilities, especially in science classes (Leete 2007, 189). Between 1970 and 1990, MARA allocated MYR700 million – 67% of its total budget – for educational purposes (Jamaludin 2003). By 1987, enrolment in the Education Ministry's residential colleges touched over 17,000, while MARA Junior Science Colleges (MRSMs) had 15,000 students (Selvaratnam 1988, 185). Bumiputera-exclusive matriculation programmes have also been established to provide an alternate route to university entrance that bypasses the national schools and the national higher school certificate examination.

At the tertiary level, new public universities were founded and a centralized government unit created to process applications and implement enrolment quotas, set at a 55:45 Bumiputera to non-Bumiputera ratio (Lee 2004a).[3] Enrolment statistics bear out this policy pursuit, showing that the targets were not just met but exceeded. In 1985, enrolment in the seven extant public higher education institutions was 67.4% Bumiputera, 25.6% Chinese, 5.9% Indian, and 1.2% others. By discipline, Malay enrolment in 1966–1967 compared to 1976–1977 showed striking gains. Within that decade straddling the inception of the NEP,

Malays increased their share from 7.5% to 21.6% in science, 1.6% to 13.4% in engineering and 15.9% to 33.6% in medicine (Santhiram and Sua 2017, 39).

In diploma courses of public institutions, Bumiputeras have consistently formed the vast majority. In 1970, these programmes were comprised of 86.5% Bumiputeras, 11.8% Chinese, 1.0% Indians and 0.7% others. By 1985, the composition has been altered to near homogeneity: 97.8% Bumiputera, 1.5% Chinese, 0.6% Indian, 0.1% others. Compared to degree programmes, Bumiputera enrolment has consistently been high in diploma-level public institutions, and hence preferential selection played a lesser role. Nonetheless, the further growth of the Bumiputera share was a striking development.

Notwithstanding these expansions, tertiary enrolment still did not keep up with increasing supply of secondary school graduates. In the early 1970s, about half of applicants were offered a place in university, but by the mid-1980s this proportion had dropped to one-fifth. Overseas and private education has eased some of the social pressures of insufficient spaces in public tertiary institutions. Many non-Bumiputeras who didn't secure a place in local universities opted to pursue higher education abroad or settle for local non-degree programmes (Lee 2004b). In 1985, among Malaysian students overseas or at TAR College, the government-affiliated private institution, 24.5% were Bumiputera, 62.2% Chinese, 12.9% Indian, 0.5% others (Malaysia 1986). In 1980, the share of students studying abroad was 47.1% of total; in 1985, the share declined but remained substantial at 37.5% (Santhiram and Sua 2017). Indeed, in 1985, there were more Chinese enrolled in tertiary institutions overseas than in Malaysia.[4]

Private tertiary education grew from the late 1980s, when a number of colleges were founded in affiliation with foreign universities or accreditation bodies to provide pre-university-level diploma or "twinning" programmes in which students could continue toward obtaining a degree from a foreign university. The Private Higher Education Institutions Act of 1996 – which permitted domestic, private, for-profit degree-granting universities – presaged a proliferation of tertiary education institutions from the mid-1990s.[5] The growth in private higher education is a crucial development parallel to Malaysia's affirmative action regime. Private higher education caters mostly to non-Bumiputeras and alleviates tensions arising from quota-based constraints in the public system (Brown 2007; Sato 2005).

The residential school and university scholarship programmes undoubtedly provided education access to many Bumiputera who otherwise would not have the opportunity. Education is the affirmative action policy sphere that also presented the broadest scope for reaching out to the disadvantaged. Research on family backgrounds of Bumiputera scholarship recipients is sparse. Malaysia's five-year plans, while providing official accounts of progress in occupational, income and wealth inequality, omitted comprehensive and vigorous integration of socio-economic class and disadvantage into the distribution of affirmative action benefits, particularly in terms of access to education.

On the whole, it is unclear whether selection processes have systematically applied socio-economic background as preferential criteria and more generally balanced the academic ability of individuals and equitable class representation of cohorts. While children of middle-class Bumiputera families would be generally better equipped to excel in higher education, those from lower-class backgrounds would be poised for upward mobility and could potentially catch up on their more privileged peers, thereby reinforcing the effects of affirmative action.

Scholarship programmes, both those open to all Malaysians and those reserved for Bumiputera, have become slightly more transparent in their operations. Reports in the late 2000s revealed that a quota has been implemented in Public Service Department scholarships, which was formally raised from 10% non-Bumiputera to 45% non-Bumiputera around 2000. However, reports found that from 2000 to 2007 the proportion of scholars who are non-Bumiputera averaged 15% at overseas institutions and 20–25% in local institutions. In 2001, a quota of 10% non-Bumiputera enrolment was also introduced in the 40 MRSMs. Meritocratic scholarships have also been announced, purportedly based entirely on academic achievements and open to all races for competitive selection. However, implementation is muddled by tendencies to dichotomize "pure merit" versus Bumiputera-reserved programmes and prospects of reform attenuated by lack of systematic incorporation of race, merit and disadvantage.

Similarly, the abrupt introduction of "meritocracy" in university admissions in 2002 provides an illusory reform that technically eludes race quotas at admissions but continually grants Bumiputeras preferential entry. Matriculation colleges, started in the 1980s to expedite Bumiputera progress into university, were massively expanded from the late 1990s. The programme's curtailed scope and rigour, however, are markedly lower than the highly demanding two-year Malaysian Higher Education Certificate (STPM). The vast majority of Bumiputera students enter university through matriculation programmes, which were 100% reserved until 2003, when a 10% non-Bumiputera quota was introduced. The "meritocracy" policy may be technically correct in its elimination of racial quotas in admissions processes and full reliance on academic grades and student portfolio, but it commits a false equivalence in placing matriculation grades on par with STPM grades and propagates misinformation in ignoring the 90% Bumiputera quota for matriculation colleges, thus ultimately doing a disservice to the ultimate objective of cultivating capability and confidence.

With regard to the distribution of educational opportunities within the Bumiputera population, recent years have seen increased attention to access for low-income households.

The BETR's programme in the education sphere, the Bumiputera Education Pioneer Foundation (*Yayasan Peneraju Pendidikan Bumiputera*, YPPB), reaches out to Bumiputeras from disadvantaged backgrounds and difficult circumstances, such as households with single parents or disabled members. YPPB sponsors enrolment primarily in technical and vocational programmes and also strives, through mentorship and supplementary activities, to inculcate more self-belief, aspirations and leadership in beneficiaries. The Bumiputera Explore Education (*Jelajah Pendidikan Bumiputera*) scheme started at UiTM in 2010 and expanded to all universities in 2016; it involved roadshows and visitations by institutions to expedite university admissions. It largely operated under the radar, but was utilized quite widely in 2016–2018 and became co-opted by political figures who would hand over university offer letters in community-based ceremonies. In MARA pre-university institutions, notably the Junior Science Colleges (MRSM), recent years have also seen more priority afforded to low-income Bumiputeras. In its education sponsorship, MARA has increasingly opted to offer loans instead of grants for higher education, although top-performing graduates can have their financial aid converted to a scholarship.

High-level occupations

The restructuring of labour markets in Malaysia abided by a mandate that "employment patterns at all levels and in all sectors . . . must reflect the racial composition of the population" (Malaysia 1971, 42). The main affirmative action interventions in this regard were comprised predominantly of the public sector and state-owned entities, with sporadic regulation of the private sector. Although the general objective was a racially representative workforce, there was no specified timeline for incrementally achieving that target, nor a systematic approach to increasing Malay penetration into the higher occupational levels. Employment practices in government and sporadic requirements directed at the private sector operated largely without codified regulations and monitoring mechanisms.

Government and statutory bodies absorbed Malay urbanization and entry into formal wage employment. As noted earlier, prior to the NEP, measures were already in place to maintain a large Malay presence in the public sector.[6] Malays comprised 62.5% of civil servants in 1970 (Malaysia 1971, 38). Under the NEP, the government augmented the public sector, especially from the 1970s until the early-1980s. Between 1970 and 1981, public sector employment grew by 6.0% per year, above the total employment rate of 3.8% per year. Correspondingly, the share of the public sector in total employment rose from 11.9% in 1970 to 15.0% in 1981 (author's calculations from Rasiah and Ishak 2001). Among Division 1 officers, the proportion of Malays rose from 39.3% in 1970 to close to 65.0% in 1987 (the latter figure includes non-Malay Bumiputera). Public sector employment is a natural extension of the university scholarship programme. Mehmet and Yip's (1985) survey of graduating scholars in the early 1980s found that 86.2% of Malays, compared to 61.9% of Chinese and Indians, worked for government and statutory bodies.

Preferential employment tended to self-generate inertia in gravitating toward higher Bumiputera representation and hence progressed without formalized rules. Increasing Bumiputera employment in some governmental bodies, notably non-administrative statutory bodies, also transpired in the absence of specific policies. For example, the state did not mandate preferential hiring of academic staff or the racial composition of university staff. Nevertheless, the application of quotas to enrolment exerted a demonstration effect of sorts on the hiring process.[7]

The remarkable entry rate of Bumiputera into occupations within the NEP's original timeframe of 1971–1990, especially in occupations broadly classified as professional, can be considerably attributed to public sector employment policies.

The proportion of Bumiputera among professionals and technicians increased from 47.2% in 1970 to 62.2% in 1990. However, progress beyond that plateaued – a point we explore further in Chapter 7.

The Industrial Coordination Act, passed in 1975, was preponderantly a measure to enforce equity redistribution, but it also required manufacturing establishments to align their workforce in accordance with the proportionality principle. Workers' ranks, it turns out, were easily filled, especially with young Malay women from villages who flocked to electronics and textile and clothing factories. Compliance at managerial levels was harder to effect, although employment aspects of the ICA were more strictly enforced before the late 1980s, through submission of Employees Provident Fund (EPF) files to ensure that the reported personnel were being paid and hence likely to be tasked with meaningful work.[8] Overall, it is likely that the effect of the ICA in terms of increasing Malay representation was limited and concentrated in non-technical responsibilities such as personnel management.[9]

In the past four decades, little emphasis has been placed on the racial composition of Malaysians within firms, and the government has few instruments to leverage on.[10] There is no general legislation of employment practices in non-manufacturing sectors, although some strive for racial diversity in a selective manner, whether for reasons of strategy or licensing requirements. From time to time, regulations have been proposed for publicly listed companies to disclose corporate social responsibility activities, including ethnic diversity of workforce, but no rewards or consequences for compliance were enunciated. The 2007 and 2008 federal budgets, respectively, proposed and reiterated a requirement to "disclose their employment composition by race and gender, as well as programmes undertaken to develop domestic and Bumiputera vendors" (Abdullah Badawi 2006; Abdullah Badawi 2007).

Recent years have witnessed policy proposals and public discourses revolving around employment practices and group representation in work places. The prospect of an equal opportunity commission recurrently arises but was elevated to an official policy recommendation in the New Economic Model of 2010. The proposal, together with the whole NEM corpus, was soon buried under a Malay nationalist backlash. However, it was fundamentally a flawed concept that took no account of public and private sector differences, and plainly lacked any specifics while suggesting that the main perpetrators of discrimination are "dominant groups," and it was thus easily stigmatized as an attack on Bumiputera preferential treatment. Nonetheless, that the notion was articulated in a national policy document signified some progress in public discourses. Consciousness of discriminatory practices have also grown, particularly with information technology rapidly disseminating job ads stating preference for particular race groups, which are patently discriminatory and unsavoury as a practice, but not necessarily reflecting racist or bigoted attitudes. Efforts at detecting discrimination should adopt more objective and nuanced methods, such as field experimental research. Conducting such an exercise, Lee and Khalid (2016) report racial disparities in call-backs for interviews among fictitiously generated Chinese and Malay job applicants of comparable quality, but they emphasize that multiple factors plausibly account for findings, including language proficiency, cultural compatibility and ethno-racial prejudice.

While legislation and regulatory structure to oversee unfair discrimination and diversity promotion will be complicated to formulate, Malaysia has more openly fostered such discourses. Since 2010, the government has expressed concern toward the under-representation of non-Malays in the public sector. The Government Transformation Programme (GTP) committed to increasing ethnic representativeness in the First GTP Roadmap, covering 2010–2012, and retained the agenda albeit less saliently in the GTP Roadmap 2.0 (Pemandu 2010, 2012). In response to pressures to increase women's representation in decision-making positions, the government has assented to policies promoting women in high-ranking public sector positions and on the boards of GLCs.

Enterprise development

The Bumiputera Commercial and Industrial Community (BCIC) has perhaps been the highest prioritized NEP objective, considering its political prominence and financial interests, as well as the government's responsiveness to progress and deficiencies. There was a staggering dearth of Bumiputera participation on owning and managing private companies at the NEP's inception. Share capital ownership in 1970 (at par value, excluding holdings of government agencies and nominee companies), according to race and citizenship, was 1.9% Malay, 22.5% Chinese, 1.0% Indian and 60.7% foreign. In the all-important agricultural sector, Malays owned 0.9%, Chinese 22.4%, Indians 0.1% and foreigners 75.3%; and similarly in mining, the distribution was 0.7% Malay, 16.8% Chinese, 0.4% Indian, and 72.4% foreign (Gomez and Jomo 1999, 20). In this context, the NEP set a 30% Bumiputera equity target – with 7.4% held by individuals and 22.6% by institutions – which directly concerned wealth ownership, but it ultimately sought to secure a Bumiputera presence and influence in the economy (Malaysia 1976).

This branch of affirmative action overlaps with Bumiputera managerial development but specifically consists of commercial production of goods and services, as distinct from public administration. One of the most pronounced areas of Malay under-representation was in management of private sector enterprise, especially in manufacturing. Three main instruments were applied. First, direct government ownership or promotion of Malay-controlled entities, which initially centred on state-owned enterprises in the 1970s to mid-1980s then shifted to privatization of formerly public entities from the late 1980s until the 1997 financial crisis, after which the emphasis fell on renationalized corporations, termed government-linked companies, with added attention to medium-scale firms since the mid-2000s. Licensing and public procurement constitute a second major route towards this objective. A third category comprises loans and microfinance, advisory services and logistical support for SMEs.

Public enterprises to privatization to government-linked companies

Throughout most of the NEP, the Malaysian government has adopted a state-centric approach to enterprise development. Various agencies were created or reinvigorated to support Malay business, particularly in the 1970s and 1980s. State-owned enterprises numbered just 22 in 1960, but burgeoned to 109 in 1970, 656 in 1980 and 1,149 in 1992, with operations across the board – in manufacturing, services, agriculture, finance and construction. To put the growth in perspective, the number of new public enterprises averaged 9 per year in the 1960s, 55 in the 1970s and 41 from 1980 to 1992 (Gomez and Jomo 1999, 29–31). The government's five-year plan expenditure on non-financial public enterprises flowed in accordance with funding needs in these enterprises.[11] State Economic Development Corporations (SEDCs) were designated a salient role in spearheading Malay business from the early 1970s, bolstered with seed funds or guarantees from government. However, ventures largely turned out unsuccessful or unsustainable, undermined by poor governance, inexperience or corruption.[12]

Through its investment arms, the Malaysian government secured ownership of hitherto British-owned companies from the late 1970s and facilitated entry of Malay managers and professionals into these entities. Takeovers of foreign-owned companies contributed to the expansion of Malays in management and executive positions. Cadres of public administrators, who had acquired some experience by this stage, were positioned to assume leadership positions in these corporations.

The 1980s witnessed major shifts in the state-sponsored Bumiputera capitalist and entrepreneurial development agenda. In the early 1980s, the heavy industries programme commenced with the establishment of the Heavy Industries Corporation of Malaysia (HICOM) and ventures into various sectors, prominently automobiles, steel and cement. These large firms were designated to be government-owned and Bumiputera-managed, with financial and operational support from Japan. The global recession of the mid-1980s stymied the launch of heavy industries, but their pre-maturity also showed up in the emergence of excess capacity, lack of competency and gross under-performance. The focus shifted again from the late 1980s to public procurement contracts and privatization of state entities, which were to facilitate the development of individuals and corporate titans in the Bumiputera Commercial and Industrial Community (BCIC), beyond agencies or institutions such as trust funds.

This policy watershed had two crucial implications. First, it positioned the private sector and the BCIC as the main target of state priorities and resources – while affirmative action programmes in education and employment continued without substantive enhancement. Second, it ushered in and pumped resources into private capital accumulation (Gomez and Jomo 1999; Jomo 2004). State-owned enterprises were handed over to a league of new, politically connected individuals. However, in 1997, the financial crisis left many of these state-sponsored Malay capitalists foundering. The largest corporations that they had been handpicked to helm were subsequently re-nationalized, and another policy reorientation took place from the mid-2000s.

The public enterprise regime was broadly reconfigured as government-linked corporations – majority-owned by government – and in some ways injected with a more corporate ethos. Government-linked companies (GLCs) in both financial and productive sectors continue to play significant roles in Bumiputera advancement, commissioned to excel as exemplars of enterprise and developers of suppliers and vendors under the GLC Transformation Programme. Systematic reforms were formulated for the entities to function better in national development, broadly construed and encompassing equity, productivity, human capital development, Bumiputera community development, as well as in performance and governance (PCG 2015). The programme sought to professionalize operations, with emphasis on the "G20" largest GLCs, and renewed their substantial roles in Bumiputera enterprise development, through direct employment as well as procurement and vendor programmes.

The enterprise development policy sphere of affirmative action has seen the most activity in recent years, under the Bumiputera Economic Transformation Programme (BETR). The BETR launched one education programme, YPPB, but rolled out numerous initiatives to promote Bumiputera entrepreneurship and company expansion. The focus of BETR's initiatives directly administered by Teraju has been on grooming independent and competitive Bumiputera companies, amidst limited resources and fiscal constraints.[13] The BETR's mainstay is the Teras programme, which screens companies based on commercial merit and potential and formally disqualifies GLC subsidiaries.[14] Tellingly, Teraju's overriding mission, declared in 2011, was to identify 1,100 high-performing Bumiputera companies by 2016. This selection process operated as a certification exercise of sorts, to provide a quality check on Bumiputera companies seeking access to government largesse and supplemented by programmes to boost these Teras companies' access to commercial bank loans.

Concurrently, the national Economic Transformation Programme (ETP) projected the creation of "Bumiputera champions" apart from the GLCs and exhorted the GLCs to contribute to this goal through their vendor development (Pemandu 2012). Bumiputera Economic Empowerment Units (*Unit Pemerkasaan Ekonomi Bumiputera*, UPEB) have been set up in every government department with Teraju's oversight. These units facilitate communication and serve as liaisons between Teras companies and the bureaucracy. Support for SMEs and for young entrepreneurs has also expanded in recent years. The SME Master Plan 2012–2020 aimed to catalyze competitive domestic firms and expressed support for the BETR, but it remained reticent on specific Bumiputera programmes (NSDC 2012). Subsequently, SME Corp introduced the Bumiputera Economic Enhancement Programme (BEEP) with financing and advisory services for Bumiputera SMEs and the Tunas Usahawan Belia Bumiputera (TUBE) programme for budding young Bumiputera entrepreneurs. Teraju also rolled out its SUPERB small-grant scheme (under MYR500,000) for young entrepreneurs to compete for funding, either by proposing new ventures or on behalf of companies three years or younger.

On the whole, the BETR is substantially different from preceding Bumiputera enterprise development policies, even though it has been dismissed as a regurgitation of the same – in modes that pre-empt debate with rather minimal engagement with the BETR's policy specifics.[15] However, the approach has been more piecemeal than systemic, with no commitment for successes to be expanded – notably, omission of reforms to the procurement system as a whole – and its future seems subject to political winds.

From 2015, the Bumiputera Economic Community was introduced as a broader banner subsuming human capital, enterprise development and wealth ownership. However, while broader in scope, the practical implications and policy specifics were, again, not formulated in a systematic and integrated manner. The shocking defeat of 60-year ruling BN in the 2018 general elections, and political turbulence of 2020 fuelled by a 'Malay unity' agenda, adds further uncertainty. In 2018, Bumiputera development agencies previously dispersed across different ministerial jurisdictions were agglomerated within the newly created Ministry of Economic Affairs, and the Ministry of Entrepreneurship was reconfigured with Bumiputera enterprise saliently within its ambit. In 2020, the Perikatan Nasional government basically reverted back to the pre-2018 structure that places Bumiputera programmes and agencies under the purview of Cabinet ministers with *de facto* portfolios within the Prime Minister's department.

Public procurement and licensing

The Malaysian state has also deployed licensing and public procurement toward developing a Bumiputera capitalist and entrepreneurial class, although these policy instruments have operated without extensively formalized and codified mechanisms. Affirmative action programmes through licensing can be differentiated by sector. For instance, the Petroleum Development Act (1974) vested ownership of oil reserves in the hands of the government and required that management of petrol stations be reserved in Bumiputera hands, and the issuing of taxi licenses has also been dictated by terms that require Bumiputera ownership – although this has been an area of conspicuous *Ali-Baba* relationships, where a Bumiputera partner merely secures a license, then subcontracts the work to other, usually Chinese, operators. The vendor development programme in the automobile sector sets up a system for development of parts suppliers. "Approved permits" have also been distributed, granting quotas to import motor vehicles. The fields of transportation, telecommunications and media have seen the issuance of licenses for big and politically strategic operations (Gomez and Jomo 1999, 91–100). The utilization of licensing for promoting Bumiputera business, in spite of the extensive measures and expenditures, has largely consisted of allocation of rents to politically connected persons.

The NEP gave impetus to utilizing the public procurement system to stimulate and finance Bumiputera commerce. The 1973 Bumiputera Economic Seminar resolved to prioritize Bumiputera operators in government transportation, supplies and service contracts. Treasury Circular Letters have served as the medium for setting out such policies. A tiered procurement framework – from the largest category A to the smallest F – was introduced in 1974, in which 100% of class F projects and 30% of the total value of other projects were reserved for Bumiputera contractors, while the remaining 70% were open for bidding among all companies, Bumiputera and non-Bumiputera. Bumiputera contractors also received price handicaps, on a sliding scale, placing Bumiputera bids on par with lower-priced, non-Bumiputera competitors – except for the largest category of contracts.[16] In 1982, a provision was introduced to prioritize members of the Malay Chamber of Commerce.[17] The parameters for classifying contracts and discounts have been adjusted from time to time, but the basic framework was retained.[18]

Support schemes for contractors feature thinly within Malaysia's development policy edifice. A "distinguished Bumiputera construction contractors" programme (*Program Kontraktor Binaan Bumiputera Berwibawa*) operated from 1993 to 2002, seeking to identify contractors with capability and potential for more direct access to contracts. Beneficiaries had to be fully Bumiputera owned, with good financial standing and track record, and would undertake to deliver the work themselves – rather than fronting for an associate –to contribute to development of Bumiputera subcontractors and vendors.[19] The programme was rather approvingly appraised after two years.[20] However, high-level attention subsequently dissipated. *The Mid-Term Review of the Eighth Malaysia Plan*, the national planning document following on the conclusion of this programme, omitted analysis while vaguely signalling continuity amid its formal closure. The document further pronounced a policy of awarding a minimum of 60% of public procurement and contracting to Bumiputera entrepreneurs, but "only competent and credible entrepreneurs will be awarded these contracts" (Malaysia 2003, 82).

From 2009 to 2012, various amendments were made (Government Procurement Division 2010). Key elements of the current system, including continuities from the past and new conditions, are worth summarizing here. The classification system added one tier and changed its nomenclature to G1 (smallest) through G7 (largest). Contractors are registered with the Construction Industry Development Board (CIDB) and must hold a government procurement certificate (*Sijil Perolehan Kerja Kerajaan*) issued by the CIDB. Bumiputera contractors must also have that status certified by the Contractor Services Centre (*Pusat Khidmat Kontraktor*). G1 contractors must be 100% Bumiputera-owned and have paid-up capital of at least MYR10,000; they also must be staffed on a full-time basis and not be engaged in subcontracting. To qualify for preferential conditions in the G2–G7 categories, Bumiputeras must hold a majority stake and maintain Bumiputera majority in employment and directorships. They must also earn a three-star rating from the CIDB, which certifies that they meet certain standards in quality, systems and safety. Some geographic limits of operation apply, with reference to place of registration. G1 contractors must operate in the district where they are registered, G2 contractors (regardless of ownership) within their state. Notably, G3 Bumiputera-status contractors may operate nationwide, while G3 non-Bumiputera-status contractors are confined to their registered state (CIDB 2016).

Policies spell out preferential conditions for award and pricing of contracts (Malaysia 2013). Work contracts valued at MYR200,000 or less, and supply contracts at the MYR100,000 threshold, are reserved for Bumiputera contractors and can be awarded by balloting or quotation. Contracts worth MYR50,000 and below can be settled by direct negotiation. One level up, G2 contractors bid for contracts worth MYR200,000–500,000, which are allocated primarily through quotation. In tendering for contractors, Bumiputera companies are entitled to a price handicap of 10% (for G2 contracts) to 7% (G3), 5% (G4), 3% (G5), and 2.5% (G6).

Political intrusion into the procurement system influences and entrenches preferential treatment. The partisanship of Bumiputera contractors has not only become embedded; it is institutionalized. The Malay Contractors Association (PKMM) was formally aligned with the former ruling Barisan Nasional (BN) coalition, and for decades, UMNO connections and patronage were intertwined with the contracting system. Some recent changes – particularly, e-procurement, competitive tenders and balloting for small contracts – have injected more integrity and transparency to the system.[21] The balloting system for small contracts provided a useful mechanism for broadly distributing rents and steady income streams, and quid pro quos such as contractors' contribution to government relief efforts during floods and other contingencies helped sustain the arrangement. The smallest category of contracts, where the vast bulk of Bumiputera contractors are located, remains a key political constituency.[22]

Under the BETR, a number of initiatives for Malay contractor development have been initiated. MARA introduced a funding scheme for contractors to obtain support in upgrading their operations. On a broader scale and with greater public scrutiny and central coordination, the "carve out and compete" programme administered by Teraju centred on Kuala Lumpur's mass rapid transit (MRT) project – the initial Kajang-Sungai Buloh line – in which about 40% of the total value of contracts were reserved for Bumiputera contractors, with official commitment to a policy of competitive selection in the award of contracts. This mode was followed for the Light Rapid Transit 3 project, where 40% of projects were carved out. More recently, the *Mid-Term Review of the Eleventh Malaysia Plan*, in reinforcing the Bumiputera Economic Community agenda and outlining policies under this banner, articulated in clearer and bolder terms the pursuit of exit paths specifically in vendor development, and it directed some stern words at those who outsource contract work, including a "stringent multi-tier exit policy" for Bumiputera vendor development programmes, warning of "appropriate action, including automatic termination, if contracts or Approved Permits awarded are sold or transferred to a third party" (Malaysia 2018, 11–14).

Loans, support and training for small and micro enterprise

The operational scale and economic significance of various programmes targeting small, and especially micro, firms are greater than the attention ascribed to them. Indeed, by the Bumiputera policy coordinating agency Teraju's tally, more than

20 institutions offer at least 150 programmes in support of Bumiputera SMEs (Teraju 2012, 64). The omission of pro-Bumiputera agencies in the literature derives from the general neglect of systematic approaches to affirmative action and selective, habitual focus on the bigger ticket programmes covered earlier. The programmes deserve more detailed coverage, but due to scant literature, a brief discussion follows. MARA's programmes for small and micro enterprises clearly constitute AA, driven as they are by MARA's overarching mission of developing the Bumiputera community.

The objectives and targeted beneficiaries of Perbadanan Usahawan National Berhad (PUNB, the National Entrepreneurs Body) and Tekun patently place them in the same policy category. Since its establishment in 1991, PUNB has financed Bumiputera ventures in small businesses, primarily in the retail sector, as well as crafts and service work such as automotive workshops and education. Tekun, founded in 1998, is mandated to serve smaller-scale operations across a broader range of sectors. Tekun is predominantly reserved for Bumiputeras, but it operates one scheme availing funds to Indians.

Efforts to inculcate entrepreneurship among students and youth, to promote self-employment and business startups, also warrant a passing mention. Entrepreneurship courses were introduced for all public university students. These are generic and rather superficial programmes. At the same time, specific programmes, involving project development and targeted at Bumiputera students, have commenced operation in recent years, such as UiTM's Malaysian Academy of SME & Entrepreneurship Development and GiatMARA's incubator scheme.

Wealth and property ownership

This policy sector is both distinguishable and intertwined with the preceding one. Increasing Bumiputera participation in management and enterprise development requires some acquisition of controlling stakes in order to exert influence over managerial and executive appointments. Property ownership can also provide security or collateral for households to undertake investment. However, the NEP's target of 30% Bumiputera equity ownership preoccupied development policy for many years, and along the way the distinction of 7% individual and 23% institutional ownership became omitted – specifically, the former, which was surpassed but seemingly not acknowledged. Bumiputera individual ownership reached 11.9% in 1985 (Malaysia 1990). Malaysia has also implemented various policies involving passive wealth holdings.

Malaysia undertook various phases in the project of increasing Malay equity ownership. Progress on this front was slow at the inception of the NEP, and from the mid-1970s pressures mounted for the state to intervene more forcefully in the transfer of assets (Lee 2007). The Industrial Coordination Act was passed in 1975 under the banner of organizing the industrial sector by requiring firms to obtain manufacturing licenses, but its underlying objective was to mandate the transfer of equity. Firms above a certain threshold in capitalization and/or workforce – a benchmark that has over time been renegotiated to exclude small and medium enterprises – had to obtain a manufacturing license, conditional on allocating at least 30% of shares to Bumiputera individuals at prices approved by government authorities. Export-oriented firms – exporting more than 80% of output – were exempted.

The government also moved aggressively in acquiring stakes, directly or through agencies, in the form of institutional representation of Bumiputera interest. State-operated Bumiputera trust funds were set up from the late 1970s, selling units and substantially investing in areas of national priority. Such trust funds have attracted broad participation, but the distribution of ownership of trust fund units has consistently been highly skewed.[23] One condition of Malaysia's political economy that worked rather fortuitously to its advantage was the large presence of foreign firms, particularly in the then lucrative and resource-based fields of mining and plantations. State investment funds played a key role in taking over these hitherto foreign establishments.

From the late 1980s, privatization proceeded rapidly and voluminously, under various arrangements such as public listing or build-operate-transfer contracts (Gomez and Jomo 1999). The 1990s saw overpowering emphasis on the BCIC, which was as much a political agenda as an economic one – a vehicle for stirring community pride and a partisan project related to UMNO funding and asset holding through nominees. More generally, initial public offerings were mandated to set aside 30% for Bumiputera at a discount. This minimal threshold, specifically for of Malaysia-based corporations on the Malaysian Bourse's Main Market, was reduced to 12.5% in 2009 – half of the minimum 25% public spread requirement – after allocations for institutional investors, which may include Permodalan Nasional and other Bumiputera funds, were taken up. The listing process may also earmark specific allocations for Bumiputera investors recognized by the Ministry of International Trade and Industry or the Ministry of Finance (Securities Commission 2017)

The establishment of entities such as PNB broadly provide Bumiputera access to financial assets, through purchasing units in these trust funds. This form of ownership, however, can be highly dispersed and diluted – with many members holding small numbers of units – and passive. The funds mainly seek financial returns, but may also undertake an interest in the strategic direction and long-term development of companies in its stable. Malaysia has, appropriately, not repeated the heady and reckless privatization of the pre-Asian crisis 1990s, but the continuing dearth of publicly listed, Bumiputera owned and controlled companies has also been a policy concern in the post-crisis era. A few initiatives have been launched to facilitate public listing, notably the Skim Jejak Jaya – established in 2007 but revamped under Teraju and private equity fund Ekuinas from 2012 – and MARA's "The Baron" programme. Equibumi, administered by SME Bank, finances share acquisitions.

The unprecedented 2018 general elections ushered in significant restructuring of the federal apparatus overseeing entrepreneurial development. The Ministry of Economic Affairs was created, powerfully subsuming the Economic Planning Unit, Department of Statistics, and various jurisdictions previously under the

Table 4.2 Malaysia: Affirmative action programmes

Programme	Basic features and notable recent developments
Higher education	
• MRSM colleges[1]	• 90% Bumiputera quota since 2000 (previously 100%)
• Matriculation colleges	• 90% Bumiputera quota since 2003 (previously 100%)
• Asasi programmes (pre-university foundation)	• Administered by universities; most programmes exclusively Bumiputera, but some do not apply ethnic quotas
• University admissions	• Quota system since 1970s; official "meritocracy" since 2002, but pro-Bumiputera preference via quotas in matriculation and Asasi
• MARA higher education institutions	• Exclusively Bumiputera: Universiti Teknologi MARA (UiTM)[2], GiatMARA and other skills-training institutes
• MARA education sponsorship	• Exclusively Bumiputera
• Public Services Department (JPA) scholarships	• De facto proportional racial quotas
• Funding and support for disadvantaged Bumiputeras	• *Yayasan Peneraju Pendidikan Bumiputera*, focusing on technical and vocational programmes
• *Jelajah Pendidikan* (Explore Education) *Bumiputera*	• Quasi-government initiative providing a second chance to enter higher education for disadvantaged Bumiputeras and those unsuccessful in previous applications; started in UiTM in 2010, extended to public institutions in 2016
High-level employment	
• Public sector employment	• Preferential selection largely redundant (predominance of Malays among candidates); since 2013, equitable representation – increasing non-Malays – a transformation objective
• GLCs	• De facto Bumiputera preference, especially in top management
Enterprise development	
• Public procurement	• Quotas, price handicaps for Bumiputera contractors: smallest contracts (tier 1 out of 7) reserved for 100% Bumiputera-owned; in tiers 2–6, ≥ 50% Bumiputera-owned afforded price handicaps; "Carve out and Compete" Bumiputera reservation for megaprojects, Bumiputera Economic Empowerment Units within each government ministry to coordinate policy and promote Teras-certified companies
• Government-linked Companies (GLCs)	• GLC Transformation (2006–2015), committed to Bumiputera preferential procurement, vendor development
• Competitive, high-growth enterprise	• Teras (selection of high-performing Bumiputera companies), coupled with Teras Fund and Dana Mudahcara (partial grant or collateral for loans), INSKEN Entrepreneurship Institute, Bumiputera Facilitation Fund for economic corridors,

(*Continued*)

Table 4.2 (Continued)

Programme	Basic features and notable recent developments
• Young entrepreneurs	• Entrepreneurship training through UiTM, GiatMARA and other MARA programmes; SUPERB grant for youth entrepreneurs
• Private equity	• Ekuinas: Controlling stakes in Bumiputera private enterprise
• Public listing of companies	• Skim Jejak Jaya Bumiputera to facilitate listing
• Capitalization	• MARA's The Baron for equity growth, effective control
• SMEs and microfinance	• Loans and support for Bumiputeras running small and micro firms (MARA, *Tekun Nasional*[3]), SMEs primarily in retail and distribution (*PUNB*)[4]; Bumiputera programmes within SME Bank and SME Corp[5]
Wealth and property ownership	
• Unit trust schemes, chiefly Amanah Saham Bumiputera	• Reservation at initial offering for Bumiputera individuals or institutional unit trust ownership
• Property purchase discounts	• Reservation of new housing developments, price discounts
• Equity requirements for initial public offerings	• 12.5% minimum allocation for Bumiputera investors (reduced from 30% in 2009)

Source: Lee (2017a).

Notes:
1 MRSMs, or MARA Junior Science Colleges, are upper secondary institutions;
2 UiTM allows non-Bumiputera enrolment in postgraduate programmes.
3 Tekun also designates Indians as beneficiaries in some of its programmes
4 National Entrepreneurship Corporation Ltd. (*Perbadanan Usahawan Nasional Berhad*, *PUNB*) has partnered with Teraju to set up Prosper Teras;
5 Bumiputera Economic Enhancement Program (finance and advisory services, SME Corp), Tunas Usahawan Belia Bumiputera (TUBE, entrepreneurship and self-employment for young adults, SME Corp), Equibumi (financing for taking over divestments or public listing, SME Bank).

Prime Minister's Department, and consolidating various agencies directly and indirectly involved in Bumiputera enterprise development, including Teraju, Ekuinas, YPPB and the SEDCs. The Ministry of Entrepreneur was revived to refill the gap of the Ministry of Entrepreneur and Cooperative Development dissolved in 2009, with a national ambit but also a clear role in overseeing Bumiputera enterprise development. Post-2020, it is safe to assume that this concentrated agenda will be sustained beyond the short-lived Pakatan Harapan government, even if further restructuring takes place.

A final noteworthy policy in Malaysia's affirmative action regime concerns property ownership. Since the 1970s, developers have been required to reserve a proportion of new housing projects and to offer a discount to Bumiputera buyers. The terms vary from state to state, with the national median quota of 30% and median discount of 7%.[24] From the mid-2000s, commercial property ownership has also received policy attention (Malaysia 2006a, 2015, 2018).

Notes

1 Malay individual ownership would include account-based or unit-based "institutions channelling private Malay funds such as *Amanah Saham MARA* and *Lembaga Urusan dan Tabung Haji* (the Haj pilgrims' fund) (Malaysia 1976, 86).

2 Pong (1993) finds that when controlling for parents' education, occupation and earnings, being Malay increased the probability of attaining secondary school education across successive cohorts, with marked difference between those of school-going age when the NEP came into effect and those who attended school before the NEP. These results are interpreted as suggesting that the gains of public expenditure were disproportionately captured by Malay families. However, the model does not control for urban/rural location and state, which bear correlations with race.

3 Exact quotas were usually not publicly disclosed, but it was reported in the early 2000s that universities observed a Bumiputera to non-Bumiputera quota of 55:45 (Jamaludin 2003).

4 Jamaludin (2003, 166) reports that in 1985, out of 22,684 students studying overseas, 73.4% were non-Bumiputera who failed to gain admission to local public universities or who were offered places in programmes not of their choice.

5 The proportion of tertiary students (degree, diploma and certificate) enrolled in overseas institutions declined from 40.2% in 1985 to 13.8% in 1995, while the share of local private institutions increased from 8.9% in 1985 to 34.7% in 1995 (Wan 2007, 4).

6 In the elite Diplomatic and Administrative Service corps, a 4 to 1 ratio of Malay to non-Malay quota was introduced in 1953 (CPPS 2006b, 5). Yusof (1994, 612) maintains that the main instrument for increasing Bumiputera participation was through hiring quotas.

7 Author's interview with Maznah Mohamed, 24 August 2007.

8 Author's interview with senior industry source, 5 September 2007.

9 Openings for Bumiputera in management and professional in oversight of assembly operations were also constrained by the flat organizational structure of factories, which offer few management or supervisory positions for a given workforce (Author's interview with the Director-General of the Economic Planning Unit, 11 September 2007).

10 Malaysia's institutional framework governing labour markets provides few instruments for enforcing employment quotas, with the possible exception of non-renewal of licenses (Author's interview with the Executive Director of the Malaysian Employers Federation, 5 September 2007).

11 Specifically, such expenditures ballooned from MYR3.9 billion (1971–1975) to MYR12.0 billion (1976–1980) and MYR27.7 billion (1981–1995), then contracted to MYR17.7 billion (1986–1990) (Muhamad Salleh and Meyanathan 1993, 19).

12 In 1981, available information on 260 companies under the purview of the Ministry of Public Enterprises showed that 94 were making losses, and 21 had yet to operate (Jesudason 1989, 98–100).

13 Teraju started with minimal budget and human resources, in the context of fiscal constraints in general, and the immense funds already committed to existing Bumiputera development agencies. It was also tasked to devise new ways of pursuing this agenda, rather than more expenditure and largesse (Author's interview with the CEO of Teraju, 3 August 2017). Concurrently, the biggest complaints registered by members of the Malay Chamber of Commerce members are the shortage of contracts and lack of transparency in the allocation process (Author's interview with the Secretary-General of the Malay Chamber of Commerce, 17 July 2017).

14 The criteria for qualifying as a Teras company are: (1) ≥ MYR10 million per annum for last three years; (2) profitable for last three years; (3) ≥ 60% Bumiputera ownership and Bumiputera CEO or managing director; (4) not a GLC or MNC subsidiary; (5) at least three-star SCORE rating by relevant certifying body; (6) good credit rating.

15 The continuation of the Bumiputera preferential policies in the 2010s, under the auspices of the BETR, have been repeatedly dismissed in the public sphere without any engagement with its contents, leaving us to surmise that such detractors simply presume that the BETR is devoid of new content and a pure rehash of existing programmes. See Kua Kia Soong, "Will Racial Discrimination Extend Beyond 2020?", *The Malay Mail*, 23 May 2015.

16 Treasury Circular Letter No. 7, 1974.

17 Treasury Circular Letter No. 3, 1982.

18 Treasury Circular Letter No. 4, 1995.

19 Treasury Circular Letter No. 11, 1993.

20 The *Seventh Malaysia Plan* reported that under programme upgraded the managerial and technical capabilities of 236 contractors, which delivered on 1,221 projects worth MYR3.6 billion (Malaysia 1996, 76).

21 Zairil Khir Johari, "Entering New Territory with Open Tenders", *Penang Monthly*, October 2011.

22 Interviews with Jamaludin Non, Deputy Secretary-General, Malay Contractors Association Malaysia on BFM radio ("Malay Contractors – Is The Cookie Crumbling?" 11 January 2018, "Open Season for Bumiputera Contractors", 5 June 2018).

23 In the late 1980s 1.3% of two million unit holders owned 75% of Amanah Saham Bumiputera (then known as Amanah Saham Nasional) shares (Jomo 2004, 14). Due to the 200,000-unit limit per ASB account holder, the concentration in the top 1% has moderated, to an estimated 17–18% in 2007–2016, but the share of the top 10% is exceedingly high, at around 77% in 2007–2013, then rose steadily to 81% in 2016. Simultaneously, the Gini coefficient of ASB accounts hovered around 0.85 (Lee and Khalid 2020).

24 National House Buyers Association memorandum to the government, "Time to Fine Tune the Bumiputera Discount", published in the *The Edge*, 5–11 November 2012 edition.

5 Affirmative action pillars and programmes
South Africa

Legal and policy frameworks

Policy-making in South Africa has not been anchored in enduring, lofty and iconic visionary statements. The democratic transition was enormously fraught with threats of violent unrest and disintegration further complicated by the imperatives of negotiating a new constitution, guaranteeing basic rights and freedoms and safeguarding against a dominant and centralized executive. At the same time, a neoliberal elite-managed macroeconomic template was laid before the political transition, placing constraints on social expenditures and expansionary macroeconomic policy. The nation had to negotiate political, economic and social tensions and contending interests, making it exceedingly difficult to galvanize energies and resources around a distinct national development framework, let alone an affirmative action platform.

The Reconstruction and Development Programme (RDP), the policy centrepiece of the April 1994 elections, referred to affirmative action in rather impressionistic terms while focusing most of its rhetorical forces on overarching national objectives and moral imperatives. It did issue a clarion call for policy interventions in the labour market – through prohibition of discrimination and promotion of blacks, women and rural communities – and particularly in the public services. The RDP also indicated the need for a "massive programme of education, training, retraining . . . to overcome the legacy of apartheid" and allowed for affirmative action to be implemented in local government contracting. However, the RDP's imprint on national policy faded soon after the democratic transition. The White Paper on the RDP of November 1994, the elected government's articulation of how the RDP would translate into policy, reduced affirmative action to the public sector. Subsequent national-level programmes focused on macroeconomic issues, minimally if at all touching on affirmative action. GEAR, launched in 1996, made no mention of AA, redress or transformation, and its successor AsgiSA similarly omitted any direct and prominent reference to AA.

Notwithstanding the flux in South Africa's macroeconomic paradigm, affirmative action became institutionalized. The constitution, adopted and signed into law in 1996, formed the bedrock for subsequent AA and anchored the country's legislative approach in general. The Labour Relations Act 1995, in stipulating that employers are not prevented from implementing policies designed to protect and advance persons disadvantaged by unfair discrimination, adumbrated various legislations to come. The most pertinent to this book's consideration rolled out successively: Higher Education Act 1997, Employment Equity Act 1998, Preferential Public Procurement Framework Act 2000 and Broad-Based Black Economic Empowerment Act 2003. The constitutional basis for affirmative action – disadvantage due to unfair discrimination – underpins these legislations. This makes the preferential treatment conditional on the persistence of such conditions. To date, policy or legal discourses have not placed a time frame or schedule of graduation or exit clauses based on the diminishing intensity of disadvantage over time.

The underpinnings of affirmative action were crystallized in the Constitution of the Republic of South Africa, which stipulates principles for safeguarding equality and prohibiting unfair discrimination while recognizing the legacy of past discrimination. Article 9 is the cornerstone of affirmative action, where it is specified that, "[t]o promote the achievement of equality, legislative and other measures designed to protect or advance persons, or categories of persons, disadvantaged by unfair discrimination may be taken."

The constitution further upholds the role of affirmative action specifically in public sector employment and public procurement. Article 195 mandates that "[p]ublic administration must be broadly representative of the South African people," while Article 217 provides for "categories of preference in the allocation of contracts" and "protection or advancement of persons, or categories of persons, disadvantaged by unfair discrimination."

The formalization of BEE in the early 2000s furnished some reference points that are worth citing. The official discourses have been reasonably clear on the specific scope, objectives and instruments, although some of the discourse can be misconstrued as setting out general policy objectives – especially poverty alleviation – that lie beyond its ambit. As articulated in the BBBEE Act 2003: "Broad-based black economic empowerment (broad-based BEE) means the economic empowerment of all black people including women, workers, youth, people with disabilities and people living in rural areas, through diverse but integrated socio-economic strategies," including asset ownership, management and control, by individuals and communities, human resources and skills development, equitable representation in the employment, preferential procurement and investment in black enterprise.

In preparation of the BBBEE Codes, a statement of principles and definitions interestingly differentiated black economic empowerment (BEE), "defined as an integrated and coherent socio-economic process that directly contributes to the economic transformation of South Africa and brings about significant increases in the number of black people who manage, own and control the country's economy, as well as significant decreases in income inequalities" (DTI 2004). However, at the same time, the "[g]overnment's strategy for broad-based black economic empowerment looks beyond the redress of past inequalities and aims to position BEE as a tool to broaden the country's economic base and accelerate growth, job creation and poverty eradication." The "broad-based" element has been contentious and can be difficult to pin down, for BBBEE is broader than BEE in emphasizing the targeted outreach to black individuals and communities but also narrower in specifying the areas of intervention. The lack of distinction between interventions involving racial preference, versus those that do not, detracts from policy clarity and coherence. The ambitious tone may also feed expectations and bring about, intentionally or otherwise, an effect of over-promising, which augments exposure to criticisms that persisting problems not under its purview – chiefly, high unemployment and mass poverty – constitute failures of BBBEE.

Perhaps prompted by the lack of an all-encompassing development vision, broader in scale and scope than the preceding GEAR and AsgiSA mandates, the government unveiled the National Development Plan in 2010. This document also discernibly responded to popular discourses of the time, in which the problems of BEE profiteering, fronting (cosmetic black involvement in ownership or as board members) and enriching politically linked "tenderpreneurs" or "BEElionaires," compounded by skills shortages and constraints in employment equity, were salient and resonant. The Plan moderated the emphasis on BEE and shifted the attention to skills development, jobs growth and poverty alleviation (Economic Development Department 2010; National Planning Commission 2012).

The growing socio-political momentum behind policy reforms would reach another fruition of sorts in the BBBEE code amendments of 2013, which sought to mitigate the fronting problem and to spur more genuine entrepreneurial development, and in the concurrent launch of the Black Industrialists Policy/ Programme (BIP). The latter addresses a specific policy lacunae: the lack of black entrepreneurs and manufacturing firms. The BIP formalizes an aspiration to promote black control, management and technology through more direct and effective measures, rather than through ownership transfers that result in passive asset holdings and limited knowledge, technological and skill acquisition.

Affirmative action programmes

Higher education

In the higher education domain, South Africa faced the dual challenge of integrating a fragmented and hierarchical system while promoting equitable access to historically white institutions. Under Apartheid, education at all levels was partially available to discriminated groups, and historically black schools, teknikons and universities were also purposely kept inferior in teacher capacity, facilities, funding and curriculum. Thus, the mandate for transformation was cast broadly, including measures to increase and improve basic education for the mass population, to reorganize or merge tertiary institutes and to pursue equitable representation in the systematically superior, historically white institutions. With institutions already segregated, emphasis was placed on integration. Any creation of racially exclusive elite schools and colleges would be at odds with the objective of deracializing education. As expounded by Badat (2012), South Africa's education system was compelled to undertake a complex and time-consuming process of simultaneously negotiating various transformations, involving all education levels and a plethora of policy concerns, including schooling quality and equitable access.

Under-provision and poor quality of primary and secondary schooling justified the priority ascribed to basic education. The composition of schools corresponds with the population of the surrounding districts; hence, pursuing racially proportionate representation would be redundant in some cases, notably in black-dominant townships or rural schools. However, it was imperative to integrate historically white institutions. These processes did not necessarily involve affirmative action measures but are an important backdrop to the transformation that has been pursued at the tertiary level. In a 1990 restructuring programme, most urban white public schools had opted for a "Model C" format, which gave schools latitude to collect fees and have jurisdiction over major decisions, including enrolment, subject to approval of the school governing authority.[1] Devolving some authority and financing to the school, it was argued, would also democratize school governance and encourage parental participation, while availing public funds to other more needy schools (Chisholm 2008; Motala *et al.* 2007). The Model C structure and user fees were preserved into the post-Apartheid era, motivated by concerns of an exodus of whites to private schools and by the prospect that such fees can reduce public funding burdens. Furthermore, the struggle for education rights had historically not been cast in racialist terms; thus the policy to provide education was "based principally on the constitutional guarantees of equal educational rights for all persons and non-discrimination" (Department of Education 1995).

However, while these political and pragmatic considerations exerted substantial weight, the policy process was also ideologically imbued with a "pro-market" orientation and attendant cost-efficiency arguments (Weber 2002). These positions outweighed the flipside of user fees, namely, its propensity to reinforce and perpetuate privilege and inequality by excluding those who cannot afford to pay – although this would be legally prohibited – and by allowing schools that charge fees to poach better teachers from other schools. Another dimension of equity stems from the reality that black households are larger and hence would face more difficulty sending children to fee-charging schools (MERG 1993, 100–102).

Education policy discourses did not acquire the language of affirmative action. While the exact reasons are unclear, they appear to stem from acceptance of the convention of confining AA terminology to employment processes, coupled with abstention from formal racial or gender targets or quotas in schools and universities. Nevertheless, we can locate policies geared towards overcoming systemic disadvantage and under-representation of blacks, under the rubric of redress and transformation. It is possible that much more was pursued than has been noticed and documented. The overwhelming share of the black population – at 90% of the national population – also moderated the need for vigorous and overt implementation of group preferences.[2] Nevertheless, it is also plausible that the official reticence on preferential policies in higher education, and the heavier social demands and policy emphasis on employment equity and BEE, account for the inconspicuousness of affirmative action in concept and terminology in the higher education sphere. Based on the literature, affirmative action *per se* began to feature more saliently as university policy in the late-2000s, particularly in the context of comparative studies of South Africa and the United States (Featherman, Hall and Krislov 2010; Nussbaum and Hasan 2012).

Another challenge in overviewing affirmative action in education is the incremental path it followed, which can be traced out in a series of official documents: government White Papers on basic schooling, training, and higher education (Department of Education 1995, 1996, 1997, 1998), discussions regarding a higher education policy framework (National Commission on Higher Education 1996) and the National Plan for Higher Education (Ministry of Education 2001). Early policy objectives were outlined in the 1995 and 1996 White Papers, which gave priority to integration of administrative bodies and expansion and improvement of basic schooling. "Affirmative action" would be applied only in the recruitment of teaching staff. The papers recognized problems of higher education, particularly its racially splintered and stratified structure, but deferred policy proposition to the newly formed Commission on Higher Education.

The need for redress in higher education had been consistently articulated with respect to unequal access based on race, gender, class and region, but measures to unify, restructure and coordinate education administration took precedence in the early post-Apartheid years. Statements on the process reflect the manifold challenges of transforming both structure and access, e.g. "[h]igher education must be transformed to redress past inequalities, to serve a new social order, to meet pressing national needs and to respond to new realities and opportunities" (Department of Education 1997). Notably, transformation and redress in education institutions have not been legislated. The National Education Policy Act 1996, which stipulates terms of reference for establishing educational institutions and formulating education policy, and the Higher Education Act 1997, which outlines a framework for restructuring and administering higher education, refrain from providing an explicit legal framework for affirmative action. Nonetheless, the Act stipulates equitable access and redress of past inequality as guiding principles, and it specifically mentions gender equality in educational access as a national policy objective. The preamble to the Higher Education Act validates the social desirability of efforts to "redress past discrimination and ensure representivity and equal access."

The transformation mandate in higher education was formulated in two layers: institutional redress and social redress. The gulfs between historically white (or advantaged) institutions (HWI) and historically black (or disadvantaged) institutions (HBI) needed to be bridged. Structural inequalities in access to higher education – due to past racial or gender discrimination, regional restrictions or inability to afford fees – were also to be rectified.[3] Initially, much policy attention was channelled toward narrowing the disparities between HWIs and HBIs. The financing framework of the mid- to late-1990s designated public funding for general operations, proportionate to enrolment, and earmarked funding for institutional redress (between HWIs and HBIs) and individual or social redress – financial aid to students, especially the National Student Financial Aid Scheme (NSFAS) (CHE 2004).

Institutional redress was relatively emphasized in the early democratic years, significantly due to alignment of higher education policy with the GEAR agenda and concomitant fiscal austerity. Funding for redress programmes plateaued in the 1995–1997 interval (du Toit 2010). Furthermore, the mid- to late-1990s saw a decline in enrolment in public higher education institutions, partly due to mismanagement of historically black institutions, but also due to stagnation in academic capability of school graduates.[4] The HBIs faced acute difficulties, *inter alia*, in collecting fees – while expectations of redress funding did not materialize – and in providing academic programmes and facilities, fuelling downward spirals in enrolment and financial sustainability. At the national level in the late 1990s, the proportion of black, especially African, students increased, as many entered public HWIs and technical universities, which saw substantially higher enrolment growth, while many whites opted for private higher education. The higher-education participation rate, however, remained static, and enrolment in sciences and engineering did not increase as desired (Imenda, Kongolo and Grewal 2004; Morrow 2008; CHE 2000).

Thus, by the late 1990s a transformation programme for higher education began to take shape more extensively and vigorously. The 1997 White Paper asserted that "changing the composition of the student body will be effected through targeted redistribution of the public subsidy to higher education. The relative proportion of public funding used to support academically able but disadvantaged students must be increased."[5] From around 2000, higher education policy shifted in some important ways, with institutional redress becoming less narrowly focused on levelling the playing field between HBIs and HWIs and increasingly geared towards social redress (CHE 2000; MOE 2001).[6] The proportion of students receiving NSFAS aid increased clearly, though still gradually, from 20% in the late 1990s to 25% in the early 2000s. Mergers and combinations of HBIs and HWIs were formally proposed, on a case-by-case basis. The number of higher education institutes fell from 36 in 1995 to 29 in 2004 to 25 in 2005, and the demarcation of HBI and HWIs was officially phased out, consonant with the shift to de-emphasize institutional redress and broaden the transformation programme in higher education.

Within ten years, higher education institutions were re-categorized, with HWIs and some merged entities termed *universities*, former HBIs and teknikons, respectively, rebranded *comprehensives* and *universities of technology*. This three-way classification has been retained to the present, with a slight modification. Hence, South Africa has 11 traditional universities, 9 comprehensive universities and 6 universities of technology.

Universities autonomously devise admissions policies and administer various forms of preferential treatment (Badat 2012). The emphasis and extent of affirmative action varies across institutions, with some focused on increasing black representation, others on catching up in academic standards. Not all institutions avail policy documents to the public, as required, but there is no doubt that affirmative action is considerably integrated into higher education. The University of the Witwatersrand makes the clearest articulation of affirmative action, or "fair discrimination," while the University of Cape Town has defended the application of race as an admission criterion. In recent years, a flourish of public debates and policy deliberations surrounding admissions policies engendered substantive revision, resulting in socio-economic status and disadvantage being increasingly incorporated – although not entirely replacing race – as a basis for granting preference.

The past decade has also seen some heightened debate on affirmative action in higher education, with pushback against preferential treatment and contentions that, as with employment equity and BEE, the black middle class and elites disproportionately benefit from transformation. Public universities remain more prestigious than private counterparts. (Established overseas universities have not set up major campuses in South Africa). The desirability of enrolling in these institutions contributes refers to public universities toward how race factors into admissions decisions. In response, some universities, saliently the University of Cape Town, have publicly defended their transformation policies and racial redress.[7] At the same time, public and policy discourses have also grown attuned to the outstanding and feasible role of higher education, among all affirmative action sectors, in taking into account socio-economic background as a selection criterion and in facilitating inter-generational upward mobility.

On the admissions front, universities have sought to expand beyond race-based selection, through adopting admissions modes that take into account socio-economic disadvantage. The University of Cape Town, for instance, operates an admissions system with three rounds: first, strictly on academic background and merit-based criteria above a certain threshold, without regard to race or other identifying feature; second, incorporating a system that provides a score corresponding with applicants' relative disadvantage (e.g. non-English spoken at home); third, balancing the composition of the student body by granting disadvantaged groups special consideration (Price 2014). As expected, whites constitute a disproportionately large share in the first round, although the cohort of high-achieving school graduates is becoming more diverse, and the second and third rounds help even out the racial composition. The university administration's primary concern in implementing this new policy – that black enrolment would substantially decline – did not transpire.[8] Variations of this admissions policy are in place in other universities besides UCT, and there will foreseeably be more modification in the years ahead.

High-level occupations and skills development

In the workplace, the Apartheid legacies of acute skills shortage, labour repression and barriers to upward mobility posed some deep and fundamental policy challenges. The formation of affirmative action policies was far from a straightforward and consensual process. From the early 1990s, a number of organizations advocated variations of AA, notably the Black Management Forum (BMF), the National African Federated Chamber of Commerce (NAFCOC) and organized labour, while others lobbied against AA, saliently the South African Chamber of Business (SACOB) (Horwitz 1996; Adam 2000). ANC policy documents mirror this mix of electoral expectation, political pressure and business clout, with *Ready to Govern* (1992) and the *RDP* (1994), both making firm and broad statements on AA, only to be circumscribed by the follow-up RDP White Paper (1994). As mentioned earlier, the latter expressed commitments to affirmative action only in public sector employment, while becoming silent on interventions to redress disadvantage in private sector employment. Bond (2000, 99) argues that the authoring of the White Paper, which was delegated to partisan individuals at the Development Bank of Southern Africa, reflects the capture of the policy agenda by neoliberal-leaning ideology and personnel.

It is not surprising that affirmative action was taken up with greater vigour in the public sector. The public services were a mainstay of pro-white affirmative action under Apartheid. However, this inherited condition made for a complicated transition towards a more representative workforce, especially at the administrative level and in highly-skilled occupations, due to limited room for manoeuvre in restructuring government offices (existing departments and officials performing crucial functions cannot be replaced) alongside shortages in skill and experience among blacks. As with all areas of transition, affirmative action was a component of a much broader transformation agenda. The 1995 *White Paper on Transformation of the Public Service* highlighted a swathe of problems: shortfalls in representativeness, popular legitimacy (the state being viewed as an Apartheid appendage) and service delivery; and operational defects or obsolescent practices such as top-down management, lack of accountability and transparency, low productivity, low pay and demotivated staff (Department of Public Service and Administration 1995). One severe constraint in the initial post-Apartheid years was the need to manage the continuation of senior and skilled staff from the previous administration, which gave rise to the sunset clause and averted mass evacuation of key government posts, and was also a vital bargaining point in transitional negotiations.

Affirmative action in the public service was formally set out in the 1998 *White Paper on Affirmative Action in the Public Service*, within the framework of the Employment Equity Bill (Ministry in the Office of the President 1994). Thus, there is little to differentiate, in principle and procedure, affirmative action in the public and private sectors. However, one distinguishing element of AA in the public service in the 1990s is the stipulation of specific targets and timeframes. The state's direct control over employment in the public sector is reflected in its rapid schedule for increasing black representation in administration, the flipside of which is the possibility of setting overly ambitious goals.[9] Another problematic aspect of affirmative action in the public sector is the widely believed disproportionate distribution of gains among sub-groups – African, Coloured, Indian – within the overarching black category.

Obstacles to effecting AA in the private sector were steeper. The state can exert only indirect influence, through persuasion or legislation, over hiring decisions, while entrenched ownership and managerial interests are disposed to pursue private interests over the social principle of equity and redress. Some blacks had enjoyed social mobility, through "black advancement" initiatives in the 1980s but had been subjected to a moving colour bar often lodged at middle level management or human resource management (Nzimande 1996). In the early 1990s, some companies began to voluntarily undertake affirmative action, largely in anticipatory compliance with future legislation and quotas. Blacks, however, remained glaringly under-represented in managerial positions, with high incidences of "window-dressing" or nominal, non-executive appointments (Adam 2000).[10] That the under-representation of blacks is due to combinations of discrimination and lack of experience and training is undeniable, but no definitive conclusion on the balance of these determinants has been, and perhaps never will be, reached. The outcome of negotiations over employment legislation reflects the dual objectives of ending discrimination and promoting opportunity – and a premise that free markets do not self-regulate towards the eradication of discrimination.

It is important to note that post-1994 affirmative action in employment was institutionalized after an interim, during which South Africa enacted basic labour legislation (Labour Relations Act 1995 and Basic Conditions of Employment Act 1997), promulgated the 1996 GEAR macroeconomic programme and set in motion the transformation agenda. The Employment Equity Act (EEA) drew significantly on Canada, which in 1995 revised federal employment law and passed the namesake Employment Equity Act (Jain, Horwitz and Wilkin 2011).

South Africa's EEA, enacted in 1998, distinguishes unfair discrimination from affirmative action and concomitantly provides grounds for prohibiting unfair discrimination. Most importantly, it establishes a legislative framework for implementing affirmative action in hiring, promotion and training. The EEA states as its chief intent the equitable representation of suitably qualified people from designated groups in all occupational categories and levels in the workforce. It makes provision for preferential treatment – i.e. fair discrimination – and numerical goals but not explicit quotas. The settlement on targets rather than quotas resulted from intensive tripartite negotiations (Thomas 2002).

From late 2010, deliberations took place over the EEA, resulting in amendments in 2013 that added local government as mandated employers, stipulated financial penalty for non-compliance and modified the language of the employer's undertaking to be in the form of steps taken, rather than mere efforts shown. These changes strengthened enforcement capacity. The status of employment equity and justification for continual implementation was simultaneously bolstered by the Constitutional Court's rulings of 2014 that upheld employment equity against a few challenges (Department of Labour 2014). Since 2016, attention has been placed on the formulation of sectoral targets – that is, rather than the racial composition of the national economically active population, affirmative action targets will separately reference eleven sectors.

A draft bill was recently initiated to institute mechanisms for issuing a certificate of compliance (South Africa 2018).

A few aspects of the initial EEA 1998 and amendments in 2013 warrant further attention. The EEA is applicable to "designated employers," which encompasses government departments and municipalities (excluding national defence and intelligence services) and companies with either 50 or more employees or turnover above various sector-specific thresholds, broadly corresponding to conventional definitions of medium-size enterprise in South Africa. Designated employers are required to: (1) submit an employment equity report (EER) of their workforce profile and their progress made towards equitable representation, disaggregated by race, gender and disability categories; (2) devise employment equity plans of 1–5 years, in consultation with employees, specifying targets for increasing the number of members of disadvantaged groups who benefit from promotion, skills development or recruitment (South Africa 1998a). Reports and plans must also be made accessible to employees. At the inception in 1998, large employers were required to submit EERs annually and others every two years; this was amended in 2013 to require all designated employers to submit annually.

The linchpin of the EEA is the stipulation that employers strive to "ensure the equitable representation of suitably qualified people from designated groups in all occupational categories and levels in the workforce" and to retain, develop and provide training for people from designated groups. Should a plan set targets that increase the representation of designated persons, then among "suitably qualified" candidates, the employer ought to give preference to blacks, women and persons with disabilities.[11] In the initial 1998 Act, compliance was assessed based on the national or regional economically active population, as well as the pool of suitably qualified persons, sectoral factors and financial circumstances. In practice, the national EAP served as the default reference, with consideration as well of the racial and gender composition of the province where employers are located.[12] The 2013 EEA amendments narrowed down the compliance criteria to the EAPs, eliminating availability of qualified persons and financial circumstances. Concurrently, clauses were added providing for the minister of labour to provide directives on compliance matters, including the referencing of national and regional EAPs in setting workforce composition targets (South Africa 2013a).

The EEA established institutional oversight of employment equity, which has also undergone some change. The Department of Labour conducts inspections and monitors compliance, pertaining to consultation, analysis, preparation and submission of the EERs, and substance of the reports. The early years witnessed some implementation struggles, clearly resulting from under-resourced offices charged with these tasks (Bezuidenhout *et al.* 2008). The process was undoubtedly onerous, then requiring EERs submitted in hardcopy to be sorted and catalogued. Shifting to online filing has immensely cut down on laborious data entry by the Department. Some provisions in the EEA were also deemed to give employers room to manoeuvre; amendments of 2013 thus included provisions that strengthened enforcement. Whereas the Department previously could only demand a written undertaking from employers who fail to prepare a plan or submit a report, it could under the new law impose fines for such infringements. A change in wording is highly significant for compliance appraisals. Since 2013, employers are audited based on "steps taken" to foster more equitable representation and train workers of the designated groups, instead of "efforts made." Whether the substance of EE plans and targets are compliant, however, remains quite subjective and can be difficult to adjudicate.

The EEA also founded the Commission for Employment Equity (CEE), comprised of tri-partite members, and mandated to advise the minister of labour on employment equity practices, codes of conduct and policy matters, and to conduct research, confer awards on employers and other actions at its discretion. Dissemination of the CEE's annual report has become a national fixture, including the data disclosed on racial representation and policy pronouncements from time to time. Through progress reports and policy advocacy, the CEE also seeks to create more awareness and apply pressure for companies to comply and to step up their efforts.

The outcomes and problems of employment equity legislation will be discussed at greater length in Chapter 8. At this juncture, we should note that South Africa's EEA has a broad scope and formalized mechanisms, since it encompasses public and private sectors, imposes self-regulatory requirements and a penalty system for non-compliance and integrates skills development as a component to enable disadvantaged employees to be upwardly mobile within firms.[13] In practice, however, employment equity has proceeded more vigorously in the public sector and in general involves preferential hiring and/or promotion more than skills development. Professional and managerial positions, hitherto the most inaccessible, became the most coveted and under the most pressure to attain equitable representation. The public sector, under the direct purview of government, absorbed large numbers of tertiary educated blacks into technical, professional and administrative occupations, coupled with a shift in public policy toward "managerialism," which has increased the proportion of management-level posts (Chipkin 2008; Edigheji 2007). Implementing employment equity in the private sector is relatively more complex and fraught with obstacles and resistance.

From 2003, the Broad-Based Black Economic Empowerment (BBBEE) entered the picture, with some implications on employment equity and skills development. The genesis and evolution of BBBEE is discussed later at greater length. In the context of employment equity, some policy features and shifts are worth pointing out. BBBEE sets targets for black advancement, whereas employment equity legislation does not specify targets and includes women and the disabled as beneficiaries. Employment equity and skills development are two of seven BBBEE elements, and in the initial 2007 codes small firms were permitted to select four of out seven elements to contribute to their score. Hence, small firms may omit employment equity and skills development altogether, while for medium and large firms the inclusion of employment equity, in particular, constitutes some duplication. At the same time, certain minimal compliance levels are higher under BBBEE. For instance, whereas the mandatory skills development levy is one percent of payroll for all employees, to obtain points under BBBEE companies must spend three percent on training black employees. The next section unpacks the score card in more detail; for now it is pertinent to note that the weightage of skills development, employment equity, ownership, management control and preferential procurement were relatively on par at the inception of the Codes in 2007. The BBBEE code revisions of 2013 increased the weightage of skills development and eliminated employment equity altogether (see Table 5.1).

By and large, then, employment equity has taken root as a legal mandate to be complied with, reinforced by the CEE's reports and public pressure on employers to show more results. From time to time, the issue escalates in the public domain, with occasional combative stances taken against employers for alleged reluctance to comply or tardiness in pursuing employment equity targets and also pushback from employers claiming their progress is hindered by deficit of skilled workers. Some parties have sought legal recourse, most prominently the Barnard case brought to the Constitutional Court, which challenged the constitutionality of some employment equity practices. The court upheld practices in hiring or leaving vacancies unfilled that are in accordance with approved employment

Table 5.1 South Africa: Affirmative action programmes

Programme	Basic features and notable recent developments
Higher education	
• Institutional redress to narrow HWI-HBI disparities	• Bridging gap between HWIs and HBIs
• Individual/social redress to increase enrolment of disadvantaged persons	• Premised on Higher Education Act 1997, public universities autonomously formulate own transformation policy, with more incorporation of socio-economic criteria in recent years
• Admissions schemes incorporating both ethnicity and socio-economic status; means-tested financial assistance.	• Institutional autonomy emphasized. AA programmes devolved to institution level; public funding available for implementing transformation plans. NSFAS offers bursaries and loans to lower-income students.
High-level employment and skills development	
• Employment Equity Act (EEA) 1998	• Designated employers consult workers and devise employment equity plans, with workforce composition and targets for increasing representation of blacks, women and the disabled. Mandatory for: • public sector (except defence) • private sector (except small enterprises) Enforcement by the Department of Labour; Commission for Employment Equity plays advisory, advocacy role.
• Skills development	• EEA scope: recruitment, promotion and skills development
• Broad-Based Black Economic Empowerment (BBBEE)	• Employment equity and skills development – elements of BBBEE scorecard

Programme	Basic features and notable recent developments
Enterprise development	
• Public enterprises/State-owned companies	• Role in facilitating black presence and accumulating experience in corporate management and cultivating black enterprises through procurement and supplier development
• Broad-Based Black Economic Empowerment	• BBBEE codes of good practice taken into account in procurement, licensing, public-private partnerships and sale of state assets. Code elements and points:

Initial version (2007):
- Ownership 20
- Management control 10
- Employment equity 15
- Skills development 15
- Preferential procurement 20
- Enterprise development 15
- Socio-economic development 5

Amended version (2013):
- Ownership 25
- Management control 15
- Skills development 20
- Enterprise and supplier development 40
- Socio-economic development 5
- Select charters accommodate industry-specific conditions

• Industrial Development Corporation	• Financial and logistical support for black-owned businesses, aligned with industrial policy priorities
• SME funding through official sources and public agencies	• Loans operated by the National Empowerment Fund, Department of Small Business and the Department of Trade and Industry
• Black Industrialists Programme	• Under IDC purview: direct promotion of black-owned enterprise, with focus on manufacturing, new and innovative ventures, and medium scale operations
Wealth and property ownership	
• BBBEE Codes and industry charters	• Transfer of shares to black individuals and groups; ownership is most vigorously tracked component of BBBEE Codes
• National Empowerment Fund	• Funding for share purchases
• Group-based/community investment funds	• Investment participants in BBBEE potentially promoting broader based ownership

Source: Expanded from Lee (2010).

equity plans; this has effectively settled major questions over the law's constitutional basis. South Africa thus proceeds with employment equity as an embedded institution, in place for over 20 years now, albeit with continual tripartite tensions and the overarching issue of skills shortages.

Enterprise development

Executive positions and board membership in large corporations

The development of black managerial and entrepreneurial capacities can be connected to three legislative or policy elements: employment equity, preferential public procurement in tandem with BEE and public enterprises/state-owned companies. Black representation in management, and in owning and operating businesses, remains one of the more elusive areas of South Africa's transformation. While employment equity can compel management to become more racially representative, dilution of decision-making power will assuredly face resistance, especially in family-based companies and medium-size firms with relatively fewer positions to reallocate. Large firms, including publicly listed companies, have greater capacity to absorb blacks into managerial ranks, but they can also create token positions or insert blacks into management posts without commensurate responsibility.

Undoubtedly, employment equity is limited in its capacity to cultivate black-owned and operated enterprises. One rationale behind employment equity is the mandate for suitably qualified persons of disadvantaged groups, previously unfairly denied recruitment or promotion, to be given opportunities to acquire experiences that can only be learned on the job, perhaps leading to such persons venturing out on their own. Slim prospects of reaching the pinnacle of management and executive power may propel capable blacks to start businesses. However, this will depend on a confluence of other ancillary factors, especially access to credit.

Black ownership, control and management of companies

One of the paramount goals of BBBEE is to promote black-owned and black-controlled companies. This socio-political imperative is driven by the terminal aspect of this objective and attendant economic influence. Black representation in management and boards can occur in a milieu of continual white dominance in ownership and control; black ownership constitutes a fuller realization of economic empowerment. There is also greater prospect of sustained progress, given the likelihood that majority ownership will be retained.

The preferential public procurement programme has been utilized as a key instrument of affirmative action in enterprise development, chiefly in the promotion of black ownership, control and management of companies. South Africa began to leverage its government contracting system to promote black-owned and operated business from about 2000. In the late 1990s, a National Black Economic Empowerment Strategy was promulgated by the Black Management Forum and then driven by the Black Business Council. Subsequently the Black Economic Empowerment Commission formulated a strategy and framework, which it presented to government in October 2000, containing preliminary ideas for a BEE Act and the formation of various implementing agencies (BEE Commission 2000).

The terms of engagement were broadly codified in the Preferential Public Procurement Framework Act (PPPFA) (2000), which stipulated allocation of 80–90 points for price and technical content and 10–20 points for specific goals, with the 80:20 ratio applying to smaller contracts and 90:10 to larger contracts. The specific goals stated in the Act include "contracting with historically disadvantaged by unfair discrimination on the basis of race, gender or disability" and "implementing programmes of the RDP." Hence, procurement practices operated with a clear template for affirmative action, although the initial terms of engagement were rather imprecise. The PPPFA preceded the systemization of BEE.

The concept of BEE, although it had been articulated since the late 1980s, was formalized through the BEE Commission's proceedings and institutionalized in the Broad-Based BEE Act (2003), which provided a legislative framework for black empowerment that had been underway through rather ad hoc and relatively uncoordinated initiatives. The BBBEE Act also empowered the minister of trade and industry to issue codes of good practice and transformation charters and established a BBBEE Advisory Council. The project met with fierce opposition. As Marais (2011, 141) notes: "There was strong public disapproval and much moral condemnation of the narrow, elitist nature of BEE. Small cliques had cornered the first generation of deals, which had been precariously engineered and were highly leveraged to enable newcomers to buy assets, effectively without financial capital of their own."

The BBBEE agenda sustained momentum. The BBBEE codes, rolled out in 2007 with a set of criteria and corresponding scores, must be taken into account in procurement, licensing, public-private partnerships and sale of state assets. The official framework articulates the following key components: direct empowerment (ownership and management); human resource development (employment equity and skills development); indirect empowerment (preferential procurement in the supply chain, enterprise development of subsidiaries or other entities). Its mechanism revolves around a metering system – the BBBEE Scorecard, audited by private firms – in which participants earn a composite score for performance across seven weighted elements. The scores map onto a grid of compliance levels, from 1 to 8, or a "non-compliant" appraisal. The DTI has appointed the South African National Accreditation System (SANAS) to accredit BBBEE ratings and verifications. The seven categories and respective score allocations demonstrate an institutional broadening of BEE. Sectoral specificities have induced the formation of BBBEE charters, of which mining stands out for being the only one with mandatory compliance, in contrast to optional participation elsewhere (Manning and Jennes 2014).

Factoring BBBEE scores into transactions with government presumably injects a competitive dimension and gives bidders a fillip to pursue the various elements of the points system. Companies earn points for their profiles and can score further in accordance with the BBBEE score of their subsidiaries and vendors or for financially assisting the development of smaller enterprises. Licensing, by forging a tighter relationship between government and license-holder, is arguably more effective than procurement in advancing black business development (Gqubule

2006). However, the magnitude of license disbursements pales in comparison to public procurement.

Recognizing that the entire BBBEE schematic is too onerous for small businesses, the codes provide exemptions and conditions for Exempted Micro Enterprises (EMEs) and Qualifying Small Enterprises (QSEs). The 2007 iteration accorded level 4 BBBEE recognition to EMEs and QSEs, with promotion to level 3 for majority black-owned entities. QSEs were allowed to choose any four out of the seven BBBEE elements to count toward their BBBEE score. The 2013 iteration upped the weightage on black ownership; both EMEs and QSEs obtain level 2 recognition for majority black ownership, and level 1 for 100% black ownership. Also, ownership is a mandatory BBBEE element for all QSEs who can elect between skills development or enterprise/supplier development for their appraisal (DTI 2013).

Public procurement remains the main leverage for BBBEE, with terms that have been amended and augmented over time. The DTI's Medium-Term Strategic Framework 2009–2012 set a schedule of progressively rising targets in the percentage of procurement spending allocated to historically disadvantaged individuals and SMMEs: 60% (2009–2010), 70% (2010–2011), 75% (2011–2012) (DTI 2009). PPPFA Regulations of 2011 aligned terms and conditions with BBBEE (DTI 2011). In 2017, public procurement terms were amended again, raising the ceiling at which the contribution of BBBEE points is 20 out of 100. Above this cut-off, the 10/90 breakdown applies. Previously, contracts above ZAR1 million in value and below would count 20 BBBEE points, but the new threshold stands at ZAR50 million, thereby increasing the scope for BBBEE to factor into public procurement decisions. Since 2017, more weightage is also placed on level 1 and 2 compliance, arising from a bigger points difference between level 2 and 3, where previously the big jump was between 3 and 4. Another requirement kicked in: 30% of large contracts must be sub-contracted to micro and small scale enterprises and black-owned businesses (IFC 2018, 41).

In practice, government procurement is exposed to misuse and abuse, most acutely through fronting. The pervasiveness of various forms of deception and manipulation prompted the 2013 redesign of the BBBEE Codes, which included checks and mitigation measures. The BBBEE Amendment Act established the BBBEE Commission, vested with responsibility and authority in oversight, monitoring, advocacy and promotion of good governance and accountability (South Africa 2013b). The amendment added a new section defining fronting, and provisions for fronting to be investigated by the Commission. Along with the generic codes, 12 sector codes have also been gazetted from 2009, mostly during 2015–2018, in recognition of sector-specific circumstances and requirements.

BBBEE has constantly had to negotiate ebbs and flows in popular sentiment toward its overall implementation and the criticism that the benefits do not reach the masses, while also responding to demands from black business and concerns toward the capacity-building objectives, and the pace of change pegged to a sluggishly growing economy. In response to slow progress in black ownership and control, and to promote more capability-building rather while also curbing tokenism in appointments, the 2013 amendments increased the weightage of ownership and effective control and skills development and merged enterprise development and public procurement to form the largest category, while eliminating employment equity. Principles and rules are stipulated for broad-based ownership and employee share ownership programmes, private equity funds, recognition of ownership after sale or loss of shares by black participants and trusts.

State-owned entities and public enterprises/state-owned companies

South Africa's state-owned entities (SOEs) encompass a wide range, at the national, provincial and local levels. While SOEs in general abide by BBBEE and public procurement regulations, the fully government-owned public enterprises or state-owned companies have been given pride of place, as institutions for pursuing AA objectives in employment and training ground for black management, within these large companies and their supply chains. The privatization agenda pushed in the early post-Apartheid years – more on ideological, neoliberal grounds than as a redistributive instrument for affirmative action – unravelled in the late 1990s, and momentum fizzled out. The scale of operations of these entities and their prominence in the economy placed them in distinctive position to be vehicles of black enterprise development. As Southall (2016, 79) compactly puts it:

> From the moment that the ANC took power, the parastatals were identified as "sites of transformation." The 300-odd "core" SOEs inherited by the ANC in 1994 employed around 300,000 people, with the "big four" – Transnet, Eskom, Telkom and Denel – making up over 75 per cent of that number. These SOEs accounted for something like 15 per cent of GDP, and under the previous government had played a major strategic role in not only priming the economy but in promoting Afrikaner upward mobility. Unsurprisingly, they were identified by the ANC as important vehicles for driving a "developmental state" and for promoting black empowerment. It was against this background that early enthusiasm for privatization, espoused by Presidents Mandela and Mbeki, came up against heavy resistance within the ANC and the Alliance. Such limited privatisation as did take place was often to be linked to BEE (with the sale of state assets to black consortia).

The prominence of public enterprises was reinvigorated in the early 2000s, together with a shift toward a more expansive role for government procurement and state agencies. A presidency-commissioned report noted that "SOEs have a significant role to play in driving the codified economic transformation policy for Government. SOEs should set the pace in achieving statutory requirements in support of Government and national priorities" (PRC-SOE 2013, 142). It also proposed an adjusted generic scorecard for SOEs.[14] While the public enterprises, now termed *state-owned companies*, are similar to government departments in terms of the state's direct influence over employment equity practices, they are largely engaged in production and are relatively more exposed than the bureaucracy to competition.[15] South Africa's experiences with poor service delivery have also raised expectations of paying consumers toward monopolies such as power utility Eskom.

Nonetheless, SOCs occupy a space in between the public services, where blacks have risen into administrative ranks but may not be sufficiently equipped for managing in competitive markets and the private sector, which has embraced employment equity unevenly. However, the socio-psychological effects on the black community of demonstrating competency and attaining success in visible ways are arguably significant.

Loans, grants and the Black Industrialist Programme

A number of programmes extend financial support for SMEs, with some specifically targeting small business. The Industrial Development Corporation was clearly primed to play a role, with its experience and established record of funding and promoting enterprise since 1940, especially in manufacturing. A 2001 amendment to the Industrial Development Act added to the IDC's objectives, "to promote the economic empowerment of the historically disadvantaged communities and persons" (South Africa 2001). Small business specifically fall under the purview of the Department of Small Business Development. Its Black Business Supplier Development Programme operates a cost-sharing grant to assist black-owned MSMEs in improving their competitiveness. The DTI awards financial assistance for BBBEE purposes, under two Support Programme for Industrial Innovation (SPII) grant schemes: Product Process Development and the Matching Scheme. Only South African companies or small- or medium-scale are eligible.

The National Empowerment Fund, founded in 1998, also extends financial assistance for enterprise development. Unfortunately, the NEF became mired in financial mismanagement and distress and was subsumed as a subsidiary of the IDC in 2017. The SME Fund, a private sector initiative launched in late 2018 with funding from 50 JSE-listed companies and the PIC, constitutes another programme under this banner.

Limited inroads by the BEE programmes, particularly in fostering effective ownership and control and participation in manufacturing activities, spurred a more direct and focused intervention. The Black Industrialists Policy (BIP) was first proposed by the BBBEE Advisory Council in 2012, with a clear target of creating 100 black industrialists by 2018. The idea was reiterated in 2014 and became promulgated as official policy in 2015 (PARI 2017). The BIP distinguishes itself from other BBBEE programmes by focusing on black-owned and managed enterprise and manufacturing operations with special reference to areas designated in the Industrial Policy Action Plan (IPAP), especially welcoming greenfield ventures and start-ups, and by administering loan financing for productive purposes. This stands in contrast to equity transfers, which were prone to acquisitive behaviour, rent-seeking and patronage.

Undoubtedly, the BIP contains elements of continuity with preceding policy interventions but with a distinct change in execution and relative emphasis, in terms of setting national champions as a priority, leveraging on public procurement and depending on development finance institutions as key implementing agencies, particularly the IDC. Its policy document makes reference to Malaysia and South Korea, seeking to emulate the developmental state achievements – although it is unclear how critically the policy formulation process incorporated lessons from the full range of Malaysia's successes and failures and its chequered overall track record (DTI 2015). The emphasis on productive and competitive enterprises through centralized, direct, state-overseen selection, however, clearly derives from these Asian predecessors and distinguishes the BIP from decentralized BBBEE and procurement.

Wealth and property ownership

Black economic empowerment is subject to various interpretations in terms of its meaning and scope and its relation to affirmative action. As with the Malaysian case of the Bumiputera Commercial and Industrial Community (BCIC), our interest in BEE recognizes the political and economic importance of ownership and control of capital, especially in its potential influence on increasing black representation in management. BEE is often thought of as a programme for redistributing ownership and wealth – and in both concept and practice, that was the case from 1994 to the early 2000s.[16]

Black corporate ownership proceeded in an ad hoc manner through the 1990s, at the initiative of white capital and through a series of mechanisms, with limited and inconsistent outcomes. The formation of the BEE Commission in 1998 and its deliberations yielded discourses on "maximalist" and "minimalist" paradigms of BEE, based on the scope of black empowerment as well as the intensity of intervention – whether the state administers programmes in a more *dirigiste* or indicative manner. The Commission decided on a maximalist approach, with expansive objectives including ownership and control over capital, employment equity and skills development (Gqubule 2006). However, up until the final Commission Report of 2001, the main thrust of BEE remained in the arena of ownership and control (Ponte, Roberts and van Sittert 2007).[17] Political funding arguably motivated BEE as well, as Marais (2011, 140–141) argues: "BEE appealed on a more profane level, too. Members' dues were insufficient to bankroll the ANC, at least not at the levels needed to function effectively and win elections comprehensively. Having a business elite 'on tap' would be a huge boon, not only to the ANC as an organization, but also to individuals within it."

As with enterprise development initiatives outlined earlier, black ownership was in a state of flux in the 1990s through to the early 2000s, experimenting with different mechanisms in sequence. Gqubule (2006) instructively demarcates waves of "capital reform," the first of which took the form of special purpose vehicles and were highly concentrated in a few entities. However, these endeavours were set back by financial crisis and exceedingly high interest rates. The second wave followed the BEE Commission Report of 2001, amid a flourish of sector charters, which deployed different instruments termed *call options, third party finance* and *vendor finance*. These transactions remained debt financed and were not coordinated.

The Commission's foundation and reports signified government's serious commitment to BEE and served notice to white capital to take up transformation more seriously.[18] Business sectors began drafting industry charters of procedures, targets and timelines for ownership transfer and broader inclusion of historically disadvantaged individuals. At the same time, public outcries over concentrations of ownership among a black, politically-linked elite compelled construction of a broader scheme for spreading benefits. Aside from criticisms of wealth acquisition, the hoped-for and hyped-up impact of a "patriotic African bourgeoisie" on transformation within firms also largely failed to materialize, whether for systemic-behavioural reasons – black capitalists are as self-interested as any capitalists – or practical reasons – having incurred heavy debt to acquire stakes, they were primarily motivated to service those loans.[19]

Some developments in the BBBEE system, reflecting continuity and change over time, merit a brief mention. One aspect of consistency concerns the placement of ownership at the top of the code. Although the weightage on ownership, at 20, matched that of preferential procurement in the 2007 codes, it was increased to 25 in the 2013 revisions, and while exceeded by the amalgamated category of enterprise development and preferential procurement, progress in ownership, alongside management control, remain politically preeminent. Concomitantly, the black ownership target of 25% has also garnered the most attention. Pressures for BEE to be truly broad-based have prompted more attention to asset distribution to investment and trust funds (operated by unions, NGOs or community groups) or employees (at a premium or for free).

Equity equivalents for multinational corporations can be approved, on a case-by-case basis, upon application to the DTI and satisfactory justification on how company policy precludes participation in BBBEE – and with proof that such policies are also consistent across the MNC's global operations. The value of equity equivalent contributions adopt the baseline of 25% of the MNCs South African operations, or 4% of total revenue of SA operations.

A few other strands of intervention that can potentially engage in advancing black ownership and control are worth mentioning to fill in this overview of affirmative action institutions. Some agencies pursue transformation in a trustee-type relationship, on behalf of the black community as a whole. The National Empowerment Fund (NEF), an agency of the Department of Trade and Industry established in 1998, provides financing for BEE equity transactions. The Public Investment Corporation (PIC), wholly owned by the South African government, has discretion to manage public pension funds to push for transformation in companies through exerting stakeholder influence.

Notes

1 Technically, schools could enrol blacks, and some did, although at a very low pace in the early 1990s (MERG 1993).
2 Author's personal correspondence with Professor Jonathan Jansen, 25 July 2017.
3 The *White Paper on Transformation of Higher Education* (1997) maintained that "transformation involves not only abolishing all existing forms of unjust differentiation, but also measures of empowerment, including financial support to bring about equal opportunity for individuals and institutions."
4 Senior certificate pass rates fluctuated along a plateau over 1990–1997 but showed an increasing trend over 1997–2002. University entrance pass rates fell from 18% in 1994 to 12% in 1999 before recovering to 17% in 2002 (SAIRR, cited in Jack 2003, 36–37).
5 Universities would be required to request "goal-oriented public funding" conditional less on enrolment size and more on a set of plans, including an academic development plan, equity plan, capital management plan, and performance improvement plan.
6 We should note that institutional redress and social or individual redress, especially with the mergers and restructuring of institutions, are conceptually but not necessarily functionally distinguishable (Personal correspondence with the Director of Transformation, University of the Witwatersrand).
7 Max Price, "In Defense of Race-Based Policy", *Mail and Guardian*, 6 January 2012.
8 Author's interview with Professor Max Price, former Vice-Chancellor of the University of Cape Town, 14 August 2017.
9 Percentage of designated group, baseline targets and timeframe

	Target	*December 1997*
Black people at management level	50% by 1999	33%
Women new recruits to the management level	30% by 1999	13%
People with disabilities	2% by 2005	0.02%

Source: Department of Public Service and Administration (1998).

10 A 1995 FSA-Contact survey reported 94% of private sector organizations had implemented some form of AA (67% formally; 27% informally), mainly at the managerial, professional and technical levels. By 1996, however, 85–95% of senior positions remained held by whites, and the black proportion of top management was a mere 3% (Adam 2000, 82). The lack of standard definitions of what constitutes AA and benchmarks for black advancement is reflected in these developments preceding the EEA.
11 The unqualified designation of women in the EEA has stirred controversy over whether white women can be considered as disadvantaged as black men, leading to assertions of a further order of priority: black female, black male, white female, white male.
12 Author's interview with Employment Equity Division official, Department of Labor, 30 November 2007.
13 The Skills Development Act, also passed in 1998, provides for the establishment of Sector Education and Training Authorities (SETAs) and a one percent of payroll levy that firms can reclaim through enrolling staff in the SETAs, irrespective of company size (South Africa 1998b). The skills development programme operates largely in tandem with employment equity for medium-scale and larger enterprises.

14 The proposed BBBEE scorecard for state-owned entities was: 15% direct empowerment (management control; ownership is a redundant criterion), 35% human resource development (15% employment equity, 20% skills development), 35% indirect empowerment (20% preferential procurement, 15% enterprise development), 15% socio-economic development (PRC-SOE 2013).

15 For example, South African Airways competes internationally, and public highways have applied competitive pressure on Transnet, the railway operator (Author's interview with senior official, Department of Public Enterprises, 5 December 2007).

16 The rhetoric of the early Mbeki Presidency is tell-tale. Speaking to the BMF in 1999, he asserted: "As part of the realization of the aim to eradicate racism in our country, we must strive to create and strengthen a black capitalist class. A critical part to create a non-racial society, is the deracialization of the ownership of productive property" (cited in Gumede 2002, 207).

17 The decision in the Commission's report to name the proposed legislation the BEE Act, instead of the commercial equity act, was made at the last minute (Author's interview with Duma Gqubule, 3 November 2007).

18 Author's interview with Roger Southall, 7 December 2007.

19 Author's interview with Lumkile Mondi, Chief Economist, Industrial Development Corporation, 28 November 2007.

Part 3

Policy achievements and reforms

Progress, shortfalls and prospects

This third batch of chapters empirically evaluates affirmative action outcomes. I compile, present and synthesize data from a range of sources to describe and analyze country performance on the primary objective of affirmative action: expanding racial representation, participation and ownership in particular spheres. I also address more qualitatively oriented questions surrounding the policy's efficacy, as well as possible adverse consequences.

This investigation sheds light on the ultimate aims of affirmative action – to cultivate capability, competitiveness and confidence in ways that can lead to the rollback of overt race preferences. Within the beneficiary group, equitable allocation of benefits and facilitation of inter-generational upward mobility enhance the policy's outreach and long-term impact. Data permitting, I consider possible disproportionalities within Bumiputera and black populations, based on ethnicity, region or class, and the efficacy of targeting the disadvantaged within the beneficiary group. This is especially pertinent to higher education. I also address questions surrounding the challenges of introducing graduation or exit clauses, the "capture" of affirmative action benefits by elites and the influence of political connections on selection processes. These questions primarily apply to the spheres of high-level employment, enterprise development and wealth ownership.

The selected data strive to cover as much as possible of the affirmative action regime and to generate findings that are comparable across both countries. This study is compelled to take into account data availability, especially in the case of Malaysia where access is more restricted and published statistics with race variables are limited. The empirical analysis seeks to inform not just policy progress but also the socio-political aspects of the policy reform debate. Hence, I also draw on public opinion surveys that reflect sentiments toward affirmative action, capturing the gravity, tensions and nuances of popular support for the policy, as well as attendant constraints on reform.

We proceed with Chapter 6 laying out the approach, scope and analytical framework of this study, with reference to empirical literature and discussion of the objectives and requirements of this inquiry. Chapters 7 and 8 analyze the achievements and shortfalls of affirmative action in Malaysia and South Africa, laying groundwork for the book's conclusion, which draws out similarities and differences in the country experiences, discusses policy implications and presents some thoughts on moving forward with affirmative action.

6 Empirical literature and analytical framework

Tracking and appraising the expansive affirmative action regimes of Malaysia and South Africa – accounting for both quantitative and qualitative aspects – present daunting analytical challenges and limitations. In line with the breadth of definitions of AA, empirical works also exhibit a broad range of approaches and focal points. This study's process of establishing a systematic approach, defining our scope and constructing a methodology builds on the gaps in single-country research on Malaysia and South Africa and the dearth of comparative work. It draws on two-country studies that have ventured further in setting up a common template for cross-country comparison. There is a plethora of literature on affirmative action, with a substantial number of studies worth referencing, but few that directly inform this study.

Individual-focused studies

Affirmative action operates at the individual level in specific ways, and there is good value in examining the experience of beneficiaries and the consequences on them. Accordingly, a considerable proportion of this research, largely within the United States, has studied specific sectors, with a large body of work on university admissions. Within this body, the scope varies – notably Bowen and Bok (1998), whose analysis is extensive but applies specifically to elite US colleges, while other sections look into hiring practices and contracting, as surveyed in Bergmann (1996) and Holzer and Neumark (2000). Yet another branch of research deals with legal cases and constitutional matters, often with examination of the circumstances of individual plaintiffs (Beckwith and Jones 1997; Cahn 2002; Curry 1996).

These studies, which illuminate affirmative action in practice and contribute substantial empirical findings to the debate, merit a mention at this juncture – and a clarification of why I omit them in shaping the framework of this study. This study is unable to replicate their work due to differences in subject matter, data quality and scope. The focus of my empirical work falls much more on the empirical policy outcomes than the legal processes – which in the case of Malaysia is also an empty quest, since affirmative action has never been constitutionally challenged. Furthermore, while constitutional issues are important and will be brought into focus in the affirmative action regime overview and referenced as context for this policy, the future of the policy hinges much less on constitutional debates than on social, political and economic developments. In-depth statistical analyses of the experience of beneficiaries usefully zoom in on policy beneficiaries at the personal level – such as university entrants or government contractors – but are unavailable or inaccessible in Malaysia and South Africa. Another reason is more basic. The national and regime-wide scope set forth in this study, encompassing AA in higher education, high-level occupations, enterprise development and wealth ownership, necessitates a more general evaluation, drawing on multiple data sources. Of course, individual-focused studies of policy beneficiaries will be referenced as supplementary material.

National-scope, multi-country studies

Compiled volumes of multi-country studies, some of which contain chapters on Malaysia and South Africa, provide insights on affirmative action experiences but tend to accommodate a wide array of subject scope and frameworks. This significantly derives from the range of countries and policy sectors involved as well as the varying specializations of contributing authors. Existing compilations of case studies generally do not impose common analytical grids, which limit their applicability to this study's research framework. Two examples merit mention. Dupper and Sankaran (2014) attain some compatibility in the sense that all chapters look at affirmative action on a national scale, although the chapters still vary; for instance, some chapters focused relatively more on education and others on employment, among countries that implement affirmative action in both sectors. Brown, Stewart and Langer (2012) adopt horizontal inequality as a conceptual theme woven through the book, which ranges in subject focus, with some chapters on education and others on employment, and a few chapters – including Yusof's (2012) on Malaysia – presenting overviews of affirmative action on a national scale. Some chapters from these volumes will be cited, primarily to compare the findings. For constructing an analytical framework, however, other literature is more instructive.

Another branch of the literature focuses on one specific policy sphere. Among the four main areas, affirmative action is implemented more frequently in higher education and employment; hence, more cross-country comparisons have been produced with these particular focal points. Featherman, Hall and Krislov (2010) collate articles on affirmative action in South Africa and the United States. They note the shared history of black subjugation and white domination, then episodes of liberation and emergent civil and political rights, while being mindful of the contrasting racial dynamics and socio-political context arising from the fact that blacks constitute the majority in South Africa, while it is the converse in the United States. Nussbaum and Hasan (2012) share the subject matter, with the addition of India as a third country case. The commonality of institutional autonomy across South Africa and the United States underscores that distinctive feature of affirmative action, and the contrast of both countries with a more quota-based system in India is instructive for our South Africa-Malaysia comparisons. The South Africa chapters in these volumes present useful references for this book.

On employment equity, Jain, Sloane and Horwitz (2003) survey and analyze the institutions and policy practices of six countries: South Africa, Malaysia, United States, Canada, Indian and Britain/Northern Ireland. Notably, they draw out differences in policy structure that are instrumental to this book: quota-based interventions and limitation to the public sector in Malaysia; legislation in South Africa, spanning both public and private sectors.

Weisskopf (2004) conducts an outstandingly original and systematic benefit-cost analysis of affirmative action in university admissions in the US and India, on a range of socio-economic criteria and based on a synthesis of existing literature. The framework encompasses a range of socio-economic outcomes that are directly affirmative-action targets or clear policy objectives, rather than highly aggregated outcomes, such as household income, which are less traceable to affirmative-action interventions. A further strength of Weisskopf's methodology is that the broader, qualitative – and sometimes intangible – goals of AA, such as learning environments, sense of group dignity and race relations, are accounted for to a meaningful degree.

The mode of analysis is also distinctive. Across the range of criteria for evaluation, Weisskopf (2004) arrives at an overall assessment of whether the outcomes are, on balance, net positive or negative, or inconclusive. The subjectivity of some evaluation criteria requires some judgments that are personal and intuitive in nature. On the whole, some elements are judged net positive and others net negative, but Weisskopf sums up the benefit-cost analysis, in line with a key objective of the research, which is to arrive at a stance for or against affirmative action. On balance, he deems the positives outweigh the negatives. This book, rather that setting out to investigate the justification for affirmative action – having established the policy as constitutional provisions and socio-political imperatives – seeks to evaluate policy outcomes and the prospects for long-term reform. Nonetheless, there is much to draw on from Weisskopf (2004) in constructing this study's methodology.

Works on Malaysia and South Africa

Obviously, studies on Malaysia and South Africa pose potentially fruitful reference points. As noted in Chapter 1, the literature empirically evaluating Malaysia and South Africa achievements in affirmative action are far less extensive than might be expected, whether we are referring to stand-alone country studies or cross-country comparisons. Furthermore, the bulk of studies on inequality in both countries address general manifestations, especially household income and personal earnings disparities, and locate the analyses in the broader public policy contexts, often without specifically and systematically conceptualizing affirmative action. Work on inequality in Malaysia and South Africa invariably draws linkages between income disparities and affirmative action, although the causal lines are indirect and often ambiguous, compared to the principal, direct and targeted policy outcomes of increasing group representation in higher education, high-level employment, commerce and industry, and wealth and property ownership.

In a similar vein, comparative empirical studies of these two countries are sparse and basically absent in the post-1995 period. Malaysia and South Africa were subjects of some comparative study in the early to mid-1990s, mostly for the purpose of drawing lessons for South Africa from Malaysia's development and redistribution programmes, including affirmative action (Emsley 1996; Hart 1994; Southall 1997). However, those studies preceded South Africa's implementation of post-apartheid majority-favouring affirmative action, and comparative work on these two countries has been scant since South Africa's affirmative action laws and programmes began to take shape. The empirical chapters of the book, it should be noted, build on my previous works which address the direct AA outcomes comparatively and in Malaysia individually, especially Lee (2015), Lee and Mondi (2018), Lee (2014a, 2014b) and Lee (2017a).

Malaysia

The literature on Malaysia that references affirmative action often enmeshes race preferential programmes broadly in the context of national development, especially the New Economic Policy. Since its introduction in 1971, the NEP has provided the impetus and imprimatur for a vast array of interventions, encompassing poverty alleviation, economic growth, industrialization and Bumiputera advancement. Affirmative action thus tends to be one of various subjects in focus, or is drawn into the discourse as an explanatory factor, among many, of broad development outcomes. A number of studies have assessed the racial dynamics of education, employment, business development and wealth ownership over time, although the overall output is rather sparse.

Restricted access to data partly accounts for the paucity of research; racial inequality was a subject of interest when official sources disseminated statistics tracking the progress of racial and ethnic inequality, especially in the *Malaysia Plans*. Such disclosures steadily diminished post-2005. Much of the extant literature covers the pre-1990s era – specifically, the NEP's official period of 1971–1990. In line with the NEP's two-pronged objectives, the literature covers both poverty alleviation and affirmative action. This dual focus is not necessarily a limitation, and indeed addresses crucial questions and policy outcomes, but it often leads to conflation of the two prongs. Empirically, these studies predominantly cover interracial inequalities in household income, and racial composition of occupational groups and equity ownership. This range of policy outcomes illustrates the NEP's second prong with broad-brushed strokes but offers superficial perspective on the ultimate goals of developing Bumiputera capability and competitiveness (Faaland, Parkinson and Saniman 1990; Hashim 1998; Jamaludin 2003; Jomo 2004; Leete 2007; Meerman 2008; Milanovic 2006; Mat Zin 2008).

Research on policy outcomes post-1990, and especially post-2000, is less voluminous and rather static, even while some shortcomings in Bumiputera economic participation persist and new challenges emerge, particularly with regard to difficulties among graduates in labour market engagement, continual dependence on public sector employment of professionals and administrators and under-representation in management and private enterprise (Lee 2005). On the issue of equity ownership specifically, Abu Samad (2002) and CPPS (2006a) have investigated Malaysia's progress toward the 30% Bumiputera target. They focus much less on affirmative action policies than on equity ownership measurement methods and their quantitative findings, which challenge the orthodoxy. Hence, these studies make for important references in the next chapter but provide little guidance for constructing a general framework.

Three assertions recur in the literature that warrant a brief discussion here, to clarify my departure from the established approaches and underscore the gaps this study seeks to fill.

First, a widely shared opinion holds that Malaysia's affirmative action deficiencies lie predominantly in equity redistribution and enterprise development – in contrast to successes in education and employment. The empirical record of racial representation at the aggregated national level is consistent with this viewpoint, and in view of the greater barriers and time-consumption of successfully owning and operating business, it is fully expected that Bumiputera progress in private enterprise, and wealth and property ownership have lagged behind education and employment (Chakravarty and Abdul-Hakim 2005; Yusof 2012; Jomo 2004). Moreover, the propensity for political patronage and corruption to vitiate policies is greater in programmes involving asset transfers and distribution of largesse. These are undeniable problems, but their relatively bumpier and skewed progress, compared to the steadier and broader gains in educational attainment, do not signify that the latter has been smooth sailing. Education is most critical to affirmative action because this policy sector imparts capability, obviates profiteering and has the most potential for inter-generational upward mobility. Achievements must be scrutinized and qualified. The sector also warrants a critical examination of the ultimate objectives, beyond the widely cited quantitative outcomes (Lee 2012).

A second conventional view pertains to the dynamics of inter-racial and intra-racial inequality. A concurrence of declining inter-racial household income inequality and rising intra-racial inequality in the 1990s prompted arguments that the former was largely resolved and had become superseded by the latter in importance. This argumentation was plausible in the 1990s, when the booming economy possibly raised premiums on still scarce high-skilled labour, and privatization policies magnified Malay income and wealth concentration at the top (Mat Zin 2008; Shari 2000). However, this assessment persists, even when the same official sources have shown a marked decline in intra-racial inequality (Lee and Khalid 2020). Accompanying this insistence that within-Bumiputera inequality has risen is a hasty assumption that affirmative action benefits are captured by the elite and do not reach the masses. The argument tends to equate affirmative action with wealth distribution, omitting a clear conceptual framework and systematic empirical corroboration. A fuller perspective of the affirmative action regime leads to conceptualization of various distributional outcomes, with contrasting effects, and *a priori* indeterminate net results. Higher education expansion may lead to income concentration among elites when a small segment has attained university degrees, but it can be the basis for middle class growth and overall lower inequality when it becomes accessible to masses of the population.

Third, a common theme in affirmative action discourse – whether official, popular or academic sources – upholds "need-based" affirmative action as an unqualified and total replacement for race-based affirmative action. I have discussed the problems with this view at length in Chapter 2. In consulting the empirical literature and its analytical underpinnings, a few points warrant a brief mention here. Various studies have identified shortcomings and failures in Malaysia's Bumiputera enterprise and capitalist class development, including political patronage and corruption, rent-seeking, debt accumulation and poor selection and monitoring of beneficiaries (Tan 2008; Gomez 2012; Chin and Teh 2017). After decades of implementation, a capable and independent Bumiputera industrial and entrepreneurial class has yet to emerge. However, to conclude from these realities that Malaysia should shift to need-based affirmative action – helping the poor instead of pandering to the elite – follows a flawed, misguided logic. The focus of such argument strays from the policy's original objective, which is not principally about helping the poor. Indeed, how could government contracts in construction or service delivery be distributed to poor households instead of company owners?

Ultimately, any rollback of preference for Bumiputera business will ride on such businesses increasingly growing in competitiveness, not on more extensive allocation of opportunities to low-income, disadvantaged households. Evaluations of the extent that affirmative action benefits the poor must be circumscribed within the policy sector where pro-poor preference can offer alternatives to race-based affirmative action – i.e. chiefly in higher education, and possibly in microfinance and savings schemes.

South Africa

In contrast to Malaysia, empirical work on racial inequality and concomitant policies has flourished in South Africa, facilitated by freer access to data and a more open public sphere.

One similarity stands out. As in Malaysia, the bulk of relevant literature focuses on household income or personal earnings, and deduces affirmative action outcomes and implications from income or earnings inequality, which are influenced by myriad other factors and policies, including economic structural change, labour market conditions, and general socio-economic development (Bhorat, Leibbrandt and Woolard 2000; Allanson, Atkins and Hinks 2002; Rospabé 2002; Van der Berg and Louw 2004; Hoogeveen and Özler 2005; Leibbrandt, Levinsohn and McCrary 2005; Seekings and Nattrass 2005; Hlekiso and Mahlo 2006; Leite, McKinley and Osorio 2006; Burger and Jafta 2012; Gradín 2018).

The dynamics of earnings and income inequality are undoubtedly important and interesting, but an extensive review of this literature takes us too far afield, given that most studies do not examine the structures and outcomes of affirmative action specifically. Two strands of the literature are worth a brief discussion.

First, the literature under the heading of *affirmative action* widely applies the official, legal definition of the policy as a component of employment equity pursuing the objective of increasing representation of the disadvantaged group. The purpose in raising this observation is not to pedantically insist that the term *affirmative action* can only be used in the manner defined for this book, but to draw out the limitations of this perspective in terms of conceptualizing and analysing the full range of racial disparity, particularly in omitting linkages between affirmative action in education and in employment. Skills shortages, including degree-holding graduates, are frequently attributed as an underlying factor for the slow progress of affirmative action in employment and are intertwined with affirmative action in higher education. However, many critical reviews of employment equity omit this interdependence. Although the education aspect is undoubtedly acknowledged, research that considers the impacts of higher education transformation on the supply of high-skilled blacks, which are integral to the progress of employment equity, is surprisingly scarce.

One specific methodology closely relates with the Employment Equity Act (EEA) and with affirmative action discourses more generally. The EEA's designation of two chapters – prohibition of discrimination and affirmative action – appears to set up income or earnings decomposition as a framework for informing the state of inequality pertinent to affirmative action. Burger and Jafta (2012) decompose disparities in employment and in earnings into the portion that can be explained by differences in productive characteristics – such as educational attainment – and the "unexplained" portion attributed to discrimination, or differential reward despite identical characteristics. The authors find that differentials between blacks and whites in labour market outcomes were persistently or increasingly due to the discrimination portion. These findings are important, but Burger and Jafta's (2012) conclusion that AA has failed to alleviate discrimination is contestable. Affirmative action's principle objective, as they clearly explain in a primer on the EEA, is to increase participation and representation of disadvantaged groups. Anti-discrimination law, of which enforcement is also very difficult, plays a complementary but subsidiary role. Hence, it is somewhat misleading to assert that persisting labour market discrimination demonstrates a deficiency of affirmative action, when the more direct policy implication is a deficit of anti-discrimination enforcement.

Moreover, their findings can also be interpreted as showing the effects of affirmative action in education, which have narrowed racial disparities, particularly in attaining degree-level qualifications, and have in turn reduced the explanatory power of differences in average productive characteristics between blacks and whites. Preferential measures to advance black educational attainment likely contribute to the relatively large unexplained portion, and thus discrimination as deduced in these decomposition exercises may well reflect gains in affirmative action. However, this conclusion cannot be pressed too hard because the persisting gap surely also arises from differentials in quality of education not captured in survey data. Thus, the unexplained portion may also be attributed to quality differences in spite of the quantitative closing of the gap in acquisition of education certificates. Gradín's (2018) decomposition analysis of the 1996 and 2001 Population Censuses and 2007 Community Survey also finds that, while workers' characteristics have improved, especially in terms of educational attainment of blacks, stratification and segregation patterns remain largely unexplained. Decomposition studies, in sum, underscore the importance of a regime-wide analysis that integrates all affirmative action sectors.

A second noteworthy strand of the earnings- and income-based empirical literature focuses on the middle class. Expanding the black middle class is important for economic, social and political reasons. This social stratum is often demarcated according to income level but corresponds with broader socio-economic development; indeed, various studies, importantly Southall (2016), apply occupation as a defining category for middle-class status. The literature on black middle-class growth provides helpful references for this study, due to various overlapping subject matters pertinent to affirmative action – especially, higher education attainment and upward occupational mobility. In addition, this research field addresses questions related to the state dependency of burgeoning new elites, which are also of interest to us. On the whole, academic works centred on household surveys, whether focused on income, earnings or occupational profiles, affirm the utility of South Africa's survey data, notably the Labour Force Survey, which will be one of the main sources here.

As with Malaysia, scholars of South Africa will be hard-pressed to find comprehensive and rigorous reviews of affirmative action that encompass all sectors of the policy regime. However, while the Malaysia literature tends to cover a range of affirmative action programmes but presents less in-depth analysis, research on South Africa has more frequently conducted separate, focused analysis of singular sectors of affirmative action. The different terminologies perhaps lend to this segmentation: redress and transformation in higher education, affirmative action as a component of employment equity, black economic empowerment predominantly in ownership and enterprise.

This study thus draws on the literature covering the specific sectors to gain a fuller appreciation of the key issues and debates, the gaps in understanding and the interactions across them. Literature on higher education transformation, notably the Featherman, Hall and Krislov (2010) volume of essays, and select articles in the *Transformation* journal furnish insightful resources. Pertinent to employment and skills training, the literature on employment equity helpfully highlights the key subject matters: access and attainment, distribution within the black population and inclusion of low-income households which stand to gain the most from upward educational mobility, and academic achievement gaps – including the supply of qualified high school graduates and higher education graduation rates.

Some works have focused on BEE, and even more specifically, the deal-making and equity ownership aspects within its expansive rubric (Gqubule 2006; Cargill 2010; Jeffery 2014). The scope of such studies is vast, spanning the chronological changes in distributive modes and transfers, which by nature are fluid and in practice not regularly tracked, especially in terms of the racial profile of ownership. This book will only draw on general findings and arguments in these works, with reference to newer, official reports that have estimated black ownership and control.

Analytical framework

This study aims to fill the gaps through focusing on the primary objectives and outcomes of affirmative action, encompassing all four policy sectors. In view of his incorporation of the multifarious interventions and various objectives of affirmative action, I draw significantly on Weisskopf (2004) in constructing an analytical framework. Although his study is focused on higher education, he sets out a wide range of evaluation criteria pertinent to the intentions and ramifications of affirmative action, without compacting the analysis down to one variable or a composite summary statistic. However, my approach departs from Weisskopf (2004) in that, whereas he weighs costs and benefits, this book will reference country attainments vis-à-vis the policy targets, mainly in terms of numerical gains but also in terms of the further, qualitative objectives of building capability and enhancing mobility. I mainly generate original findings from raw national survey or census data, or collate and compute statistics from official reports to obtain new insights from published – but largely under-tapped – sources.

It may be helpful at this juncture to register three points that clarify the scope and focus of my analysis. First, income inequality does not feature as centrally in this book as it does in the literature – whether works claiming to focus on affirmative action or those more broadly tackling racial or ethnic inequality. The literature on inequality in Malaysia and South Africa overwhelmingly focuses on income, as discussed earlier. Middle-class expansion and narrowing income gaps are concomitant developments to affirmative action, but focusing on those socio-economic outcomes somewhat detracts from a precise handling of affirmative-action policies, which first and foremost target participation and ultimately seek to broadly cultivate capability, competitiveness and confidence as a pre-requisite for preferential treatment to be rolled back.

Second, the declared grand ambitions and overpromises in policy statements are misplaced building blocks for empirical analysis of affirmative action. This is strikingly demonstrated in Malaysia's New Economic Model's profession of replacing race-based AA with need-based AA and South Africa's BEE discourse that subsumes unemployment and all manifestations of underdevelopment within its ambit. These imprecise, overblown and somewhat misguided pronouncements readily foreshadow condemnations of affirmative action for failures that are outside the policy's scope, especially persisting poverty or lagging socio-economic development of low-income households (Gomez 2015; Jeffery 2014).

Third, following on the earlier discussion of the Malaysia literature, this book does not engage at length with the questions of inter-group and intra-group inequalities which recur in the literature – specifically, the argument that affirmative action has increased intra-racial inequality. In Malaysia, critique of the system emerged in the 1990s, when conventional wisdom held that the benefits of economic growth and redistributive policy were accruing to a narrow elite. In corroboration, official data showed rising household income inequality, as captured in the Gini coefficient. However, so ingrained is the perception of rising intra-Bumiputera that it endures until the present, despite the official statistical series showing continuous and steep decline in this dimension of inequality since 2004 (Lee and Khalid 2020). Likewise, in South Africa, empirical evidence of rising intra-racial inequality concurred with observations that the uppermost crust of the black population was seizing a disproportionate share of benefits.

However, we should be more measured in thinking about this relationship and the evidence for evaluating it. Importantly, affirmative action encompasses much more than wealth transfers and big business contracts, which are the overwhelming focus of the critique that the policy exacerbates intra-racial disparity. While such outcomes do transpire and are problematic, these critiques omit higher education attainment, upward occupational mobility and SME support, which may have inequality-reducing effects. These trends may also widen the gaps between middle-income and low-income households. Whether this unequivocally constitutes a negative outcome and a fault of affirmative action, as typically argued, is open to question, especially when various structural problems, such as low wages, lie beyond the remit of affirmative action.

The causality is less deterministic than is often maintained. The mainstream critique of affirmative action spotlights income and wealth concentration at the top as evidence of regressively implemented affirmative action that skews the distribution of benefits in favour of politically connected elites, thus increasing the gap between the rich and the rest. This is further taken as an indictment of affirmative action, typically for "not benefiting those it intended to help." The enrichment of a corrupt and parasitic elite is a clear-cut undesirable outcome, but the channelling of opportunities to the upper class of professionals and managers is a precise objective of affirmative action. Thus, the disbursement of benefits to "the elite" cannot be dismissed as an unqualified failure or distortion; the decisive question is whether the beneficiaries deliver on those opportunities, and whether implementation averts hoarding.

Ideally, the allocation of benefits should also abide by apolitical, non-partisan norms, but this is never fully achievable. A political economic reality, particularly in the context of an incipient capitalist class, is the scarcity of independent industrialists and entrepreneurs. Disqualifying the "politically connected" from receiving any rent transfers might shrink an already small pool of potential recipients. The situation calls for pragmatic award of opportunity to industrialists with capability or potential and strict monitoring of project delivery and productive gains. The utilization of rent for learning and capacity building, rather than the absence of any political connection, ultimately matters more for the development of Bumiputera and black capability and competitiveness.

Template

Chapters 7 and 8 will adhere to the following template, drawing on Lee (2015), which examined Malaysia and South Africa comparatively in higher education and employment, and Lee (2014a, 2014b) which evaluated AA across all sectors in Malaysia. I evaluate the increase in Bumiputera or black representation aligned with the principal objectives of affirmative action. This progresses through the four policy sectors of higher education, high-level occupations, enterprise development and wealth ownership. Along the way, I explore attendant, supplementary developments that reflect attainment of the further policy objectives of developing capability, mobility, competitiveness and confidence, which impact on the capacity and readiness to undertake difficult and necessary policy reforms.

Topics are specific to each policy sector. In higher education, questions surrounding graduate employment and labour market mobility, unemployment more broadly and inter-generational upward mobility are germane and important. In terms of racial representation in high-level occupations, the sectoral distribution – particularly, across public sector and government-owned entities versus private firms and organizations – is a crucial supplementary element. For enterprise development, broader ramifications arise, revolving around the performance of government-linked companies or state-owned companies, public procurement policies, and financial and business support in developing capability – especially of small and medium firms – and in expanding into specific economic activities, notably manufacturing. In the fourth sector of wealth and property ownership, policies and empirical evidence are more unique to each country and data are scarcer, but we are able to draw out some insights from available sources. The analysis proceeds, mindful of the data constraints. The more limited and country-specific the empirical evidence, the more circumspect we need to be in making cross-country comparisons.

The chapters will also make observations on policy coordination, strategic planning and operational implementation, laying the groundwork for later discussion of policy modifications and reforms. Emphatically, affirmative action is also sustained by political imperatives and pressures, social dispositions and sentiments. To unpack the question of popular support for the policy, I draw out relevant information from various opinion surveys.

The contentions and dilemmas regarding preferential treatment for majority groups and access to opportunity for minority groups, of course, must be part of the analysis. These issues apply across the AA regime, and the general sentiment and tensions will permeate all policy sectors to some extent. Chapters 7 and 8 will each focus on the sector in which these dilemmas are particularly salient, in each country. Chapter 7 will discuss majority-minority contentions in Malaysia with reference to higher education. Chapter 8 will explore analogous debates in the context of South Africa's employment equity. Although wealth transfer policies – under the BCIC in Malaysia and BEE in South Africa – have perhaps been the most prominent in media coverage and most controversial in public discourses, affirmative action in Malaysia's higher education and South Africa's employment spheres are arguably the broadest in scope and the most intense sites of contestation over preferential treatment and fair opportunity.

Data sources

The chapters will tap into multiple sources, collating direct and supplementary data pertinent to policy outcomes. The country-based evaluations rely on data availability and official statistical transparency, in which both countries bear some fundamental differences. Raw, microdata are generally unavailable for research in Malaysia, particularly when race and ethnicity enter the frame, and statistical disclosures are also rather sparse and uneven across time. This research, like much of the literature touching on affirmative action in Malaysia, also relies on official documents, including the *Malaysia Plans* that have been the main conduit of statistics tracking the NEP since 1971. The five-year plans have furnished household income, occupational representation and equity ownership, but are less substantive and less consistent in reportage of racial representation in higher education and enterprise development. Since 2010, less and less has been disclosed in five-year *Malaysia Plans*. To fill in the gaps, I thus draw on other data publications, including the Labour Force Survey Report. Some statistics are not published with any regularity, and sometimes they enter the public domain through parliamentary proceedings, media reports and government statements. These types of references also contribute to the analysis of Chapter 7.

In contrast, South Africa has practiced more openness and transparency in its stewardship of national survey data. Access to micro data is unhindered, particularly through Statistics SA's online platforms that avail these resources including complete sets of national surveys or an interface for extracting selected statistics. While Malaysia has over time steadily restricted disclosures on race and ethnicity, South Africa has consistently reported on race. These conditions enable macro analysis of policy outcomes in Chapter 8, drawing considerably on the Labour Force Survey to inform policy outcomes in employment and education, as well as regular publications of the government labour and education agencies. Specifically, higher education reports and the Commission of Employment Equity's annual reports permit observation of time trends. Data on enterprise development and ownership are more scant; and unlike Malaysia, the absence of a standardized development planning document precludes such outlets for presenting official statistics. The analysis therefore compiles insights from various official sources, including BBBEE Commission reports, research reports and government-commissioned studies.

This research strives to collate and analyze the most recent data, and to cover the post-1990s period in both countries. Although Malaysia's experience with intensive affirmative action took off from NEP's inception in 1971, the period since 1990 holds significance as the official post-NEP era, marked by under-research amid various policy shifts and continuities. For South Africa, the birth of a new democratic republic in 1994 inexorably marks the start, but much of the empirical data, especially time-consistent sources, are available from the late-1990s or early-2000s.

7 Affirmative action outcomes in Malaysia

This chapter looks at Malaysia's progress and shortfalls in affirmative action. The evaluation begins with post-secondary and higher education, where I piece together data from assorted sources to track Bumiputera enrolment and academic achievement. This is followed by a consideration of graduate quality and employability, where disaggregations by public and private universities lend insight, and of inter-generational mobility, for which education data are most useful. For the next stage of high-level occupations, I reference official data sources that have traced changes over time, and again, probe public and private sector differences that reflect lateral mobility, and to some extent, capability and competitiveness. Moving on to the enterprise development sphere, I synthesize data on the various elements of GLCs: board membership, public procurement, SME ownership and control, as well as support programmes offering loans, grants and support. Wealth and property ownership draw on the official data series on equity ownership while also addressing the empirical debate and alternate estimates of Bumiputera ownership and paying some attention to trust agencies and property. Before the concluding portion, this chapter collates insights from a number of surveys on public opinion and popular support for AA.

Post-secondary and higher education

Empirical data on Bumiputera advancement in tertiary education are quite patchy and inconsistent, unlike occupational representation and other statistics that government sources consistently tracked in development plans until the mid-2000s. Nonetheless, a range of sources paint a picture of substantial quantitative gains. Institutions and financial assistance established for Bumiputera educational advancement, at late secondary and post-secondary stages and in TVET institutions, grew immensely and continue to provide access and support. Sharp differentiations have emerged at the secondary school level, where 15% of Bumiputera students are enrolled in TVET, compared to 4% of Indians and 1% of Chinese (Khazanah Research Institute 2018). Preferential admissions to university have also continually played a role in facilitating degree-level attainment.

Enrolment and attainment

From various sources, we can assemble images of affirmative action progress over time, or at least a current snapshot of extensive operations. The racial distribution of educational enrolment – the key indicator of interest – has not been disclosed regularly and completely.

Secondary and post-secondary programmes have continuously promoted upward educational mobility:

- The MARA Junior Science Colleges (MRSM), 100% Bumiputera until 2000, when a 90:10 Bumiputera to non-Bumiputera quota was introduced, saw enrolment increase from 3,470 in 1980, 10,900 in 1990, 15,400 in 2000 to 30,000 in 2009, as reported in the *Malaysia Plans* (Malaysia 1986, 1991, 2006a, 2010b). The latest figure indicates a plateauing in MRSM enrolment, with 29,100 in 2018 (Education Planning and Research Division 2018).
- Pre-university programmes, including matriculation and foundation, which in parallel with MRSMs applied a 90:10 apportionment in 2003, grew from 2,000 in 1980 to 9,000 in 1990, then burgeoned further to 28,700 in 2000 and 34,400 in 2009 (Malaysia 1986, 1991, 2006a, 2010b).[1] These enrolment figures have not been tallied in subsequent development plans, but available sources generate a compatible estimate of 36,200 for 2017, comprised of 22,700 in matriculation colleges (Education Planning and Research Division 2018) and 13,500 in university-run foundation programmes.[2]
- MARA operates various other programmes, particularly in technical and vocational education. Data on change over time are difficult to obtain, but it is fair to surmise that the programmes have been substantially sustained or increased through the past decades. For example, GiatMARA offers training at 231 centres, with an intake of 21,700, while MARA Skills Institutes and MARA High Skills Colleges have over the years reportedly produced 6,073 graduates. Universiti Kuala Lumpur, providing degree level technical education, conferred degrees or diplomas on 5,961 graduates. MARA also maintains six Professional Colleges (Lee 2017a).

Matriculation and foundation programmes have in recent decades crucially facilitated Bumiputera entry to higher education, but the quality and rigor of these pre-university fast tracks are questionable. The preferential component directly benefits Bumiputera students through the 90% enrolment quota. Matriculation graduates subsequently enjoy better prospects of university admissions, compared to holders of the STPM higher education certificate, the main pathway for non-Bumiputeras. In 2019, among STPM graduates, 24,375 were admitted to a university, or 73.4% of the total 33,197. In contrast, 20,269 out of 20,907 matriculation graduates, 96.9% of the total, were offered a place in public universities.[3] For the 2018–2019 intake, STPM graduates made up 54.6%, while matriculation students made up 45.4% of intake into public universities. Studies have found that students from matriculation colleges underperform in terms of academic ability relative to those obtaining comparable grades in the Malaysian Higher Education Certificate (STPM), the predominant passage for non-Bumiputeras to apply for university admission (Othman *et al.* 2009). Wan and Cheo (2012) also find differentials in the scholastic ability of STPM and matriculation university entrants.

The labelling of university admissions as "meritocracy," with academic grades and points for extra-curricular activities as the entry criteria, thus displacing racial quotas, is illusory and effectively compounds a deficient system. The emotionally empowering notion that Bumiputera elevation to university is based purely on merit not only overlooks or denies the quality disparities between the programmes that render their equivalence false and misleading, but also precludes attention to Bumiputera capability development in the education sphere. The scarce 10% non-Bumiputera quota also induces competition to pursue matriculation colleges – and disappointment among high-achieving students who are not offered a place. I discuss this issue at greater length in a later section on distribution of education opportunity.

The primary objective of increasing Bumiputera representation in higher education calls for evaluation of the racial composition. Chapter 4 traced out the rise in the Bumiputera proportion of enrolment, most pertinently at the degree level, where preferential treatment is more pronounced and consequential. The group's share of university enrolment rose from 40% in 1970 to 67% in 1985, as reported in the *Fourth Malaysia Plan* and *Fifth Malaysia Plan* (Malaysia 1981, 1986). The practice of reporting these statistics, however, was abruptly stopped – even while racial distribution of employment and equity ownership continued.

Nonetheless, a series can be cobbled together from the literature. Referencing the Second National Economic Consultative Council's report, the Bumiputera share of degree-level enrolment was reported at 66% in 1990 and 70% in 1995 (Khoo 2005). A similar figure of 69% was reported for 2002 (Santhiram and Sua 2017). These figures suggest a plateauing of Bumiputera representation in universities – at a level not far off the national demographics. However, more complete sources have indicated a continually rising Bumiputera proportion of total enrolment. Mukherjee *et al.* (2017) report that the group's share at the degree level was 81.8% in 2005 and rose further to 83.1% in 2008. For degree, diploma and certificate programmes combined, Bumiputeras consistently constituted 84–85% in 2005–2008. The study's provision of the gross total enrolment numbers, and direct data sourcing from the Ministry of Education, lend credibility to this distributional portrait of higher education.

The effect of affirmative action is undeniable; besides the 90% Bumiputera matriculation quota discussed earlier, various fully reserved programmes have continually expanded. The upgrading of Bumiputera-exclusive MARA Institute of Technology to Universiti Teknologi MARA (UiTM) in 1999 bolstered the institute's capacity to produce degree-level graduates. In 2018, UiTM enrolled 165,600 out of a total 538,600 in the public university system (Education Planning and Research Division 2018).

It is common knowledge that racial and ethnic composition varies across public institutions – a continuation of patterns empirically reported in the past (Malaysia 1981, 1986). Student bodies remain more diverse at the older, comprehensive and urban-based Universiti Malaya, Universiti Sains Malaysia and Universiti Kebangsaan Malaysia (national university). Various newer universities, while not reserved like UiTM, are predominantly Bumiputera in enrolment.

Reports on Bumiputera participation within study disciplines, in which massive racial disparities stood out at the onset of the NEP (Chapter 4), have not been found in this study's literature search. Nonetheless, it is safe to presume that Bumiputera students have steadily increased their presence across the board, including in the scientific, technical, engineering and professional fields where they were formerly conspicuously under-represented. At the same time, concerns remain over persistent academic achievement gaps at the point of graduation and relative concentration in social sciences and humanities, which may curtail employment prospects of fresh graduates.

Labour force statistics trace out the expansion of higher education across time, and differentials between races, shedding light on affirmative action's effects on attaining academic certificates (Figure 7.1). Malaysia enhanced its workforce profile; the share with tertiary education – holding a certificate, diploma or degree – increased across the board. The statistics also reflect the effects of affirmative action: the increase was most rapid for the Malay population which, post-2000, exceeded all other groups. In 2013, the latest year that official statistics disaggregate Malays and non-Malay Bumiputeras, Malay attainment of formal qualifications is highest of all, followed by Chinese and Indian by slight margins, and non-Malay Bumiputeras by a conspicuously wide margin. Tertiary education

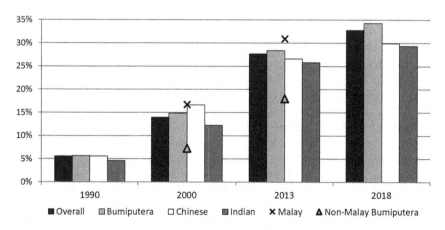

Figure 7.1 Malaysia: Share of labour force with tertiary education, by race and ethnicity, 1990, 2000, 2013

Source: Department of Statistics (Malaysia) (1990, 2000, 2013a).

Note: The last year these data were differentiated by ethnicity was 2013.

opportunities have expanded, but disparities within the Bumiputera population persist, particularly with non-Malay indigenous groups lagging.

Non-Bumiputera access weighs heavily as a socio-economic and political issue. Perceptions of unfair opportunity arguably bear greater consequence in higher education compared to the other policy sectors of employment, enterprise development and wealth ownership. Public higher education opportunity resonates especially among Chinese, Indian and other minorities, in contrast to primary and secondary schooling where clearer social bargains have provided equitable educational access and cultural-linguistic expression. Additionally, the stakes are high, due to the potential upward mobility and economic benefits of holding university-level qualifications, compounded over many years by the lack of private institutions – unlike the employment sphere, where private sector alternatives to the public sector have perennially existed.

The burden of private higher education weighed heavily, especially before the mid-1990s. Up until then, students not admitted to the limited spaces in Malaysia's public universities, or not getting offers to their preferred field of study, pursued higher education options that involved overseas universities – either for the entirety of the programme or for part of it, through credit transfers or partnerships between foreign universities and local colleges. Presumably, many of these were non-Bumiputeras with adequate academic qualifications and solid chances of getting admission to the public system if not for racial quotas and preferences.

The mid-1990s ushered in a sea of change. Public tertiary education burgeoned; institutions were rapidly established in every state of Malaysia; university colleges were upgraded to university status. Private tertiary education institutions expanded under the Private Higher Education Institutions Act of 1996, which permitted domestic private for-profit degree-granting universities. Those who could afford the private institutions' fees had a backup in the event of non-admission to the public institutions. Increasingly, many would opt out of the public tertiary system altogether and set out on a private education trajectory of private pre-university programmes upon completion of secondary school. The option of student loans, through the National Higher Education Loan Programme (PTPTN) established in 1997, has also enhanced accessibility of private higher education.

By 2000, private institutions accounted for 45% of the national tertiary student population and marginally increased that proportion over the next half decade. At the degree level, however, the share of private institutions in total enrolment rose considerably, from 24% to 31% during 2000–2005. Tertiary institutions proliferated such that by 2005, Malaysia had 11 private universities (alongside 11 public universities), 11 university colleges (compared to 6 in the public system) and 5 branch campuses of foreign universities. The number of private colleges swelled to 632 in 2000, then settled back at 532 in 2005, reflecting fast – and somewhat reckless – growth (Malaysia 2006a).[4] The number of Malaysians studying abroad remains substantial, but it has dwindled as opportunities to obtain degrees domestically have grown.[5] In 2017, public higher education institutions accounted for 50.9% of total enrolment of 1.21 million, 27.2% of certificate and diploma (total 409,700) and 53.7% of degree level undergraduate, postgraduate and professional programmes (total 795,500).[6]

The expansion of private higher education has played a crucial compensatory and complementary role within Malaysia's continuing affirmative action regime. Nevertheless, public university entry remains a major policy issue, with continual need to balance equitable representation, academic merit and the overall capability development through attending university and graduating with skills and qualifications. The illusory meritocracy in admissions, due to the 90% Bumiputera quota in matriculation programmes, undermines the pursuit of excellence and fair opportunity. Undeniably, the imperative of maintaining Bumiputera higher education access demands that policy reforms cannot abruptly reduce the majority group's representation; steady and constructive transitions are required. These issues were rekindled in the wake of the 2018 general elections, in which the winning Pakatan Harapan coalition promised to recognize the Unified Examination Certificate (UEC) conferred by independent Chinese secondary schools, which is accepted for university admissions in private sector and outside of Malaysia but not in public universities within. The government also made a one-off offer of 1,000 places to B40 Chinese students and eventually increased the overall enrolment of matriculation colleges while retaining the 90–10 Bumiputera-non-Bumiputera quota, as a concession to pressures for non-Bumiputera access to the prized pre-university programme (Lee 2019). This move, however, merely postpones the government's reckoning with the dilemma of preferential treatment and fair opportunity.

This 90–10 breakdown applies as well to MRSM enrolment, with a varied result in that the 10% non-Bumiputera quota has been undersubscribed. This outcome underscores the need for more systematic approaches beyond altering racial quotas, toward the goal of diversifying enrolments and safeguarding equitable access to education. News reports show uneven take-up of the non-Bumiputera quota, with only 70% (7% out of the 10%) filled in 2004. In 2008, non-Bumiputeras comprised almost 12% of the total, only to see their participation fall precipitously to 1% in 2018. However, subsequent to the 2018 general elections, interest appears to have picked up, with up to 8% of the 10% taken.[7] This unevenness suggests that the solution rests not simply in setting racial quotas, but also in addressing location, compatibility and educational prospects – and public trust.

Contentions have also intermittently arisen over the award of public services department (PSD) scholarships, which unlike other scholarships reserved for Bumiputeras, are open to non-Bumiputeras and have faced scrutiny from time to time. As with university enrolment, a formal written policy has not been traced, nor official declarations publicly recorded, but it is believed that a 55:45 Bumiputera to non-Bumiputera has been in effect, and in the 2000s attention was given to non-Bumiputera opportunities to win these scholarships, especially to study overseas. The PSD scheme also apportioned some scholarships to be awarded through open competition, and some according to ethnic quotas, with provision also for East Malaysian Bumiputeras and the socially disadvantaged (Wan 2010).[8]

Data on the distribution of scholarships are exceedingly scarce; most of these public disclosures happen through parliamentary proceedings. In 2009–2011, out of an average of 1,780 scholarships per year, 56.6% were awarded to Bumiputeras and 43.4% to non-Bumiputeras. However, sponsorship for studying abroad abruptly shrank to 300 in 2012, and the Bumiputera share also rose slightly to 60%.[9] In subsequent years, funding for study abroad was steeply reduced, falling in 2016 to 20 for the very top students to go anywhere, and 200 for study in countries with lower tuition fees, specifically Japan, South Korea, Germany and France. The model of sponsorship also shifted to loans convertible to grants upon averaging high scores in university.[10] Public scholarships have increasingly facilitated enrolment in domestic universities, and the racial-proportions scholars strikingly contrast overseas counterparts. Of the 58,500 PSD scholarships awarded for domestic study in 2000–2008, 12.7% went to non-Bumiputeras overall. The share did rise from 9.2% in 2000–2002 to 17.5% in 2006–2008 (Mukherjee *et al.* 2017). More recent data are not available, but the occasional public grievance of minority group members who perceive unfair opportunity, although perhaps less vociferous than in the past, reflect continuing dilemmas. Affirmative action in Malaysia in the future will need to address contending interests in education sponsorship and strike an amenable balance.

A general point must be registered here: Malaysia's education system has, from the inception of many higher education institutions and through legislation controlling academic thought and partisan allegiance for many decades, overtly maintained political interests – not just of the Bumiputera agenda but of UMNO/BN regime maintenance specifically. The utilization of admissions and sponsorship as tools of political patronage, and placement of institutions in political constituencies, is strikingly demonstrated in the *Jelajah* (explore) scheme, in which members of parliament handed out admissions offers at constituency outreach ceremonies (Lee 2017a). While the practical and psychological effects are difficult to prove empirically, such acts that make recipients politically beholden must have adverse effects on independent, critical and innovative thought.

Graduate employment and labour market mobility

Affirmative action in higher education seeks to equip beneficiaries to gain employment more capably, robustly and self-sufficiently. The transition of graduates to the labour market to a meaningful extent reflects the qualitative side of the policy, which is increasingly crucial to the efficacy of affirmative action, given that Malaysia has attained mass access to higher education. Serious questions over the quality of tertiary education have arisen in the past decade, especially with growing concern over graduate unemployment and its disproportionate incidence among Bumiputeras.

Differentials in unemployment to an extent reflect varying capacity of graduates to participate in the labour market. Labour force statistics shed some light by allowing us to observe unemployment rates based on educational attainment (Table 7.1). Most germane to affirmative action is the time trend, within the

Table 7.1 Malaysia: Unemployment rates within race group, by highest education; 1995, 2007 and 2013

	Overall Malaysia			Bumiputera			Chinese			Indian		
	1995	2007	2013	1995	2007	2013	1995	2007	2013	1995	2007	2013
Primary	1.7	2.2	1.9	2.7	2.6	1.9	0.8	1.6	1.5	1.5	2.8	2.0
Secondary	4.0	3.6	3.4	6.0	4.1	3.5	1.7	2.5	2.8	3.2	4.3	4.4
Tertiary	3.1	3.9	3.9	3.8	4.8	4.4	2.3	2.2	2.8	2.6	4.0	3.5
Overall	3.1	3.4	3.4	4.6	3.9	3.5	1.5	2.2	2.6	2.6	4.0	3.9

Source: Author's calculations from Department of Statistics (1995, 2007, 2013a).

Table 7.2 Malaysia: Unemployment rate within Bumiputera, 2007 and 2013

	2007		2013	
	Malay	Non-Malay Bumiputera	Malay	Non-Malay Bumiputera
Primary	2.1	3.9	1.5	2.6
Secondary	3.6	6.8	3.0	6.2
Tertiary	4.3	9.5	3.8	8.0
Overall	3.5	5.8	3.1	5.5

Source: Author's calculations from Department of Statistics (2007, 2013a).

tertiary qualified labour force, of Bumiputeras consistently registering higher unemployment rates. Malay and non-Malay Bumiputera differentials also persist, with the latter consistently registering higher unemployment, even those attaining tertiary education (Table 7.2). Concern with youth unemployment tends to give disproportionate attention to university graduates, but diploma and certificate holders – included in these data, which aggregated all levels of tertiary education – also encounter difficulties securing jobs. Interestingly, Bumiputeras with secondary-level qualifications have lower unemployment compared to Indian counterparts in 2007 and 2013.

These patterns concur with the perspective that group-preferential treatment, which is most salient at the tertiary level, probably under-equips the average beneficiary for labour force participation. The higher levels of Indian unemployment within the secondary-qualified workforce, converse to the pattern at for tertiary-qualified workers, somewhat reinforce this point. The situation has induced government intervention, through special programmes to enhance employability of fresh graduates, most prominently the graduates training scheme SL1M (*Skim Latihan Graduan 1Malaysia*), with a focus on language and soft skills. The programme has been predominantly executed by government-linked companies since its launch in 2011,[11] and it was rebranded and reconfigured as Professional Training & Education for Growing Entrepreneurs (PROTÉGÉ) in 2019. While not designated for a particular group, Bumiputera fresh graduates have comprised the vast majority of participants.

Large-sample labour market data that directly include racial identity are almost entirely absent. However, we can make a few deductions on tertiary education outcomes based on firm-level surveys. The World Bank's (2005) survey of employers and employees, sampling 902 firms in Peninsular Malaysia, reported managers' assessments that lack of capable university graduates constitutes the most severe constraint on higher technological investment. Employees' assessment of their most lacking skill for performing their job competently ranked English proficiency first (47%), far ahead of professional and technical skills (14%), the second major deficiency. This self-appraised lack of English language deficiency was found to be more acute on the Malay-dominant East Coast, where the population is predominantly Malay.

We may deduce from these findings that Malay, as well as non-Malay Bumiputera, graduates are more likely to face difficulty securing employment in professional occupations. This World Bank (2005) survey conducted in 2003, and a follow-up four years later, found that about one-third of respondents regard Malaysians trained abroad to be more competent and capable than Malaysians trained locally (World Bank 2009). Other surveys obtain similar results. Jobstreet, the noted employment portal, asked managers to rank the reasons for not recruiting fresh graduates. Of 3,800 respondents, the most widely cited factor, again, was poor command of English – a disadvantage that is presumably more widespread among graduates of Malaysia's Malay-medium public universities (Jobstreet 2005).

Interview selection processes, the first stage of labour market participation, also shed light on perceived quality differentials between Malay and non-Malay fresh university graduates. Lee and Khalid (2016) conducted a field experiment – a correspondence study – on racial discrimination by sending fictitious résumés of comparably qualified Malay and Chinese fresh graduates to actual job openings and observing whether one group got called for interview significantly more than the other. Call-back differentials reflect racial discriminatory practices.[12] The study finds a high magnitude of bias favouring Chinese applicants over comparably qualified Malays. However, the results do not merely signify prejudice, bigotry and more blatant manifestations of racist attitudes. Various inter-related factors can be posited as plausible explanations for the findings, including cultural and lingual compatibility (many firms are Chinese-owned SMEs), negative perceptions or past experiences of Malay/Bumiputera graduates or expectations that well-qualified Malay graduates will be attracted to work in government or GLCs, where their prospects might be better than at a private firm.

The relative concentration of graduates in private versus public sectors provides some insight into their relative mobility and capacity to secure employment, with the assumption that recruitment, retention and promotion processes are more open and competitive in the private sector. This is obviously a generalization, especially following on the research showing that private sectors extend preferential treatment to Chinese job applicants over comparably qualified Malays

Table 7.3 Malaysia: Bumiputera and non-Bumiputera proportions of tertiary-educated managers and professionals, by sector (public versus private), 2000

Total employed	Bumiputera	Non-Bumiputera	Total
	58.0	42.0	100
Public sector managers	85.0	15.0	100
Private sector managers	40.9	59.1	100
Public sector professionals	80.3	19.7	100
Private sector professionals	43.9	56.1	100

Source: Lee (2012).

and they may do so to counterbalance the Malay preferential treatment in the public sector (Lee and Khalid 2016). The 2000 Population Census disaggregates degree holders by degree type and employed persons by sector, permitting analysis of employment patterns by race, sector and educational qualification (the 2010 census has not been availed for research). As reported by Lee (2012), Bumiputera professionals and managers are concentrated in the public sector – and this applies to all graduates, whether of local or foreign universities, who are more highly regarded by employers in general (Table 7.3).

Graduate tracer studies, which are mandatory and conducted throughout the higher education sector, are a potentially rich data source on labour market entry experiences. An official report from the 2018 graduate tracer surveys does not disaggregate by race, but it shows stark contrasts between public and private university graduates that we can safely presume to still broadly correlate with race (Ministry of Education 2019). Among public university graduates, 28.1% worked in the public sector (government GLC, statutory body), 58.2% in the private sector (domestic firms and MNCs) and 13.7% in NGOs. Private university graduates are distributed across sectors as follows: 11.9% public sector, 73.3% private sector, 14.9% NGOs.

Another aspect of the graduation-to-work transition is the option of self-employment and start-ups, which is systemic in scope, but has also been addressed through Bumiputera agencies targeting Bumiputera young adults. UiTM operates a number of entrepreneurial training modules and programmes, which aimed to groom 4,500 entrepreneurs over the period 2016–2020. About 1,480 graduated from this programme in 2017 (SME Corp 2018). The incubator programme operated by GiatMARA technical colleges reportedly developed 1,730 entrepreneurs during the *Tenth Malaysia Plan* 2011–2015 (Malaysia 2015, 3–5). The efficacy of these programmes remains under-researched, but disclosures so far indicate small and incipient steps.

Inter-generational upward mobility

The distribution of higher-education opportunity within the Bumiputera population – specifically, the extent to which disadvantaged households benefit and attain inter-generational upward mobility – has been consistently, albeit rather ambiguously, interwoven with affirmative action in Malaysia. The integration of socio-economic background into the selection of policy beneficiaries has not followed clearly articulated and officially sanctioned policy. Certain programmes (notably, residential schools and micro and small business support) target rural and/or low-income households, but there is no cited official policy document stipulating these criteria. Likewise, empirical inquiry into the income or class profile of affirmative action beneficiaries is quite scant. However, two substantial policy interventions provide reference points for tracing out policy practices across time: MARA Junior Science College (MRSM) enrolment, and university scholarships and admissions.

MRSMs are highly pertinent because these residential colleges were formally designated to serve poor households, especially rural residents. They have also been recurrently faulted for deviating from this initial mission. In the mid-1970s, children of urban middle class households reportedly constituted 63% of the MRSM student body (Selvaratnam 1988, 191). The perception that middle-class and privileged Malays have taken disproportionately large share of spaces in MRSMs has persisted, albeit more anecdotal accounts than empirical evidence. Mounting attention to the B40 in recent years has come to bear on the award of MRSM places. In the 2010s, admissions decisions gave priority to excelling students from low-income families and rural residents, without a specified quota.[13] The PH government intensified this B40 emphasis, setting a 65% target for MRSM enrolment in 2018. This was duly met, with the share of B40 students among the 11,000 newly enrolled – 6,600 entering at secondary school form one (year 7) and 4,500 entering at form four (year 10) – rising from 44% in 2018 to 68% in 2019. The share of the M40 and T20 in 2018 were evenly split at 28% apiece.[14]

This pattern likely ensues from merit-based selection, in which T20 candidates are advantaged and thus over-represented, but it also mirrors another problem of the M40 potentially being squeezed out. On the class-based distribution of government scholarships, research has found that the allocation of university scholarships lacked outreach to the poor. Mehmet and Yip's (1985) widely cited survey, conducted at the 1982–1983 graduation ceremonies and capturing 45% of the five domestic universities' graduating cohort, found the distribution of scholarships skewed towards children of high-income families in general, but more markedly among Malays. They found that, while families earning above MYR1,000 per month constituted 10.3% of the national population, 25.5% of scholarships were awarded to students in this category. Within the Malay community, this top income bracket constituted 4.9% of the population, but 22.9% of scholars.

Newer research is scarce, but it is safe to maintain that a substantial share of Bumiputera scholarships has continually accrued to middle- and upper-class households. Ball and Chik's (2001) survey of Bumiputera scholars in the late 1990s offers some information – specifically of returnees from studies abroad. They characterize the distribution as following a "slightly regressive" pattern, with respect to family socio-economic status, household income and parents' education. At the same time, a somewhat high 58% of scholars had fathers who only attained primary schooling, reflecting considerable inter-generational mobility. These findings are unsurprising, given the mass provision of secondary education and burgeoning access to tertiary education for lower-income households, although the study's small sample size calls for circumspection.[15] The class profile of government scholarships remains largely undisclosed in official documents and under-researched in more recent times. However, it is plausible that the distribution is not as upwardly skewed as older studies found, due to broadening access to secondary schooling, which has expanded the talent pool applying for scholarships, as well as increased options for other scholarships and self-financing for overseas university education among high-income households of all groups, including Bumiputeras.

Similarly, more recent reports on university enrolment indicate considerable proportionality in the class profile of university enrolment. In 2010, 60% of public higher education graduates came from households with MYR2,000 or less income per month; 47% of counterparts in private institutions (Russayani *et al.* 2013). For reference, 33.4% of Malaysia's households received monthly income below MYR2,000 (Malaysia 2010b). The University of Malaya disclosed that almost half – precisely 46% in May 2019 – of its undergraduate population are from the B40 segment and 12% from a "lowest income" category, with 32% from the M40 and 10% from the T20.[16] Providing a rare insight to the interface of class and race, Khalid's (2018) report of a social mobility study – based on respondents' recollection of their parents' socio-economic status – painted portraits of substantial inter-generational education mobility, measured in terms of the subsequent generation attaining a higher tier of education (among the three, primary/secondary/tertiary). This was obtained for all, with Bumiputera on par with Chinese, though Indian households slightly lagged. The study also noted the contribution of public scholarships, in that recipients, relative to non-recipients, are four times more likely to attain tertiary education.

Yayasan Peneraju Pendidikan Bumiputera (YPPB), which specifically targets youth from challenging backgrounds for financial assistance and mentoring in technical and vocational programmes, merits a brief mention. In the first few years of its operations (2012–2016), YPPB helped 14,000 students get enrolled and disbursed MYR260 million in grants. Its mission and operational strengths warrant consideration for expansion and replication – for Bumiputera empowerment to more effectively facilitate inter-generational upward mobility – and for extension to a broader base, particularly the Indian community.

High-level occupations

To track the policy of promoting Bumiputera upward-employment mobility, public documents have reported statistics showing racial representation by occupation groups. We can observe a few patterns from 1970 to 2013, focusing on high-level occupations which are the principal targets of affirmative action. Figure 7.2 presents occupational group profiles derived from labour force surveys

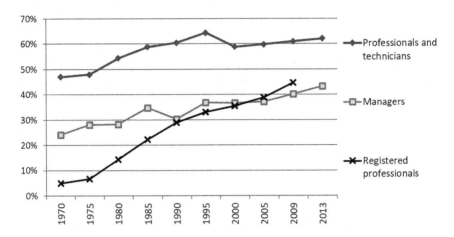

Figure 7.2 Malaysia: Bumiputera representation in high-level occupations, 1970–2013
Sources: Malaysia (1971, 1981, 1986, 1991, 1996, 2006a), Department of Statistics (2009, 2013a).
Notes: 1970 and 1975 for Peninsula only; occupational classifications changed in 1980 and 2000.

and professional association membership rolls. We should note modifications to Malaysia's occupation classification system in 2000 likely account for the disjuncture observed before and after that year, particularly in the professional and technician categories. Labour force survey data show Bumiputeras steadily increasing their presence in professional and technical positions in the 1970s and 1980s, but progress slowed down from the 1990s through the 2000s, captured in the flatter slope. These figures encompass public and private sectors and include teachers (in the professionals category) and nurses and skilled health workers (in the technicians category).[17]

Professional association rolls, another empirical reference, similarly chart a rising Bumiputera share of registered members, more steeply from 1970 to 1990 and more gradually thereafter. This data mainly cover the private sector, and the patterns vary across occupations. While the overall picture is one of slowing Bumiputera mobility into professional organizations from the 1990s, the pace has been sustained in a few categories – in particular, architects, dentists and lawyers. The underlying causes of the slowdown in Bumiputera entry have not been rigorously examined. We may posit a few plausible factors related to education policy in general, and affirmative action in particular. Systemic issues concerning quality and employability of graduates, including the shortage of capable engineers highlighted in firm-level surveys, may translate into more acute Bumiputera under-representation in certain fields. Given the pre-requisite of tertiary-level qualifications and industry certification in various sectors, it is also possible that waning preference for professional study programmes has constrained mobility into professional occupations.

The shortfall is most pronounced at management level. This is intertwined with the enterprise development and ownership policy spheres – in sum, the programme of developing an independent Bumiputera Commercial and Industrial Community (BCIC). Statistics on the racial profile of managers reflect relatively slow and inconsistent progress. From 1970 to 1995, Bumiputera representation in management had increased gradually, but remained static over 1995–2005, before rising again until 2013.

How have these developments been manifested inter-generationally? Akin to the educational mobility referenced earlier, successive generations have also moved up occupationally. Khalid (2018) cross-tabulates the occupational skill level – in three tiers, low, middle and high – of parents and children. The majority of children whose parents worked in low-skill and middle-skill jobs graduate to work in middle-skill and high-skill jobs; this upward mobility was highest among Chinese, followed quite closely by Bumiputeras, with Indians further behind, particularly in showing a lower share of the successive generation becoming high-skilled workers. Indian children of high-skilled working parents, however, are the most likely among the three groups to also attain high-skill jobs, while Bumiputeras in the parallel situation are more likely to move downward to middle-skill jobs. We may deduce that affirmative action has impacted on this process, but arguably with less than desired efficacy in terms of inculcating self-reliance and self-confidence among beneficiaries.

Sectoral distribution: public sector and private sector

Malaysia's promotion of Bumiputera occupational advancement operated predominantly in the public sector, as well as government-controlled entities. Undeniably, Bumiputeras have advanced within private sector entities, but the public sector has demonstrably played an instrumental role in fostering Malay upward mobility and raising a Malay middle class, during and beyond the NEP (Embong 1996; Torii 2003; Abdul Aziz 2012). This policy sphere basically applies to the public sector and GLCs, given the absence of regulation in private sector employment, except for broad indication of preference for companies with Bumiputera employees in public procurement. The public sector and "G20" top GLCs employ 1.6 million and 225,000 Malaysians, respectively, accounting for about 15% of total employment of citizens. Malay quotas of between 75–80% have been reported for specific ranks of officials, mostly in authoritative corps, such as the Administrative and Diplomatic Service (PTD), police, judicial and legal services, and customs services. These would constitute less than 15% of the public service employment. There are no specific quotas for professional and technical services, but non-codified race preference is clearly practiced (Lim 2013).

As noted in Chapter 4, rapid expansion of employment in government in the 1970s and 1980s, amid an urbanizing and increasingly educated population, substantially absorbed the burgeoning Bumiputera labour supply. Employment trends of recent decades reflect continuing dependence of affirmative action on government employment. The public sector's share of employment expanded between 2000 and 2005, from 10.4% to 11.3%, and by a greater margin among management and professional occupations – from 11.3% to 17.0%. In 2005, 52.5% of Bumiputera professionals, compared to about 22.4% of Chinese professionals and 30.8% of Indian professionals, worked as teachers and lecturers, predominantly in government.[18] One of the steps taken to solve the unemployed graduate problem in the early to mid-2000s was to intensify public sector hiring. The education ministry contributed massively to the net increase in public sector employment at managerial and professional levels – accounting for 89.5% in 1996–2000 and 74.5% in 2000–2005.

The implementation of quotas and biases has been less overt – compared to education quotas, for instance – and over time effectively self-reproducing, as non-Bumiputeras have withdrawn from the public sector and its increasing Bumiputera homogenization renders group preferences largely redundant. As widely known and observed anecdotally, but scantly documented empirically, the racial composition of the public sector reflects general predilections and perceived career prospects. The Bumiputera share of public sector employment was reported at 76.9% in 1999 (Khoo 2005, 19) and 84.8% in 2005 (MCA 2006, 4). Lee (2012) finds higher proportions of Bumiputera managers and professionals in the public sector, based on the 2000 Population Census. Bumiputera graduates of overseas universities are also more likely to work in government – due to a plausible range of factors, including obligation to fulfil scholarship bonds, but also a combination of security and career prospects. The issue should not be simplistically reduced to overt preferential treatment and quotas; the major race groups vary in inclination toward seeking public sector employment. Woo's (2016) survey of university students confirms differences in predilections and perceptions, with Malay respondents indicating more positive disposition towards public sector careers, and higher propensity to seek employment there. Similarly, Khazanah Research Institute's (2018) nationally representative survey of tertiary-level students found substantial differences: 30% of Bumiputeras declare a preference to work in government, slightly above Indians (26%) and starkly more than Chinese (9%). Interestingly, matching shares within all three groups – 25% of Chinese and Indians, 22% of Bumiputeras – prefer to start their own business.

Sabah and Sarawak indigenous peoples are particularly aggrieved about Malay dominance in the civil service. The political elite of these states have continuously voiced dissatisfaction at recurrent appointments of non-Sarawakian and non-Sabahan natives, especially Peninsular Malays, into top government positions.[19] This problem is multi-layered, in light of the indigenous peoples' Bumiputera status and the terms of the Malaysia agreement which grant elements of autonomy to Sabah and Sarawak. The complexities notwithstanding, moving forward will require intentional and constructive solutions.

To be fair, the government has expressed some concern toward the under-representation of non-Malays in the public sector; the Government Transformation Programme commits to racial representativeness in the First GTP Roadmap, covering 2010–2012 (Pemandu 2010, 2012). Despite the GTP Roadmap 2.0 being more reticent on this front, we can observe some efforts toward diversifying the government workforce, although wide disproportionalities persist. From 1980 to 2003, Chinese representation in the civil service fell from 29.7% to 8.2%, while that of Indians declined from 9.8% to 5.2%. Applications for jobs by non-Bumiputera have dwindled over time to miniscule proportions. In 2006, 1.8% of applications were from Chinese, and 2.5 % from Indians.[20] Reports show further decline in non-Malay ethnic representation; in 2014, Chinese comprised 5.2% of the civil service, and Indians 4.1%.[21] At the same time, the public services draw a small but relatively well-qualified stream of Chinese applicants. The share of Malay, Chinese and Indian among recruits in 2008 was 78.6%, 4.4% and 4.5%; in 2011: 71.0%, 8.0% and 5.4% (Woo 2015). In 2015, Chinese comprised 1.7% of total applicants, but 4.1% of total appointments.[22]

Employment in GLCs reflects their adherence to Bumiputera empowerment, although the resulting profile is less disproportionate compared to the bureaucracy. The workforce composition of the G20 top GLCs is 79% Bumiputera, 10% Chinese, 8% Indian, and 3% others, on the whole, and in executive positions, 73% Bumiputera, 19% Chinese, 6% Indian, and 2% others (PCG 2015). However, the topmost CEO positions are predominantly, if not exclusively, held by Bumiputeras. GLCs, accounting for an estimated five percent of the employed population, are somewhat limited in their numerical impact on Bumiputera representation at the national level. Nonetheless, they play significant signalling and demonstration roles, projecting Bumiputera corporate leadership and taking the lead on policy initiatives such as promoting women in boards and management.

Enterprise development

Evaluating Malaysia's endeavours to develop Bumiputera enterprise is as multifaceted as the array of programmes that have pursued this agenda. This policy sphere operated for decades, from the 1970s in into the 2010s under the aegis of the Bumiputera Commercial and Industrial Community (BCIC). In the aftermath of the Asian financial crisis, which saw the implosion of Malaysia's gigantic privatization exercise and creation of Bumiputera capitalists and rapid expansion into business, this agenda was comprehensively reset. From a priority on heavy industries, privatization and large corporations and conglomerates under Mahathir Mohamad (prime minister from 1981 to 2003), his successor Ahmad Badawi (2003–2009) channelled more attention to SMEs and initiated the GLC Transformation Programme (Chin and Teh 2017). Subsequently, Najib Razak (2009–2018) launched the Bumiputera Economic Transformation Programme in 2011. Throughout these shifts in the overarching theme and relative emphases, and introduction of new programmes, many embedded policies and programmes have continued to operate essentially unchanged. Around 2015, the agenda was rebranded the Bumiputera Economic Community (BEC), with some attempt to broaden the scope beyond business and entrepreneurship, but this policy sphere continually predominated within the BEC.

This section considers contemporary policy achievements and shortcomings arranged according to the three main policy instruments: public procurement, government-linked companies, and loans, grants and training. Within each section, I evaluate the scale and profile of operations, and where possible, track the growth over time, and consider the policies' achievements in promoting capability and competitiveness.

Public procurement

Malaysia's public procurement system is a heavyweight within Malaysia's affirmative action regime, owing to the magnitude of rents disbursed and the direct control of the state. Government construction projects awarded to local contractors amounted to MYR23.8 billion in 2015 and MYR41.4 billion in 2016 (CIDB online data). The number of contractors grew from about 2,000 contractors in 1972 to 41,000 by 2010. The system promotes Bumiputera firms in construction and services-based operations, through reservation of contracts in the smallest category (class G1, formerly F) and price handicaps and other preferential terms for larger categories, with the largest contracts formally subjected to fully open tender. Class F has obviously been the focal point, due to the reservation policy; indeed, three quarters of all Bumiputera contractors are in this smallest class. Unsurprisingly, it has also seen surges of growth, notably in the early 2000s. In 2002–2003, 14,700 class F contractors were registered, in response to government allocations of small projects in parliamentary constituencies.[23] Accordingly, amid federal budget tightening, the number of G1 contractors shrank, reportedly to 23,000 in mid-2018. However, Malay contractors retain political clout, as demonstrated by assurances that the reservation policy will remain under the newly elected Pakatan Harapan government in 2018, the first non-UMNO-led coalition to hold federal power (Lee 2018). True to form, the 2020 Federal Budget speech announced the registration of 946 new G1 contractors within the month of September 2019, nonchalantly adding that "existing and new registered contractors will get to bid for government jobs" (Lim 2019). No attempt was made to invigorate the procurement system.

In terms of breadth of participation, public procurement mainly affects SMEs; hence it is pertinent to provide statistics on the overarching picture. In 2010, SMEs contributed to around 30% of Malaysia's GDP, while Bumiputera SMEs contributed only 13%. The government targeted raising this share to 20% in 2020 (Pemandu 2011, 226). Bumiputera-controlled companies also accounted for 25% of the 800,000 registered companies in Malaysia around 2010 (Teraju 2012, 56). Bumiputera SMEs have continuously comprised a minority among total establishments, with a slight increase in the past decade, but a persistently high concentration of micro and small operations. Bumiputera SMEs accounted for 38.4% of Malaysian-owned SMEs in 2005 (247,900 out of 645,100); this share increased to 40.6% in 2015 (357,800 out of 877,700). The proportion that are small-scale increased, but that of medium-scale remained miniscule. Among Bumiputera SMEs, 88.3% were classified as micro, 10.5% small, 1.2% medium in 2005, and 83.5% micro, 15.1% small, 1.4% medium in 2015. For comparison, among non-Bumiputera SMEs in 2005, 69.9% were micro, 25.9% small, 4.3% medium (data are not available for 2015).[24]

We can crudely estimate the prevalence of public procurement among Bumiputera enterprises by juxtaposing the number of registered small Bumiputera contractors against the "small" scale enterprises, omitting those classified as micro, under the assumption that establishments of that scale will not have the capacity to participate in public procurement. Taking a snapshot of 2015, the year for which SME data have be reported, and an approximation of 30,000 class F contractors, we find that both are virtually equivalent, since the 11% share of small enterprises among 250,000 SMEs translates into 27,500. Registered government contractors do not necessarily draw all revenue from public procurement, but these figures reflect a significant dependency.

The procurement system has performed poorly in terms of the cultivation of capability and competitiveness. It should be acknowledged that this is scarcely a policy objective. Bumiputera representation in ownership, management and the high-level occupations do feature as criteria for project tenders, but without a clear and systematic framework, especially given the increased emphasis on cost efficiency in recent years. Moreover, race-based quotas are specified within Article 153's provisions, and Malay contractors' interests are institutionally embedded and politically mobilized. At the same time, public procurement has been leveraged for various purposes, such as green building and industrialized building systems. The utilization of public procurement for fostering forward-looking change and developmental objectives suggests the potential for the system to facilitate the growth and catch-up among Bumiputera enterprises.

The current system actually incentivizes stasis, containing features that discourage growth and development. Focusing preferential programmes on small and medium companies may correspond with the greater capacity of Malay contractors to compete at those scales (McCrudden and Gross 2006), but it also perpetuates their concentration at the lower end. Expectedly, Bumiputera reservation of small contracts and the balloting system with no limit on repeated award of the rents has induced the vast majority to stay small. Three-quarters of Bumiputera contractors are in classified as G1, the smallest of seven tiers needing paid-up capital of only MYR5,000–10,000, and almost all remain there. In 2011, less than 0.2% of them (47 out of about 29,000) graduated to a higher class (REFSA 2011). Growth and technological upgrading are constrained by various factors, especially financial constraints and lack of breakthrough in attaining economies of scale. But the system has no formalized mechanisms that promote scaling up or improving performance – including the price handicap system that compensates for higher prices without quality requirements.

Some initiatives under the Bumiputera Economic Transformation Programme, launched in 2011, have also sought to enhance quality and performance in public procurement. The Teras scheme that effectively certifies high-performing companies functions in tandem with public procurement – as a means for facilitating competent companies for public projects. Its core feature of identifying reputable and capable Bumiputera firms for special consideration in contract awards,

resembles interventions in the 1990s, but with added criteria and operational features that relatively enhance the potential to build capability of contract recipients.
Teraju reports that in the first eight years (2011–2019), 1,090 companies were
endorsed.[25] Large projects have operated on a "Carve out and Compete" basis.
The initiative's showcase Kuala Lumpur's inaugural mass rapid transit (MRT) saw
372 companies securing contracts worth MYR10.5 billion, or close to 50% of the
total. A further MYR54.2 billion of opportunities in 13 mega projects have been
identified, but the future of this programme is uncertain post-2018, under new
administrations. The outcome of contracting in the MRT remains to be rigorously analyzed, but timely delivery and smooth rollout generally reflect well on
the project. It also set a constructive precedent of transparency in contract awards,
which are posted online.[26] MARA's SPiKE (*Skim Pembiayaan Kontrak Ekspres*, or
Express contract support scheme) set up under the Bumiputera Economic Transformation Programme to provide financing of up to MYR1 million for G1-G5
contractors, reportedly extended assistance, amounting to MYR1.25 billion, to
18,200 contractors in 2013–2015 (MARA 2014, 2015). However, the efficacy
and continuity of these measures are unclear.

Another aspect of reforms – in terms of graduating out of preferential
assistance – is steeply challenging, and negligible in the policy discourses. In
an exceptional episode, Malaysia was prompted by the external pressure of the
Trans-Pacific Partnership Agreement to specify terms for foreign participation,
and to secure concessions for its preferential system. The eventual terms – while
presently in abeyance, given the uncertainty over the TPPA – are instructive. The
domain of formal Bumiputera preferences remained intact: small contracts would
not be touched; only large contracts would be opened, with a gradual widening. Specifically, foreign competitors could bid for projects above MYR300 million, a threshold that would slide to MYR100 million in 20 years. However, the
agreement preserved a 30% Bumiputera carve-out in government procurement,
Petronas' exclusive rights to petroleum and policy autonomy, performance and
national requirements, foreign equity limits for certain sectors (notably, retail
and automotive), and operations of specific entities, such as Teraju, Ekuinas and
MARA. GLCs could also continue ascribing preferential treatment to a maximum 40% of annual budgeted purchases (PwC 2015, 33 and 246). Unsurprisingly, the terms only applied to the largest of projects, which attract multinational
corporations' interest.

The impetus for sustained and effective reforms to facilitate Bumiputera contractor capabilities cannot derive from extraneous sources; it must spring from
within Malaysia. This endeavour also requires acknowledgment of the challenges facing Malay contractors, most saliently, their lack of financial resources
and access to established supply chains, which curtail upscaling and price competitiveness. However, the system also poorly serves its intended beneficiaries in
some major ways, such as poor regulation that allows failed contractors – even
those terminated in previous contracts – to bid anew for contracts, possibly under
a new company, and exploitation of bidding mechanisms to inflate prices. The
Malay Contractors Association, on record, welcomes more competition *among*

Malay contractors to facilitate quality and to more equitably allocate opportunities within this political-economic constituency.[27] Whether rhetoric translates into reality remains to be seen. Nonetheless, it bodes well that certain critical stances toward enhancing affirmative action in public procurement are increasingly articulated. Another fundamental hurdle concerns the value placed on private, independent enterprise, which arguably has not been not widely valued in the past, particularly during the heady 1990s when political alliances offered better prospects (Sloane 1999).[28] Increasing emphasis on entrepreneurship, alongside recognition that the capacity of the public sector and GLCs to absorb the skilled workforce will likely decline, potentially offers a window of opportunity for enterprise development initiatives to gain traction.

Government-linked companies and publicly listed companies

Malaysia's journey toward cultivating the Bumiputera Commercial and Industrial Community is the most storied of all affirmative action interventions, with a succession of marquee programmes: SOEs in the 1970s, foreign corporation takeovers and state-owned heavy industries in the early 1980s, and privatization from the 1980s until the Asian financial crisis of 1997–1998. The 1990s also saw growing influence of public investment agencies, also termed *government linked investment companies* (GLICs). In the aftermath of the cataclysmic collapse of the mass privatization project and renationalization of numerous corporations, GLCs were thrust back to the forefront of the Bumiputera agenda.

This section focuses on the post-AFC era. From the onset, attempts to empirically appraise GLCs face a challenge of information gathering on an expansive category of corporate entities, on which there is no data repository nor even a range of defining features. A widely applied convention defines GLCs as companies in which the government, represented by the GLICs, exercises control through majority equity ownership or special shares. Various entities that arguably fit the term *government-linked* and that have clearly played key roles in Bumiputera enterprise development are generally omitted in the GLC literature, including Petronas and FELDA, and are also missing here. Notwithstanding the scarce research on GLCs more broadly defined, recent work on the conventional notion of GLCs provide substantial material that inform another aspect of Malaysia's affirmative action.

The scale of GLCs is well established. GLICs hold majority ownership of 35 publicly listed companies, and these 35 GLCs in turn accounted for 42% of Bursa Malaysia's capitalization in 2013 (Gomez *et al.* 2017). They operate across an array of sectors, saliently, in telecommunications, banking, aviation, property, plantations, automotive and utilities (PCG 2015). The market share of GLCs is more challenging to compute and has received less attention; official documents have omitted estimation attempts. Menon and Ng (2013) report that in 2012, GLCs accounted for 93% of income in utilities, 80% in transportation and warehousing, and over 50% in agriculture, banking, formation and communications, and retail trade. What effect does GLCs' economic presence and power have on private investment? Menon and Ng (2013) note that GLCs invest at a higher rate than private companies, and trace this to their superior reserves and political proximity that confer added leverage and privilege. They further argue that GLCs crowd out private capital, significantly accounting for Malaysia's anaemic private investment rate since the late 1990s.

This debate lies beyond this book's scope, but it is germane to the question of divestment of GLCs, on which policy articulation is inconsistent and implementation is slow – partly because it relates back to the Bumiputera agenda.

GLCs have registered substantial growth and development. The G20, in particular, have emerged from the 2006–2015 GLC Transformation Programme as visible demonstrations of dynamism, competitiveness and regional presence of corporations helmed by Malay professionals and managers. Comparing governance profiles and political influence from the 1990s to the 2010s, Gomez *et al.* (2017) note the much greater presence of professionals in management, and less overtly political appointments, especially of UMNO figures. Retired civil servants and private sector individuals have also increasingly been appointed to GLC boards, replacing past prevalence of partisan affiliation. The current profile of directorships in the largest companies is telling. A data compilation of the largest 100 publicly listed companies at the end of 2019 found that 42% of a total 837 directors are Chinese, 41% Malay and 5% Indian.[29] This inquiry by RHL Ventures also sorted the age profile and occupational profile, saliently noting the heavy seniority presence, with 95% above 40 years and three-quarters holding more than two directorships, hinting that the system's generational bias precludes younger leadership.[30] The general composition also show the presence of a Malay old guard, largely made up of retired civil servants.

The largest companies have the means and impetus to diversify their board, but independently forged inter-racial partnerships, which are more likely co-equal partnerships than appointments for political expediency, are more elusive. Indeed, the lack of Bumiputera and non-Bumiputera partnerships has been cogently documented. The Center for Public Policy Studies (CPPS) (2006a) found that, out of 757 publicly listed firms in the year 2000, only 18 (or 2.4% of the total) comprised of independent joint ventures with Bumiputera and non-Bumiputera owners, with 12 of them in manufacturing, and 5 in construction – where partnerships might be induced by profiling and positioning for public procurement.

The broad challenge remains to leverage on these achievements in the GLCs widely, and to generate some ripple effects on the private sector. GLC vendor development continues to be a priority on paper, although in practice, procurement has become more driven by financial bottom lines (Khalid 2014). The extent of progress in instituting more efficient, effective transparent systems is difficult to ascertain, but this is clearly an area needing further consolidation in the foreseeable future.

The state of the GLCs presents a few policy implications and some dilemmas for the Malaysian government. First, concentration of political power, particular in the Ministry of Finance, Inc., exposes the system to moral hazard and risks of patronage and corruption, which has ramifications on the GLCs' efficacy in driving Bumiputera enterprise development. Second, efforts to reduce GLC market power entail some degree of divestment, which will reduce potential dividends received by government or by unit trust and pension account holders in the GLICs, both of which pose political quandaries. Third, financial implications of divestment are also significant. The better-performing GLCs will be more attractive and feasible privatization prospects – and simultaneously inflict largest loss of future income. Fourth, the Bumiputera question arises again, in terms of who will buy the divested shares. The imperative of transferring ownership with at least a proportionate, if not dominant, share to Bumiputera interests remains – but the low levels of private wealth ownership suggest the pool of potential buyers is small, and borrowing for takeovers carries high risks. Management buy-out, another form of transfer from public to private hands, has been floated from time to time, including in the recent *Mid-Term Review of the Eleventh Malaysia Plan* (Malaysia 2018). This strategy provides the advantage of new owners possessing first-hand experience in managing the company and a direct stake in its long-term success and sustainability. Of course, any such moves must still be pursued with great caution and circumspection.

Various other agencies designated to promote Bumiputera enterprises operate behind the scenes and independent of critical scrutiny. Among these, Ekuinas merits a specific mention and brief overview. While it was established in conjunction with the removal of Bumiputera equity requirements in selected service sub-sectors, it plays a more significant role in cultivating Bumiputera enterprise than expanding Bumiputera ownership, and as a private equity firm it adopts an approach different to other public agencies. As of 2018, Ekuinas had attained control through buy-out of Malaysian companies (approximately 40% of its portfolio), investment in Malaysian or Bumiputera companies (37%) and acquisition of non-core assets (23%) (Ekuinas 2018). Seventy percent of Ekuinas firms are private, 30% are publicly listed.

Among the main modes are through franchising and participation in value chains. Bumiputera holdings have accounted for about three-quarters of equity in the companies under Ekuinas' watch, which are concentrated in the oil and gas, education and retail sectors. By 2018, it reported increases of MYR6.6 billion in shareholders' value (doubling the capital invested), and of 25% and 27%, respectively, in the number of Bumiputera management and Bumiputera employees, since it exerted control over the companies. Hence, nearing its first decade of operations, it is reasonable to say that Ekuinas has been a steady and productive endeavour, with hits and misses – as well as a notable policy experiment. Its future prospects and continual role in Malaysia's affirmative action regime warrant a deeper analysis and critical consideration.

Loans, grants and ancillary support

The outcomes of Malaysia's manifold financial, technical and advisory programmes for Bumiputera enterprise, which are predominantly targeted at SMEs, are decidedly under-researched. Reports of fund allocations and recipients provide quantitative reference points, but the qualitative results are more difficult to appraise and absent in the literature. The importance of these programmes demands their due coverage in this study, despite the admittedly thin empirical analysis.

A wide range of programmes operate, largely behind the scenes, to promote Bumiputera micro and small business. While overshadowed by larger and more prestigious programmes, they importantly cater to Bumiputera firms, the vast majority of which are concentrated at these levels. We survey them based on implementing agency:

- MARA runs numerous training modules for entrepreneurship, skills and technological absorption, and provides funding for renovation, upgrading and business growth. By its self-reporting, these programmes groomed 103,500 entrepreneurs and provided financing for 21,100 ventures in 2014 and 2015. MARA's Strategic Transformation 2011–2020 aspires to take enterprise development to the next level, beyond dispensing opportunity and funding (MARA 2014, 2015). MARA's The Baron initiative reports the facilitation of 40 corporate entrepreneurs, after expenditures of MYR148 million (MARA 2015). However, the extent that these interventions spur capability and competitiveness remains to be seen.

- PUNB provides SME support to a sizable pool, but evidence suggests a considerable distance to go in cultivating truly dynamic enterprise. PUNB has 2,222 companies in its registry (excluding Prosper Teras, of which data are unavailable), with the majority in the Prosper Runcit scheme (1,741). Automotive workshops and petrol stations or gas distributors constitute the two largest sectors – constituting 12% and 11% of the total.[31]

- Tekun, a microfinance scheme, disbursed financing to 473,982 entrepreneurs totalling MYR4.29 billion, from 1992 to mid-2016.[32] As a microfinance scheme, it is constrained in terms of innovative and technological capacity. There is limited evidence of beneficiaries being induced toward higher competitiveness. Tekun is also mired in heavy losses and debt, with a former CEO on trial for corruption. It recorded a loss of MYR209.28mil at the end of 2015 due to several failed financing schemes, according to the 2016 Auditor-General's report.[33] A thorough clean-up and revamp is in order, and was given impetus with the change of government in 2018, which vowed to prosecute corruption and halted the past patronage practice of politicians providing support letters for Tekun loan applications.

- Among Teraju-administered programmes, the Teras endeavour that selects high-performing Bumiputera companies has, besides public procurement, also delivered benefits in terms of bank loans. Teraju's provision of MYR332 as collateral to banks multiplied to MYR3.14 billion in loans to Teras companies (Teraju 2017). From its start in 2014 until January 2018, the SUPERB grant for young entrepreneurs awarded MYR80 million for 259 businesses, of which 183 are considered "start-ups."[34]

- SME Corp's BEEP reported that, until end 2015, 512 Bumiputera companies had received grants amounting to MYR61.3 million. Most of the approved projects were for product and process upgrading, product packaging, certification and quality management systems. The Tunas Usahawan Belia Bumiputera (TUBE, for budding Bumiputera youth entrepreneurs) programme of small loans for young adults (18–40 years) was launched in June 2015. By end 2015, TUBE 1.0 had registered 443 participants and generated combined sales of MYR17.8 million, alongside 848 job opportunities. From a MYR10 million allocation, TUBE 2.0 targeted 500 young entrepreneurs including 100 graduates who had completed the SL1M training programme. In 2017, MYR14.9 million was spent to assist 994 beneficiaries (SME Corp 2018).[35]

- A number of other programmes merit a mention, but data are insufficient to provide an evaluation. These include initiatives by the Malaysian Timber Industry Board and Malaysia Automotive Institute to support Bumiputera businesses or sub-contractors in terms of export capacity, sales and profitability, and the Sarawak Ministry of Industrial and Entrepreneur Development which assists market access of Bumiputera SMEs in the state (SME Corp 2018).

This overview, viewed together with public procurement and GLCs, emphatically shows the range and diversity of Bumiputera enterprise development programmes. We can also note that each programme serves designated purposes and target groups, with no major duplications. However, the continual lack of major breakthroughs also stands out and must be a policy priority looking forward. Most recently, the 2020 Budget allocated MYR445 million for Bumiputera SME development – mostly loans and grants – under Tekun, PUNB, SME Corp, Pelaburan Hartanah and Teraju, in a quotidian manner, maintaining these programmes with minimal attempt at rejuvenation.

Wealth and property ownership

Malaysia's endeavour of expanding Bumiputera ownership has focused primarily on equity, but implicitly broader constituents of wealth and property have also received policy attention.

Bumiputera equity ownership was studiously monitored under the NEP, which set a target of 30% (7.4% held individually, 22.6% by institutions). A consistent official data series is available from then until 2008, showing growth in Bumiputera holdings, particularly of Bumiputera individuals, from 1970 to 1990. The 7.4% individual target was surpassed by 1985. Nominee companies and trust agencies also held substantial shares. However, since 1990, the statistics show a plateauing trend, with the combined holdings of Bumiputera individuals and trust agencies holding at 19% in both 1990 and 2000, nudging up to 22% in 2008. The government stopped reporting these disaggregated data after the mid-2000s;

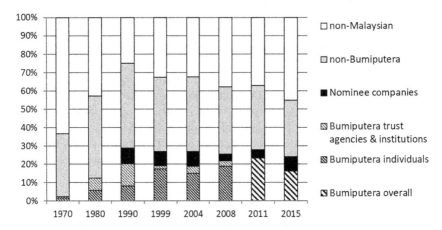

Figure 7.3 Malaysia: Equity ownership by race and nationality, percentage of total, 1970–2015

Source: Malaysia 1976, 1991, 2001, 2006a; Ministry of Economic Affairs 2019.

Notes: Par value; disaggregation of Bumiputera ownership into individual and trust agencies and institutions are not available for 2011 and 2015.

nominee holdings appeared to decline in the late 2000s, but grew again post-2010. The more recent data show Bumiputera ownership – individual and institutional combined – rising to 23% in 2011, then falling back to 16% in 2015. It is questionable whether Amanah Saham Bumiputera has been properly accounted for.

These official statistics have been mired in controversy, methodological and political. Three main critiques of the calculation method have been articulated: the opacity of shares held through nominees, the application of par value instead of market value and the omission of government ownership (Jomo 2004; CPPS 2006a).

The official figures for Bumiputera ownership during the 1990s strain for credibility in the face of contemporaneous political economic developments, implicitly providing some validation of research that found evidence of more substantial gains. Amid Malaysia's privatization boom that transferred enormous wealth to newly created Bumiputera capitalists, the Bumiputera share of equity only inched up marginally, from 19.3% in 1990 to 20.6% in 1995. Alternate estimates include Abu Samad's (2002) analysis of KLSE equity ownership data concluded that the 30% threshold was reached by 1997. Bumiputera individual and institutional ownership – excluding nominees – of publicly listed shares, based on par value, passed 12.0% in 1998, 19.0% in 1991 and 26.0% in 1994, reaching 33.7% just prior to the Asian financial crisis. CPPS (2006a), employing a different methodology that combines par value and market value, and most distinctively includes government ownership, attributes 45% of equity ownership to Bumiputera interest.[36]

Undoubtedly, the debate is not merely empirical. The political side of this debate concerns the arguable vested interest of the government and policy beneficiaries in under-declaring achievements – in order to justify perpetuation of preferential treatment as long as the country has not reached the 30% target. We should note that equity allocation by fiat has been gradually dismantled over the decades. Export-oriented, large manufacturing firms have been exempted from formal Bumiputera equity rules for quite some time, and in 2009 such rules were liberalized in service sectors. A minimum 12.5% Bumiputera allocation remains in place for public listings. Nevertheless, voluminous wealth transfers under privatization in the 1990s, and the establishment of Ekuinas to fill in the expected gap in the wake of that 2009 intervention, demonstrate the political proclivities and pressures for measures to boost Bumiputera equity holdings. The government has acknowledged that, by 2005, beneficiaries of Bumiputera reservation had sold off MYR52 billion of the MYR54 billion worth of shares received from public-listed companies.[37]

The specialized programmes for promoting Bumiputera ownership, which is interlinked with management control and entrepreneurship, continue running on a limited scale. Ekuinas, discussed earlier for its role in enterprise development, plays a dual role in contributing to Bumiputera equity ownership. However, its Bumiputera holdings, valued at MYR5 billion in 2018, amount to a drop in the bucket. The Jejak Jaya Bumiputera programme reported that, as of December 2019, the 15 companies for which it facilitated public listing reached a market capitalization of MYR11.35 billion, up from MYR5.2 billion at their listing.[38]

Conversely, account-based Bumiputera investment funds, which provide a more direct basis to assess Bumiputera personal wealth compared to GLIC holdings, constitute a large segment of publicly listed shares. Towering above all, Permodalan Nasional alone holds one sixth of the capitalization of publicly listed companies, and its biggest fund Amanah Saham Bumiputera had 8.6 million unitholders and 137.3 billion units in 2014, accounting for about 31% of the industry nationwide. However, distribution within ASB is highly concentrated at the very top. In 2016, the bottom 50% held less than 2% of total ASB units, while the top 1% held about 81%. These wide gaps between segments translate into a Gini coefficient in the range 0.83–0.85 for the period 2007–2016. It should be noted that ASB's cap of a maximum 200,000 units per individual provides a check against more runaway accumulation at the top. The highly unequal distribution results from millions of tiny accounts (Lee and Khalid 2020).

This section is probably not complete without a note on property ownership. Bumiputera quotas and discounts are cemented as measures to facilitate housing ownership, sometimes to engineer diversity in residential neighbourhoods. Data showing racial distribution are unavailable in official sources, but we can deduce from the appeals by housing developers for permission to put unsold Bumiputera-quota houses on the open market that higher end property ownership is lower within the Bumiputera population. Commercial property also received more attention under the *Ninth Malaysia Plan,* and new initiatives corresponded with a modest increase in Bumiputera ownership, from 11.7% in 2005 to 14.0% in 2008 (Malaysia 2010b). This issue continues to be a policy priority, although more recent ownership statistics have not been disclosed.

The overarching story is complex. While progress in Bumiputera wealth and property ownership likely lags other affirmative action spheres, pursuing accelerated change poses greater perils, due to the risks of rent-seeking and corruption.

Public opinion and popular support

Public sentiments and popular support for affirmative action constitute another vital dimension of the policy's sustenance and durability in Malaysia, as well as the scope for reform. A number of surveys shed light on sentiments toward Bumiputera preferential policies and support for their continuation (Lee 2017b). Two important insights emerge. First, Malaysians are sharply divided in sentiments toward majority-favouring policies and fair treatment: a clear majority of Bumiputeras support continuity and deem the system as fair; minority groups show widespread misgivings and perceive broad unfairness in opportunities availed to them.

This subject is fraught with complexity of interests and emotional baggage, and discourses surrounding it, even in academic settings, tend to take on polemical angles. Nonetheless, a few carefully conducted surveys merit our attention. Al Ramiah, Hewstone and Wölfer (2017), enquiring about attitudes toward in-groups and out-groups, seek responses from a Peninsula-wide representative sample, on a 1 to 5 scale, of level of comfort with Malays receiving special privileges. Malays are decidedly positive, averaging almost 4 per 5, while Chines and Indians display some unease, respectively answering closer to 2. Less than half of Malay respondents (47%), but overwhelming majorities of Chinese (85%) and Indians (88%), agree with implementation of "fair competition for everyone so that no one group gets special privileges." The study also finds a considerably higher proportion of Malays than Chinese and Indians regarding their group interests as protected by the government, and perceiving economic policies as fair. Chinese indicated a higher interest in emigrating. Similarly, Merdeka Center (2015) informs the perception of fairness and stark variations across groups. Opinion toward the economic system – that it is fair vs. unfair – is split as follows: Malays (46%, 46%), Muslim Bumiputera (38%, 42%), non-Muslim Bumiputera (33%, 58%), Chinese (9%, 85%), Indians (29%, 67%).

Unquestionably, sentiment, perception and opinion toward receiving preferential treatment within the Bumiputera population are pivotal. Merdeka Center (2010) sheds some light on this front through some precisely worded statements presented to Malays/Bumiputera respondents. Sizable majorities deem the policy necessary and beneficial: 73% agreed with the stance "Malays/ Bumiputeras need all the help they can get to move ahead so programs like the NEP should be welcome;" only 21% concurred with the contrasting view, "Assistance such as the NEP doesn't help Malays/Bumiputeras in long run as it makes them dependent." Correspondingly, 59% held the stance, "As the original inhabitants of this country, Malays/Bumiputeras should continue to be accorded with special rights and privileges," while the statement, "People should be treated and accorded the same rights in Malaysia regardless of race or religion" reflected the opinion of 40%.

The issue of race-based policies is intertwined with, and often regarded as inextricable from, race-based politics which shaped Malaysia throughout Alliance-Barisan Nasional rule from 1957 to 2018. A common extension from this view equates public approval of BN's mode of race-based parties with parallel shifts in attitudes toward race-based policies. Such positions equate rejection of race-based parties and politics with rejection of race-based policies. This is a conflation of two phenomena that do not necessarily have to move in tandem.

Emphatically, attitudes toward race-based politics, which may lean toward less pronounced differentiation, do not translate into identical attitudes toward race-based policies. Al Ramiah, Hewstone and Wölfer (2017) ask whether "all political parties should be racially mixed," to which 62% of Malays respond affirmatively, along with 80% of Chinese and 83% of Indians. These findings should be tempered by the possibility that respondents may consider a coalition of race-based parties as "racially mixed" parties. Regardless of the conception of political entities, survey evidence indicates that representation of group interest matters. Merdeka Center (2015) unambiguously finds that Malaysians value political representation of communal interests and concerns, whether or not race-based parties govern the country: 38% of respondents agreed with the statement that one's "communal group should be united under BN to ensure their survival into the future," while 42% were more aligned with: "more room should be given to opposition party to voice the community's interest." In other words, even if parties are not based on race, they are expected to represent racial and ethnic groups' interests – which presumably includes Bumiputera preferential policies and fair opportunity for minorities.

The 2018 general election and its aftermath drive home the durability of race-based policies despite political reconfigurations. The winning Pakatan Harapan coalition, constituted differently from its predecessor, ushered in a new form of politics not revolving around race-based parties under a Malay hegemon. The inclusion, and leadership, of Malay-based parties were key to its victory, as well as its campaign platforms which emphatically gave assurance of retaining and reinforcing Bumiputera policies, and markedly avoided promising to abolish or even reform affirmative action. At the same time, expectations of reform are heightened, particularly among the Chinese and Indian electorate that overwhelmingly voted for PH. The political upheavals of 2020, resulting in the overthrow of PH and seizure of power by the Perikatan Nasional coalition anchored in "Malay unity," underscore the current and future political vicissitudes alongside constancy, and likely expansion, of Bumiputera/Malay preferential policies. These issues will be addressed in Chapter 9, where I unpack the policy implications.

Conclusion

Policy outcomes presented and discussed in this chapter reflect the magnitude and complexity of Malaysia's affirmative action regime and sturdy majority support for its continuation. Considerable data provide material for analysis, but the treatment here has been far from exhaustive. Gaps in data disclosures curtail our view, even of quantitative policy objectives, and the subjective and sometimes intangible nature of some qualitative outcomes limits such evaluation. However, a summary may be helpful at this juncture, as an attempt to condense and synthesize a sprawling subject.

Affirmative action has massively allocated opportunity in higher education – both academic and technical streams – but fallen short in promoting capability. The evidence confounds a common tendency to view affirmative action in education as an unqualified success, while asserting that the problems with the policy regime lie in the other policy spheres, especially politically-linked business and wealth accumulation (Yusof 2012; Gomez 2015). For sure, education holds out the greatest potential to promote Bumiputera capability and has significantly facilitated inter-generational upward mobility, while averting the more conspicuous failures and abuses more likely to transpire in the distribution of largesse. Rent-seeking, profiteering and corruption are much less prevalent in higher education admissions and scholarships; such deviances are mitigated by the fact that university admissions and degrees do not yield windfall profits and cannot be sold off like contracts or financial assets. The relative lesser abuse, however, does not insulate affirmative action in education from critical analysis – although the literature largely omits such scrutiny, particularly on the qualitative aspects. The error of another popular critique of affirmative action – that it has only benefited a small sliver of Bumiputeras (Chin 2009)[39] – is underscored by Malaysia's experience in the higher education sphere, where large swathes of lower- and middle-income classes have benefited.

The overarching story of affirmative action in Malaysia's higher education thus remains threefold: extensive allocation of opportunity, shortcomings in developing capability and competitiveness, untapped potential to transition away from race-based to need-based and to more effectively target and empower the disadvantaged. Education administration continually lacks coherence and consistency in integrating academic achievement and socio-economic disadvantage, or merit and need in popular parlance, into admissions, scholarships and financial assistance processes. More systemic deficiencies in the higher education system (Wan, Sirat and Abdul Razak 2018), rooted in myriad factors including preferential selection in appointments, also constrain the capacity of the sector to empower graduates with knowledge, skills and confidence, especially in public institutions which constitute the predominant pathway for Bumiputeras.

In the sphere of employment, the evidence points to considerable promotion of Bumiputera representation in high-level occupations, but the pace of change slowed down from the 1990s, and the community continually relies more on the public sector and GLCs when pursuing career paths. The broader ramifications of these tendencies are not straightforward. Group representation clearly remains a priority; affirmative action in the public sector holds pride of place among the various spheres of intervention, due to the influence, prestige and security of employment, and the constitutional provision of Bumiputera reservation based on a narrow interpretation of Article 153. Broader questions related to racial and ethnic representation in government also arise, and have been manifest in various ways, including recent efforts to draw more non-Bumiputeras into the public sector and recurrent discontent in Sarawak and Sabah toward perceived neglect of indigenous Bumiputeras in high-level promotions.

Affirmative action policy will need to continually strive to balance individual capability and group representation – ideally, with phase-in of more open competition for positions and promotion primarily based on merit. Lessons from recent achievements – especially the GLC Transformation – can potentially be harnessed as replicable examples, drawing on the G20 largest GLCs that have attained racial diversity in decision-making positions. Levers over the private sector are modest, and intervening in workforce composition by fiat is not advisable. However, there is room for introducing better practices and perhaps setting employment conditions for public procurement, in a clear and constructive manner. The imperative of affirmative action remains, but Malaysia can explore possibilities in instituting a more professionalized system that can more effectively groom talent and leadership, while progressively shifting away from overt group preference toward diversity-oriented employment practices.

An overarching theme of the overview of enterprise development programmes is the extensive range and diversity of programmes and implementing agencies, each serving particular purposes and socio-economic segments. Malaysia's efforts to groom Bumiputera enterprises also draw on public procurement and GLC vendor development, as well as various government programmes, involving loans, grants and advisory support. Much of the critique in the literature highlights the continual extensiveness and state-centricity of these measures. The BEC, the most recent iteration of this agenda massively pursued under the BCIC aegis for many years, remains dependent on government (Chin and Teh 2017). The ambitions, missteps and failures of Malaysia's massive 1980s–1990s privatization exercise are widely researched, shedding light on specificities of that chapter in history – with lessons that remain resonant for the present. Tan's (2008) focus on the deficiencies of Malaysia's monitoring and disciplining mechanisms, alongside rampant profiteering and patronage, is particularly pertinent to programmes seeking to groom medium to large firms.

The disproportionately higher share of Bumiputera companies in the micro and small range, and continual difficulties in graduating to medium scale, dynamic and competitive enterprises, constitute deep policy challenges. As also emphasized in Chapter 2, affirmative action in enterprise development is predominantly reinforced by merit-based selection, with emphasis on capability rather than disadvantage, although sunset clauses can be introduced on repeat beneficiaries. Calls for elimination are hasty, especially without evidence that private financial institutions will adequately fill the gap. Of course, there is much room for improvement to more effectively extend financial, technical and advisory assistance. These alternatives can be expanded, and duplication of institutions mitigated. However, the overriding fault is perhaps less about overlap or duplication, than the disparate manner of operations – specifically, the lack of coordination in setting priorities and targets, and of critical evaluation of outcomes and transmission of lessons learned across the programmes.

Shifts in policy orientation and operation of the past decade – focusing on performance, relying less on government funding and extending beyond the GLC orbit – are significant, albeit piecemeal. The challenges of effectively cultivating these abilities and replicating successes on a broader scale remain steep. In some ways, Malaysia has gone back to basics, with implicit acknowledgment that fast-tracking attempts of the past have fallen short, and that there is still a long way to go, to take this policy sphere to a higher gear of professionalism and dynamism, with competition ingrained as the norm rather than referral or connection, and with resolve to accumulate capital and acquire track records and to institute proper accounting and governance structures, in order to facilitate credit access and participate more directly in commercial banking and financial markets.[40]

In the further quest to roll back race preferential treatment, it is also essential for Bumiputera enterprise to be independent and innovative. The shortfall is most acute here.

As noted in Chapter 2, the scope for incorporating need-based preference is very limited; family background and socio-economic status can possibly be considered for graduates' first jobs or microfinance, but beyond these incipient stages of participation, when it comes to career advancement, particularly appointment to decision-making positions, Bumiputeras must be selected primarily on competency and capability, not disadvantage.

Affirmative action programmes in wealth and property ownership have fallen short of targets in many ways, but registered one NEP achievement that has, rather peculiarly, eluded the attention of policy makers and scholars: Bumiputera individual ownership. Undeniably, political pressures for continual pursuit of this 30% equity target are persistent and entrenched, and may not be placated by the possibility that the threshold has been surpassed based on measurements besides the official sources, or with credible inclusion of unit trust holdings. Interestingly, while the 30% target has become emblematic of the NEP's unfinished business, it is in this policy area that rollback of distribution requirements has actually taken place, including removal of equity requirements for export-oriented manufacturing and service industries, and reduction in Bumiputera quotas for listing companies.

Lesser weightage on the 30% target is warranted, concomitant with the need to reemphasize Bumiputera capability and competitiveness. Moreover, this particular policy sphere, given adverse tendencies for rent-seeking and the exceeding challenges of achieving parity, also warrants more searching questions about whether sunset clauses and exit strategies should kick in sooner, and whether proportionality should be an ultimate goal. For the near and medium term, the clarion call of returning to the basics of developing capabilities and bolstering earnings and income, which fosters more sustainable wealth accumulation, resounds as an integral and inter-dependent element of affirmative action alongside enterprise development.

Notes

1 Matriculation programmes operate in 15 matriculation colleges and 2 MARA colleges, while Asasi (foundational) programmes are offered in various universities. Among the Asasi programmes, 6 are reserved for Bumiputera (including Universiti Teknology MARA (UiTM), Asasi Sains UM (Universiti Malaya), Asasi Islamic University of Malaysia (IIUM)) and 5 are open to all, including Asasi Islamic Studies UM, Asasi Universiti Putra Malaysia (UPM), Asasi Universiti Kebangsaan Malaysia (UKM) (Higher Education Department 2017).
2 Data downloaded from data.gov.my.
3 "STPM vs Matriculation Students: Who Stands a Better Chance?", *Malaysiakini*, 7 May 2019.
4 A staggering 200 private colleges were shut down in 2002.
5 The number of Malaysian university (degree-level) students studying abroad diminished from 103,700 in 2001 to 53,900 in 2006 (Wan 2007, 4).
6 Author's calculations from Ministry of Education data accessed at data.gov.my
7 "Mara Colleges Hope to Attract More Non-Bumis", *The Star*, 10 August 2004; "More than 3,000 Non-bumis in Mara Colleges", *The Star*, 15 May 2008; "Hanya satu peratus isi kuota bukan Bumiputera MRSM" (Only one percent of non-Bumiputera quota filled), *Berita Harian*, 11 November; "MARA Announces MRSM Admissions Results 2019", *Minister of Rural Development's Press Statement*, 4 January 2019.
8 Specifically, 20% were for academic excellence, 60% for ethnic population, 10% for Sabah and Sarawak Bumiputeras, and 10% for the socially disadvantaged. The weightage of selection criteria also varied across these four categories, with academic performance weighted highest in the first group, and socio-economic background factoring larger in the latter two groups (Wan 2010).
9 Lisa J. Ariffin, "JPA Scholarships Awarded Fairly, Defends MP", *Free Malaysia Today*, 29 October 2013.
10 "JPA Bursaries only for Studies Locally", *Malaysiakini*, 28 January 2016.
11 In February 2017, publicly listed companies were directed to participate, even threatened with disqualification from public procurement if they did not ("Public-listed Companies must Join SL1M to Get gov't Contracts: Najib", *New Straits Times*, 21 February 2017).
12 Lee and Khalid (2016) conducted a field experiment, sending 3012 fictitious résumés of comparably qualified Malay and Chinese fresh graduates to 753 private sector job openings, and recorded callbacks to observe differences in treatment based on race. They controlled for quality, mainly based on cumulative grade point average, with two Malay and two Chinese applicants – one each representing an above average and below average students – for each vacancy. They found that even below average Chinese were substantially more likely to be called for interview compared to above average Malays. At the same time, skills such as Chinese language proficiency were found to give an advantage to both Chinese and Malay applicants. The factors beneath such discriminatory practice are complex and cannot be reduced to bigotry or racist ideology, although the study suggests employers quite heavily prejudge based on identity. While the study does not conclusively explain the roots of discriminatory treatment of job applicants, the authors posit that the findings are due to a combination of cultural and lingual compatibility, negative presumptions about the validity over of high-scoring Malays, concerns over the ability to attract and retain high-achieving Malays whose prospects are bright in the public sector and GLCs, and related to that, a sense that the private sector plays a role in counterbalancing the pro-Malay disposition of the public sector and GLCs.
13 "High Performing Students from Lower Income Groups Get Priority in MRSM", *New Straits Times*, 6 December 2017.

14 "MARA Announces MRSM Admissions Results 2019", *Minister of Rural Development's Press Statement*, 4 January 2019.

15 Ball and Razmi (2001) conducted a mail questionnaire, sampling 538 from a total 2,708 Bumiputera overseas graduates. Out of these, 365 addresses were obtained and 222 respondents mailed back questionnaires.

16 The cut-offs for these categories are: lowest income (below MYR1,000), B40 (income below MYR3,855 per month), M40 (MYR3,856–8,319), T20 (MYR8,320 and above) ("Funding Cuts Fuel UM's Endowment Fund Initiative", *The Edge Malaysia*, 15–21 July 2019).

17 The full term is *technicians and associate professionals*, but for brevity I omit the latter phrase.

18 Author's calculations from Malaysia (2006a).

19 "Malays Top Appointments in State's Federal Civil Service", *The Borneo Post*, 31 October 2012; "3,539 more Sabahans Join Federal Civil Service", *The Borneo Post*, 22 November 2012.

20 Public Services Department Director-General, cited in *The Star*, 25 December 2007.

21 "Lack of Non-Bumis in Civil Service Must be Addressed", *Free Malaysia Today*, 9 May 2015.

22 Author's calculations from Public Services Commission open source data downloaded from data.gov.my

23 Mastura Jaafar, "Kaji hala tuju dasar kontraktor kelas F" (Study the policy direction for class F contractors), *Utusan Malaysia*, 17 June 2005.

24 Author's calculations from PwC (2015, 243) and unpublished Economic Census statistics.

25 Teraju website (www.teraju.gov.my).

26 Lists of balloting and winning contractors are publicly available (www.mymrt.com.my/en/bumiputera-participation). While it is unclear whether the reports are independently scrutinized, the disclosure is a noteworthy act of transparency.

27 BFM radio interviews with Jamaluddin Non, Deputy Secretary-General, Malay Contractors Association Malaysia: "Open Season for Bumiputera Contractors," 5 June 2018 (https://bfm.my/podcast/evening-edition/evening-edition/open-season-for-bumiputera-contractors); "Doing Away with Government Project Quota," 28 May 2019 (https://bfm.my/podcast/morning-run/morning-brief/mb-doing-away-with-government-project-quota).

28 As Sloane (1999, 137–138) observed: "Innovative expansion through networking – not economic intensification – had become the Schumpeterian (and perhaps Islamic) symbol of Malay entrepreneurial success. Few Malay entrepreneurs saw the value in building something from the ground up. They believed that alliances made through networking were crucial to economic success."

29 "Malaysian Corporate Boards Lack Diversity, Overseas Experience", *Bernama*, 10 January 2020.

30 The author thanks RHL Ventures for sharing their research findings.

31 Data compiled by the author from PUNB's website (www.punb.com.my/index.php/my/direktori-usahawan).

32 "Audit Report: TEKUN's Losses at RM209m, Bad Debts at RM411m", *The Malay Mail*, 31 July 2017.

33 "Auditor General's Report: Tekun's Failed Schemes Led to RM209mil Losses", *The Star*, 31 July 2017.

34 Data compiled from Teraju website (www.teraju.gov.my/skim-usahawan-permulaan-bumiputera-2/).

35 Another SME Corp initiative, the Bumiputera Export Promotion Programme (Program Galakan Eksport Bumiputera, GEB), seeks to enhance SME export

market potential and to increase the number of Bumiputera SMEs penetrating international markets through integrated financial assistance. In 2017, MYR28.3 million was spent to provide assistance to 20 SMEs.

36 CPPS (2006a) account for the exclusion of government ownership in the official statistical series by adding GLIC holdings of publicly listed companies, estimated to be about 40% of the Malaysian bourse. Assigning 70% of omitted government holdings as representing Bumiputera interest, in rough proportion to the group's population weight, CPPS (2006a) concluded that Bumiputera stood at 45%. The study adopts the official figure of 20% Bumiputera ownership based on par value, but references market value when adding government ownership. Notwithstanding this discrepancy – an externally imposed one, in view of data inaccessibility – a dual structure of sorts in ownership is clear: private, individual Bumiputera equity holdings remain low, institutional ownership which represents Bumiputera "interests" and account holders maintains a substantial portion of the financial markets.

37 Shannon Teoh, "Pro-bumiputera Policy Tough to Scrap", *The Straits Times*, 4 August 2017.

38 Data compiled from Teraju website (www.teraju.gov.my/skim-jejak-jaya-bumi putera/)

39 Chin (2009) cites Sowell's (2004) woefully biased and hasty conclusion on this matter. See footnote 5, Chapter 9.

40 Author's interview with Husni Salleh, CEO of Teraju, 3 August 2017.

8 Affirmative action outcomes in South Africa

This chapter unpacks South Africa's achievements and shortfalls in affirmative action. In higher education and employment, an abundance of data enables macro analyses. We observe racial representation in public university enrolment and academic achievement, considering both quantitative and qualitative outcomes, including persistent effects of socio-economic disadvantage and challenges of graduates' transition to the labour market. I then evaluate policy outcomes in the employment sphere, particularly group representation in high-level occupations, and the attendant issues of public and private sector differences and underlying factors that constrain the implementation of employment equity. This section hosts the most extensive discussion, in view of the importance and magnitude of its impact and the polarizing debate surrounding it. I then investigate the progress of enterprise development in line with the major programmes under this policy sector – group representation in executive positions and on boards of large companies, the situation of black-owned companies and BBBEE scorecards, state-owned companies, and loans, grants and ancillary support – mustering the available evidence which provides various snapshots, albeit with less breadth and granularity than the higher education and employment spheres. The fourth policy sector of wealth ownership references equity distribution, specifically the shares of publicly listed companies of which estimates are available.

Higher education

Empirical evaluation of affirmative action outcomes in South Africa begins with higher education, from the more quantitative angle of enrolment, certification and graduation, to the more qualitative aspects – still captured in numerical data but broadly reflecting achievement and capability. In line with the contours of South Africa's higher education landscape, public institutions predominate, both in terms of the numerical share of enrolment and the relative prestige of their degree-level qualifications. Happily, public higher education statistics, including disaggregation by race, are also reported regularly by the Council on Higher Education, Department of Basic Education, and Department of Higher Education and Training. Hence, we can sketch out changes in the profile of university enrolment and other outcomes germane to affirmative action.

Enrolment and attainment

The student composition of higher education institutions changed, with blacks growing both in terms of gross numbers and as a proportion of total enrolment (Figure 8.1). The early democratic years witnessed challenging adjustments, resulting in a steeper decline in the share of whites and growth in black, especially African, enrolment amid contraction in total public higher education enrolment, from 571,000 in 1995 to 566,000 in 1999. Subsequently, however, a growth trajectory was resumed, touching 674,000 in 2002, 741,000 in 2006, 893,000 in 2010, 984,000 in 2013 and 976,000 in 2016. Within the black population, African students gained the most, followed by Coloureds, while the share of Indians has held steady. Student bodies have become more reflective of the populace. In 1995, the profile was 50.3% African, 5.8% Coloured, 6.5% Indian and 37.5% White; in 2016, 72.6% African, 6.4% Coloured, 5.2% Indian and 15.8% White. In this 1995–2016 interval, the number of Africans annually enrolled in university increased by 144%, exceeding that of Coloureds (88%) and Indians (36%), while the number of whites dropped by 29%. The proportion of blacks remains higher among enrolled students than among graduates, but both show a rising trend (Figure 8.2).

Demographic and structural factors, alongside affirmative action policies, have substantially contributed to the expansion of black higher education enrolment and attainment. The African population's overwhelming majority, coupled with constitutional mandate of racial representation and the common sense that opening up to black students is socially, economically and morally the right course of action, have inexorably driven the increasing share of Africans and blacks in

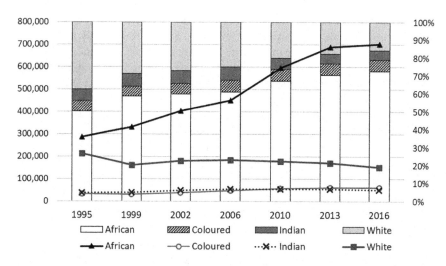

Figure 8.1 South Africa: Enrolment in public higher education, by race (number and share of total), 1995–2016

Sources: CHE (2004, 2013, 2018), Department of Education (2004, 2008).

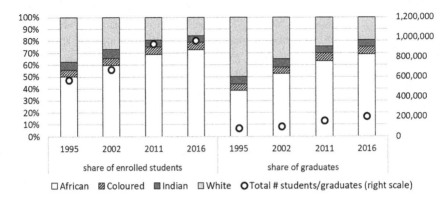

Figure 8.2 South African public universities: number of enrolled students and graduates, by race, 1995–2016

Source: Author's calculations from CHE (2004, 2018).

enrolment. Some institutions are more constrained or path-dependent, due to cultural and language factors, demographics in the institution's vicinity and mergers that have sustained mainly white and mainly black campuses within the same institution.[1]

Redistribution across institutional types unfolded in a phenomenon unique to South Africa. The early post-apartheid years saw a growing proportion of black students enrolled in historically white institutions (HWIs) and a declining proportion in historically black institutions (HBIs) – also known as historically advantaged or disadvantaged institutions. In 1993, 49% of black students were enrolled in HBIs and 13% in HWIs; in 2003, 32% were in HBIs and 42% in HWIs – with the remainder in distance learning (Ministry of Education 2001; Department of Education 2005). Restructuring of public higher education had contributed to the redistribution; from 1995 to 1999, HBIs lost 28,000 students to HWIs, or 25% of their total enrolment. Restructuring and mergers, from 2001 onwards, further reconfigured the sector (du Toit 2010). Student populations in a major portion of universities and technical institutes were already predominantly black. Preferential access and increasing black enrolment thus has not been the main challenge in various institutions. Figure 8.3 shows the variance in enrolment profiles across the current classification, with black and especially African shares higher in comprehensive universities and universities of technology, and lower in traditional universities – but continuing to rise across the board.

Of course, admissions policies have come into play in significant ways. The mandate for redress or transformation is issued to universities in general, but it applies more forcefully to the historically white or historically advantaged institutions, presently termed *traditional universities*. Affirmative action is more consequential

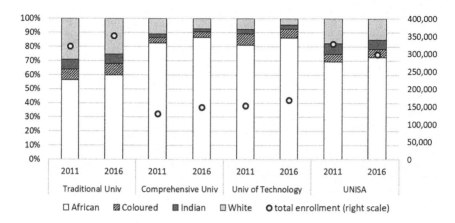

Figure 8.3 South Africa: Enrolment in public higher education by institution type and race, 2011 and 2018

Source: Author's calculations from CHE (2018).

within a further subset of prestigious institutions in the major cities, where black participation is lowest. However, they enjoy greater capacity and reputation to attract higher academic achievers around the country and to strive for student composition beyond the local demographics. *Inter alia*, the Universities of Cape Town, the Witwatersrand, and Kwazulu-Natal, have grappled more intensively with increasing student diversity in admissions policies. Universities have autonomously devised measures to facilitate transformation, and partly in response to critiques of race as a criterion, have in recent years incorporated targeting based on socio-economic disadvantage. Notably, the momentum of rising black enrolment persisted amid modified admissions practices, bringing relief to some administrations concerned at the possibility that black enrolment might fall.[2]

Expectedly, the challenge of transformation is more serious and complex in programmes with high academic entry requirements, such as engineering and medicine. In 2000, Africans constituted 51% of all graduates, but their proportion varies across fields, from 85% in education, 74% in public administration and 58% in social science to 39% in business and commerce and 32% in science, engineering and technology (Subotzky 2003, 370). Figures 8.4 and 8.5 show recent patterns in the composition of enrolled students and graduates, by academic areas. Africans comprise a growing proportion of enrolment in three broad categories of business and commerce, the humanities, and science, engineering and technology (SET) and held steady in education. However, in comparing the number of annual graduates between 2011 and 2016, we observe that Africans' share increased more steeply in business and commerce and the humanities, held constant in education and actually declined in SET.

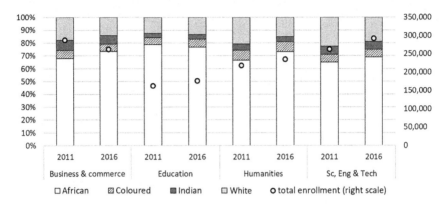

Figure 8.4 South Africa: Enrolment in public higher education, by study discipline and race, 2011 and 2016

Source: Author's calculations from CHE (2018).

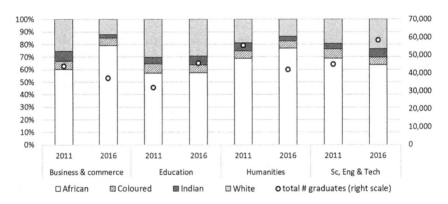

Figure 8.5 South Africa: Graduates in public higher education, by study discipline and race, 2011 and 2016

Source: Author's calculations from CHE (2018).

For completeness, our discussion of educational attainment should account for private institutions. South Africa's public institutions have delivered the mammoth share of overall higher education; this chapter's much more extensive coverage of public HEIs corresponds with their weight within higher education on the whole. Nonetheless, the share of private sector counterparts should not be discounted – especially when it has grown over time (Table 8.1). Private HEIs are not directly mandated to engage in transformation, but they are germane to our consideration given the possibility that they may fill gaps in public higher education or provide opportunities for those seeking different programme offerings

Table 8.1 South Africa: Higher education enrolment, public and private institutions, 2011 and 2016

	Public HEIs (group % of total)		Private HEIs (group % of total)		Share of private HEIs in total enrolment	
	2011	*2016*	*2011*	*2016*	*2011*	*2016*
African	640,442 *(68.7%)*	701,481 *(72.6%)*	56,988 *(60.8%)*	99,972 *(67.1%)*	*8.2%*	*12.5%*
Coloured	59,313 *(6.4%)*	61,963 *(6.4%)*	7,526 *(8.0%)*	11,223 *(7.5%)*	*11.3%*	*15.3%*
Indian	54,698 *(5.9%)*	50,450 *(5.2%)*	5,913 *(6.3%)*	10,494 *(7.0%)*	*9.8%*	*17.2%*
White	177,365 *(19.0%)*	152,489 *(15.8%)*	23,311 *(24.9%)*	27,212 *(18.3%)*	*11.6%*	*15.1%*
Total	931,818	966,383	93,738	148,901	*9.1%*	*13.4%*

Source: Author's calculations from Department of Higher Education and Training (2018).

or failing to gain admission to public institutions. There is no marked pattern of blacks being disinclined to private institutions, although Africans depend on public institutions slightly more than others. Africans constituted a rising share in private higher education, increasing from 60.8% in 2011 to 67.1% in 2016, while that of Whites has decreased – possibly due to increasing numbers going abroad to study. The share of private HEIs in total higher education has increased within all groups, but by 2016 remained lower among Africans, and notably highest among Indians (rightmost columns).

Achievement and participation

Achievement gaps continue to constrain academic progress of South Africa's black majority, differentiating higher education graduates in terms of quality and impacting on the extent to which affirmative action facilitates economic and labour market participation, as well as inter-generational upward mobility. It is necessary to locate this analysis in the context of basic schooling, which precedes affirmative action interventions and sets attainable limits on aspirational goals. South Africa's schools have faced enormous and complex systemic problems, as addressed by voluminous studies. Accommodating higher education admissions policies must work with the given supply of school graduates and prospective university entrants. Fisher and Scott's (2011) substantive evaluation of education in South Africa noted that tertiary education participation rates remain low for the African and Coloured communities and that black students take considerably longer to graduate and are more likely to drop out.

Post-apartheid South Africa inherited a highly stratified schooling system, with large swathes crippled by decades of neglect, discrimination and ennui. A decade after democratization, it was clear that stratification of the education system persisted, and had possibly intensified, as racially diversifying urban middle and upper classes increasingly enjoy the advantages of being educated in previously white schools and HWIs (Morrow 2008). More recent trends in these areas will be examined in this section. Jonathan Jansen and Salim Badat, both drawing on direct personal experience of governing universities, expound the complexities of affirmative action in the context of apartheid's debilitating educational legacy (Jansen 2010; Badat 2012). The first decade of democracy saw scarcely any increase in number of Africans with university-entrance matric passes; the figures remained static at 50,000 annually (du Toit 2010). This severely limited the prospects for upward educational mobility.

Racial and ethnic disparities have persisted, though the gulf has been gradually bridged, due to increasing entry of blacks into better-performing schools and efforts to improve basic education on the whole. National Senior Certificate examination pass rates, one indication of preparedness for higher education, maintained the 70–78% range from 2011 to 2018, touching that upper limit in 2013 and 2018. This marks an improvement from decades before, but the momentum has also somewhat stalled. In terms of inter-group disparities, disclosures are less overt and regular in official annual publications, although it was reported that in 2016, 42% of Africans and 43% of Coloureds achieved matriculation, compared to 77% of Indians and 87% of Whites.[3]

Nonetheless, we can deduce racial dynamics based on provincial outcomes from annual education statistical documents. In 2016, 704,533 students were enrolled in grade 12, and 610,178 wrote the examination. Among the latter, 72.6% passed the examination, 26.6% qualified for bachelor's programmes, 29.4% for diploma, 16.5% for higher certificate. That 13% of those enrolled did not take the examination is a broader problem – which would also look worse if school dropouts are factored in.[4] Focusing on the exam takers here, we can observe significant differentials. Pass rates vary across provinces, from the highest 88.2% in Free State, to 85.9% in Western Cape and 85.1% in Gauteng, and at the lower end, 62.5% in Limpopo and 59.3% in Eastern Cape. In terms of the proportion qualifying for bachelor's programmes, Western Cape recorded the highest at 40.9%, followed by Gauteng (36.2%) and Free State (35.8%), with Kwazulu-Natal (24.5%), Eastern Cape (18.9%) and Limpopo (18.4%) lagging the most (Department of Basic Education 2018).[5]

At university, the inter-racial gap has been substantial in completion rates, and greater in terms of length of time taken to graduate. Kraak (2003) reported on engineering student progress rates, from a six-year longitudinal study conducted over 1995–2000, finding that African and white students registered completion rates of, respectively, 55% and 75%. However, the percentage graduating within the minimal period was just 6% among Africans, compared to 51% among Whites. The proportion graduating within six years was 41% for Africans and 72% for Whites. These gaps have narrowed on aggregate (Table 8.2). Comparing success rates in public institutions, we observe Africans on a catch-up trend, with the differential between White and African students narrowing from 17 percentage points in 2002 to nine percentage points in 2016 at the

Table 8.2 South Africa: University success rate in public institutions, by race (percent), 2002–2016

	Undergraduate				Postgraduate	
	2002	*2006*	*2011*	*2016*	*2011*	*2016*
African	68	72	74	77	66	66
Coloured	74	76	77	80	70	72
Indian	80	79	78	81	67	68
White	85	85	84	86	81	81
Overall	74	76	76	79	71	70

Source: Department of Education (2003, 2008); Department of Higher Education and Training (2018).

Note: Full-time equivalent passes per full-time equivalent enrolment.

Table 8.3 South Africa: Participation in public higher education institutions (percent), 1993–2016

	1993	*2004*	*2011*	*2016*
African	9	12	14	16
Coloured	13	12	14	15
Indian	40	50	47	47
White	70	60	57	50
Overall	17	16	17	18

Sources: Breier and Mabuzela (2008), CHE (2004, 2018).

Note: Enrolment in higher education per 20- to 24-year-old population.

undergraduate level. In postgraduate study, however, the disparity is higher and static over 2011–2016.

Graduation and participation statistics reflect the general hierarchy. Among students who enrolled in three-year degree programmes in 2011, 55% of Africans had graduated by 2016 and 45% had dropped out. This is similar to graduated-to-dropped out splits of 56:44 among Coloureds, but Indians and Whites do better, at 61:39 and 65:35, respectively. Parallel patterns prevail in four-year degrees, with the shares of the 2011 starting cohort graduating and dropping out at 63:37 for Africans, 60:40 for Coloureds, 66:34 for Indians and 70:30 for Whites (CHE 2018). Again, racial disparities persist, but not necessarily to an alarming degree based on these data sources. However, the panoramic picture of educational attainment, reflected in participation of 20- to 24-year-olds, shows persistent gulfs amid changes in line with affirmative action (Table 8.3). Between 1993 and 2016, the share of the 20- to 24-year-old population enrolled in public higher education institutions increased only slightly among Africans, from 9% to 16%, and by an even lesser margin among Coloureds, from 13% to 15%. The corresponding proportion rose from 40% to 47% among Indians and declined from 70% to 50% among Whites.

Transition to the labour market

We now turn to the labour force and employment, the subsequent test ground of the efficacy of affirmative action in higher education. Labour force data also provides empirical material to check for consistency with the earlier analyses of higher education data. This sub-section, and the following section on employment equity and labour market dynamics more broadly, report findings derived from the Labour Force Survey, which is deemed a reasonably reliable source for examining the demographic composition of the workforce (Bezuidenhout *et al.* 2008). I compute labour market information from the September LFS for 2000–2007, and the Third Quarter LFS for 2008–2018.

Trends in educational access and attainment charted earlier find parallels in the labour force. The proportion of tertiary qualified workers rises within each race group, particularly from the early 2000s to 2018 (Figure 8.6). White workers continue to be the most highly educated. Although their enrolment in public higher enrolment has declined, they have managed to obtain qualifications through other channels. The Indian labour force has also retained relatively high, and rising, educational attainment. Within the African and Coloured labour force, the proportion with tertiary qualifications has slowly crept upwards, most consistently for the former.

Viewed from the angle of racial composition within similarly qualified workers, these trends translate into a rising share of blacks among workers with complete secondary schooling, and moderately steeper gains among diploma and degree holders (Figure 8.7). The most recent labour force surveys put the share of blacks among diploma holders at just above 80%, and that of degree holders at about 65%. Zooming in further on degree-level qualifications, the share of Africans has

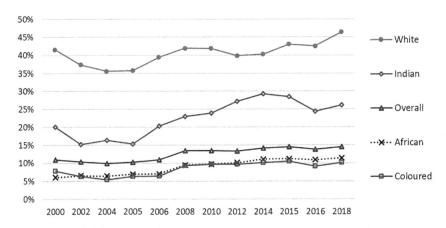

Figure 8.6 South Africa: Tertiary educated workers as share of labour force (% total), 2000–2018

Source: Author's calculations from Labour Force Survey raw data.

Note: *Tertiary educated* refers to post-secondary certificate, diploma and degree.

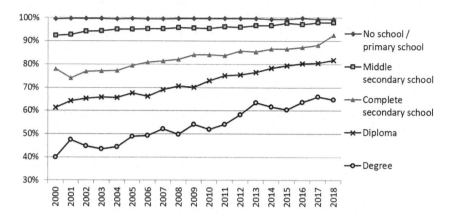

Figure 8.7 South Africa: Share of blacks in labour force, by education attained, 2000–2018

Source: Author's computations from Labour Force Survey raw data.

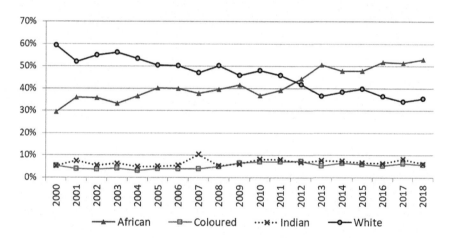

Figure 8.8 South Africa: Composition of degree holders in the labour force, by racial group, 2000–2018

Source: Author's computations from Labour Force Survey raw data.

risen the most, and in almost a mirror reflection of this trend, the share of whites has dropped (Figure 8.8).

How about educational attainment across generations? The more that higher education facilitates inter-generational upward mobility, the greater the positive ramifications for South Africa's transformation. This issue merits a brief discussion, on two aspects: first, affordability and financial hurdles to entry or completion; second, preparedness and adaptability of students from disadvantaged backgrounds. South Africa's university fees are a major obstacle to upward mobility, to overcoming disadvantages blacks encounter that are augmented by class and social stratification (Jansen 2010; Badat 2012). Financial aid schemes, by design, generally favour disadvantaged students, tend to be pro-poor in orientation and are viewed as mainly benefiting black students.[6]

However, the inadequacy of the financial assistance, and its increase relative to rising costs, have continuously posed major challenges to broadening participation. South African tuition fees increased 93% between 2000 and 2004, while National Student Financial Aid Scheme (NSFAS) allocations increased by just 48%. This lag in financial aid curtails tertiary education opportunities disproportionately for students of low-income families (Breier and Mabuzela 2008, 290). In recent years, NSFAS funding has been sustained, but with uneven progress in terms of the numbers assisted. NSFAS funded students totalled 216,874 in 2011 and 225,950 in 2016, but among final-year students, the total fell from 28,464 in 2011 to 22,461 in 2016. Cost coverage rose, with the average grant per tuition cost rising from 113% in 2011 to 144% in 2015, and average grant per full cost also increasing, from 44% in 2011 to 56% in 2015, hence still leaving borrowing students with a funding hole to fill (author's calculations from CHE 2018).

The disadvantaged circumstances of many students also help explain the high drop-out rate in university. A large portion of high school graduates are inadequately prepared, and South Africa's universities arguably were not sufficiently mindful of challenges faced by blacks who were the first generation to enter university. Zoch (2016) finds, as expected, that parents' education and household income are significantly correlated with the chances of completing matriculation and getting into university. Thus, despite remedial classes and other forms of assistance, the racial achievement gap remains very wide (Jansen 2010). The Fees Must Fall protest and campus unrest in 2015–2016, while rooted in a multiplicity of factors and resorting to tactics that are difficult to condone, were nonetheless expressive of material conditions and genuine frustrations on the ground.

The issues of graduate unemployment, and of qualitative differences between graduates that impact on "employability," are integral to discussions surrounding affirmative action. An empirical overview and brief discussion on unemployment and lateral mobility are warranted at this juncture.

South Africa's unemployment rate is markedly differentiated by race and education level. As shown in Figure 8.9, the broad unemployment rate for the black labour force as a whole is exceedingly high, hovering in the 40–45% band in the early 2000s and remaining at 36–40% over the past decade. Unemployment in the white labour force has been sustained in the 6–9% range. White degree holders register exceptionally low unemployment rates of 2–3%, and for post-secondary diploma holders it is quite steady, around 5%. Among diploma-holding blacks, unemployment has followed a U-shaped curve, declining from the upper 20s to almost 10% in 2008, but rising in the post-global financial crisis era to the lower 20s. Unemployment rates of degree-holding blacks followed a similar pattern, declining from 15% in 2001 to 5% in 2007, then climbing upwards to 8–10% in 2016–2018.

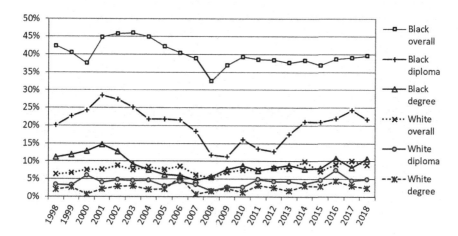

Figure 8.9 South Africa: Unemployment rate (broad), by education attained and race, 1998–2018

Sources: Author's computations from the October Household Survey and Labour Force Survey.

Labour market mobility of graduates to an extent reflects capability and versatility, while also deriving from direct policy outcomes related to relative intensity of employment equity practices. Graduate tracer studies could potentially shed light on this matter, but these are yet to be conducted systematically and consistently in South Africa, thereby precluding such information on a national scale (Senekal and Munro 2019). This data scarcity notwithstanding, two graduate tracer studies are worth extracting. Moleke (2005), as referenced earlier, also investigated graduates' employment experiences. At a basic level, the occupational profile of graduates varies by race. A considerably larger proportion of white graduates are in managerial positions, and moderately larger proportions of black graduates hold supervisory and administrative jobs.[7] A much higher share of African graduates secured their first job in the public sector – 76.7%, compared to 39.0% of white counterparts. The survey also found major differences between graduates of historically white institutions (HWIs) and historically black institutions (HBIs) in the length of time taken to secure a job after graduation and in the share of unemployed (across all study disciplines), with HBI graduates registering slower transitions into employment.

Rogan and Reynolds' (2016) investigation of the 2010–2011 graduating cohort of Rhodes University and the University of Fort Hare (UFH) finds that socio-economic disadvantage remains substantially coterminous with race and that the effects begin from schooling and extend beyond graduation. Rhodes, an historically white institution, has changed complexion, but white students remain in the majority, at 57%. In contrast, UFH's student composition is 93% African, and less than 5% white. The schooling background is also illuminating. At

Rhodes, 50% came from public elite (model C) schools and 30% from private elite schools, with 5% from public low-cost schools; whereas the background of UFH students shows a starkly different profile: 53% public low cost, 34% public elite, 4% private elite. Completion rates vary across institution; for instance, in science, engineering and technology, 60% of Rhodes students completed their studies, compared to 48% in UFH. More striking are the differentials in unemployment, with UFH graduates registering 20%, almost three times higher than Rhodes counterparts at 7%. Econometric analysis finds a statistically significant higher risk of unemployment for UFH graduates and African graduates, after controlling for gender, field of study and academic scores. Importantly, Rogan and Reynolds (2016) also investigate job seeking modes, finding Rhodes graduates substantially more likely to use personal contacts and social media, while UFH graduates depend on newspaper ads, or enter employment that is linked to their bursary.

High-level and skilled occupations

South Africa's endeavours to transform labour markets, specifically in the high-level positions to which blacks were systematically denied entry under apartheid, have been extensive, complex and contentious. The heightened expectations for change in this policy sphere compelled decisive action institutionalized in employment equity legislation, but out of the same historical conditions, the deep-seated disadvantages of the black population have also posed complications for policy implementation. This section reports on progress in increasing black representation in high-level occupations, accounting for some variations by sector and employer type. I also consider the ramifications of affirmative action on questions of merit and the context of skills shortages and unpack the debate surrounding the implementation of employment equity. Labour Force Surveys and the Employment Equity Reports supply the bulk of data, supplemented by other sources.

Group representation

This chapter's evaluation of affirmative action in occupational representation draws first on the Labour Force Survey – and only includes the formally employed, since the informal economy lies outside the ambit of employment equity enforcement. Black representation in employment increased in the post-apartheid era, notably in the high-level occupations prioritized by affirmative action and other skilled occupations such as the technical and clerical categories (Figure 8.10). These trends are consistent with Southall's (2016) seminal work on the black middle class, which references the 1997 October Household Survey and the 2014 South Africa Survey to similarly plot rising black representation in high-level occupations.

The sub-samples of the nine occupation groups are smaller than those of education categories, entailing some outlier situations, notably in 2007, which sees a spike in black representation among managers and professionals, and simultaneously a plunge among technicians. Nonetheless, we can generally discern

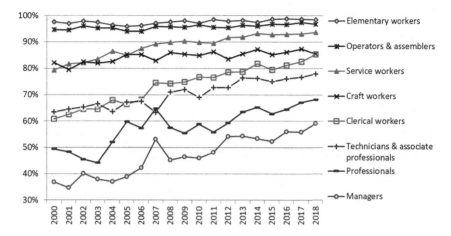

Figure 8.10 South Africa: Proportion of blacks within occupation groups, 2000–2018
Source: Author's computations from Labour Force Survey.
Note: Formal employment only.

trends over time. In professional employment, blacks increased their proportion from the 45–50% range in the early 2000s to almost 70% by 2018. A parallel pattern holds in management ranks, where black representation rises from around 40% to 60%. Focusing on the two main targets of affirmative action and disaggregating by the four population groups, we can observe Africans steadily rising as a proportion of managers and professionals and whites correspondingly declining, especially over the period 2010–2018, while Coloureds and Indians maintain their level of representation throughout almost two decades (Figures 8.11 and 8.12).

The racial profile of occupational groups are the primary policy targets due to labour market hierarchies and the history of repression toward black upward mobility. Within occupations, the distribution across different industries is a matter of supplementary interest to our inquiry, particularly if there are persistent concentrations of blacks in particular sectors. In 2017–2018, about 5% of black professionals were in manufacturing, while 20% were in the financial and business services and 65% in "community, social and personal services," compared to about 10%, 35% and 45% of white professionals in these respective industry categories.[8] No clear trends emerged when comparing these findings across time. Unsurprisingly, black professionals are considerably more likely to be in services, consistent with the high proportion who are teachers. These industry-based patterns point back to the education pipeline and the qualifications of degree-holders in the labour market.

Employment Equity Reports offer an alternate data source, based on employers' submissions to the Commission on Employment Equity. All companies and

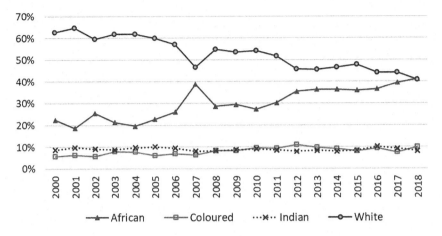

Figure 8.11 South Africa: Racial composition of managers, 2000–2018
Source: Author's computations from Labour Force Survey.
Note: Formal employment only.

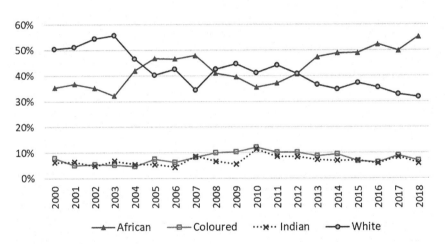

Figure 8.12 South Africa: Racial composition of professionals, 2000–2018
Source: Author's computations from Labour Force Survey.
Note: Formal employment only.

government departments above a threshold size are mandated to regularly submit EERs. One advantage of this data source is the disaggregation of management top, senior and middle levels, which helps profile the ultimate decision-making positions. The reports also sort occupations into broad categories subsuming "professionally qualified and experienced specialists or mid-management" and "skilled technical and academically qualified/junior management/supervisors/

foremen/superintendents," which I simply refer to as, respectively, *professionals* and *skilled workers*. Employer compliance was rather patchy during the early years, including by government offices, but compliance has increased and stabilized over time.[9] Bi-annual reporting for smaller establishments probably accounts for year-to-year fluctuations in the number of reports submitted, and indeed we observe more regularity in the latter years, notably since the 2013 EEA amendments that required all employers to file EERs annually.

As shown in Figures 8.13 and 8.14, black representation has increased over the two decades since the Employment Equity Act was passed in 1998, with variations

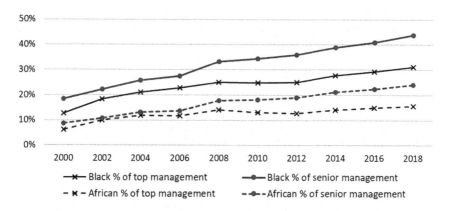

Figure 8.13 South Africa: Black and African share of top management and senior management positions, 2000–2018

Source: Author's compilations from *Employment Equity Reports* (Department of Labour).

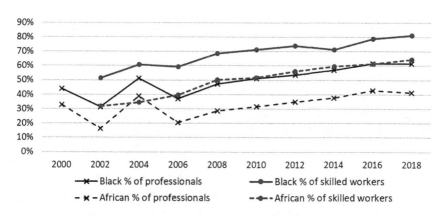

Figure 8.14 South Africa: Black and African share of professional and skilled positions, 2000–2018

Source: Author's compilations from *Employment Equity Reports* (Department of Labour).

Note: Professionals include middle management.

within the black category and lagging gains among Africans in some aspects. The charts show the composition of South African employees, for consistency across time, since foreign employees were excluded in the Employment Equity Reports prior to 2006 (Department of Labour 2007). As expected, the level of black representation runs inverse to the occupational hierarchy. Blacks, and especially Africans, remain more disproportionately under-represented in top management, followed by senior management, then professionals and skilled workers. Across time, we observe slowly rising proportions of blacks in all categories. The over-all levels of black representation in high-level and skilled occupations are less than the estimates computed from the Labour Force Survey presented here. In part, the form and limitations of the data explain the differentials; employment equity data derive from employer reports of workforce composition, rather than stratified random sampling, and importantly exclude small businesses and the self-employed.

Fluctuations in the profile of professionally qualified and middle management in the 2000–2006 interval possibly reflect compliance variations in report sub-mission, these swings being more likely due to the large number of positions in these occupational categories which makes the data susceptible to the presence of different employers, especially large organizations, in the sample. In particular, the considerably smaller average firm size in reports analyzed in 2002 and 2006 coincides with lower black representation at professional and middle manage-ment positions.[10] As firm size increases, in most cases the number of professional and middle management positions would grow at a higher rate than the number of senior and top management positions. Smaller firms offer less opportunity for horizontal expansion of employment at these levels, and hence fewer positions in which preferential selection can be afforded to blacks.

The trends are steadier in the past decade, corresponding with the broader compliance with reporting requirements. All designated employers report annu-ally, and procedures have been streamlined. The results from 2008 onwards thus carry added weight; differences within the black population also warrant atten-tion. Black representation rises from 25% in 2008 to 31% in 2018 in top manage-ment, and from 33% in 2008 to 44% in 2018 in senior management. Africans constitute about half of blacks at both management levels. The African share of top management remains static, at about 13–15% across 2008–2018. The share of Coloureds also remains the same, but that of Indians rises from 6% to 10%, and is the main contributor to the overall increase in black representation. In senior management, Africans register a more steadily rising share, from 18% of the total in 2008 to 24% in 2018. Indians also increase their share, from 8.5% to 11.5%. Among professionals and skilled workers, the share of blacks rises from 47% in 2008 to 61% in 2018, and from 68% to 81%, respectively. African employees drive these changes; their share of professionals increasing from 29% to 41%, and 50% to 64% among skilled workers.

These results are not surprising and are comparable to other firm-based sur-veys. Human resource consultancy P-E Corporate Services reported increasing black representation among executives and top management: 8% in 1996, 16% in

2000, 23% in 2005, 26% in 2010 and 37% in 2016. As a proportion of management, blacks constituted 10% in 1996, 19% in 2000, 29% in 2005, 33% in 2010, 36% in 2016 (Leepile 2018).[11] The Breakwater Monitor survey, another useful reference specific to the late 1990s, computed the proportion of blacks in management at 7.0% in 1994, 12.7% in 1998 and 20.3% in 2000. However, blacks constituted 35% of management recruits in 2000 (Horwitz and Bowmaker-Falconer 2003, 616–622).[12] Within the black managerial population, the persistence of black under-representation in lead operational and strategic decision-making positions – and concomitantly, their concentration in human resources and public relations – are widely observed, and empirically corroborated by Mohamed and Roberts (2008).

We can observe employment equity in operation, juxtaposing employment, recruitment and promotion numbers. Figures 8.15 and 8.16 report on 2008 and 2018, including foreign employees and combining recruitment and promotion data for two years, to smoothen over fluctuations that can arise from large one-off exercises. In line with employment equity objectives, blacks comprise a larger share of promotions than of the workforce in all four categories – and follow rising trends over time. Notably, blacks' share of recruitment is higher than their share of numbers employed in top management and senior management but lower in professional and skilled occupations. These patterns suggest greater inclination to recruit black managers, perhaps in response to the scrutiny on these positions, as well as availability of blacks to take up such appointments. The lesser share of blacks among professional and skilled recruits indicates possible concerns over the availability and capability of tertiary-level qualifications

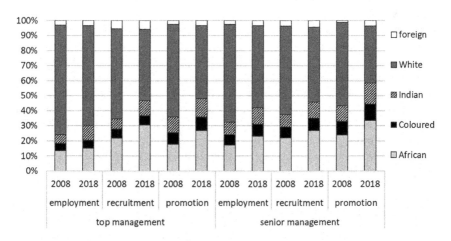

Figure 8.15 South Africa: Racial composition of employment, recruitment and promotion of top and senior management, 2008 and 2018

Source: Author's compilations from *Employment Equity Reports* (Department of Labour).

Note: Recruitment and promotion are averaged over two years, 2007–2008 and 2017–2018.

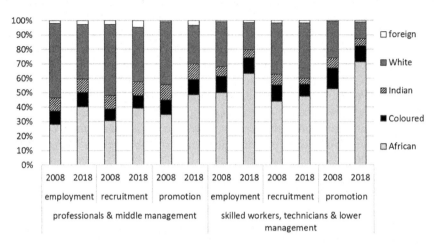

Figure 8.16 South Africa: Racial composition of employment, recruitment and promotion of professional and skilled positions, 2008 and 2018

Source: Author's compilations from *Employment Equity Reports* (Department of Labour).

Note: Recruitment and promotion cover two years, 2007–2008 and 2017–2018.

or competency for skill-specific jobs. These findings concur with the view that employment equity progresses in tandem with educational advancement.

Data on registered professionals and trainees serve as useful reference points. In 2004, 2.1% of chartered accountants were African, 1.4% Coloured, 6.0 Indian and 90.3% White. Among trainees, 15% were African, 4% Coloured, 14% Indian and 66% White (van Zyl 2008, 380).[13] More recent data are available specifically in the engineering corps. From 2010 to 2019, the share of blacks among professional engineers increased from 10.0% to 16.4%, and from 5.1% to 10.9% for Africans. Increases among new registrations was considerably greater, with the share of blacks rising from 36.4% to 50.6% (22.6% to 34.6% for Africans). In the professional engineering technologist category, the share of blacks grew from 21.4% to 41.2% overall, and from 47.2% to 71.8% for new registrants, with Africans contributing the bulk of these increases (author's calculations from ECSA 2010, 2019). These figures reflect both persistent racial gaps and slow but distinct progress towards redressing disproportionalities.

Case study: university staff

Employment equity encounters higher hurdles in more specialized jobs requiring advanced qualifications. Changes in the profile of university staff, which are reported based on full registries rather than surveys, provide a distinctly reliable and informative data source. Affirmative action holds a unique importance, and faces unique challenges, in university staffing and leadership (Badat 2018;

Habib 2016b). The state of employment equity in universities arguably impacts on affirmative action in other significant ways; increased presence of blacks in academic and management roles can boost the positive demonstration effect of visible black career advancement, especially to the benefit of black students. At the same time, the advanced qualifications required of university academic staff also pose major constraints on the scope and pace of change, given the depth of expertise and specialization, plus duration of time taken to complete post-graduate, especially doctoral, degrees. Unsurprisingly, by 2001, Africans constituted only 20% of academic staff (16% in the now traditional universities, 29% in comprehensive universities and 17% in the universities of technology). Whites comprised 69% overall, and 73% in the traditional universities, 65% in comprehensives, 63% in universities of technology. Similar disproportionalities held in terms of executive and management positions (CHE 2004).

Recent years have seen slight increases in black representation in senior management, academic and administrative posts in public universities (Figures 8.17 and 8.18). This quantitative progress bodes well, especially in academic positions which have been growing in absolute numbers and changing in racial composition within a five-year period. Undoubtedly, much room for progress remains. By 2016, blacks were still considerably under-represented in senior management and academic strata, and when grouped by qualification, we also note narrowing but still large disparities, with the black share of PhD-holding staff increasing but not yet reaching 50%.

The starting point was emphatically very low, but progress in transformation has also been slow. A mere 71 black doctoral candidates (9.6% of the annual total) graduated in 1994; this increased to 580 (45.6%) in 2007 (Badat 2010, 22). However, pursuing an academic career entails other push and pull factors.

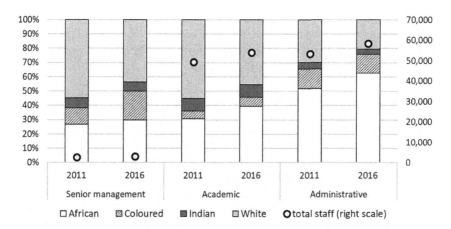

Figure 8.17 South Africa: Racial composition of public university staff, 2011 and 2016

Source: Author's calculations from CHE (2018).

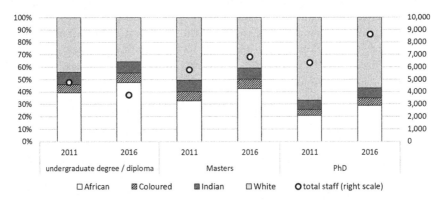

Figure 8.18 South Africa: Public university academic staff, by highest qualification, 2011 and 2016

Source: Author's calculations from CHE (2018).

Habib (2016b) critiques the lack of support for Master's and doctoral students and of enabling environments for black academics to settle down for long and productive careers. Diversifying academia is difficult, despite many universities allocating funds for recruitment of black scholars and making substantial efforts at employment equity appointments. Durrheim *et al.*'s (2007) qualitative survey of black academics found qualified support for affirmative action on the whole, with prevailing tensions within the academic community. In contrast to white academics, who tend to be more concerned with "procedural fairness," black academics are "primarily interested in ends, and criticized the policy for failing to eradicate the inequalities of apartheid in practice" (Durrheim *et al.* 2007, 127). The high clearance bar of advanced formal qualifications is compounded by the need for sustained outputs – which in turn depend on collaborative work and publications assessed by external parties. South Africa's further progress in this specific field will be crucial, and continually challenging.

Sectoral distribution: public and private sectors

The public sector has evidently facilitated black mobility into managerial and professional positions. We again draw on the Labour Force Surveys and employment equity report (EER) summaries. The LFS series shows higher proportions of managerial and professional blacks working in the public sector – encompassing national, provincial and local government offices and public enterprises – compared to the private sector (Figures 8.19 to 8.21).[14] Simultaneously, the across-time patterns show striking parallels. In both public and private sectors, the share of blacks rises roughly 20 percentage points among managers and 10 percentage points among professionals. That blacks have increasingly experienced upward mobility in the private sector is arguably the more noteworthy trend, given that

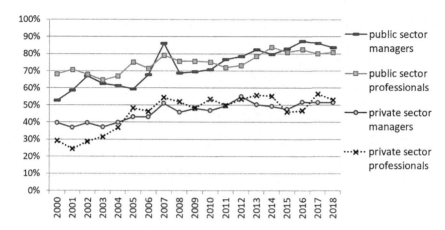

Figure 8.19 South Africa: Proportion of blacks among managers and professionals, public sector and private sector, 2000–2018

Source: Author's computations from Labour Force Survey raw data.

Notes: Formal employment only; public sector includes government and state-owned companies.

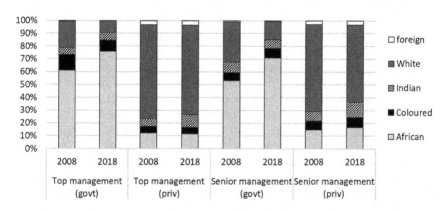

Figure 8.20 South Africa: Racial composition of top and senior management, government and private sector, 2008 and 2018

Source: Author's compilations from *Employment Equity Reports* (Department of Labour).

the public sector is expected to be the driver of employment equity. In 2018, 25% of African managers worked in the public sector and SOCs, with the balance in the private sector and non-profits, compared to 11% for Coloureds, 8% for Indians and 5% for Whites. In professional qualified positions, likewise, the proportion working in the public sector and SOCs is markedly higher for Africans (51%) than for Coloureds (29%), Indians (22%) and Whites (20%).[15]

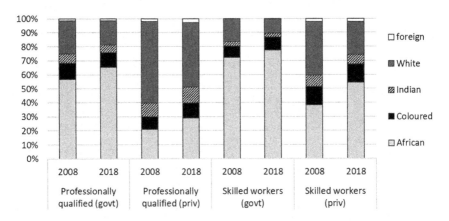

Figure 8.21 South Africa: Racial composition of professional and skilled positions, government and private sector, 2008 and 2018

Source: Author's compilations from *Employment Equity Reports* (Department of Labour).

The inclination of blacks, particularly Africans, toward public sector employment derives from various factors, including the concentration of tertiary-qualified blacks in services, especially education, and the greater latitude for employment equity enforcement in government departments or government-owned entities. The changes could actually be even larger, if not for limited expansion in government recruitment, coupled with scarcity of adequately skilled blacks, which have likely constrained the capacity of the public sector to absorb blacks into high-level employment. The entry of highly educated and upwardly mobile blacks into private sector employment proceeded in the early- to mid-2000s, continuing previous trends but bolstered by employment equity law from 1998.

The public services employment roll is an even more direct and complete data source for informing the composition of government employment. This repository, which has been disclosed to researchers, permits computations based on a full registry instead of a sample. Figure 8.22 shows differentials in annual employment growth by occupational and skill categories, amid almost no net change in the overall size of the public sector across the 1995–2010 period. Managerial and supervisory positions grew substantially more on the whole, thereby availing places to recruit black employees. The racial composition at five-year intervals, displayed in Figure 8.23, show steady gains in black representation in high-level occupations.

Target-setting and job redelineation have both contributed to these outcomes. The government set aggressive affirmative action targets and reached them, including the 50% mark for black representation at management, which was attained by 1999 (Naidoo 2008, 109–110). However, the increase in black representation in management within public services is attributable in part to changes in job

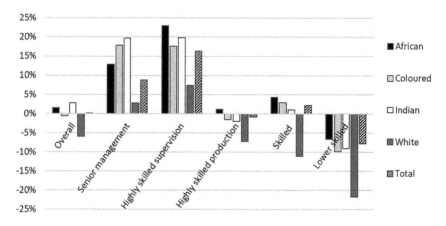

Figure 8.22 South Africa public services: Average annual growth of employees, by occupation and skill level, and race, 1995–2010

Source: Author's computations from Cameron and Milne (2011).

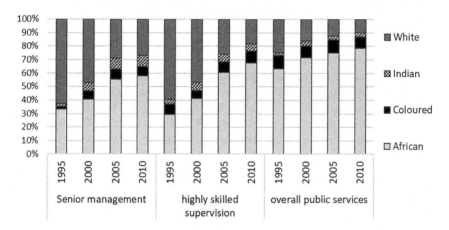

Figure 8.23 South Africa public services: Racial composition of selected occupation groups and overall, 1995–2010

Source: Author's computations from Cameron and Milne (2011).

demarcation. This organizational shift is consistent with the increase in number of managers concurrent with falling total employment, as shown.

Affirmative action in the public sector undeniably comes with attendant complexities and controversies, particularly service delivery problems. Alongside efforts to increase black representation in managerial positions, South Africa adopted new structures and practices of public administration, revolving around higher proportions of administrators in the overall workforce and expansion of their role. These shifts, aligned with "new public management," translated into the substantially higher growth in managerial positions and downsizing of less-skilled positions as mirrored in Figure 8.24, but also, as argued by Chipkin (2011), set up many inexperienced appointees for failure, whose accelerated promotions were compounded by increased devolution of responsibility to them. Another phenomenon in public service employment that impacted on service delivery is the practice of not filling vacancies due to affirmative action considerations. This is consistent with the law and upheld by the Constitutional Court, on condition that leaving vacancies unfilled arises from the lack of a suitably qualified candidate of the designated group and conforms with the organization's employment equity plan. Nonetheless, problems may arise if the practice recurs on a widespread scale.

Some politically tinged elements of employment equity are more acutely controversial, specifically, the ANC's "cadre deployment." This deliberate and unambiguous political project traces back to the party's 1985 National Consultative Conference, which focused on the liberation movement's internal organization, and to discussion documents of 1996 which raised the issue of "cadre development" and called for more attention to "strategic deployments" to positions in the civil service, the military, police and intelligence services (Mkongi 2013; Netshitenzhe 1996). The impetus of those galvanizing efforts is understandable, taking into account the political necessity of cohesively securing levers of power, at a time that administrators from the Apartheid era were retained and cohorts of the liberation struggle were seeking influential positions while lacking governmental experience. However, the pervasiveness and duration of such a campaign are questionable, and contrary to governance principles of the democratization process. Cadre deployment, persisting into the 2010s, has been singled out in academic analysis as a major problem of public administration (Kanyane, Houston and Sausi 2013; Southall 2016; Habib 2016a).

Analysis of employment equity

The gravity and immensity of employment equity in South Africa warrants a synthesis of policy outcomes and debates at this juncture. The first decade after the passage of employment equity law in 1998 saw intensive and polarizing debates, with one side pressing the lack of compliance, slow progress and foregone benefits, against another side stressing skills shortages, unfair treatment of non-beneficiaries and added business costs. Subsequently, at the start of the 2010s, there was a discernible shift in national policy discourses toward reemphasis on employment, skills, and poverty, as skills shortages became more widely acknowledged and public backlash has surfaced against wealth accumulating excesses of politically connected BEE beneficiaries (Economic Development Department 2010; National Planning Commission 2012).

Of course, employment equity law remains intact, and the BBBEE scorecard in 2013 increased the weightage of skills development, management control and enterprise development. Since the mid-2010s, debates surrounding the process and application of employment equity law – which set out parameters but leave some latitude for interpretation – have perhaps reached a state of settlement. Significantly, South Africa has attained more legal clarity on the basis and bounds of affirmative action and unfair discrimination, in light of Constitutional Court judgments, particularly the Barnard case as it is popularly known.[16] Undoubtedly, the country faces ongoing challenges in spurring progress while exercising objective judgment on whether the pace and magnitude of change are adequate. Gains in black representation are demonstrably steady but gradual, as empirically captured in the data reviewed earlier.

But opinion is divided on the reasons for the slow progress, and the question of whether black advancement could or should have progressed faster. For context, reference to the principal model for South Africa's employment equity law bears mentioning. That Canada was also deemed to have made sluggish progress on employment equity compliance, based on a Human Rights Commission report of 1999, thirteen years after the enactment, speaks to the challenges of propelling the desired change (Thomas and Jain 2004, 42).

Did the policy interventions make a difference? Racism against blacks is no longer institutionalized, rampant and brutal as under apartheid, but prejudice can certainly persist, and the marked socio-economic disadvantage and network effects of recruiting within social and professional circles can perpetuate black under-representation starkly in the upper echelons. Thomas (2002) highlights the importance of top management's commitment to the cause, and the role of the legislative approach in confronting tendencies for established "old boys networks" to favour the status quo.

At this juncture, the more constructive and fruitful endeavour is to examine employment equity in practice, rather than question its establishment. More than two decades after its passage, the question of repeal or replacement is a political nonstarter. Undeniably, accepting that employment equity law is deeply embedded and impossible to rescind in the foreseeable future does not presage simple answers. The contribution of the legal mandate is difficult to ascertain precisely, but it is harder to deny that its presence has propelled black occupational advancement. Employers' complaints reflect difficult labour market realities, but also demonstrate that they are under pressure to comply, which further entails that many blacks – with women and the disabled – have enjoyed faster upward mobility than would be the case without the law.

Progress of employment equity – realization of the constructive objectives with mitigation of negative side effects – hinges on factors related to support systems, human resources and macro policy implementation. Undeniably, black recruits and employees on average lag behind white counterparts in terms of academic achievement, highlighting the need to lend support and avail meaningful career paths. The issue of employee turnover and mobility may also arise in this context. While the evidence is mixed, it is plausible that competition for highly qualified blacks, in particular, augments turnover, which potentially constitutes a business cost and disrupts public service delivery. On the whole, then, this complex of outcomes demands comprehensive and objective acknowledgement of the potentialities, pitfalls and supplementary requirements for effective and productive implementation.

Qualitative data and firm-level studies can add some insight here. Various studies, conducted mostly after the first decade of employment equity enforcement, found limited evidence of active implementation. Based on fieldwork interviews with officials and employers, Bezuidenhout *et al.* (2008) observed that government capacity to monitor employment equity was significantly lacking. Schreuder, van Heerden and Khanya (2007) found that firms attach higher priority to equity transfers than employment equity and enterprise development. The study also reports skills shortages, the existence of a small black elite, and high turnover as the most-cited perceived impediments. Oosthuizen and Naidoo (2010), based on interviews with employers and employees, characterize employment equity practices as being in compliance mode, while grappling with skills shortages and mismatch, lack of training and development, perceptions of "reverse discrimination," brain drain and varieties of discontent, including hierarchy within the Black designated group – African first, then Coloured and Indian.[17]

Studies also corroborate the importance of moving from the letter of the employment equity law to its spirit, and disseminating knowledge and appreciation of its underlying intention. Furthermore, a transition from the instrumentalist view and technical adherence to group representation targets, toward embracing diversity, can help sustain the pursuit of employment equity. Zulu and Parumasur (2009) find minimal commitment among companies toward managing cultural diversity, and that employees play a limited role in workplace transformation. Nkomo's (2011) case study of a multinational and public university (formed through a merger) observed ambitious goal-setting and ancillary interventions (diversity workshops, EE committee, targeted recruitment, cultural awareness days). Nonetheless, white male-dominated management displayed less inclination toward transforming attitudes and within-organization cultures. Both blacks and women expressed "frustration with everyday racism and sexism" (Nkomo 2011, 126). The outcomes are traced to the prevalence of hierarchical organizations, profit-motivated diversity interventions, lack of mandate from top leadership which precludes vision/ethos filtering down to middle management, and denial, particularly among white staff, of continuing effects of apartheid in the workplace.

Scarcity of black graduates with in-demand skills, coupled with employment equity imperatives, has given rise to perceptions that job-hopping is more prevalent among black workers, who consequently command high wage premiums to be recruited or retained (e.g. SAIRR 2007). Research over the years has shed some light on this multi-faceted question. Moleke (2005), drawing on a tracer survey of 2,672 graduates between 1990 and 1998, found a higher percentage of Africans still in their first job compared to whites. This outcome is significantly due to a higher proportion of Africans in the public sector, mostly teachers, who tend to retain their jobs over the long term. Nonetheless, the results do not support generalized assessments about the incidence of job-hopping in the African labour force, while leaving open the possibility that highly-qualified Africans are exceptionally mobile. The survey, it should also be noted, was conducted before passage of employment equity legislation.

Another source of information addresses questions over staff turnover in the public sector. Computing public service payroll data, Naidoo (2008) reports high mobility rates in public services over 1998–2002, specifically at the senior management level. The high vacancy rate on average (22.3% in 2004–2005) stems more from mobility than from creation of new posts, and most of the turnover involves internal movement – between departments within the public service.[18] This lends support to the view that job-switching derives from competition between government departments to meet employment equity targets amidst a scarcity of qualified and experienced candidates (Chipkin 2008). However, mobility of white managers has also been high. Over 1998–2002, among senior management that changed jobs within national government, 46% were African and 40% white, both of which are close to the groups' shares of employed senior management (Naidoo 2008, 120–121). High turnover in public sector employment correlates with employment equity and skills shortages, but, as the surveys here suggest, also appears to be part of more systemic problems of workplace relations and combinations of push and pull factors.

Some studies focused on the private sector yield noteworthy findings. Khanyile and Maponga (2007) conducted a survey of professionals to investigate the contention of higher turnover among blacks.[19] They found that 52% of African respondents remained in the same company since starting their career, compared to 25% of white respondents. However, black professionals are more inclined to move, with 41% looking for another job, against 16% of whites. This survey also enquires, through discussions with groups of black professionals, the sources of job satisfaction and reasons for wanting to change jobs, finding that push factors – being denied responsibilities or appraised unequally – play a prominent role. Nzukuma and Bussin (2011), investigating the underlying factors for turnover among African senior managers in service sectors, conclude that self-determination in career development, and lack of support from top management, are greater motivations than material reward.[20] It is plausible that the impetus underlying employment decisions for Africans, and Blacks more generally, vary along career paths, with remuneration more impactful at early stages, while the quest for more fulfilling and autonomous roles weigh heavier for those reaching senior management.

The skills development aspect of employment equity is less tangible, and on the face of the evidence, a lower priority in practice. It is expected that promotion of blacks to managerial positions took primacy in the early post-apartheid years, as the more immediate demand in the dismantling of the racist regime. The 1990s transition was complicated by the fact that the vast majority of black candidates lacked experience and formal qualifications, compared to privileged white counterparts. South Africa's intent to continue transforming labour markets in the 2020s will encounter persisting, if not intensifying, need for skills and experience, which demand greater weightage attached to qualifications, competency, skills and experience in facilitating black upward mobility.

A general observation worth noting here is that managers and professionals receive a considerable share of skills training as reported in the EERs. Companies may have a predilection to show progress on skills development for high-level employees, but the disproportionately lesser benefit to middle ranking employees should be a policy concern.

The phenomenon of minimal compliance applies here as well. Skills development funding levies are also mandatory for employers, which, partly due to the struggling reputation of the Sector Education and Training Authorities (SETA), further lends to disengagement. Companies may opt to pay the levy as a sunk cost without reclaiming it through enrolling employees in training programmes. Nonetheless, there is substantial scope – and under-explored potential – for making the skills development component of affirmative action more expansive and effective. The BEE code revisions in 2013 recognized this, with the weightage on skills development increasing from 10 to 15. Such interventions, continually focused on upward mobility, maintain the thrust of affirmative action.

Enterprise development

Executive positions and board membership in large corporations

Black representation in executive positions and decision-making roles is a key objective of BEE. Employment equity also addresses racial representation in top management positions, but the sphere of large corporations warrants a specific analysis – especially considering the concentrated economic power at the twilight of apartheid and continuing into the democratic era. Transformation of the management and boards of JSE-listed companies reflect the balance of economic influence and power. Empowerdex (2012) tracked JSE-listed companies' board composition, finding a continuous increase in black directors, from 15 in 1992 to 98 in 1997, 307 in 2003, and 1,046 in 2012.

One-off inquiries of publicly listed companies furnish more details, although different sampling limits the comparability of these snapshots. Wu, Khoza and Ngcobo (2002), investigating the top 115 JSE companies found that, out of 1,333 directorships, historically disadvantaged individuals hold 180 positions, or 13.5% of the total. This broad HDI category subsumes blacks, women and the disabled.[21] In 2002, almost one decade after the democratic transition, just one CEO was an HDI, along with four executive chairmen, three COO/CFO, 22 executive directors, 15 non-executive chairmen, 135 non-executive directors. In sum, 83% of total directors occupied non-executive roles. One decade later, the predominance of non-executive black directors persisted. Empowerdex's (2012) data compilations from all JSE companies found that, from 2006 to 2012, the number of black directorships increased from 485 to 1,046, and the share of non-executives among these directors stagnated, at 81% in 2006 and 83% in 2012.[22] Head-hunting firm Jack Hammer's data compilation of South Africa's 40 largest companies found that blacks constituted 10–15% of CEO positions between 2012 to 2018, and about 21% of executive teams, mostly in corporate service roles such as human resources, marketing, legal and corporate affairs, with few still in strategic, operations or finance positions (Jack Hammer 2015; Jack Hammer 2018).

More recently, PwC (2019) reported on the racial composition within topmost and executive director positions of 365 JSE-listed companies, as of April 2019.[23] Among CEOs, 10.2% are African, 1.7% Coloured, 2.2% Indian, 85.9% White, while the profile of CFOs is more disparate, with 4.6% African, 3.2% Coloured, 2.5% Indian, 89.7% White. Information on non-executive directorships were not disclosed in this report. However, blacks have considerably advanced into executive director positions, where 29.5% were African, 10.2% Coloured, 20.4% Indian, 40.0% White. High-profile cases of leadership change may be outlying cases, but nonetheless contribute to popular perceptions. In this context, the 2016 appointment of a white CEO at mobile telecommunications firm MTN, popularly upheld as an exemplar of BEE, induced polarizing reactions. Political and racialist rhetoric aside, constructive lessons can be derived from this outcome, which confirms the continual deep-seated challenge of BEE in the context of scarce talent and experience, but also the commendable willingness to be more pragmatic rather than take an intransigent stance on racial preference for the CEO position.

Black-owned companies and BBBEE scorecard elements

Data limitations are quite acute in the area of black-owned companies. This is technically subsumed under the BBBEE framework, in which grooming black-owned enterprise is an ultimate objective. However, it is challenging to evaluate the outcomes of BBBEE, including black ownership, due to the composite nature of the scorecard which is difficult to disaggregate, and also different interpretations of the complex scoring criteria in the verification process (Shai, Molefinyana and Quinot 2019). The lack of an authoritative monitoring agency with the means and resources to compile and compute data compounds the empirical inadequacies. The BBBEE Commission was only established in 2016; prior to that, BEE-related public agencies served mainly in advisory capacities.

Ownership databases require immense accounting efforts in compiling data and tracking changes due to sale and purchase. Absent nationally representative data, sector-specific samples provide some snapshots – and have indicated limited progress in black-owned companies. Analyzing the first decade of democracy, Sanchez (2008) noted a slow expansion of blacks in establishing and operating small and medium scale enterprises, especially in engineering and technical fields. Mohamed and Roberts (2008), in a survey of engineering firms, found minimal procurement of technical or material products from BBBEE firms, and a number of transactions involved ambiguous or misleading classification of BBBEE status.[24]

Schreuder, van Heerden and Khanya (2007), surveying compliance with the BBBEE codes across its seven elements, found generally low levels of engagement, especially among small firms. Respondents indicated making efforts in ownership transfer, skills development and employment equity, but on average performed poorly in the categories of preferential procurement and enterprise development.[25] Arguably, procurement targets are ineffectually low and susceptible to selective compliance.[26]

Ownership of micro, small and medium enterprises (MSMEs) paint a broad-brushed but instructive picture. African-owned MSMEs constituted 79% of the total in 2008, but fell to 71% in 2013, before rebounding to 76% in 2017, while Coloured- and Indian-owned combined for 8–10% across the 2008–2017 period. The share of White-owned companies rose from 12% in 2008 to 16% in 2017 (IFC 2018). Stark differences emerge when disaggregated by scale. In 2010, the share of African firms – predominantly self-employed individuals, among those in the micro category – varied from 75% among micro to 39% among small, and 31% among medium. Contrastingly, White-owned operations comprised 8%, 36% and 46%, respectively, at micro, small and medium scale. Indian-owned and Coloured-owned firms registered disproportionately larger shares than their population share, with Indian firms notably high among the medium-scaled, at 15%, and Coloured among small-scaled, at 16%.

South Africa's complex procurement system poses further research challenges, as noted earlier. Our concern here is with operations and growth of black-owned companies, especially SMEs, through the primary instrument of public procurement, as well as licensing and subcontracting. The overwhelming presence of large companies in the South African economy placed the spotlight upon them in the BEE discourse, policy implementation and empirical research. The ownership aspect has also taken centre stage and debate has been quite vigorous, as overviewed in the next segment. The multiple elements of the BBBEE scorecard, compounded by the policy's fluidity and voluntary participation, complicate the process of translating composite scores into distinct empirical policy outcomes. The absence of an established data registry and a well-resourced monitoring agency, alongside changes in BBBEE terms and conditions, limited data availability – until the formation of the BBBEE Commission in 2016, which has begun to publish data from BBBEE certificates. Perspectives of SME owners and operators are also pertinent. Pike, Puchert and Chinyamurindi's (2018) survey of SMEs and public procurement in East London captured – in one locality – a range of opinion, with more respondents highlighting problems with the competency of selected of contractors and non-delivery of projects, and allegations of tender corruption, but some viewing BBBEE positively. These reinforce the reality that BBBEE is a work in progress, needing vigilant execution and possibly further modification.

The BBBEE Commission has incrementally consolidated its monitoring capacities, reflected in the successive *National State of Transformation and Trend Analysis Reports* of 2016 to 2018, which collate and synthesize data from certificates submitted to the Commission. The vastly different samples across time render them not comparable. The numbers suggest improved compliance, with the tally of large enterprises increasing from 851 in 2017 to 1,061 in 2018. However, due to changes in reporting requirements, the number of qualifying small enterprise fell from 871 to 588 and exempted micro enterprise plummeted from 1,139 to 25 (BBBEE Commission 2019). Compliance of state-owned entities and organs of state are exceptionally low, with only 29 reporting in 2018. The distribution of large companies based on BBBEE levels is worth referencing. In 2018, 21.1% were at levels 1–2, 25.4% at levels 3–4, 10.7% at levels 5–6, 19.4% at levels 7–8, while 23.4% were non-compliant. The Report also computes the average BBBEE points achieved as a percentage of available BBBEE points, which varies by scorecard element. In the order they are listed in the scorecard, the achieved rates were 56% for ownership, 46% for management control, 50% for skills development, 61% for enterprise and supplier development and 73% for socio-economic development. JSE-listed companies are obligated to submit BEE reports, but only 161 out of 371 complied in 2018, with 18.6% at levels 1–2, 32.3% at levels 3–4, 12.4% at levels 5–6, 13.7% at levels 7–8 and 23.0% classified non-compliant or with no data (BBBEE Commission 2019).

Public procurement, as the primary instrument of BBBEE, warrants a brief note. The 2013 report of the Presidential Review Committee on SOEs, commissioned in 2010, furnishes some pertinent findings. BEE suppliers accounted for 50% of government and SOE procurement and 8.5% in the private sector (PRC-SOE 2013). Companies that were 50% black-owned and 30% black women-owned accounted for 13.0% and 0.6%, respectively, of procurement by government or SOEs and the private sector. For qualifying small enterprises and exempted micro enterprises, the corresponding shares were 18.1% and 3.7%. The data are scarce and not tracked across time. Nonetheless, it is reasonable to extrapolate from these figures that distribution of procurement contracts to black empowered companies through public procurement has progressed at a modest pace. Assessing the capability development aspect requires more data.

BBBEE expectedly features marginally in private sector procurement. However, South Africa has seen some initiative in "sustainable public procurement" – which integrates other objectives besides cost and quality, including supplier diversity. The South African Supplier Diversity Council (SASDC) was established in 2011, as part of a network of five supplier diversity councils: Australia, UK, Canada and China (Rogerson 2012). The key objective of diversity is to increase the participation of black suppliers, which the SASDC certifies through its own mechanisms. By January 2020, the SASDC consisted of 28 corporate members and reported 761 certified black suppliers employing 20,800 workers in its network, with ZAR500 million in spending between corporates and suppliers. While a notable programme, its magnitude, averaging close to ZAR60 million per year,[27] is dwarfed by annual public procurement budgets of about ZAR500 billion (Mazibuko 2018).

State-owned entities and public enterprises/state-owned companies

South Africa has 715 state-owned entities in total, at all spheres of government – including commercial entities, agencies, regulators and others (PRC-SOE 2013).[28] The more commercially-oriented and strategically-located entities, termed *public enterprises* in the first decades of democracy and presently state-owned companies (SOCs), have been utilized for promoting a black managerial class and enterprises through the procurement chain. The largest of these, and other strategic or more complex operations, come under the Department of Public Enterprise's oversight: Transnet, South African Airways (SAA, and subsidiary SAA Express), Eskom, Safcom, Denel and Alexkor.

SOEs pursue employment equity vigorously, but stand out for appointing blacks to top management and executive positions, thus also play a signalling role in the broader scheme of affirmative action by demonstrating black capability in commercial enterprise. This poses challenges in terms of securing suitably qualified candidates, and managing scrutiny and potential controversy arising from the high-profile visibility of personnel changes. Among the largest SOCs, Eskom and South African Airways have been engulfed in operational and financial difficulties, due to multiple factors related to industry structure and public policy, which have also caused, and perhaps resulted from, high turnover of CEOs. Among high profile cases were the resignations of Eskom's and SAA's black CEOs in mid-2019 and appointment of white CEOs. Reactions were polarized, and symptomatic of a still-racialized society but also one capable of exercising sober judgment and handing the reins to more experienced leadership. Denel, likewise, while appointing a white CEO in early 2019, reported that blacks constituted over half of its executive team, 61% of its workforce and 84% of new appointments in 2018.[29]

SOEs' procurement amounts to 25% of total government procurement expenditure (PARI 2017) and is highly concentrated in the large companies: Eskom, Transnet and SAA account for around 70% of total SOE procurement (PRC-SOE 2013). The Presidential Review Committee on SOEs is worth referencing again; its 2013 report identified policy challenges and provided some broad-brushed analysis. Among the chief findings were that SOEs have progressed further than the private sector in employment equity but still lag in terms of black representation in technical roles, and that SOEs fall short of compliance targets. In preferential procurement of selected major SOEs, compliance averaged 15 out of 20 (based on the BEE scorecard). The enterprise development element registered high scores, but the report deemed this as loosely defined and prone to abuse. Therefore, on the whole, BBBEE through SOE procurement shows a chequered record.

Loans, grants and ancillary support

South Africa's interventions in cultivating black-owned companies through provision of loans and grants has leveraged on existing institutions such as the IDC and newly created agencies such as the National Empowerment Fund, as well as incentive schemes under the Department of Trade and Industry, and most recently, the Black Industrialists Programme. Data are scant, and some programmes are only recently launched, but their progress merits a cursory update.

Funding for black enterprise has stemmed from three main sources – IDC, NEF and DTI.

The annual value of IDC's loans approved to "black-empowered companies," meaning companies with 25% or more black shareholding from 1993 to 2001, increased from about ZAR0.2 billion in 1994 to ZAR1.2 billion in 2001. The volume continually rose with some year-to-year fluctuation, and with 50% or more black-owned companies – a category differentiated from 2002 – receiving more than half the loans. IDC funding for BEE spiked at ZAR6.5 billion in 2010, hovered thereafter in the ZAR5–6 billion range from 2012–2015, then rose again to ZAR8–10 billion in 2018–2019 (IDC 2010, 2015a, 2015b, 2018, 2019). By proportion, black-owned companies have been increasingly prioritized, and above all, those classified as black industrialists.[30]

The National Empowerment Fund, in its first decade, facilitated 86 transactions worth ZAR496 million,[31] of which 78% by number were for starting up or expanding businesses, and 75% by value were for buying equity in white-owned businesses (Schreuder, van Heerden and Khanya 2007). The NEF received further seed funding of ZAR2.4 billion in 2005, all of which was disbursed by 2010, and was subsequently self-financed through lending and investment activities. However, it became embroiled in a scandal in 2013, which triggered a moratorium on its operations. Until 2017, when it became reconstituted as a subsidiary of the IDC, the NEF had approved ZAR8.5 billion in support of 839 black-owned companies.[32] The DTI's schemes principally target black-owned small-scale and especially medium-scale enterprises. Data on the amounts disbursed and number of recipients in the Support Programme for Industrial Innovation (SPII) and Technology and Human Resource for Industry Programme (THRIP) were not found in publicly accessible sources.

Two recent initiatives stand out for their focus on SMEs and potential to groom industry players in more dynamic and effective ways, with a stress on directly black-owned, capable and competitive players: the SME Fund, and especially the Black Industrialist Programme (BIP). Information on these programmes' progress is scant. The SME Fund, financed by 50 listed companies and the PIC, was only launched in late 2018 and hence, it is too soon to evaluate. The BIP, under IDC oversight, has targeted 100 beneficiaries by 2018. By October 2018, 128 projects with proposed investment amounting to ZAR11.1 billion had been approved.[33] Black industrialists received ZAR4.9 billion in 2017, ZAR7.8 billion in 2018, dropping again to ZAR6.0 billion in 2019. The total amount approved for black industrialists over 2014–2018 was ZAR21.4 billion, or 93% of the five-year target of ZAR23 billion set in the 2016 financial year (IDC 2019). In 2019 the programme was budgeted ZAR40 billion for the following 4–5 years, to foster 400 black industrialists.[34]

Public demands intensified for the government to disclose BIP beneficiaries from June 2017. The DTI relented a year later, in June 2018, garnering fierce reactions at the appearance of politically connected individuals, which prompted castigation that it is a new form of black elitism and ANC patronage.[35] The IDC has defended its selection process, maintaining that it conducted rigorous and impartial selection of BIP beneficiaries. There is scarce information to reach more definitive conclusions. Appraisals of the profile of recipients, however, should be tempered with acknowledgment that, in view of the scarcity of entrepreneurs in general, insistence on party non-affiliation may be too rigid and limiting a precondition. The pool of non-ANC-linked businesses is presumably growing and should be tapped, but South Africa's trajectory has shaped the political economy such that capable entrepreneurs have arisen from within the ANC establishment. Ultimately, capability and competitiveness – with stringent oversight and accountability – will impact on the BIP's success more than political non-affiliation.

Wealth ownership

This study focuses on South Africa's efforts to redistribute equity ownership – the principal area of wealth-related affirmative action. Indeed, the discourse – and fierce debate – over BEE and wealth ownership revolve singularly around the dimension of shareholdings. These interventions intersect with black-owned companies and blacks on corporate boards as discussed earlier, but the specific goal of transferring shares entails distinct policy channels and implications. Full books have been written on this aspect of BEE alone, delving into the complexities of transactions. Gqubule (2006) and Cargill (2010) notably provide detailed accounts of the process, including the rather ad hoc and experimental manner that deals and wealth transfers unfolded in the 1990s through to the more formalization of BBBEE in the early- to mid-2000s.

Two forms of data provide the means for empirical analyses: BEE deals and ownership of publicly listed companies. Besides volume of transactions and transfers, other characteristics are also of interest, especially the control conferred and the participation of broad-based constituents, such as employees, community organizations and trade unions. The 2000s witnessed a flourish in BBBEE deals, particularly in the half decade following the BBBEE Act 2003, as noted by Horwitz and Jain (2011) and Patel and Graham (2012). Specifically, there was a spike in the number of deals in 2004–2006, followed by a slowdown in 2007–2009, just as the BBBEE Codes were promulgated – but the global financial crisis also struck. Another problematic feature of the early waves of BBE deals is that they were dependent on capital gains; subsequent deals were more reliant on dividends.[36] In terms of the distribution within BEE beneficiaries, broad-based groups constituted a small segment, but saw their share of total deals increase from 7.6% in 2004 to 14.0% in 2006. The decline in volume of BEE deals in 2007–2009 was accompanied by an increase in the share of broad-based beneficiaries (Patel and Graham 2012). The growth spurt also concurs with Sartorius and Botha's (2008) survey of 72 publicly listed companies, in which they find most complying with BEE as a political economic imperative and selecting BEE partners based on potential to add value and grow market share, but also to expand benefits broadly and assist in transformation.

Some fundamental, structural problems with BEE deals have been robustly critiqued, particularly the practice of debt-financing, which facilitated deals under more buoyant conditions that were vulnerable to downturns and resulted in passive rather than productive and innovative engagements. Cargill (2010) and

Gqubule (2006), in particular, have made cogent observations. Increased political weight behind the agenda propelled share acquisitions from the early 2000s. However, while relatively lesser in volume, BEE of the 1990s possibly transferred more control and meaningful participation. As Cargill (2010, 51) writes: "Contrary to perception, more of the real thing occurred in the first wave of BEE than in the period after the adoption of the various BEE polices, codes and sector charters, all of which took shape from 2003." On the BBBEE Act and Codes,

> [T]he evidence suggest that earlier black corporate shareholding initiatives provided a basis for productive investment outcomes. The Codes stalled this trend. Further, investment companies with a strong broad-based shareholder flavour display a type of corporate entrepreneurship that is barely evident among the individual BEE investors.
>
> (Cargill 2010, 56)

Institutional investments that are less wedded to personalities deliver better for long-term investments and steady returns to shareholders – providing a positive scope for broad-based investor groups or trusts and employee-ownership.

Gqubule (2006) highlights how the formation of black entrepreneurial class in the first post-Apartheid decade was limited to a small set of sectors, and was most effective in licensing, due in part to the economic domain carved out for the licensee which gives room to grow and develop the business, and in part to the government's greater leverage over the beneficiary that augments monitoring and disciplinary efforts. More generally, he critiques the lack of innovative vigour, and notes the pace of ownership redistribution derives from economic growth and macroeconomic conditions, especially interest rates. He also rebuts the call for abolishing BEE policy because it has concentrated wealth in a handful of blacks. Gqubule (2006, 35) writes,

> The real story is that hundreds of capital reform initiatives have delivered negligible equity to black companies. The key issue is not that a few people have been enriched through capital reform, but that so few have been empowered. . . . The other side of the futile and sterile debate about enrichment versus empowerment is that the so-called BEE oligarchs are not real oligarchs. Their companies are still small, even by South African standards.

The prevalence of a quantity-quality trade-off should not surprise, in view of the dearth of black entrepreneurial capacity and experience. That broad-based groups and employees tend to maintain longer-term interest is another expected outcome, given the greater stake such investors would hold in the growth of the business rather than short-term gains. These conditions and outcomes have factored into the BBBEE process, which has been compelled to respond to fronting, wealth concentration and profiteering. Policy modifications in the 2010s, including the BBBEE code revisions of 2013, have also been prompted by popular disaffection and public backlash, and protracted economic malaise. The question of political connection of beneficiaries, however, is not uniformly negative as some-times regarded. The more productive or promising BEE share ownership and licensing deals do not stand out for absence of political linkage, but for acumen, ability or charisma. Partisan interest certainly can, and often does, detract from productivity gains and capability development, but a blanket disqualification of beneficiaries on the basis of political affinity limits the pool of capable candidates. The decisive issue, and policy challenge, is to more credibly and stringently select and monitor progress among the nascent black capitalist and industrial class, of which many, having emerged under the state's aegis, will likely have cultivated some political relationships.

Emphatically, many implementation and structural issues persist. A number of contentious elements of the BBBEE system, particularly the lock-in period which reduces liquidity and restricts black shareholders' latitude, the "once empowered always empowered" clause that allows companies to claim points even after black shareholders have sold off their stakes to non-blacks, ownership accounting that does not factor in debt and variances across different industry charters, will con-tinue to be debated (Gqubule 2017).

Public debate over ownership also erupts from time to time, with a notable crescendo in 2015, triggered by the presidency's contention that that black direct ownership in JSE-listed companies amounted to a mere 3%. This clashed with estimates disseminated by the JSE, which commissioned a study that put black ownership at 23% of the top 100 companies,[37] comprised of 10% black owner-ship and 13% in indirect ownership via institutions, predominantly the public sector pension fund (JSE 2015). This had followed on a similar work of 2011 that reported 8% direct black ownership and 9% of pension fund and mandated investments attributed to blacks. The presidency subsequently issued a rejoinder, reiterating the initial disclosure and explaining its sources and basis – and suggest-ing that the 3% referred not just to ownership but also direct control (Maharaj and Medupi 2015).[38] The debate is partly about definitions of ownership and control; the disparity in the nominally comparable metric of direct black owner-ship indicates the need for more candour and consensus on the existence and consequences of different methodologies (Gqubule 2017).

Black ownership in the mining sector is significant, as the sector steeped in historical injustices, bearing arguably the heaviest imperative for transformation. BEE charters have been fiercely contested and intensively conflictual, and the gains in ownership, while exceeding the national average, remain low. At end 2014, black ownership comprised 16.1% of the top 25 mining companies, but net value – after accounting for debt incurred to acquire the assets and removing non-empowerment participants in BEE transactions – was equivalent to 9.6% (Gqubule 2016).

Popular attitudes toward affirmative action

A further aspect of our inquiry into affirmative action concerns public opinion and sentiment toward the policy. Broadly, surveys more directly capturing policy support find a majority favouring AA, with disparities across groups. More recent surveys seeking views on allocative outcomes and labour market procedures but not precisely capturing opinion toward law and public policy, find support for competency in appointments and also observe disparities across groups, most markedly between Africans and Whites. On quotas in sports teams, a question consistently asked across questionnaires, we see a gravitation of support away from such intervention. Consistent disparities within the Black category, mirroring a sense of exclusion among Coloureds and Indians, are a cause for concern.

The South Africa Social Attitudes Survey (SASAS), a series conducted from 2003 to 2009, is perhaps the data source most directly addressing public sentiment towards affirmative action policy (Roberts, Weir-Smith and Reddy 2011). I draw on Roberts (2006) and Durrheim (2010), which report findings from the 2003 and 2004 SASAS, respectively.[39]

The SASASes also capture popular sentiment toward a range of policies, providing material for instructive comparison. Most pertinent to this study is the degree of support for basic provisions, in which the 2003 SASAS showed broad and overwhelming support, with more than 80% within all groups, and 90% nationwide, supporting the view that government is responsible for providing employment and basic livelihood (Roberts 2006). The surveys affirm the higher priority that South African society places on basic needs and livelihoods, but importantly, also demonstrate that such opinion can coincide with support, particularly in the majority group, for affirmative action.

An overall majority support preferential measures to promote blacks in business and occupational advancement, but the matter is starkly polarizing. In the 2003 and 2004 SASASes, the statement, "there should be preferential hiring and promotion of black South Africans in employment," received over 60% support overall, but overwhelmingly, Africans were favourable (80% agreeing or strongly agreeing) and Whites were opposed (13–16% in agreement), while the support of Coloureds and Indians was not much higher than that of Whites.[40] Stratifying the sample, Roberts (2006) found higher support among lower income respondents, with 81% and 75% of "poor" and "vulnerable" respondents, respectively, in agreement, compared to 54% of those classified as "wealthy." The SASASes observe similar patterns regarding preferential contracts and support for black business.[41] On quotas for sports teams, similar patterns of racial disparity hold, but by lesser margins, with 62% of Africans and 18% of Whites supporting such a policy (Durrheim 2010).[42]

A contrasting survey was conducted at the same time as the early SASASes, and has sometimes been cited as evidence of popular rejection of affirmative action (du Toit 2004). It asks a different set of questions, some of which are rather emotively charged.[43] The statement "affirmative action policies turn able-bodied white men into second class citizens in their own country" elicited polarized responses, with about 70% of Whites in agreement but only around 30% of Africans, and larger shares but still a minority (less than 40%) of Coloureds and Indians. These results are expected. However, on whether "young people entering the job market for the first time should be exempted from affirmative action policies," there is less disparity, with almost 80% of Whites, and over 70% of Coloureds and Indians, agreeing, along with nearly 50% of Africans. In both of these questions, more highly educated and higher income earners are more likely to agree.

An annual series of surveys by the South African Institute of Race Relations (SAIRR) from 2014 onwards have been conducted in a similar vein of probing public sentiment on policy priorities and outcomes and procedural scenarios, but unlike the SASAS, these findings do not capture public opinion toward the policy *per se* (SAIRR 2017, 2018, 2019).[44] The presentation of alternate positions regarding appointments processes also, arguably, elevate the role of "merit" in ways that potentially bias responses. Among the salient repeated questions across the survey's iterations is, "Who should be appointed to jobs in South Africa?" The answer "appointments on merit, with special training for the previously disadvantaged" receives broad support of 60–70% overall, with majorities of all groups agreeing.[45] However, the statement presents a somewhat internally inconsistent picture: if the previously disadvantaged require special training, can they be appointed solely on the basis of "merit"? The statement is premised on a disparity and implies that some who are less capable or less experienced can be appointed, yet sets up an unqualified merit-based appointment process (SAIRR 2017, 2019).[46] The question also contains elements of qualified support for affirmative action; for instance, the findings may be interpreted as favouring affirmative action specifically in skills development, or appointment on preferential terms conditional upon subsequent training. However, the reports derived from these surveys generally take the findings as a rejection of affirmative action.

Nonetheless, there is some value in referencing these surveys, which discernibly reflect a popular demand for competency, especially in positions with public consequence. Problems with public service delivery may also reside in the background of the broad reception for merit-based appointments, although again, the findings are not as decisive as the SASAS in reflecting opinion toward the policy and expected roles of government in affirmative action. The SAIRR surveys also probe the issue of racial quotas in sports teams, with a line of questioning that is comparable to the SASAS. In contrast to the SASAS, these surveys find all groups overwhelming rejecting quotas, in contrast to the gaps between Africans and Whites ten years prior. This suggests that support for merit-based appointment have increased across time, and South Africans may be less concerned with racial representation. However, the issue of sports teams must be handled circumspectly. Their exceptional visibility, and the visceral and vicarious impact of their success, set them apart from ordinary employment. This is partly reflected in the lesser emphasis on racial representation in sports teams compared to employment in general, in the SASAS. The SAIRR findings suggest that the term *quota*, evidently with negative connotations, is a trigger point in surveys that appears to swing opinion against such policies – but respondents, especially Africans, still value group representation.[47]

Conclusion

South Africa's voluminous data availability and public dissemination of statistics has made for an extensive analysis. This chapter concludes with some condensed notes. Black representation has increased in higher education enrolment and graduation. However, various developments are cause for concern, including a drop in the share of science, engineering and technology graduates. Socio-economic disadvantage also persists and disproportionately affects blacks and especially Africans, compounded by challenges of affordability and financial resources, institutional quality and reputation, which still matter despite attempts to narrow gaps and dilute the distinction between HWIs and HBIs. Basic schooling system deficiencies exert legacy effects and place the disadvantaged and privileged on different trajectories. But it must be accepted that AA in higher education must proceed simultaneously; it cannot wait until basic schooling is fixed. The recent implementation of class-based preference in university enrolment mark a positive step. In the transition to work, holding a diploma or degree qualifications matters immensely. Black graduates register lower unemployment rates than average, but still higher than white graduates. Blacks remain more reliant on public sector and state-owned entities for employment.

Higher up the occupational ladder, Black representation in professional and management ranks have steadily increased, in both public and private sectors. Entry into the top and senior management strata, however, has been slow. Blacks have advanced in greater volume in the public sector, as expected, but the rapid pace of change has been a double-edged sword; accelerating the formation of a black professional and managerial corps has come at some expense of competency and service delivery. The ANC's execution of cadre deployment, in particularly, has been faulted for both politicizing appointments and undermining government performance. Within the Black category, Africans have gained the most ground, moving in the direction of proportionality with the economically active population. But this has also been a source of friction, with Coloureds and Indians perceiving themselves in subsidiary status to Africans. Employment equity law has propelled the changing race profile of high-level occupations, although the exact contribution is difficult to estimate. The incidence of adverse consequences, including inexperience and incompetency, and brain drain, must be acknowledged, but role of affirmative action is as impossible to deny. The debates will persist. Ultimately, however, moving forward pre-eminently entails effective and prudent implementation of deeply mandated legislation and policy.

Likewise, the imperative remains for policy interventions to promote black participation in enterprise. The very reasons that compel affirmative action – South Africa's economic structure, where the commanding heights are characterized by immense, oligopolistic concentration in key sectors, notably mining, which have high entry barriers – also greatly encumber the quest for breakthroughs and sustained progress. The share of blacks in executive positions and management control has witnessed slow gains. State owned companies, which have sought to develop and demonstrate Black managerial capability and supplier development primarily through procurement, have progressed more than the private sector on these fronts, but in recent years commercial woes in a few entities have prompted some moderation of the agenda, with a few whites appointed CEO.

More generally, public procurement has been the chief instrument for BBBEE, and its effects are presumably quite extensive. However, the data are rather patchy. The BBBEE Commission was only established in 2016 and its data repository is still tentative, sufficient only for impressionistic observations. The Commission reports poor compliance of both private companies and government departments in submitting BBBEE certificates. In the 2018 dataset of large companies and JSE-listed companies, of which compliance was still low but relatively higher than average, one-fifth registered levels 1 or 2, while one-quarter were deemed non-compliant or without data.

Amid the array of AA programmes, enterprise development is in some ways more contingent on an effective and dynamic developmental state because the intervention involves selecting and monitoring companies that must deliver more complex outcomes with broader ramifications. This elicits more general questions surrounding state capability and public trust that has eroded in recent years. The efficacy of public procurement, state-owned companies and state-sponsored financing and support are constrained by operational deficiencies, in terms of personnel, technical knowledge and structural factors such as the level of centralization/decentralization (Ambe and Badenhorst-Weiss 2012) and widespread unethical practices (Mazibuko 2018), most saliently the "state capture" scandal of the Zuma Presidency (PARI 2017). Patronage and rent-seeking that have arguably become endemic to the ANC also contribute to a deleterious pursuit of personal enrichment and political popularity at the expense of national developmental benefits (Ndletyana 2015). The increased priority of more bottom-up processes for grooming SMEs and black industrialists through rigorous selection and financial support, with more modest quantitative targets and emphasis on performance and delivery, mark constructive change and a potentially more sustainable and productive mode of visibly empowering black business. The track record of SOCs is mixed, with some chronically beset with commercial malady and managerial turmoil, but they are hindered by broader systemic woes and remain institutions that can help foster BBBEE.

The milestones, deficiencies and dilemmas of BEE are widely articulated, from more measured analyses (Gqubule 2006; Cargill 2010; Manning and Jennes 2014; Southall 2016) to more polemical positions (Jeffery 2014). BEE's challenge and dilemma are well summed up by Horwitz and Jain (2011, 314), who maintain that it "arguably . . . may be an overly mechanistic rather a transformative process although measures of progress in these areas may well be needed." The shortfalls in cultivating dynamic, innovative and competitive black-owned enterprise underscore the limits of a standardized, compliance-based approach that redistributes existing assets. At the same time, disparities in participation and wealth ownership remain unacceptably high, and the moral imperative of apartheid redress, while perhaps less forceful than two decades ago, still bears substantial weight and is also counterbalanced by need to address the backlashes against BEE provoked by black wealth concentration, corruption and profiteering amid chronically high unemployment and public service deficiencies. Less BEE does not necessarily translate into more jobs for the masses, but public pressures for more effectively and genuinely engendering broad-based outcomes have borne some fruit in amendments tackling the problem of fronting and facilitating more employee and broad-based group ownership. The imperative of transformation remains pronounced in terms of South Africa's persistent structural inequalities, with particularly sectors, especially mining, maintaining economic power and influence, and high concentration of large corporations. The impetus on ownership transfers to reach broad-based groups remains pertinent, in the context of historical redress.

Alongside continual efforts to transform resource-based sectors and the commanding heights, expanding ownership and participation more generally, and in a bottom-up manner, entails more attention to black SMEs. The relative scarcity of data disclosure and official reportage are perhaps reflective of the lesser priority ascribed to SME development; the little information mustered shows, unsurprisingly, black-owned SMEs constitute a small proportion, particularly in manufacturing. The challenge of making breakthroughs, not just in transferring ownership or appointing blacks prominently but above all in facilitating black-owned and operated enterprises, is compounded by the requisite technical sophistication. The Black Industrialists Policy distinctly seeks to promote black participation in this specific sector, to operate more directly through stringent selection and monitoring, and to start out with a small, select set of beneficiaries.

A built-up process must advance in tandem with the increase in talent and experience. The scarcities remain real and acute. There is perhaps some acceptance that the preference for blacks to lead SOCs may need to be tempered. It is prudent for the government to establish a discourse that recognizes these realities and depoliticizes the decision-making. At the same time, reactions to prominent politically-linked figures receiving benefits can also arise from overly dogmatic predispositions.

Affirmative action is embedded in South Africa and is perhaps more institutionalized in law than in any other country. Does the government have popular mandate? It is fair to say, from public discourse and opinion surveys, that concentration of wealth entwined with BEE, and public service delivery associated with affirmative action and ANC cadre deployment, fuel popular discontent, and these sentiments are reflected in opinion surveys. However, the surveys do not indicate public endorsement for abolishing employment equity law or abandoning BEE.

At this juncture, the premises, findings and analyses of this book prescribe a constructive, productive and conciliatory path forward, focused on making affirmative action more effective in developing capability, distributing opportunity in a truly broad-based manner and demonstrating achievement and success to be further built upon.

Notes

1 The University of the Free State and University of Pretoria are examples of transformation driven by demographic factors. At the University of Stellenbosch, with its strong Afrikaans undergraduate culture and enrolment trends, coupled with low density black African townships in the vicinity, enrolment patterns have been more difficult to change. North West University maintains a largely white campus in Potchefstroom and a black campus in Mafikeng partly because the latter, with an established black identity, was merged into the former, an historically white university. The author thanks Professor Jonathan Jansen for these insights (Author's personal correspondence, 25 July 2017).

2 Author's interview with Professor Max Price, then Vice-Chancellor of the University of Cape Town (14 August 2017).

3 Nicola Jenvey, "Black Graduates Struggle the Most to Find Employment", *University World News*, 29 September 2017.

4 Of the cohort starting school in 2007, who would be age eligible to take the NSC in 2018, the share who took the NSC is estimated to be around 40% ("South Africa's School-Pass Rate Rose to 78.2% in 2018", *Bloomberg*, 4 January 2019).

5 For reference, the share of blacks in the economically active population of South Africa's provinces are: Eastern Cape (93.0%), Free State (95.4%), Gauteng (86.6%), Kwazulu-Natal (96.7%), Limpopo (97.7%), Mpumalanga (94.6%), North West (93.7%), Northern Cape (93.0%), Western Cape (85.0%) (Department of Labour 2019).

6 Author's personal correspondence with Professor Jonathan Jansen, 25 July 2017.

7 Among whites, 22.6% were managers, 57.2% professionals, 4.4% supervisors, and 10.4% in administrative positions. Among Africans, 10.8% were managers, 59.9% professionals, 7.7% supervisors, and 13.1% administrators (Moleke 2005).

8 Author's calculations from the Labour Force Surveys (2017 third quarter and 2018 third quarter).

9 In 2004, the CEE received 9,389 reports encompassing 2,534,525 employees (for an average of 270 per employer). In 2010, the corresponding totals were 18,534 reports and 5,280,037 employees (averaging 285), and in 2016, 26,255 reports and 7,071,449 employees (averaging 269).

10 The number of EERs received in 2002 and 2006 stand out, at 6,990 (2002) and 6,876 (2006), compared to 12,980 in 2000 and 9,389 in 2004 (*Employment Equity Report 2006–2007*).

11 These surveys in the mid-2000s covered 850 companies employing over 1.5 million people ("Black Women Getting Top Management", *Business Day*, 8 December 2008).

12 Two caveats are attached to this survey: first, participation is voluntary, and respondents are disproportionately large firms.

13 These changes transpire on the back of steady but slow gains in enrolment in this particular professional field. Among accounting majors, 2.2% were African, 1.1% Coloured, 5.6% Indian, and 88.8% White in 1991. By 2001, these shares were 9.0% African, 2.7% Coloured, 9.7% Indian, and 76.5% White. Private sector programmes have been initiated to address these racial disparities, but their impact is necessarily limited, while shortfalls in the public higher education and training systems persist (van Zyl 2008, 379–383).

14 LFS data have been found to be reasonably compatible with public services employment data. Naidoo (2008), analyzing the 2006 public service payroll, reports Africans constituting 57% at senior management and 73% overall, while the contemporaneous LFS finds Africans to constitute 57.3% of managers and 71.2% of government employees.

15 Author's calculations from the *Commission for Employment Equity Annual Report 2018–2019.*
16 The full name of this case is: *Solidary obo Barnard* v. *South African Police Services* (Case no. CCT 01/14).
17 Oosthuizen and Naidoo (2010) register a caveat about the small sample of 21 organizations, with 105 interviews, which requires circumspection in extrapolating the study, while simultaneously acknowledging the ways this qualitative study complements more common quantitative research.
18 For example, between 1998 and 2002, 91% of mobility of senior managers in national government occurred within the public services (Author's calculation from Naidoo 2008, 120).
19 Khanyile and Maponga's (2007) sample comprises 2,000 respondents, the majority of which earn above ZAR10,000 a month.
20 Nzukuma and Bussin (2011) interviewed 208 respondents in various service industries.
21 Wu, Khoza and Ngcobo (2002) arrived at a sample of 115 by setting a size threshold of capitalization above ZAR1 billion.
22 Empowerdex (2012) also disaggregates by gender. The 1,046 total black directors comprised 702 male and 344 female, and the balance within the 177 executive directors (142 male, 35 female) and 865 non-executive directors (560 male, 309 female) show black women disproportionately in non-executive roles.
23 Specifically, PwC (2019) reports on 1,198 executive positions, of which there are 335 CEOs, 310 CFOs, and 435 executive directors.
24 Mohamed and Roberts (2008) sample 25 firms in metals and engineering industries.
25 Respondents fell short least of all in the ownership element of the BEE scorecard (60.3% of the target level), ahead of skills development (43.8%) and employment equity (36.7%) (Schreuder, van Heerden and Khanya 2007).
26 Author's personal correspondence with Duma Gqubule, 11 January 2019.
27 Data obtained from the SASDC website (www.sasdc.org.za, accessed 3 January 2020).
28 A recent search on publicly available sources finds 171 "public entities" under national government, and 93 under provincial governments. (Author's compilations from officially listed entities, https://nationalgovernment.co.za/, accessed 3 January 2020.)
29 "Denel Defends Appointment of White Male CEO as 'Top Candidate'", *Fin24,* 14 January 2019.
30 In 2015–2019, the IDC's "transformation" funding allocation by proportion were: 36% for black-owned companies (with 35% for black industrialists); 25% for black-empowered companies; 17% for woman-empowered companies; 7% for youth-empowered companies (IDC 2019).
31 These disbursements derive from 102 approved transactions worth ZAR692 million.
32 "NEF Merges with IDC to Advance Development of Black Industrialists", *Engineering News,* 15 February 2017.
33 "Market Access Still Poses a Challenge for Black Industrialists", *DTI Media Statement,* 4 October 2018 (www.thedti.gov.za/editmedia.jsp?id=5614).
34 Duma Gqubule, "Funding Empowerment", not dated, *Business Media MAGS.*
35 Loyiso Sidimba, "SA's Elite Cashing in", *IOL News,* 21 June 2018.
36 Author's personal correspondence with Colin Reddy.
37 The top 100 listed companies accounted for 90% of market capitalization in 2018, and 96% in 2019 (PwC 2019, 4).

38 The presidency's numbers derive from the NEF, which employed direct owner-ship as defined in the BBBEE codes. The 2015 JSE figures have been challenged for lack of disclosure of methodology. However, the estimates are comparable with another JSE-sponsored exercise four years prior based on JSE data of 2010. The press release for a 2011 study also commissioned by the JSE, includes a link to presentation slides by Trevor Chandler & Associates, the consultancy that con-ducted the study, which explains various steps and data sources – but also without detailing the process for arriving at 8% direct black ownership. Both indicate that they follow DTI guidelines on computing ownership. However, the 2015 press release omits supplementary information.

39 Roberts (2006) accessed half the 2,500 sample of the 2003 SASAS; Durrheim (2010) utilized 2,744 observations from the 2004 SASAS. Roberts (2006) pre-sents the findings in the positive – the share of respondents agreeing or strongly agreeing – while Durrheim (2010) adopts the obverse angle of the proportion who neither agree nor strongly agree. The SASAS questionnaire is administered on a 5-point Likert scale, presumably with midpoint answer of neither agreeing nor disagreeing. It is not entirely clear where Durrheim (2010) places ambivalent respondents, but I convert his findings by taking the balance against 100%, and find that the results are compatible with Roberts' (2006).

40 The support levels, in full, were in 2003: 60% overall, 80% Africans, 17% Col-oureds, 31% Indians, 15% Whites 15% (Roberts 2006); and in 2004: 65% overall, 80% Africans, 25% Coloureds, 25% Indians, 13% Whites (Durrheim 2010).

41 The support levels in 2003 for preferential contracts and support for black busi-ness were 66% overall, 72% Africans, 20% Coloureds, 26% Indians, 13% Whites in 2003 (Roberts 2006) and 61% overall, 73% Africans, 30% Coloureds, 24% Indians, 16% Whites in 2004 (Durrheim 2010). Roberts (2006) disaggregates responses to this question by income group, reporting 74% and 71% of "poor" and "vulnerable" respondents, respectively, in agreement, compared to 50% of those classified as "wealthy."

42 The full results for support for race quotas in sports teams: 54% overall, 62% Afri-cans, 35% Coloureds, 32% Indians, 18% Whites (Durrheim 2010).

43 Du Toit (2004) obtains a nationally representative sample of 3,500.

44 These SAIRR surveys obtain nationally representative samples of around 2,000.

45 The proportions agreeing were, in 2015: 70% overall, 71% Africans, 67% Col-oured, 84% Indian, 59% Whites (SAIRR 2017). And in 2018: 60% overall, 55% Africans, 67% Coloured, 69% Indian, 68% Whites (SAIRR 2019).

46 The 2017 SAIRR survey adopts a slightly different angle "when hiring, black peo-ple should be appointed over whites, if they have potential, are trained," to which 31% of all respondents agree, ranging from 38% of Africans to 13% of Coloureds, 16% of Indians, and 9% of Whites. This scenario more closely approximates affirm-ative action, but in posing the scenario as blacks over whites, the findings must also be taken with circumspection in view of the potential emotive trigger point (SAIRR 2018).

47 Interestingly, the 2017 SAIRR survey found disparities between race groups when the issue of player selection was juxtaposed with group representation in the team: 58% on the whole agreed with picking "best players, even if the team is not broadly representative," with levels ranging from 51% among Africans to 91% among Whites (SAIRR 2018). Whereas the 2016 and 2018 surveys found, on a narrower statement "sports teams should be selected on merit, not quotas," upwards of 70% agreed on the whole, and the gaps between races were smaller.

9 Taking stock and looking ahead

This book embarked from the premises that systemic disadvantage of a majority population group and inter-group socio-economic disparities pose profound national problems and that efforts to redress such conditions are politically imperative. Colonialism in Malaysia and Apartheid in South Africa systemically excluded a majority race from moving up and fully participating in the economic mainstream. In these countries' respective post-colonial and post-Apartheid eras, persistent under-representation of the Bumiputera of Malaysia and blacks of South Africa in positions conferring social esteem and economic influence induced constitutional provisions and established policy platforms for affirmative action, buttressed by the political dominance of these groups. Chapter 2 exposited definitions of AA and debates and contentions integral to the policies' objectives, instruments and outcomes. The majority-favouring, expansive and intensive character of affirmative action regimes in Malaysia and South Africa markedly distinguish them from other countries implementing some form of AA.

While outstanding globally as the two most extensive AA regimes, the closer we look at these countries, the more their differences emerge. Chapter 3 examined the historical circumstances that shaped AA regimes, giving rise to a more discretionary, centralized and quota-based system in Malaysia, contrasted with more statutory, decentralized and target-oriented modes in South Africa. Chapters 4 and 5 followed up by detailing the AA programmes in both countries in the main policy sectors of higher education, high-level employment, enterprise development, and wealth and property ownership. The third, and largest, portion of this book empirically evaluated AA outcomes. Chapter 6 surveyed literature to identify gaps in the research on Malaysia and South Africa and build an analytical framework. The achievements and shortfalls were then presented and discussed in Chapters 7 and 8, focusing on the post-1990 era, encompassing direct and indirect policy objectives and referencing data capturing quantitative and qualitative aspects. Ultimately, this book seeks to inform the policy implications for both countries, moving forward.

Where do Malaysia and South Africa go next in their pursuit of parity through preferential treatment? How do AA regimes more effectively cultivate capability and competitiveness to enhance the prospects of graduating and exiting from the current overtly race-based system?

Concluding this book, this chapter condenses, compares and contrasts the main findings on policy outcomes. In line with the distinctive and unique features of each policy regime, my summary of policy outcomes first accounts for country-specific features, then draws out cross-country comparison. I take stock of the situation, summarizing each country's policy achievements and shortfalls in point form (Table 9.1) and elaborating on the comparative angles.

I then cast our eyes forward, to consider the prospects for further progress and possible reform. Applying the systematic framework outlined in Chapter 2, I sketch out some contours of current and future policy prospects specific to the contexts of Malaysia and South Africa but also applicable to other countries. I begin with the need for a coherent, consistent and systematic grounding in policy objectives, instruments and outcomes, obviating the muddled, misguided and sometimes polemical discourses that present partial or false policy alternatives. Next comes a presentation of policy options, addressing the four main policy sectors distinctly, and as part of an integrated policy regime. This process incorporates need-based enhancements to replace race-based preferences where appropriate – primarily in higher education, but also in microfinance and savings schemes – and merit-based enhancements in order to raise the efficacy of affirmative action in building capability and competitiveness, accompanied by graduation and exit clauses. The latter apply more acutely in high-level employment, enterprise development and wealth transfers.

Some subjects in policy debate seem perpetually mired in dilemma or stalemate, with opposing sides holding polarized and seemingly irreconcilable positions. I engage with two dilemmas, surrounding the dynamics of racialized identity and the prospect of majority groups relinquishing privileges. I briefly unpack these problems, which clearly require multi-pronged solutions alongside AA. The discussion identifies ways that AA can bolster its contribution to social cohesion and reinforces the case that the policy must proceed with focused, robust and effective implementation as pre-requisites for the majority – who must be the driving force of change – to gain sufficient capacity and confidence in order to phase out overt preferential treatment.

This book arrives at a complex time in history, with tension, fluidity, continuity and opportunity intermingling in the public sphere. Societies are polarized, economic conditions are sluggish and labour markets tenuous; wealth disparities occupy the popular imagination. At the same time, basic social provisions are firmly established, and sustainability, equity and inclusion are mainstreamed in development policy. Political change swept across both nations in the late 2010s, pregnant with common yearnings for justice and accountability but polarized opinion toward preferential policies. Defence of affirmative action overwhelmingly emanates from the majority, beneficiary group; denunciation of affirmative action typically resounds from minorities – and a sliver of the majority group.

What possibilities for constructive and conciliatory outcomes might be conceivable? This chapter concludes the book by reiterating the need for clear distinction between provision of basic needs and poverty alleviation which operate on the basis of equality, versus AA which redresses under-representation and promotes upward mobility. Ultimately, Malaysia and South Africa must steadfastly focus AA on developing capability, competitiveness and confidence of the majority.

Taking stock

This section synthesizes Chapters 7 and 8, with a focus on comparative policy outcomes. Some of the contents are omitted for brevity and simplification; lack of compatible data across countries constrain the analysis in some areas. Table 9.1 condenses the contents.

Higher education

In the higher education realm, evidence shows substantial quantitative gains in line with affirmative action objectives in Malaysia and South Africa. The scope for expanding tertiary-level enrolment and mechanisms for redistributing opportunities are broader and simpler compared to the other AA spheres, and hence potentially more numerically attainable, as evidenced by the increases in the proportion of graduates in the Bumiputera and black workforces. However, while AA expands the degree-qualified labour force, it does not necessarily improve – and may well diminish – academic achievement and graduate capability. These outcomes demonstrate the need for critical appraisal of qualitative ramifications, besides tracking progress in group representation.

Malaysia's experience demonstrates the potential adverse effects of preferential treatment on academic outcomes. Unquestionably, many contributing factors come into play, but the distinct impact of maintaining an illusory meritocracy in university admissions warrants policy attention. Racial preference in the easier matriculation college route to university ultimately disserves the Bumiputera community by under-equipping students, doing little to narrow achievement gaps, compounded by the false assurance of parity stemming from the official rhetoric of "meritocracy." Moving forward, reinvigorating pre-university programmes must be a first-order priority specific to AA; narrowing achievement gaps at this stage is pre-requisite for reforming admissions systems toward genuinely incorporating merit-based selection alongside need-based preferences, and perhaps eventually instituting a singular university entrance examination (Lee 2019). Malaysia also needs to seek out solutions to systemic problems of its public universities that inhibit academic rigour and graduate quality.

This book's analysis confounds a common view in the AA literature which omits critical attention to education, implying that the problem only lies with the enterprise development and wealth distribution sectors. On this note, South Africa should mindfully avoid the pitfalls observable in the Malaysian education system. South Africa's demographics and constitutional non-racialism may provide buffers against the creation of racially exclusive institutions and maintenance of a parallel system for AA beneficiaries, but such prospects should still be purposefully averted.

Table 9.1 Malaysia and South Africa: Major affirmative action policy outcomes

Policy sector	Malaysia	South Africa
Higher education	• Rapid expansion of enrolment • Share of Malays with higher education certification exceeds national average, but non-Malay Bumiputeras lagging • Substantial Bumiputera educational advancement, facilitated by Bumiputera-exclusive programmes and admissions quotas • "Meritocracy" in university admissions: illusory, detracts from academic rigour and ultimately disserves Bumiputeras • Bumiputera graduates are less able to secure skilled employment, particularly in the private sector • Bumiputera graduates are more dependent on public sector employment • Diversity is lacking in many universities and higher education institutions; system is politicized and partisan • Increased access has facilitated inter-generational upward mobility, but sponsorship and admissions lack structure and consistency in taking into account socio-economic disadvantage	• Steady expansion of enrolment • Black – especially African – students lag in participation rates and attainment, especially in completion and graduation; these gaps remain large but are narrowing • Persisting disparities between graduates of historically white institutions (HWIs) and historically black institutions (HBIs) – legacies endure although classifications have been phased out • Black socio-economic disadvantage persists; stark deficiencies in quality of basic schooling for the majority • Black graduates register higher unemployment rate, are more dependent on public sector employment • With decentralized university system, institutions devise own transformation plans, incorporating socio-economic disadvantage and group representation criteria – potentially facilitating upward mobility and expanding the scope of non-race-based selection
High-level employment	• Increasing Bumiputera representation at management and professional levels over 1970s-1990s; slower gains since the mid-1990s • Bumiputera dependence on the public sector for upward occupational mobility, with concentration among teaching and health professionals • Low Bumiputera representation in some specialized, highly skilled occupations	• Increasing black representation at professional and managerial levels • Employment equity law has spurred hiring and promotion of blacks, especially Africans, but progress is slower in senior and top management • Greater gains in the public sector; steady increases in the private sector

Policy sector	Malaysia	South Africa
	• Public sector is Malay dominated and difficult to diversify, holds potential for grooming capability • GLCs are more racially diverse; professionalized leadership demonstrates ability, builds confidence	• Low black representation in some specialized, highly skilled occupations • Skills and experience shortage are major constraints; shortfalls in employers' commitment and support systems for black employee advancement • ANC's "cadre deployment" and overly accelerated managerial promotion has compromised on public service delivery • SOCs and SOEs are at the forefront; scarcity of talent and experience have induced a more tempered approach
Enterprise development	• Bumiputeras in top GLCs visibly demonstrate capability and confidence, but GLCs on the whole have a chequered track record • Bumiputera share on boards of large, publicly listed companies show marked formation of Malay corporate old guard, but generational transition is unclear • Shortfall of Bumiputera participation across industries and in SMEs • Concentration of small Malay contractors in public procurement; system lacks incentives to expand and improve capability and quality • Loans, grants, advisory services operate expansively, but have failed to make decisive and momentous breakthroughs • Recent programmes under Teraju strive to cultivate capability and competitiveness, but resources are limited and operations more selective than systemic	• Substantial black participation in managing and staffing SOEs and SOCs but chequered track record; recent leadership changes and appointment of white CEOs • Black representation on boards of large, public listed companies shows slow but steady progress • Shortfall of black participation across industries and in SMEs • BBBEE certificates: available data show slow progress to top levels, considerable missing data or non-compliance • BBBEE approach – mechanistic, accounting- and compliance-based – is warranted for historical redress but limited in capacity to spur new and innovative enterprise • More direct interventions, especially the Black Industrialist Programme, hold out potential for breakthrough – with rigorous selection and monitoring

(*Continued*)

Table 9.1 (Continued)

Policy sector	Malaysia	South Africa
Wealth and property ownership	• Equity ownership: original NEP target for Bumiputera individual ownership is surpassed, institutional target not met – but issue is also clouded by measurement problems • Savings schemes, notably ASB, highly unequal • Housing and commercial property ownership continually salient in policy, but with scant progress reporting	• Equity ownership target not achieved, by some estimates black share is still extremely low; persisting debates over measurement method • Flourish in BBBEE deals in 2000s, sluggish since the global financial crisis • Since 2013, promotion of broad-based group participation and curbs on fronting, but slowdown in BBBEE deals on the whole
Popular sentiments and public support	• Substantial support for continuity of affirmative action among Bumiputeras, particularly Malays • Racially polarized opinion on the system's fairness; minorities uneasy about perpetual Malay special privileges	• Black majority support for affirmative action, but racially polarized opinion • Solid support for appointments based on merit, competency and access to training, but no conclusive repudiation of affirmative action

Source: Author.

South Africa's AA challenges in higher education also have unique elements, chiefly the HWI/HBI Apartheid legacies, which persist despite mergers and reconfigurations. The current traditional/comprehensive/university of technology/ UNISA classification, while not racially delineated, remains stratified and characterized by racial patterns. The share of blacks in enrolment has increased all around but remains significantly lower in the top-tier institutions and unevenly distributed across study fields, with black enrolment and graduation in SET particularly lagging. The student bodies of many lower-tier institutions are also overwhelmingly black; persisting or widening quality gaps vis-à-vis the leading and more integrated institutions impedes the cultivation of capable, competitive and confident black professionals, managers and entrepreneurs. Socio-economic disadvantage, deriving substantially from widespread deficiencies in basic schooling, continually impacts on higher education achievement.

The general picture of quantitative achievements and qualitative shortfalls extends to labour market entry, the next stage after graduation from higher education in both countries. Lesser employment prospects of Bumiputera public university graduates and dependence on the public sector derive from numerous factors, but the effects of enrolment quotas and racially exclusive programmes cannot be discounted. The practice of sponsoring the cream of the crop to study abroad buffers AA beneficiaries from more competitive settings and effectively deprives local public institutions of Bumiputera talent. In South Africa, racial disparities in university enrolment have steadily narrowed, but the magnitudes remain wider in graduation and duration to completion, and shortfall of black, especially African, achievement is more acute more technical fields. Quality difference perceivably accounts for persistently higher unemployment rates of black diploma- and degree-holders compared to white counterparts.

The shortcomings notwithstanding, education remains the AA policy sphere with the most potential for facilitating inter-generational upward mobility and for jointly bridging racial and class divides. The experiences of both countries show the possibilities for targeting disadvantaged and low-income households *within* the Bumiputera and black populations. The larger the share of disadvantaged, low-income recipients within the beneficiary group, the greater the prospects of the current generation improving on their forebears. The proportion of disadvantaged among Bumiputera and black higher education students has not been precisely quantified, but evidence points to Malaysia's B40 considerably benefiting from various AA programmes, while the implementation of South Africa's financial aid system is believed to reach out to low-income households. However, in admissions schemes, the incorporation of socio-economic disadvantage and family background, alongside academic achievement and talent, has not been systematically developed in Malaysia, and is at an incipient stage in South Africa, although various universities have made a promising start.

High-level occupations

On affirmative action in the labour market, some cross-country similarities prevail – despite contrasting mechanisms. The public sector and state-owned entities play prominent roles in facilitating upward occupational mobility. In Malaysia, this follows directly from the *de facto* confinement of affirmative action in employment to the public sector and GLCs. In South Africa, although employment equity mandates apply to both the public sector and private sector, blacks have seen more progress in the former, with steady gains in the latter, especially in professional positions while under-representation remains pronounced in senior management and especially top management. AA has also, across both countries, proceeded slower in certain occupations requiring highly specialized qualifications or experience.

Some differences in policy implications merit consideration. Malaysia's Bumiputera-, especially Malay-dominant, public sector has created a milieu that largely precludes the need for race preferential treatment, in view of the scant interest among non-Bumiputeras. But the inertia also perpetuates dependence on government to absorb Bumiputera graduates into technical and professional positions. The situation calls for a reorientation of public sector employment policy towards a more balanced racial composition, and Malaysia's government, and the GLCs under its watch, have made some overtures in this direction, but there is considerable room for growth. Undoubtedly, Bumiputera presence has also grown in the private sector, whether through mobility between public and private sectors, or career development fully in the latter, in tandem with increased higher education attainment. The public sector has functioned as a training ground of sorts for professionals and administrators to transition to commercial settings, especially in the context of government-linked companies. But the scope of these channels for upward occupational mobility will narrow in the future; growth of public sector employment, in all likelihood, will not keep up with labour supply. Malaysia's reliance on more "organic" processes of promoting Bumiputera upward mobility through higher education – without legal mandates such as employment equity – will foreseeably need to intensify, with expansion of self-employment and business start-ups.

The achievements and shortfalls of employment equity in South Africa, and the complexities and nuances of its mandatory enforcement with employer-specific terms, have been discussed at length in Chapter 8. In brief summary, black upward occupational mobility has progressed, though at a slower rate in the higher echelons. South Africa's experience in implementing employment equity, arguably on a larger scale than any other country, reveals the potential and peril, the impetus and limits, of this statutory and mandatory approach. The process has involved compromises (with occasional overreach), self-regulation and employer autonomy coupled with official oversight and top-down pressure. Employment equity has been criticized from opposing ends of a spectrum, faulted for too little progress (in view of obstinate employers) and too much pressure (given skills shortages). It has faced legal challenges – and as a consequence, South Africa has significantly settled the EEA's constitutionality and appropriate practice.

The greater progress in the public sector and SOEs is inevitable; these entities fall directly under the state's purview, and the democratic transition could not politically proceed without meaningful and visible change in the racial profile of the bureaucracy, especially after the "sunset clause" period which facilitated continuity of Apartheid era appointments. The private sector's slow pace of transformation derives from skills shortages, among other things, but employment equity compliance has also provided an extra push that compels employers to look beyond immediate networks and comfort zones. Blatant forms of politicization are more clearly detrimental, particularly the ANC's cadre deployment widely blamed for undermining public service delivery. More generally, though, the question of whether the state's leverage has been prudently utilized, and whether employment equity oversight can be improved, will remain vigorously debated.

Enterprise development

The development of a managerial and entrepreneurial class has proven exceedingly difficult among affirmative action endeavours in both Malaysia and South Africa. Government-linked companies (GLCs) in Malaysia and state-owned companies (SOCs) in South Africa continually provide employment and training grounds for managers and professionals and apply racial preference in procurement and contracting decisions. These state-owned entities are designated a substantive and symbolic role; they occupy a major portion in major sectors of both economies, with high profile leadership positions. The success of commercial operations under Bumiputera and black leadership potentially contribute to raising the esteem of the group in general, demonstrating achievements that can serve as sources of encouragement and models for emulation.

The reality is a mixed bag. Malaysia's GLCs, particularly the largest corporations, have achieved a considerable measure of success, but a mottled picture emerges when more entities, under federal and state government oversight, enter the frame. South Africa's SOCs have posted uneven track records, including high profile struggles, although some cases of under-performance – particularly of Eskom and South African Airways – should be tempered against possible overgeneralization, and with acknowledgement of macroeconomic conditions unconducive for growth, regardless of AA. SOEs are arguably the most similar component of AA across both countries, in which Malaysia has clearly set some precedents. However, the capacity for South Africa to emulate Malaysia in developing a managerial class through state-owned or state-affiliated companies is constrained by peculiar conditions. South Africa lacks some advantages Malaysia enjoyed, notably the existence of a bureaucratic elite that transferred skills acquired in public administration to management in the corporate sector in the 1980s and 1990s, in plantation companies, banking and other activities (Southall 1997, 23).[1] Nonetheless, given the certainty that SOCs will continue their assigned lead role in BBBEE, the policy should press on in pursuit of a robust balance of representation and competency. Another surety across both countries concerns the capacity for state-owned entities to cultivate an independent and broad entrepreneurial class. These goals will remain circumscribed by the limited scale and scope of SOEs, compared to the private sector which remains much larger and spread over more sectors and differently sized operations.

Publicly listed companies, which in Malaysia include many GLCs, are sites of AA, targeting board membership and executive positions. Malaysia and South Africa have made progress, particularly in the former where there are now equal numbers of Malays and Chinese on the largest 100 companies' boards. The senior age profile, and heavy presence of retired bureaucrats, however, raises questions on generational divides and inwardness of the process, underscoring the limits to which these interventions can contribute to the broadening of participation in commerce and industry. In South Africa, listed company boards remain preponderantly white; the advancement of blacks, particularly Africans, has been slow. The apartheid history and concentration of power in large conglomerates add political pressure and some moral force toward change at the top strata embodied in these board positions. However, the extremely few beneficiaries involved and prevalence of non-executive roles, should factor into the relative priority ascribed to this policy arm.

Allocation of government procurement, licensing and contracting constitutes another set of interventions – deploying more direct instruments – for developing entrepreneurial capacity. Malaysia's procurement system, which reserves the smallest tier of contracts for Bumiputeras, engineers a high concentration of Bumiputera contractors in that category, and it has arguably under-utilized the leverage at the government's disposal for cultivating more SME capability and competitiveness. In South Africa, public procurement provides the prime inducement for private firms to participate in BBBEE and confers leverage on the state to exert change. The outcomes are difficult to evaluate; while BBBEE certificates differentiate companies by compliance levels, these data provide a composite picture with scant disaggregation of the various elements, each of which warrants its own examination. The distribution of composite scores shows modest progress, with a minority reaching the top levels. Preferential policies are also incorporated into the procurement systems of Malaysia's GLCs and South Africa's SOCs; these programmes have not stood out for significant successes, although it should be acknowledged that the literature is sparse.

This book generally concurs with the established view that affirmative action in cultivating enterprise must be pursued with caution and restraint, especially to avert being vitiated by unproductive wealth accumulation, rent-seeking, fronting, corruption and political patronage (Jomo 2004; Southall 2005). Malaysia's privatization exercise from the 1980s, one of the largest ever executed, came to a cataclysmic halt during the 1997–1998 Asian financial crisis. The external shock notwithstanding, the policy was mortally marred by poor execution and trumped by vested interests of political-business elites (Tan 2008). South Africa's BBBEE regime technically provides incentives for firms to compete on terms that are codified and audited. Still, the pitfalls in these schemes can be immense, especially where lucrative contracts and fast windfall profits are at stake, and are compounded by corruption and dearth of oversight that have come to the fore in both countries. Recent enhancements to the regulatory framework, saliently Malaysia's declared commitments to transparency in procurement and South Africa's BBBEE enhancements to combat fronting, will need consistent and resolute follow through.

The shares of Bumiputera-owned or black-owned enterprises among SMEs, the broadest empirical measure and a more compatible cross-country indicator, show limited progress in increasing participation. However, both countries have in recent years paid increasing attention to grooming more dynamic, capable and competitive SMEs, through the procurement systems as well as grant and loan schemes. Greater competition for contracts and regulation against fronting have been emphasized lately in both countries, and the prospect of graduating out of special assistance has been raised in Malaysia. Despite many years in implementing numerous financial, logistical and advisory schemes, Malaysia has not made the desired breakthrough. South Africa, having witnessed the inadequacies of the BBBEE approach of redistributing existing assets, often held passively, ventures into new territory with the BIP. While too early to appraise, by design it holds out potential to make a more meaningful impact on black-owned enterprise.

Wealth and property ownership

Programmes for redistributing wealth or promoting accumulation have been among the most strenuously pursued in both countries, but are also mired in empirical contestations. Estimating wealth is difficult in any context, due to complexities in pricing assets and liabilities and tracing ownership. Unsurprisingly, tracking of progress in this policy sector – most prominently, the share of Bumiputera and black equity holdings in the economy – has been pointedly contested. In Malaysia, where much policy rhetoric and public discourse have fixated on the 30% Bumiputera equity target, and debate has revolved around the application of par value versus market value, and the exclusion of government-linked investment funds in the official account, which reports Bumiputera ownership still considerably short of 30%. A reminder of the original NEP articulation can help resolve this imbroglio, by establishing that the 7.4% individual ownership has been surpassed and shining the spotlight on institutional ownership, which remains an important vehicle for Bumiputera wealth. In South Africa, BEE transactions have been uneven across time and sluggish in the past decade. The distribution debate references 25% black ownership, based on BBBEE compliance targets. Similar to Malaysia, this debate significantly revolves around the inclusion/exclusion of institutional investment, especially pension funds of which blacks constitute the majority and incorporation of debt that encumbers share purchases. Upper-end estimates still fall short of 25%; excluding institutional funds and accounting for debt generates exceedingly low estimates of black net ownership.

These debates will persist, as surely as the ownership agendas will continue. The equitability of distribution also constitutes an important policy issue, in which both countries have common and unique experiences. Evidence, directly or indirectly, points to the problem of high concentration of wealth ownership at the top. Malaysia's unit trust funds, while involving millions of Bumiputeras as unit holders, shows highly skewed ownership patterns. South Africa's increased emphasis on broad-based groups as BBBEE beneficiaries acknowledges the shortcomings of the policy in reaching out to the "person on the street."

Looking forward

This book's thrust bears reiterating: affirmative action in Malaysia and South Africa is a socio-political imperative, and that the policy is coherent, reasonable and defensible as a temporary measure that needs to be implemented effectively – in order that graduation and exit plans can be pursued. Both countries have made gains and fallen short, and the prospects of such reforms remain elusive. I will focus on policy requirements and reform options that can make affirmative action more effective, while being mindful of the socio-political conditions and constitutional provisions that tend to perpetuate the policy. This chapter will also consider policy implications and lessons for other countries, particularly in middle- and low-income brackets, that are grappling with racial or ethnic inequality and affirmative action as a remedial intervention.

Affirmative action policies, laws and programmes are constitutionally authorized, majority supported and interwoven with the social and political fabric of Malaysia and South Africa. As discussed in Chapters 4 and 5, the constitutional provisions for AA are, explicitly or implicitly, contingent on the prevalence of group disadvantage. Reforms and rollbacks are consistent with the spirit, if not the letter, of the law. The policies are embedded, continually bathed in imperatives and controversies, and animated by debate over achievements and deficiencies.

Where do these countries go from here? This section presents some thoughts, proposals and prescriptions on moving forward, building on the framework of need-based and merit-based enhancements outlined in Table 2.1. These ideas are summarized in Table 9.2 and discussed thereafter.

My focus is on building a systematic framework, with some specific applications but not a comprehensive plan – due to limitations of space in this book and also limitations of information and imagination. Government, polity and society of Malaysia and South Africa must research, collate and deliberate the comprehensive range of policy options.

Policy framework and reform prospects

Moving forward, Malaysia and South Africa must start on the right footing. In order to do this, both countries need to establish clarity and coherence in the overarching framework, to systematically grasp the purpose, scope and mechanisms of their respective AA regimes. This is far from a mere theoretical construct for academic ends; AA discourses and actual policy design often spin in fruitless spirals of misplaced expectations and misguided policy design, which in turn fuel unduly adversarial and truculent debate. Both countries tend to perpetuate polarized stand-offs, eluding direct engagement on the original purpose and specific instruments of AA, with parties talking past each other. This section builds on the framework and approach applied in this book, in ways that – hopefully – engage critical debate and pursue viable reforms.

The proposed policy framework and reform guidelines comprise three key applications.

1 Adopt a systematic approach

The paramount need for affirmative action to be grounded coherently and systematically has been expounded in Chapter 2, but it is worth reiterating here with reference to the policy achievements and shortcomings reviewed earlier and policy options moving forward. The principal objectives, instruments and outcomes – increasing a disadvantaged group's participation and upward mobility, through preferential measures, in spheres where they are under-represented – remain intact, 50 years after the advent of Malaysia's NEP and 25 years beyond South Africa's democratic transition. Affirmative action must resolutely cleave to this systematic framework, which also specifies the key policy sectors and identifies precise mechanisms of each sector. The discussion of the preceding chapters has also drawn out some patterns of thought that detract from this systematic approach, which two merit a brief discourse.

First, discussion of policy alternatives often becomes mired in conflation and imprecision. In Malaysia, this predominantly takes the form of uncritical

Table 9.2 Malaysia and South Africa: Major affirmative action policy implications

Policy sector	Malaysia	South Africa
Policy framework	• Systematic framework fundamentally pursuing development of capability, competitiveness and confidence, encompassing AA across the four main sectors and featuring sector-specific programmes that incorporate: • need-based and merit-based enhancements • exit and graduation prospects, timelines and milestones • Reform to make programmes more effective, as precursor to broader reform, especially in pre-university, contracting, SME support • Redress socio-economic disadvantage more systematically, especially in education • Focus on capability, competitiveness and confidence – empowerment that consolidates the majority's readiness to roll back overt preferential treatment • Empowered Bumiputera and black elites are positioned to demonstrate graduation from preferential assistance, and should do so in constructive and visible ways • Fundamental shift to multi-pronged pursuit of equality and fairness, balanced with equitable representation and diversity	
	• Jettison conflation of poverty alleviation and "pro-B40" programmes with AA; cease propagation of muddled and incoherent notions of "need-based AA" • Attention to intra-Bumiputera disparities and omitted groups, especially Indian and *Orang Asli*	• Jettison conflation of policies targeting poverty and unemployment with AA; discard fragmented view of AA/redress/transformation/BBBEE • Attention to disparities within black population, and between African sub-groups
Higher education	• Pre-university must be rigorous to effectively equip Bumiputeras, as precondition for removal of overt group preference • Shift to applying equal access and equitable representation as dual principles, with decentralized admissions, autonomous institutions and systematic consideration of socio-economic disadvantage • Distinguish need-based bursaries from merit-based scholarships; set up prestigious scholarships with funding amount aligned with financial need	• Basic schooling deficiencies and socio-economic disparities remain the principal challenge, inhibiting blacks' progress to higher education – especially enrolment in SET • Continual application and innovation of university admissions – accounting for disadvantage • Education bursaries and scholarships, and financial aid in general, to promote equitable access and inter-generational upward mobility, including prestigious scholarships with funding aligned with financial need

(*Continued*)

Table 9.2 (Continued)

Policy sector	Malaysia	South Africa
High-level employment	• Fair employment to legislate against unfair discrimination and provide guidelines for pursuing affirmative action in the public sector, and diversity more broadly	• Employment equity enforcement can follow more measured pace and moderated targets – possibly by sector, or referencing professional qualifications and registrations • Incentivize and support new ventures by experienced AA beneficiaries
Enterprise development	• Exert more pressure to increase competitiveness and scale, especially to groom medium-scale enterprises • Procurement and vendor development: competitive selection, apply limits to repeat benefits, conditions for graduation and exit • Microfinance can distinctly shift from race-based to need-based selection and improve outreach to disadvantaged groups	• BBBEE: more effective promotion of management control, skills development and enterprise development through procurement and support for suppliers and subsidiaries • Efforts to cultivate viable, innovative enterprises should continue, notably through ensuring effective execution of the BIP and programmes supporting new, black-owned companies
Wealth and property ownership	• Return to original NEP individual and institutional equity ownership targets • Incorporate need-based preference in pro-poor savings schemes • Property ownership should operate primarily on socio-economic grounds; property discounts for middle- and high-income Bumiputeras are a distinct case for policy graduation	• Emphasis on active and broad-based ownership in redistributive programmes • Priority on black ownership in new and innovative ventures

Source: Author.

regurgitation of "need-based affirmative action" *as a complete and systemic replacement for* race-based affirmative action, rather than as a complementary measure contingent on sector-specific situations. Indeed, various need-based and merit-based enhancements of race-based AA are already in place, but Malaysia must strive for a correct, precise and honest discourse and for systematically introducing reforms specific to each policy sector. Wrong-footing of South Africa's AA discourses arises more from disparate and fragmented conceptions, with higher education transformation often excluded from broader discourses of AA or BEE, or with AA applied exclusively to employment equity and not coherently integrated with BEE, which in turn is often associated with the gamut of development issues such as poverty and unemployment. BBBEE rhetoric, where it veers toward overpromise, also muddles the discourse and exposes itself to assessments of failure for outcomes that it is not responsible for in the first place.

A first point of clarification is that AA is not principally about poverty alleviation or mass employment. Pro-poor elements, where applicable, can be incorporated to reinforce AA's efficacy (Brown and Langer 2015). While acknowledging the sense of justice undergirding needs-based and means-tested assistance, we must also be mindful of the patent limits to which these modes can replace the existing AA regimes.[2] The underpinning objective and impetus – in country-specific and sector-specific ways – must continually anchor policy formulation and revision. In Malaysia, the emphasis should rest relatively more on promoting capability and participation and enhancing inclusiveness, as foundations for effectively and sustainably narrowing income and wealth disparities. After protracted implementation, the onus is increasingly on effective execution alongside measures that facilitate graduation and exit, or transition to other modes of fostering diversity. In South Africa, the moral imperative of redress for past unfair discrimination and black mobility into commanding heights remains sturdy, but it must be tempered with the need for more judicious implementation and, like Malaysia, more emphasis on capability and competitiveness, alongside a broadening of benefits within the black population. Pro-poor and universalist policies must be seen as complementary to AA and must be placed in context of each policy sector.

Second, aligned with the policy objectives described here, policy targets and empirical analyses must also focus on the direct policy outcomes and primarily on inequality between groups. Consequently, the beneficiary group's higher education attainment, representation in high-level occupations, participation in owning and operating business, take precedence over household income in formulation and evaluation of AA. Household income undeniably remains a paramount indicator of well-being, and must feature in public policy more generally. The ramifications of AA on household income warrant attention – but as a second-order and more indirect outcome, one that is also dependent on a multiplicity of other economic structures and policies, including labour force participation, quantity and quality of jobs, wage versus profit shares and urban-rural divides.

Additionally, AA discourses should be circumspect in handling the intra-group inequality versus inter-group inequality debate, which typically arises in the context of household income. A refrain heard in both countries, that intra-racial income inequalities have risen as a result of AA and hence policy should address intra-group inequalities *instead of* inter-group inequalities, commits considerable over-simplification and imprecise argumentation – and in the case of Malaysia, empirical error as well. Much of the discourse into the 2010s too readily presumes that intra-Bumiputera inequality is rising, omitting or ignoring evidence of falling inequality (Lee and Khalid 2020). The crux of the argument cuts across both countries, although it is more pronounced in South Africa: AA, in omitting benefits to the poor masses and only benefiting the elite, raises inequality. Mass unemployment derives from many factors, largely unrelated to AA, although some contribution of AA cannot be denied.

A clearer conception of AA recognizes that there are multiple, simultaneous effects associated with AA, some of which are possibly inequality reducing and others inequality raising. A different dimension of inequality also yields a different pattern of inequality. The policy objective of promoting upward mobility, including highly remunerating positions, possibly increases gaps between the topmost and the rest to a greater extent than in the absence of AA. But to solely focus on this angle biases the perspective, particularly when the majority of AA interventions address the growth of middle classes, which may reduce inequality. Additionally, such effects may also change over time; for instance, as earnings premiums on higher education rise, then diminish. In sum, the effects of AA on inequality, especially of household income, are much less determinate than they are often made to be, and it is unclear that removing AA will reduce inequality, when it may well cause lesser growth of the middle class.

To be sure, the intra- and inter-perspective has policy relevance. But the decisive point should be that, while AA can strive to extend benefits to the poor – where applicable – the principle, systemic objective is the beneficiary group's presence in middle classes and upper strata. Countries should make efforts to progressively distribute opportunity as much as possible, such as by prioritizing the disadvantaged in higher education, focusing on SMEs and introducing graduation and exit clauses to limit repeat beneficiaries and hoarding. Sustained attention to equitable distribution of opportunity within the beneficiary group, and to socio-economic disadvantage as an underlying premise for extending preferential treatment, should incline policy targeting to excluded groups, such as the marginalized *Orang Asli* and Indian populations in Malaysia, and Coloureds or particular African ethnic groups in South Africa. However, these efforts to reduce intra-group disparities do not detract from the consistent primary objective of narrowing inter-group inequality, in participation and capability.

2 Reinforce and reform affirmative action by integrating need-based and merit-based selection

Policy alternatives are not confined to a dichotomy of maintaining versus abolishing the status quo of current laws, codes, programmes, quotas and targets. Malaysia and South Africa have much room to robustly enhance efficacy and pursue reforms, some of which may be more robust and pivotal, others subtle and incremental. Policy regimes can integrate more need-based selection, where appropriate, to target the disadvantaged and to impose sunset clauses and limits on those who have benefited. In some but not all policy sectors, need-based preferences can go a meaningful distance toward replacing race-based preferences, and eventually various mechanisms can be employed for upholding fairness, equity and diversity. The regimes should also expand the scope for merit-based selection in allocating opportunity to Bumiputera and black beneficiaries with capability and potential to showcase success and achieve competitiveness – again, specific to policy sectors – alongside plans to graduate or exit out of special assistance and roll back overt racial preference. The sector-specific components are salient; hence I discuss each distinctly in this section.

Higher education

In discussing policy options moving forward, the primacy of education must be established and reiterated here. Advocating for an emphasis on education can come across as a threadbare platitude; but in the specific context of AA, the impact and ramifications of higher education stand out among the other policy sectors. Higher education is potentially the most impactful instrument because it principally imparts capability and knowledge, delivers benefits on a mass scale, considerably obviates rent-seeking and holds the most potential for reaching the disadvantaged and promoting inter-generational upward mobility (Khalid 2018; Matambo and Ani 2015).

Schooling systems and higher education admissions differ quite substantially, but some policy reform possibilities in scholarships and financial aid are broadly applicable across both countries. Malaysia and South Africa can both enhance the distinction between need-based bursaries and merit-based scholarships, to concurrently promote equity and excellence, and to balance of majority and minority interests. A further modification to competitive, merit-based scholarships can also be weighed. Given the reality that middle-income and high-income candidates will be well-poised to compete academically, due to their advantaged schooling and upbringing, it is worthwhile considering the establishment of prestigious non-fully funded scholarships with the grant award proportionate to ability to pay. Hence, empowered Bumiputeras and blacks – alongside non-Bumiputeras and whites – can continue to access these opportunities and recognition of talent in an equitable manner, rather than be disqualified from scholarships.

Malaysia's more extensive preferential programmes raise questions starting from secondary and pre-university programmes. The current mode of 90% Bumiputera quotas or Bumiputera-exclusive enrolment has become entrenched. The implications vary across MRSMs, matriculation colleges and other pre-university programmes, but all such institutions must be more rigorous and effective in equipping students for university entry. This is also a pre-requisite for potential transition to a single university-entrance examination, provided the problems arising from parallel programmes are resolved.[3] For MRSMs, their specific mandate to serve rural populations – with attention to quality of education – should be re-emphasized, alongside the increased share of admissions to lower-income students in recent years.

South Africa's education challenges are in a sense more deep-seated, considering the issues in basic schooling. Clearly, advancement of blacks to higher education will correspond with the state of primary and secondary school. The conduct of AA, however, is relatively less complicated, since the system is less steeped in race-based preferential treatment. Strenuous and sustained efforts must close the quality gaps between institutions and enhance the contribution of university education to the upward mobility of graduates. University admissions, which are devolved to each institution, some of which have increasingly adopted socio-economic disadvantage as a selection criterion, should continue modifying and refining their mechanisms to promote black enrolment and student diversity without overtly and directly targeting race.

High-level employment

A shared strand of affirmative action in employment across Malaysia and South Africa is the primary role of the public sector and state-owned entities. This will likely persist, but with the Bumiputeras over-represented and blacks, especially Africans, continuously increasing their share in administrative and professional ranks and heading toward proportionality, it is timely to begin considering some longer-term implications. The visibility of professionals and administrators in the bureaucracy can exert a signalling effect, demonstrating successful upward mobility through competently filling the roles. The onus remains on the system to select capable officers and deliver public services, which are also crucial for sustaining talent in the pipeline and facilitating possible relaxation of affirmative action in the future.

Moving forward poses different options from the onset. Bumiputera representation in high-level occupations, past and present, operates in a more *de facto* manner rather than a clearly enunciated law or policy, predominantly through recruitment and promotion in the public sector and GLCs. The route of a mandatory system such as employment equity law lacks historical or moral bases. Nonetheless, it is timely, judicious and worthwhile for Malaysia to enact fair employment legislation, and establish a fair employment commission, to oversee unfair discrimination, bring about some clarification of AA policy in the public sector and GLCs and provide guidance for pursuing diversity across both public and private sectors.

South Africa employment equity is deeply embedded and, while understandably on an expansion and intensification path, will need to continually need to strike a balance of effective enforcement with tempered expectations and moderated pace. The next steps arguably require more by way of recalibrating the targeting mechanisms, for instance by referencing workforce composition by industry (Bezuidenhout *et al.* 2008), or using baselines corresponding with the supply of tertiary qualified candidates, or perhaps even more specifically pegging targets to job-specific qualifications and skills, such as registration of professionals. For the latter case, it is worth considering setting targets slightly above the current levels, taking into account projected increases in supply of graduates and registered professionals. This responds to the criticism that the EAP is a more static reference and shaped by existing biases, including higher male labour force participation. These modifications potentially enhance policy responsiveness and its integration with the overall AA regime, especially higher education. However, the outer bound of employment equity remains – it essentially redistributes within existing employers. Thus, it will continually encounter resistance in the upper reaches of management, especially in small and medium family-owned businesses. South Africa might explore options in incentivizing and supporting new ventures started by AA-facilitated appointments, who have gained work experience and may be ready to lead on their own.

Enterprise development

This is arguably the most exacting of the four policy sectors. Enterprise development entails effective ownership and operational, decision-making and risk-taking roles, more than both employment and wealth holdings which may demand less in terms of investment, resourcefulness, networks and experience. At the small-scale end, particularly in Malaysia and its Bumiputera microfinance schemes, there is room to revert from race-based to need-based preferences, or to target disadvantaged population groups outside the Bumiputera orbit. The principle of need-based assistance can also be applied in the converse direction – instead of assisting the disadvantaged, disqualifying those who do not need assistance from receiving further preferential treatment or graduating recipients out of repeatedly receiving preference.

However, for the most part it is incumbent on enterprise development programmes to effectively and productively execute the goal of developing capability and competitiveness in as broad-based a manner as possible, for the ultimate purpose of graduating and exiting from overt racial preferences. The range of programmes is expansive, but these themes run throughout, from the voluminous public procurement and licensing machinery, to loans and grants, and advisory and training services.

A few considerations specific to Malaysia can be raised here. In the corporate sphere, Malays have secured a substantial presence in management of GLCs and on boards of GLCs and large listed companies. The forthcoming challenges are to transition to the next generation and to make a structural shift toward broader participation across all sectors and beyond the established mobility within GLCs or from senior civil service positions to corporate boards. In promoting Bumiputera entrepreneurs, recent policy discourses in Malaysia have duly emphasized the need to be vigilant and punitive against rent-seeking and subcontracting and also to be open to experimentation, improvisation and support for risk-taking, including second chances for first-time failing Bumiputera entrepreneurs (Malaysia 2018). The importance of policy design and implementation to deliver on these intentions, and to avert past rent-seeking proclivities, must be stressed.

Malaysia's public procurement, as well as GLC vendor development, remain extensive instruments for enterprise development. A few modifications merit consideration. In rural areas, instead of Malay ownership as the qualifying criterion for small contracts, the existing requirement of local registration – within the district a contract is awarded – can adequately safeguard local interests, while indirectly continuing to provide opportunity to Malay contractors. In urban areas with higher density of operators, the focus within the Malay preferential system can shift to more competitive selection, new incentives for the smallest scale G1 contractors to move up, by setting limits on the repetition of contracts preferentially received at the G1 scale, or bonus points for scaling up to G2 or beyond.[4] The prospect of slower economic growth foreshadows the need to get more mileage out of public expenditures. Bumiputera preference is associated with efficiency losses, but other factors also weigh in, for instance the pricing system based on the average of bids, which can be manipulated through collusion, including submission of multiple bids at inflated prices. Price handicaps for Bumiputera contractors, as per official policy, therefore must be either replaced or reinforced with a points system for technological upgrades or quality improvements.

In South Africa, enterprise development remains the primary domain of BBBEE. Its underwhelming track record and problematic execution have continually invited scrutiny and prompted policy shifts to better align its mechanisms with genuine economic empowerment. The recentness of BBBEE Code revamps, with priority placed on management control, skills development and enterprise development, and novel establishment of the BBBEE Commission, with designated roles in data compilation and policy evaluation, renew the agenda with significant productive potential and hence deserve another trial period for achievements to be realized. This compliance-based approach undoubtedly has its limits. Beyond redistribution, BBBEE must resolutely seek to build capabilities and resourcefulness and to be a springboard for new ventures. Likewise, it is imperative to cultivate dynamism and innovation, which demands rigorous selection and strenuous monitoring of the BIP and programmes directly supporting the creation or enhancement of black-owned enterprise.

Wealth and property ownership

This policy sector often captures most attention, due to the vested interests of beneficiaries and the conspicuous, often elite enriching, trait of many transactions. Malaysia's pro-Bumiputera wealth ownership policies stand out globally and are also uniquely mired in impasse regarding the measurement of progress and justification for policy continuation and the issue of equitable distribution. A fresh approach to the perpetually unresolved matter of the 30% Bumiputera target, with its entrenched adversarial interests, can take the simple form of reverting back to the original NEP articulation of individual and institutional ownership. Acknowledging that the individual targets have been reached directs attention to institutional ownership, where attention can be further channelled constructively, toward facilitating broader and more inclusive participation. An opportunity also opens up for policy targeting based on income or need regardless of race, particularly in savings schemes for low-income households such as ASB and ASN. At the other end of the class spectrum, wealth ownership schemes that continually benefit well-heeled Bumiputeras are among the AA programmes ripe for phasing out. Bumiputera middle classes and elites who are poised to afford property purchases should make the first move in relinquishing discounts, which is justified on grounds that they do no longer need preferential treatment, and reinforced by this opportunity to positively and concretely demonstrate how empowered Bumiputeras can graduate out of receiving privileges and stand on their own feet.

Discussion of South Africa is brief in proportion to South Africa's wealth ownership policies within the AA rubric, which are considerably less than Malaysia's in scope and also more in flux due to BBBEE policy shifts. Looking forward mainly involves sketching out principles. Wealth held through institutions, notably public sector pension funds, impacts on economic ownership and security of blacks proportionate to their presence in the public services, but this institution generally operates outside the ambit of affirmative action. Policy implications therefore circle back to BBBEE-facilitated asset transfers, predominantly company shares, in which policies should in principle ensure that active and broad-based ownership takes precedence over passive ownership and upwardly skewed distribution.

3 Devise long-term, sector-specific plans for transitioning away from overt race-based preference

The preceding discussion does not frame a timeline of policy actions on the near and far horizons, although clearly some proposals can roll out sooner while others will need more time. My long-term outlook is rooted in the normative and pragmatic stance that AA, particularly in the form of overt race-based preferences of Malaysia and South Africa, is in principle a transitory intervention, a means to an end. This theme resonates in the literature.

However, while sharing that common ground, I depart from the tendencies in writings on Malaysia and South Africa to eschew long-term planning and to assume, explicitly or implicitly, that achieving targets or passing time thresholds constitute grounds to phase out AA. Emphatically, reaching certain targets and milestones do not automatically indicate a readiness to relinquish preferential treatment. Policy-making involves setting targets, and achieving them can prompt or sustain reform efforts. But more decisively, the readiness and capacity for reform depends on the beneficiary group being economically equipped and socio-politically confident and determined to undertake the exceedingly daunting and difficult challenge of exiting a system conferring preferential treatment. Phasing out of preferential treatment must be systematically programmed into AA mechanisms, and not merely scheduled as an expiry date. This issue is more pronounced in Malaysia. Since the NEP set a timeframe of 1971–1990 and projected some targets, most saliently 30% Bumiputera equity, the focus continues to be on tracking progress and keeping time-based limits in view, with the implicit implication that the when targets are achieved or if deadlines pass, the policy can be abolished. The policy, in turn, is presented as a monolithic edifice to be dismantled all at once. This further predisposition in the discourses, to omit differences across sectors, should also give way to a sector-by-sector formulation of timelines and milestones.

It suffices at this point, and in accordance with my limited resources, to present guideposts rather than roadmaps. The complexity of overseeing the distant arc of affirmative action, and the need for vast data and information alongside intensive debate and compromise among all interested parties, demand a national conversation.

Three points stand out. First, a long-term reform agenda will need to establish a driving narrative and a resolute adherence to it. Execution of AA must sustain momentum in expanding the disadvantaged beneficiary group's participation and capability, and avoid being side-tracked to deal with problems that are not under its purview. Reforms can proceed more coherently and effectively on condition that Bumiputeras and blacks are sufficiently empowered. Analysis and policy monitoring must also consistently shine the light on AA-relevant outcomes, with due consideration of the ways it can reach out to the poor and other ways that it must select based on merit and talent, and critically assess the balance of successes and failures. In this area of policy appraisals, another challenge stems from heavily biased, imprecise or outright erroneous pronouncements of unqualified failure – with the implication that such failures compel abolition of AA.

Reforms to race-based AA must strive for steady transitions, with candid and credible efforts to mitigate adverse repercussions on the majority group's access to socio-economic opportunity. Self-defeating policy loops have replayed, particularly in Malaysia. Mainstream policy discourses err not only in cleaving to pro-poor policies as alternatives to AA, the flaws and illogic of which have been discussed at various points throughout this book, but also misplace confidence that invoking a "help the poor" slogan will assure Bumiputeras that all their interests will continually be safeguarded – while, again, ignoring marked differences between policy sectors and clear limits to pro-poor preferential treatment. The vacuity of these assurances stirs public unease and impels the government to backpedal on proposals to introduce change, thereby forestalling real and systematic reform.

Policymaking must acknowledge the legitimate concern that vaguely articulated reforms may reverse the gains Bumiputeras and blacks have made under AA or constrict the opportunities preferentially offered to them. Moving forward, it is imperative to provide assurance that policy reforms will continually facilitate upward mobility for Bumiputeras and blacks and maintain safeguards against reversals to the progress made under AA. For instance, policies can articulate that increasing the scope of pro-poor preferential selection for university entry will especially benefit the disadvantaged in the racial majority, but admissions processes will continue to give consideration to racial and ethnic diversity and equitable representation through direct and indirect means. South Africa's experience in university admissions provides some lessons for Malaysia to consider.

Policy discourses induce expectations. In particular, questions of the equitability and productivity of AA call for more circumspection than the influential view that AA only benefits an "elite" rather than the poor. Unfortunately, Sowell (2004) has been repeatedly cited, especially his egregiously opaque and sweeping claim that affirmative action in Malaysia has benefited a mere five percent of Malays, which grabs attention but amounts to a reckless quest to confirm preconceived conclusions.[5] This stance, besides conflating AA with poverty alleviation and basic needs provision, also fuels false expectations that AA can be dismantled because the masses presumably do not benefit from it anyway. Of course, skewed distribution of benefits undermines some AA programmes, particularly when wealth distribution induces unproductive profiteering and corruption. However, more systematic analyses will avoid simplistic dismissals of AA on the grounds that it eludes the masses. AA in higher education has opened up opportunities to lower-income households (albeit with room for improvement); enterprise development targets a range of potential beneficiaries, including micro and small business, but also medium- and large-scale entities. To maintain coherence and momentum, policy discourse should steadfastly focus on AA objectives and instruments and recognize the specific ways it reaches out to broad and narrow segments within the beneficiary group.

Second, sector-specific operations demand sector-specific reforms, involving both timelines and milestones. The paramount need to conduct AA on a sector-by-sector basis extends to long-term planning. Far horizons are generally omitted in policy discourses, and where reform plans appear, conventional thinking gravitates to expiry dates, with no differentiation across policy sectors, thus implying that the system, from higher education to wealth ownership, can be shut down all at once.

However, there are eminent reasons to roll back AA according to each sector's mechanisms and potentialities. Deliberations within each country will need to address specific conditions and needs. Nevertheless, in general AA in higher education holds out greater potential to undertake reform in nearer future because class-based/need-based selection can already be introduced, the supply of students is readily available to enjoy educational mobility and need for experience is considerably less than in employment or enterprise. In contrast, the case can be made for AA in employment and enterprise development to roll out reforms over a longer horizon, or in accordance with more stretched out milestones. Different sectors can adopt a blend of timelines or milestones – whichever may be deemed appropriate or effective. Timelines fix transition or expiry dates, milestones trigger changes when targets are achieved. It is not the place here to generalize which countries or policies should adopt timelines versus milestones, or combinations of both. But a range of possibilities should be explored, beyond the predilection to rely on expiry dates.

Another aspect of policy targeting concerns segments within the beneficiary group and forms of assistance that hold out potential for demonstrable relinquishing of privilege. The Bumiputera and black elite are poised – and, arguably, morally obligated as the most substantially empowered within the beneficiary group – to play a lead role in foregoing preferential treatment, the impact amplified by their visibility and influence. Some policies in Malaysia readily present such opportunities, notably wealth ownership interventions and discounts in property purchase.

A third point of long-term policy change and reform concerns the adoption of a broader menu of policy options. Policy reform does not equate with full elimination of AA. Indeed, public policies will continually need to address equitable representation, whether based on race, ethnicity, gender or other population group, particularly in public universities and government departments. However, countries undertaking the imperative of promoting equitable representation can and should look beyond racial quotas and other overt preferential treatment. The menu of policy options can be broadened, toward measures such as preferential boosts or points systems and outreach mechanisms (expanding the pool of candidates of designated groups) (Weisskopf 2006; Sabbagh 2012).

Limitations and dilemmas

Emphatically, Malaysia's and South Africa's problems with race and inequality are more extensive and complex than I have managed to address, due to limited scope and space of this book and gaps in the literature. This book's focus on affirmative action's principal goals of redressing under-representation and developing capability also set boundaries on our coverage; portions of the analysis lack substantiation and nuance. Among the complementary subjects omitted from more in-depth engagement are racial discrimination (especially in the labour market), effects of affirmative action on emigration, ramifications of racial diversity in workplaces, the multiplicity of barriers to Bumiputera/black enterprise (access to capital, skills shortage, inadequate experience, etc.) and non-financial, culturally-entwined forms of wealth, especially land.[6] There is a sizable literature on most of these topics for readers to explore.

Some of the greater expectations placed on affirmative action, however, warrant attention in this penultimate segment of the book. Like many diverse and divided societies, Malaysia and South Africa aspire for integration and cohesion. Racial identity and privilege create tensions in these quests. It will be remiss for this book to ignore these important, if intractable, issues.

Affirmative action undeniably creates new dilemmas, even as it tries to resolve old ones. It seeks to foster integration and cohesion, in which race, ethnicity, gender and disability are no longer barriers to opportunity and participation, by utilizing these categories to preferentially distribute opportunity. It is part of grandiose national projects of "unity in diversity" or "rainbow nation" and more nuanced notions of "cosmopolitan citizenship" (Bentley and Habib 2008). AA is also critiqued for entrenching racial consciousness, conforming to past categories and excluding hybridity, in ways antithetical to these national aspirations (Gomez 2012; Alexander 2007; Maré 2011; Ruggunan and Maré 2012). In principle, these concerns are legitimate and constructive, but the practical alternatives are also challenging. There is some scope for referencing language, schooling and other variables representing socio-economic background in selection processes, whether to replace or proxy for race and ethnicity, but as reiterated throughout this book, such options apply primarily in education but scarcely to other policy sectors.

That AA sustains racial identity and labels cannot be denied, but it is also exceedingly difficult to prove the counterfactual that such phenomena would dissipate in the absence of AA. The policy requires formal identification and draws lines between policy beneficiaries and others, but people also self-identify by their own volition, according to race, ethnicity, language, region and other normally accepted categories. Moreover, regardless of the strength of affiliation with racial identity, increased interaction – through diversity in places of learning, living and work – arguably yields positive benefits through fostering understanding and breaking down barriers. The extent to which higher education institutions function as sites of social interaction among peers, although not a subject of this book's analysis, is crucial to maintain as context. Studies in that field have generated mixed findings. If social polarization remains while campuses are increasingly diverse, it is highly plausible that the situation will be worse if campuses are mono-racial.[7] Increased diversity in the middle and upper classes of Malaysia and South Africa are substantive and symbolic achievements not to be overlooked (Abdul Aziz 2012; Embong 2018; Horwitz and Jain 2011; Southall 2016).

The racial dynamics of division and cohesion have been prolifically researched, particularly in political and sociological studies. Baharuddin (2010) perceptively proposes "social cohesion" to encapsulate Malaysia's "stable tension," sustained by continuous effort in preserving group identities, representing interests and processing compromises. Challenges to cohesion increasingly derive from religious fault lines or the magnification of conflict when religion fuses with race (Lee 2017b). Seekings (2008) characterizes South Africa as having improved race relations but with "limited social deracialization." While evidence suggests that widespread, blatant occurrences of discrimination are no longer prevalent, perceptions of race and opportunity, whether or not based on objective data, can drive behaviour. For instance, belief among whites that their career opportunities are foreclosed can influence their decisions, including emigration. Race is also deep-seated, persisting due to multidimensional, structural reasons (MacDonald 2006).

There are no simple and straightforward solutions. Of course, inclusive policies regarding culture, language and religion can foster cohesion. Racialized politics tends to be divisive; less racialized politics arguably stand to benefit Malaysia and South Africa – but such trajectories are exceedingly hard to engineer. The struggles of mixed-race parties in Malaysia to gain broad traction, and persistently sharp racial voting patterns in South Africa for political parties not constituted along racial lines, demonstrate the durable and complex underpinnings of racial representation. Proposals to reduce or eliminate racial categorization are noble and worth experimentation, but in Malaysia and South Africa, the majority of names immediately give away racial or ethnic identity. The problem of "brain drain" is salient in both countries and undeniably related to AA, but also attributable to various other factors, including corruption, crime, political culture and better career prospects and income-earning opportunities abroad regardless of race-based policies at home.

How then should we situate AA in the context of broader national agendas and political structures? Since elimination of AA is not foreseeably feasible, the onus rests on effective execution and systematic forward planning, with mitigation of adverse effects on both non-beneficiaries and beneficiaries, as outlined here. A constructive starting point will be to acknowledge the current importance and embeddedness of racial representation in esteemed and influential positions, while continually probing limits. The principle of proportionality – representation corresponding with the profile of relevant populations – holds legitimacy as the baseline for AA objectives, but solutions must be sought on a sectoral basis. This critical, if discomforting, question must be posed: can social cohesion be attained without proportionate wealth ownership and economic power? On one hand, wealth disparities reproduce across generations and can set different groups on divergent trajectories; on the other hand, wealth redistribution is the most vulnerable to corruption and patronage, and pursuit of it also perpetuates consumerism and accumulation inimical to sustainable development principles.

On these questions, and on the general challenge of AA across all spheres, countries must deliberate and reach accommodation and compromise.

The prospect of possible resistance to reforms also needs critical consideration and candid dialogue. In essence, the question is: can the majority groups of Malaysia and South Africa relinquish privilege? Bumiputeras and blacks enjoy preferential treatment to a range of opportunities. The formalized privilege intends to accelerate learning and work experience, but it can depreciate into a sense of entitlement which undermines the intended productive gains and may also stigmatize policy beneficiaries, including those who are genuinely capable. These aspects of affirmative action are often clouded in polemics and presumptions, with political motivations and self-interest often overstated as the motivation to maintain the policy. A more sober and objective perspective should see that the spectre of loss of privilege is unnerving to ordinary people who benefit in material ways and have structured their lives and hopes around affirmative action policies.

Moving forward, these dilemmas present challenges and opportunities. Race and privilege are both durable and dynamic. Affirmative action must continually grapple with the complexities arising from racial preference as a defining and operational feature that differentiates groups, while also playing transitory roles in promoting the disadvantaged group's socio-economic advancement and fostering more diverse settings for learning and working. Deeply embedded identity and proudly retained heritage positively contribute to the countries' multi-racial, multi-lingual and multi-religious composition, but they also constitute divides that need to be bridged. Again, AA must strike a balance of conferring preferential treatment while striving for those afforded opportunities to augment capabilities such that preference becomes redundant and that diversity can be pursued through less overtly preferential mechanisms.

As implausible as it may seem, but specifically in majority-favouring AA regimes, where the beneficiary group wields electoral power, the impetus and momentum of reform – of rolling back privileged access – must derive from the majority. They must, in turn, be adequately enabled, secure, competitive and confident.

The policy concludes when beneficiaries achieve success and graduate, not declare failure and abandon.

The present moment: fluidity, continuity, opportunity

This book arrives at historic junctures in Malaysia and South Africa. Both countries are experiencing fluidity in political power and economic conditions and continuity, if not reassertion, of affirmative action. Economic slowdown constrains the capacity to pursue AA. We can also glimpse some opportunities for affirmative action to undertake change. Malaysia experienced a watershed in 2018, when the Barisan Nasional alliance lost power after continuously ruling for six decades. "Rice bowl" issues such as cost of living and public services were momentous in the campaign. Pro-Bumiputera affirmative action had been enmeshed with BN, but the incoming Pakatan Harapan coalition essentially preserved the system – even promised various enhancements. Twenty-one months later, PH collapsed, due to realignments and defections galvanized around a "Malay unity" agenda, supposedly restoring pro-Malay policies perceived or besmirched as under threat by the PH government.

Two years into the Ramaphosa presidency, South Africa plods along with sluggish economic growth and chronically high unemployment, compounded by the government's struggling efforts to restore confidence and integrity shattered by the venal Zuma administration (PARI 2017).[8] The gravity of fundamental challenges may temper expectations of the magnitude and pace of affirmative action, but the agenda remains firmly in place, with added impetus to return to more basic issues of higher education affordability, employment generation and black-owned SME growth.

In both countries, extensive social assistance programmes, notably South Africa's social grants, are extensive and embedded. Both countries grapple with the global trend of heightened awareness to inequality and exclusion. Popular demands for effective and empathetic service delivery, for economic stewardship that looks out for the common person, potentially expand the common ground and national consensus around public programmes that are premised on equality and basic rights and that operate on the basis of need, means and socio-economic conditions – regardless of race or other form of identity. Heightened global uncertainty, and distress in the aftermath of the Covid-19 pandemic, will compel countries to mobilize resources that cater to the masses.

We should not extrapolate too much from the current moment on to the future of affirmative action. But the conditions suggest the possibility for Malaysia and South Africa to clearly distinguish the remedial actions taken to care for citizens and residents from the ongoing, if perhaps more tempered and equitable, implementation of AA. Poverty, employment and public services are fundamental and crucial, and indeed should take precedence in policy design and public funding allocations. Popular consciousness of inequality and equitable distribution may also incline programmes to focus more on education for the disadvantaged, development of micro and small enterprise, upscaling to medium-scale operations and wealth ownership of ordinary households. Such shifts are undeniably not guaranteed, but they will be welcome and wholesome in potentially fostering a more sustained and progressive AA.

Ultimately, however, Malaysia and South Africa will need to stare deeply to the distant horizons and reckon with final destinations. And if seeking closure, then formulate the possibilities for rolling back the current AA regimes, setting milestones and timelines for exit or graduation. Among the beneficiaries, there will need to be a "critical mass" that becomes amenable to phasing out the policy in its current form, having acquired capability, competitiveness, confidence and self-reliance.

Will disparities persist in Malaysia and South Africa, or will the countries edge close enough for parity between groups? Will race-preferential treatment be retained or become redundant and relinquishable? These are the questions waiting to be answered in the decades to come.

Notes

1 Malaysia's takeover of foreign companies, in some cases through hostile means, presents another recourse not available to South Africa.

2 Jain (2006, 51) emanates a hint of justice promised in means-based AA, which "would not permit the occurrence of unjust advantage, as benefits would be extended to individuals upon their classification through a combination of wealth and income analysis, as economically disadvantaged, irrespective of race." However, this position is weakened by the omission of proposals on how wealth and income can operate as selection criteria across the range of existing policy contexts, even within his main focus of employment. Income and wealth can conceivably apply in the hiring of fresh graduates, but surely becomes exceedingly difficult or problematic when it comes to promotions or high-level appointments.

3 Malaysia's parallel pre-university programmes continually pose a profound policy challenge. While this concluding chapter takes a rather prescriptive stance, we must be mindful of the complexity involved. Malaysia's Education Blueprint, 2013–2025 proposed to enhance the appeal of Form 6 (Ministry of Education 2013). Subsequently, Form 6 colleges have increased in number, 5 in 2013 and 14 in 2017. They remain in the minority within the broader scheme of the three modes of Form 6. In 2017, there were 78 schools offering Form 6 in a separate block within a mainstream school, and 538 offering Form 6 within the same compound as the mainstream school. The colleges, by providing STPM instruction in a more concrete and programme-specific setting, concomitantly entrench the position of the matriculation colleges. On the other hand, these investments in pre-university colleges may open windows of opportunity. The expansion of STPM colleges – especially if constructed in urban areas – may serve to complement rural-located matriculation colleges, and possibly even lay foundations for future merger of these parallel university entrance programmes.

4 Other possible modifications include incentives for partnerships and consortia to bid for larger contracts (e.g. set aside some G4 contracts for G2 and G3 to jointly pursue), points for moving up a tier (e.g. award points for a G1 contractor who moves up to G2, applicable for the first 2–3 years after that move) and sunset clauses that limit the number of contracts or time periods one can receive preferential treatment (e.g. 3 contracts, or 6 years) (Lee 2018).

5 Sowell (2004), while sub-titled "an empirical study," performs no empirical analysis of his own – and conveniently cites an obscure book chapter, published in 1984, which he acknowledges is an "early" study of the NEP, but one that claims that no more than five percent of Malays benefited from such policies. Without furnishing any details of that study, which by then is also 20 years outdated, Sowell (2004, 74)

concludes his chapter on Malaysia with a tendentious assertion that "in Malaysia no more than 5 percent of the Malays have been estimated to have actually benefitted from such programs." The book's handling of Malaysia is gravely discredited by the apparently wilful omission of abundant existing literature which would paint more credible and nuanced portraits of policy outcomes.

6 The omission of land ownership in this book, noted in the introduction, is worth reiterating. Although it is a key asset with major implications on wealth dynamics – a source of gaping disparity in South Africa, a mixed picture in Malaysia – the complications associated with land distribution, and deep entanglements with power, culture and food production, necessitate separate academic and policy research.

7 Yahaya, Tey and Yeoh's (2004) campus survey paints a portrait of university students tolerant and amicably coexisting across racial lines but polarized when it comes to friendships and social circles. Soudien (2010) unpacks the heterogeneity of undergraduates' perspectives and complexity in social interactions, with informal segregation but also friendships fostered across colour lines, amid recurrent racism against black students. Those studying in HWIs may have their confidence bolstered, but also imbibe a status consciousness that complicates their sense of identity and relations with their community.

8 Norimitsu Onishi and Selam Gebrekidan, "'They Eat Money': How Mandela's Political Heirs Grow Rich Off Corruption", *New York Times*, 16 April 2018.

Bibliography

Abdul Aziz, Rahimah. 2012. "New Economic Policy and the Malaysian Multiethnic Middle Class." *Asian Ethnicity* 13, no. 1: 29–46.

Abu Samad, M. Fazilah. 2002. *Bumiputeras in the Corporate Sector: Three Decades of Performance, 1970–2000.* CEDER Research Reports Series, No. 1.

Adam, Kanya. 1997. "The Politics of Redress: South African Style Affirmative Action." *The Journal of Modern African Studies* 35, no. 2: 231–249.

Adam, Kanya. 2000. *The Colour Of Business: Managing Diversity In South Africa.* Basel: P. Schlettwein Publishing.

African National Congress (ANC). 1955. *The Freedom Charter.* Adopted at the Congress of the People, Kliptown, 26 June. www.anc.org.za/ancdocs/history/charter. html (accessed 22 March 2009).

Aihara, Akihito. 2009. "Paradoxes of Higher Education Reforms: Implications on the Malaysian Middle Class." *International Journal of Asia-Pacific Studies* 5, no. 1: 81–113.

Alexander, Neville. 2007. "Affirmative Action and the Perpetuation of Racial Identities in Post-apartheid South Africa." *Transformation: Critical Perspectives on Southern Africa* 63: 92–108.

Allanson, Paul, Jonathan P. Atkins and Timothy Hinks. 2002. "No End to the Racial Wage Hierarchy in South Africa?" *Review of Development Economics* 6, no. 3: 442–459.

Al Ramiah, Ananthi, Miles Hewstone and Ralf Wölfer. 2017. *Attitudes and Ethnoreligious Integration: Meeting the Challenge and Maximizing the Promise of Multicultural Malaysia.* Final Report: Survey and Recommendations Presented to the Board of Trustees, CIMB Foundation.

Ambe, Intaher M. and Johanna A. Badenhorst-Weiss. 2012. "Procurement Challenges in the South African Public Sector." *Journal of Transport and Supply Chain Management* 6, no. 1: 242–261.

Ambikaipaker, Mohan. 2013. "Anti-polarization Identity Politics in Malaysia: Critical Race Subjects and the Theatre of Leow Puay Tin." *Postcolonial Studies* 16, no. 4: 340–357.

Anand, Sudhir. 1981. *Inequality and Poverty in Malaysia: Measurement and Decomposition.* Oxford: Oxford University Press.

ANC. 1994. *Reconstruction and Development Plan.* www.anc.org.za/show. php?doc=rdp/rdpall.html (accessed 9 December 2008).

ANC. 2007. *Economic Transformation for a National Democratic Society.* Policy Discussion Document.

ANC (Department of Economic Planning). 1992. *Ready to Govern*. ANC Policy Guidelines for a Democratic South Africa Adopted at the National Conference, 28–31 May. www.anc.org.za/ancdocs/history/readyto.html (accessed 27 November 2008).

Andaya, Barbara Watson and Leonard Y. Andaya. 2001. *A History of Malaysia*. Honolulu: University of Hawai'i Press.

Badat, Salim. 2010. *The Challenges of Transformation in Higher Education and Training Institutions in South Africa*. Paper commissioned by the Development Bank of Southern Africa.

Badat, Salim. 2012. "Redressing the Colonial/Apartheid Legacy: Social Equity, Redress, and Higher Education Admissions in Democratic South Africa." In *Affirmative Action in Higher Education in India, United States, and South Africa*, edited by Martha Nussbaum and Zoya Hasan, 121–150. New Delhi: Oxford University Press.

Badat, Salim. 2018. "On Black Professors, Deracialization, Transformation." *The Conversation*, November.

Badawi, Abdullah Ahmad. 2006. *The 2007 Budget Speech*. Putrajaya: Ministry of Finance.

Badawi, Abdullah Ahmad. 2007. *The 2008 Budget Speech*. Putrajaya: Ministry of Finance.

Baharuddin, Shamsul Amri. 2010. *Unity in Diversity: The Malaysian Experience*. Bangi: Institut Kajian Etnik (KITA), UKM.

Ball, Rob and Razmi Chik. 2001. "Early Employment Outcomes of Home and Foreign Educated Graduates – the Malaysian Experience." *Higher Education* 42: 171–189.

BBBEE Commission. 2019. *National Status and Trends on Black Economic Empowerment Report*. Pretoria: Broad-based Black Economic Empowerment Commission.

Becker, Gary. 1971. *The Economics of Discrimination* (2nd Edition). Chicago and London: University of Chicago Press.

Beckwith, Francis J. and Todd E. Jones, eds. 1997. *Affirmative Action: Social Justice or Reverse Discrimination?* Amherst, NY: Prometheus.

BEE Commission. 2000. *Black Economic Empowerment Commission Presentation Prepared for the Portfolio Committee on Trade and Industry*. Black Economic Empowerment Commission, 13 September.

Benabou, Roland. 1996. "Equity and Efficiency in Human Capital Investment: The Local Connection." *Review of Economic Studies* 63: 237–264.

Bentley, Kristina and Adam Habib. 2008. "Racial Redress, National Identity and Citizenship in Post-Apartheid South Africa." In *Racial Redress and Citizenship in South Africa*, edited by Adam Habib and Christina Bentley, 3–32. Cape Town: HSRC Press.

Bergmann, Barbara R. 1996. *In Defense of Affirmative Action*. New York: Basic Books.

Bezuidenhout, Andries, Christine Bischoff, Sakhela Buhlungu and Kezia Lewins. 2008. *Tracking Progress on the Implementation and Impact of the Employment Equity Act Since its Inception*. Research Commissioned by the Department of Labour, South Africa.

Bhalla, Surjit and Homi Kharas. 1992. "Growth and Equity in Malaysia: Policies and Consequences." In *Malaysia's Economic Vision*, edited by Teh Hoe Yoke and Goh Kim Leng, 41–88. Petaling Jaya: Pelanduk.

Bhorat, Haroon, Murray Leibbrandt and Ingrid Woolard. 2000. "Understanding South Africa's Inequality." In *Development Issues in South Africa*, edited by Ibrahim A. Elbadawi and Trudi Hartzenberg, 14–50. New York: St. Martin's Press.

Bond, Patrick. 2000. *Elite Transition: From Apartheid to Neoliberalism in South Africa*. London: Pluto Press.

Bowen, William G. and Derek Bok. 1998. *The Shape of the River: Long-Term Consequences of Considering Race in College and University Admissions*. Princeton: Princeton University Press.

Bowles, Samuel and Herbert Gintis. 1975. "The Problem with Human Capital Theory – A Marxian Critique." *American Economic Review* 65, no. 2: 74–82.

Breier, Mignonne and Mahlubi Mabuzela. 2008. "Higher Education." In *Human Resources Development Review 2008*, edited by Andre Kraak and Karen Press, 278–299. Cape Town: HSRC Press.

Brown, Graham. 2007. "Making Ethnic Citizens: The Politics and Practice of Education in Malaysia." *International Journal of Educational Development* 27, no. 3: 318–330.

Brown, Graham and Arnim Langer. 2015. "Does Affirmative Action Work? Lessons from around the World." *Foreign Affairs*, March/April.

Brown, Graham K., Frances Stewart and Arnim Langer, eds. 2012. *Affirmative Action in Plural Societies: International Comparisons*. Basingstoke: Palgrave Macmillan.

Burger, Rulof and Rachel Jafta. 2012. "Affirmative Action in South Africa: An Empirical Assessment of the Impact on Labour Market Outcomes." In *Affirmative Action in Plural Societies: International Comparisons*, edited by Graham K. Brown, Frances Stewart and Arnim Langer, 80–99. Basingstoke: Palgrave Macmillan.

Cahn, Steven M., ed. 2002. *The Affirmative Action Debate*. London and New York: Routledge.

Cameron, R. and C. Milne. 2011. "Representative Bureaucracy in the South African Public Service." *African Journal of Public Affairs* 4, no. 2: 18–35.

Cargill, Jenny. 2010. *Trick or Treat: Rethinking Black Economic Empowerment*. Johannesburg: Jacana.

Chakravarty, Shanti P. and Roslan Abdul-Hakim, 2005. "Ethnic Nationalism and Income Distribution in Malaysia." *The European Journal of Development Research* 17, no. 2: 270–288.

CHE. 2000. *Policy Report: Towards a New Higher Education Landscape: Meeting the Equity, Quality and Social Development Imperatives of South Africa in the Twenty-first Century*. Pretoria: Council on Higher Education.

CHE. 2004. *South African Higher Education in the First Decade of Democracy*. Pretoria: Council on Higher Education.

CHE. 2013. *Vital Stats: Public Higher Education 2011*. Pretoria: Council on Higher Education.

CHE. 2018. *Vital Stats: Public Higher Education 2016*. Pretoria: Council on Higher Education.

Chin, James. 2009. "The Malaysian Chinese Dilemma: The Never Ending Policy (NEP)." *Chinese Southern Diaspora Studies* 3: 167–182.

Chin, Yee Whah and Benny Teh Cheng Guan. 2017. "Malaysia's Protracted Affirmative Action Policy and the Evolution of the Bumiputera Commercial and Industrial Community." *SOJOURN: Journal of Social Issues in Southeast Asia* 32, no. 2: 336–373.

Chipkin, Ivor. 2008. "Set-up for Failure: Racial Redress in the Department of Public Service and Administration." In *Racial Redress and Citizenship in South Africa*, edited by Adam Habib and Christina Bentley, 129–152. Cape Town: HSRC Press.

Chipkin, Ivor. 2011. "Transcending Bureaucracy: State Transformation in the Age of the Manager." *Transformation: Critical Perspectives on Southern Africa* 77: 31–51.

Chisholm, Linda. 2008. "The Meaning of Racial Redress in South African Schools, 1994 to 2006." In *Racial Redress and Citizenship in South Africa*, edited by Adam Habib and Christina Bentley, 230–262. Cape Town: HSRC Press.

Chung, Tsung-Ping. 2003. "Returns to Education: Updates for Malaysia." *Applied Economic Letters* 10: 837–841.

CIDB. 2016. *Contractor Registration Requirements and Procedures Handbook*. Kuala Lumpur: Construction Industry Development Board.

CPPS. 2006a. *Corporate Equity Distribution: Past Trends and Future Policy*. Kuala Lumpur: Centre for Public Policy Studies.

CPPS. 2006b. *Towards a More Representative and World Class Civil Service*. Kuala Lumpur: Centre for Public Policy Studies.

Crankshaw, Owen. 1996. "Changes in the Racial Division of Labour during the Apartheid Era." *Journal of Southern African Studies* 22, no. 4: 633–656.

Crouch, Harold. 2001. "Managing Ethnic Tensions through Affirmative Action: The Malaysian Experience." In *Social Cohesion and Conflict Prevention in Asia: Managing Diversity through Development*, edited by Nat J. Colleta, Teck Ghee Lim and Anita Kelles-Viitanen, 225–262. Washington, DC: World Bank.

Curry, George E., ed. 1996. *The Affirmative Action Debate*. Reading, MA: Addison Wesley.

Darity, William, Jr. 1982. "The Human Capital Approach to Black-White Earnings Inequality: Some Unsettled Questions." *The Journal of Human Resources* 17, no. 1: 72–93.

Darity, William. 2013. "Confronting those Affirmative Action Grumbles." In *Capitalism on Trial: Explorations in the Tradition of Thomas E. Weisskopf*, edited by Jeannette Wicks-Lim and Robert Pollin, 215–223. Northampton: Edward Elgar.

Department of Basic Education. 2018. *Education Statistics in South Africa 2016*. Pretoria: Department of Basic Education.

Department of Education. 1995. *White Paper on Education and Training*. Notice 196 of 1995, Parliament of the Republic of South Africa, Cape Town, 15 March.

Department of Education. 1996. *The Organisation, Governance and Funding of Schools* (Education White Paper 2), General Notice 130 of 1996, Pretoria, February.

Department of Education. 1997. *A Programme for Higher Education Transformation* (Education White Paper 3), Pretoria, 15 August.

Department of Education. 1998. *A Programme for the Transformation of Further Education and Training* (Education White Paper 4), Pretoria, 25 September.

Department of Education. 2003. *Education Statistics in South Africa at a Glance in 2002*. Pretoria: Department of Education.

Department of Education. 2004. *Education Statistics in South Africa at a Glance in 2003*. Pretoria: Department of Education.

Department of Education. 2005. *Education Statistics in South Africa at a Glance in 2004*. Pretoria: Department of Education.

Department of Education. 2008. *Education Statistics in South Africa 2006*. Pretoria: Department of Education.

Department of Higher Education and Training (DHET). 2018. *Statistics on Post-School Education and Training in South Africa: 2016.* Pretoria: Department of Higher Education and Training.

Department of Labour. 2000–2019. *Commission for Employment Equity Annual Report.* Pretoria: Department of Labour.

Department of Public Service and Administration. 1995. *White Paper on Transformation of Public Service.* Pretoria: Government Gazette.

Department of Public Service and Administration. 1998. *White Paper on Affirmative Action in the Public Service.* Notice 564 of 1998, Pretoria: Government Gazette.

Department of Statistics. 1990. *Labour Force Survey Report.* Kuala Lumpur: Department of Statistics.

Department of Statistics. 1995. *Labour Force Survey Report.* Kuala Lumpur: Department of Statistics.

Department of Statistics. 2000. *Labour Force Survey Report.* Kuala Lumpur: Department of Statistics.

Department of Statistics. 2007. *Labour Force Survey Report.* Kuala Lumpur: Department of Statistics.

Department of Statistics. 2009. *Yearbook of Statistics.* Kuala Lumpur: Department of Statistics.

Department of Statistics. 2010. *Labour Force Survey Report.* Kuala Lumpur: Department of Statistics.

Department of Statistics. 2013a. *Labour Force Survey Report.* Kuala Lumpur: Department of Statistics.

Department of Statistics. 2013b. *Population Distribution and Basic Demographic Characteristics Report 2010.* Kuala Lumpur: Department of Statistics.

Department of Statistics. 2019. *Graduate Statistics 2018.* Putrajaya: Department of Statistics.

Department of Statistics. Various Years. *Annual Statistical Yearbook.* Kuala Lumpur: Department of Statistics.

DTI. 2004. *The Codes of Good Practice on Broad-Based Black Economic Empowerment.* Pretoria: Department of Trade and Industry.

DTI. 2009. *Medium Term Strategic Framework 2009–2012.* Pretoria: Department of Trade and Industry.

DTI. 2011. *Leveraging Public Procurement.* Presentation at the Annual Small Business Summit, Bloemfontein, 11 October. Department of Trade and Industry.

DTI. 2013. *Broad-based Black Economic Empowerment Act (53/2003): Issue of Codes of Good Practice.* Pretoria: Government Gazette, Republic of South Africa, No. 36928.

DTI. 2015. *Black Industrialists Policy.* Pretoria: Department of Trade and Industry.

Dupper, Ockert. 2005. "Remedying the Past or Reshaping the Future? Justifying Race-based Affirmative Action in South Africa and the United States." *The International Journal of Comparative Labor Law and Industrial Relations* 21, no. 1: 89–130.

Dupper, Ockert. 2014. "Restraint, Deference and Reasonableness: Affirmative Action in South Africa." In *Affirmative Action: A View from the Global South,* edited by Ockert Dupper and Kamala Sankaran, 253–279. Stellenbosch: SUN Press.

Dupper, Ockert and Kamala Sankaran, eds. 2014. *Affirmative Action: A View from the Global South.* Stellenbosch: SUN Press.

Durlauf, Stephen. 1996. "A Theory of Persistent Income Inequality." *Journal of Economic Growth* 1, no. 1: 75–93.

Durrheim, Kevin. 2010. "Attitudes Toward Racial Redress in South Africa." In *South African Social Attitudes – The 2nd Report: Reflections on the Age of Hope*, edited by Benjamin Roberts, Mbithi wa Kivilu and Yul Derek Davids, 31–42. Cape Town: HSRC Press.

Durrheim, Kevin, Merridy Boettiger, Zaynab Essack, Silvia Maarschalk and Chitra Ranchod. 2007. "The Colour of Success: A Qualitative Study of Affirmative Action Attitudes of Black Academics in South Africa." *Transformation: Critical Perspectives on Southern Africa* 64: 112–139.

du Toit, André. 2010. "Social Justice and Postapartheid Education in South Africa." In *The Next Twenty-five Years: Affirmative Action in Higher Education in the United States and South Africa*, edited by David Featherman, Martin Hall Martin and Marvin Krislov, 87–109. Ann Arbor, MI: University of Michigan Press.

du Toit, Pierre. 2004. *Affirmative Action and the Politics of Transformation*. A Study Commissioned by the FW de Klerk Foundation. Panorama, South Africa: FW de Klerk Foundation.

Economic Development Department. 2010. *The New Growth Path*. Pretoria: Economic Development Department.

ECSA. 2010. *Annual Report 2009–2010*. Johannesburg: Engineering Council of South Africa.

ECSA. 2019. *Annual Report 2018–2019*. Johannesburg: Engineering Council of South Africa.

Edigheji, Omano. 2007. *Affirmative Action and State Capacity in a Democratic South Africa*. Johannesburg: Centre for Policy Studies.

Educational Planning and Research Division. 2018. *Quick Facts 2018: Malaysia Educational Statistics*. Putrajaya: Educational Planning and Research Division, Ministry of Education Malaysia.

Ekuinas. 2018. *Annual Report*. Petaling Jaya: Ekuiti Nasional Berhad (Ekuinas).

Embong, Abdul Rahman. 1996. "Social Transformation, the State and the Middle Classes in Post-Independence Malaysia." *Southeast Asian Studies* 34, no. 3: 56–79.

Embong, Abdul Rahman. 2018. "Ethnicity and Class: Divides and Dissent in Malaysian Studies." In *Divides and Dissent: Malaysian Politics 60 Years after Merdeka*, edited by Khoo Boo Teik, special issue, *Southeast Asian Studies* 7, no. 3: 281–307.

Empowerdex. 2012. *JSE Black Directorship Analysis (2006–2012)*. Johannesburg: Empowerdex.

Emsley, Ian. 1996. *The Malaysian Experience of Affirmative Action: Lessons for South Africa*. Cape Town: Human and Rousseau.

Faaland, Just, J. R. Parkinson and Rais Saniman. 1990. *Growth and Ethnic Inequality: Malaysia's New Economic Policy*. London: Hurst.

Faruqi, Shad Saleem. 2008. *Document of Destiny: The Constitution of the Federation of Malaysia*. Petaling Jaya: Star Publications.

Featherman, David, Martin Hall and Marvin Krislov, eds. 2010. *The Next Twenty-five Years: Affirmative Action in Higher Education in the United States and South Africa*. Ann Arbor, MI: University of Michigan Press.

Fernando, Joseph M. 2015. "Special Rights in the Malaysian Constitution and the Framers' Dilemma, 1956–57." *The Journal of Imperial and Commonwealth History* 43, no. 3: 535–556.

Fernando, Joseph M. and Shanthiah Rajagopal. 2017. "Fundamental Liberties in the Malayan Constitution and the Search for a Balance." *International Journal of Asia Pacific Studies* 13, no. 1: 1–28.

Fine, Ben and Zav Rustomjee. 1996. *South Africa's Political Economy: From Mineral-Energy Complex to Industrialization?* London: Hurst.

Fisher, Glen and Scott Ian. 2011. "The Role of Higher Education in Closing the Skills Gap in South Africa." Background paper 3, 'Closing the Skills and Technology Gap in South Africa' Project. World Bank Human Development Group, Africa Region.

Fryer, Roland G. Jr. and Glenn Loury. 2005. "Affirmative Action and Its Mythology." *Journal of Economic Perspectives* 19, no. 3: 147–162.

Gerakan. 1984. *The National Economic Policy – 1990 and Beyond.* Penang: Parti Gerakan Rakyat Malaysia (Gerakan).

Gomez, Edmund Terence. 2012. "Targeting Horizontal Inequalities: Ethnicity, Equity, and Entrepreneurship in Malaysia." *Asian Economic Papers* 11, no. 2: 31–57.

Gomez, Edmund Terence. 2015. "The 11th Malaysia Plan: Covertly Persisting with Market-Friendly Affirmative Action?" *The Round Table* 104, no. 4: 511–513.

Gomez, Edmund Terence and K.S. Jomo. 1999. *Malaysia's Political Economy: Power, Profits, Patronage.* Cambridge: Cambridge University Press.

Gomez, Edmund Terence, Thirshalar Padmanabhan, Norfaryanti Kamaruddin, Sunil Bhalla, Fikri Fisal and Sunil Bhalla. 2017. *Minister of Finance Incorporated: Ownership and Control of Corporate Malaysia.* Singapore: Palgrave Macmillan.

Gomez, Edmund Terence and Ralph R. Premdas. 2013. *Affirmative Action, Ethnicity, and Conflict.* London and New York: Routledge.

Gomez, Edmund Terence and Johan Saravanamuttu, eds. 2013. *The New Economic Policy in Malaysia: Affirmative Action, Ethnic Inequalities and Social Justice.* Singapore and Petaling Jaya: NUS Press, ISEAS and SIRD.

Government Procurement Division. 2010. *Malaysia's Government Procurement Regime.* Putrajaya: Government Procurement Division, Ministry of Finance.

Gqubule, Duma. 2006. "The True Meaning of Black Economic Empowerment." In *Making Mistakes Righting Wrongs: Insights into Black Economic Empowerment,* edited by Duma Gqubule, 1–38. Johannesburg and Cape Town: Jonathan Ball.

Gqubule, Duma. 2016. *South African Mining at the Crossroads: An Analysis of the Mining Charter 2004–2014.* Johannesburg: Centre for Economic Development and Transformation.

Gqubule, Duma. 2017. "Black Ownership on the JSE." 26 January. Centre for Economic Development and Transformation.

Gradín, Carlos. 2018. "Occupational Segregation By Race in South Africa After Apartheid." *Review of Development Economics* 23: 553–576.

Griesel, Hanlie and Ben Parker. 2009. *Graduate Attributes: A Baseline Study on South African Graduates from the Perspective of Employers.* Pretoria: Higher Education South Africa.

Gumede, William. 2002. "Down to Business, but Nothing to Show." In *Thabo Mbeki's World: The Politics and Ideology of the South African President,* edited by Sean Jacobs and Richard Calland. London: Zed Books.

Habib, Adam. 2016a. *South Africa's Suspended Revolution: Hopes and Prospects.* Athens, OH: Ohio University Press.

Habib, Adam. 2016b. "Goals and Mean: Reimagining the South African University and Critically Analyzing the Struggle for its Realization." *Transformation: Critical Perspectives on Southern Africa* 90: 111–132.

Habib, Adam and Vishnu Padayachee. 2000. "Economic Policy and Power Relations in South Africa's Transition to Democracy." *World Development* 28, no. 2: 245–263.

Hart, Gillian. 1994. "The New Economic Policy and Redistribution in Malaysia: A Model for Post-Apartheid South Africa?" *Transformation: Critical Perspectives on Southern Africa* 23: 44–58.

Hashim, Shireen Mardziah. 1998. *Income Inequality and Poverty in Malaysia*. Lanham, MD: Rowman and Littlefield.

Henderson, Jeffrey and Richard Philips. 2007. "Unintended Consequences: Social Policy, State Institutions and the 'Stalling' of the Malaysian Industrialization Project." *Economy and Society* 36, no. 1: 78–102.

Hermann, Dirk. 2007. *The Naked Emperor: Why Affirmative Action Failed*. Pretoria: Protea.

Hirsch, Alan. 2006. *Season of Hope: Economic Reform under Mandela and Mbeki*. Scottsville: University of KwaZulu-Natal Press.

Hirschman, Charles. 1986. "The Making of Race in Colonial Malaya: Political Economy and Racial Ideology." *Sociological Forum* 1, no. 2: 330–359.

Hlekiso, Thami and Nthabiseng Mahlo. 2006. "Wage Trends and Inequality in South Africa: A Comparative Analysis." *Labour Market Frontiers* October: 9–15.

Ho, Khai Leong. 1992. "Dynamics of Policy-Making in Malaysia: The Formulation of the New Economic Policy and the National Development Policy." *Asian Journal of Public Administration* 14, no. 2: 204–227.

Holzer, Harry and David Neumark. 2000. "Assessing Affirmative Action." *Journal of Economic Literature* 38: 483–568.

Hoogeveen, Johannes G. and Berk Özler. 2005. *Not Separate, Not Equal: Poverty and Inequality in Post-Apartheid South Africa*. William Davidson Institute Working Paper No. 739.

Horwitz, Frank M. 1996. "Executive Development: Facing the New Realities." *Journal of European Industrial Training* 20, no. 4: 11–16.

Horwitz, Frank M. and Angus Bowmaker-Falconer. 2003. "Managers." In *Human Resources Development Review 2003*, edited by Andre Kraak and Helene Perold, 610–632. Cape Town: HSRC Press.

Horwitz, Frank M. and Harish Jain. 2011. "An Assessment of Employment Equity and Broad Based Black Economic Empowerment Developments in South Africa." *Equality, Diversity and Inclusion: An International Journal* 30, no. 4: 297–317.

IDC. 2010. *Annual Report: Towards a New Development Growth Path*. Johannesburg: Industrial Development Corporation.

IDC. 2015a. *Integrated Report: Advancing Industrial Development*. Johannesburg: Industrial Development Corporation.

IDC. 2015b. *IDC's Support to Black Industrialists*. Presentation at the Black Industrialists Indaba, 25–26 March. Gallagher Convention Centre, Midrand.

IDC. 2018. *Annual Report: Partnering for Inclusive Industrialisation*. Johannesburg: Industrial Development Corporation.

IDC. 2019. *Annual Report: Towards a New Development Growth Path*. Johannesburg: Industrial Development Corporation.

IFC. 2018. *The Unseen Sector: A Report on the MSME Opportunity in South Africa.* Washington, DC: International Financial Corporation.

Iheduru, Okechukwu C. 2004. "Black Economic Power and Nation-building in Post-Apartheid South Africa." *The Journal of Modern African Studies* 42, no. 1: 1–30.

ILO. 1958. *Convention 111.* Geneva: International Labour Organisation (ILO).

ILO. 2003. *Time for Equality at Work.* ILO Conference 91st Session, Report I(B). Geneva: ILO.

ILO. 2007. *Equality at Work: Tackling the Challenges.* ILO Conference 96th Session, Report I(B). Geneva: ILO.

Imenda, S. N., M. Kongolo and A. S. Grewal. 2004. "Factors Underlying Teknikon and University Enrolment Trends in South Africa." *Educational Management, Administration and Leadership* 32, no. 2: 195–215.

Jack, Hammer. 2015. *Executive Report – Volume Three.* Cape Town: Jack Hammer.

Jack, Hammer. 2018. *Executive Report – Volume Five.* Cape Town: Jack Hammer.

Jack, Vuyo. 2003. *Ten Years of Black Economic Empowerment.* Johannesburg: Empowerdex.

Jain, Harish C., Frank Horwitz and Christa L. Wilkin. 2011. "Employment Equity in Canada and South Africa: A Comparative Review." *International Journal of Human Resource Management* 23, no. 1: 1–17.

Jain, Harish C., Peter Sloane and Frank Horwitz. 2003. *Employment Equity and Affirmative Action: An International Comparison.* Armonk, New York: M. E. Sharpe.

Jain, Sumeet. 2006. "Affirmative Action: An Evolving Remedy." In *Transformation Audit,* 44–54. Cape Town: Institute for Justice and Reconciliation.

Jamaludin, Faridah. 2003. "Malaysia's New Economic Policy: Has it been a Success?" In *Boundaries of Clan and Color: Transnational Comparisons of Inter-Group Disparity,* edited by William Darity and Ashwin Deshpande, 152–174. London and New York: Routledge.

Jansen, Jonathan. 2010. "Moving on up? The Politics, Problems, and Prospects of Universities as Gateways for Social Mobility in South Africa." In *The Next Twenty-five Years: Affirmative Action in Higher Education in the United States and South Africa,* edited by David Featherman, Martin Hall Martin and Marvin Krislov, 129–136. Ann Arbor, MI: University of Michigan Press.

Jeffery, Anthea. 2014. *BEE: Helping or Hurting?* Cape Town: Tafelberg.

Jenkins, Laura Dudley and Michele E. Moses, eds. 2014. *Affirmative Action Matters: Creating Opportunities for Students Around the World.* London and New York: Routledge.

Jesudason, James V. 1989. *Ethnicity and the Economy.* Singapore: Oxford University Press.

Jobstreet. 2005. "Survey of Managers on Reasons Why They Do Not Hire Some Fresh Graduates." Press statement, 9 May 2005. http://pesona.mmu.edu.my/~ytbau/tes3211/job_survey_2005.pdf (accessed 20 July 2009).

Jomo K.S. 2004. *The New Economic Policy and Interethnic Relations in Malaysia.* Identities, Conflict and Cohesion Programme Paper No. 7, UNRISD, Geneva.

Jomo K.S., ed. 2007. *Industrial Policy in Malaysia.* Singapore: Singapore University Press.

JSE. 2011. "JSE Releases Second Study on Black Ownership on the Exchange." JSE press release, 5 October.

JSE. 2015. "Black South Africans Hold at Least 23% of the Top 100 Companies Listed on the Johannesburg Stock Exchange." JSE press release, 20 February.

Kanyane, Modimowabarwa H., Gregory F. Houston and Kombi Sausi. 2013. "State of South African Public Service in the Context of Macro Socio-Economic Environment." *Journal of Public Administration and Governance* 3, no. 1: 126–141.

Khalid, Muhammed Abdul. 2014. *The Colour of Inequality*. Petaling Jaya: MPH.

Khalid, Muhammed Abdul. 2018. "Climbing the Ladder: Socioeconomic Mobility in Malaysia." *Asian Economic Papers* 17, no. 3: 1–23.

Khanyile, Nomsa and Rudo Maponga. 2007. *Rolling Stones: Job Hopping among Black Professionals*. Johannesburg: TNS Research Surveys.

Khazanah Research Institute. 2018. *The School-to-Work Transition of Young Malaysians*. Kuala Lumpur: Khazanah Research Institute.

Khoo, Boo Teik. 2005. *Ethnic Structure, Inequality and Governance in the Public Sector: Malaysian Experiences*. Democracy, Governance and Human Rights Programme Paper 20. Geneva: UNRISD.

Kistner, Ulrike. 2011. "Under New Management; the Ambiguities of 'Transformation' in Higher Education." *Transformation: Critical Perspectives on Southern Africa* 77: 136–151.

Kraak, Andre. 2003. "HRD and the Skills Crisis." In *Human Resources Development Review 2003*, edited by Andre Kraak and Helene Perold, 661–687. Cape Town: HSRC Press.

Kraak, Andre. 2008. "The Education-Economy Relationship in South Africa, 2001–2005." In *Human Resources Development Review 2008*, edited by Andre Kraak and Karen Press, 1–25. Cape Town: HSRC Press.

Lee, Hock Guan. 2005. "Affirmative Action in Malaysia." *Southeast Asian Affairs* 2005, 211–228.

Lee, Hwok-Aun. 2007. "Industrial Policy and Inter-ethnic Income Distribution in Malaysia: Industrial Development and Equity Ownership, 1975–97." In *Industrial Policy in Malaysia*, edited by Jomo K. S., 216–244. Singapore: Singapore University Press.

Lee, Hwok-Aun. 2010. "Racial Inequality and Affirmative Action in Malaysia and South Africa." PhD diss., University of Massachusetts, Amherst.

Lee, Hwok-Aun. 2012. "Affirmative Action in Malaysia: Education and Employment Outcomes since the 1990s." *Journal of Contemporary Asia* 42, no. 2: 230–254.

Lee, Hwok-Aun. 2014a. "Affirmative Action: Hefty Measures, Mixed Outcomes, Muddled Thinking." In *Routledge Handbook on Contemporary Malaysia*, edited by Meredith L. Weiss, 162–176. New York: Routledge.

Lee, Hwok-Aun. 2014b. "Affirmative Action in Malaysia: Solid Grounds, Long Arms, Shallow Roots." In *Affirmative Action: A View from the Global South*, edited by Ockert Dupper and Kamala Sankaran, 137–167. Stellenbosch: SUN Press.

Lee, Hwok-Aun. 2015. "Affirmative Action in Malaysia and South Africa: Contrasting Structures, Continuing Pursuits." *Journal of Asian and African Studies* 50, no. 5: 615–634.

Lee, Hwok-Aun. 2016. "Affirmative Action Regime Formation in Malaysia and South Africa." *Journal of Asian and African Studies* 51, no. 5: 511–527.

Lee, Hwok-Aun. 2017a. "Malaysia's Bumiputera Preferential Regime and Transformation Agenda: Modified Programmes, Unchanged System." *Trends in Southeast Asia 2017 No. 22*. Singapore: ISEAS.

Lee, Hwok-Aun. 2017b. "Surveys Reveal Fault Lines – And Common Ground – in Malaysia's Ethnic Relations and Policies." *ISEAS Perspective 2017 No. 63.* Singapore: ISEAS.

Lee, Hwok-Aun. 2018. "New Regimes, Old Policies and a Bumiputera Reboot." *The New Mandala*, 16 September.

Lee, Hwok-Aun. 2019. "Quality, Equity, Autonomy: Malaysia's Education Reforms Examined." *Trends in Southeast Asia 2019 No. 13.* Singapore: ISEAS.

Lee, Hwok-Aun and Muhammed Abdul Khalid. 2016. "Discrimination of High Degrees: Race and Graduate Hiring in Malaysia." *Journal of the Asia Pacific Economy* 21, no. 1: 53–76.

Lee, Hwok-Aun and Muhammed Abdul Khalid. 2020. "Is Inequality Really Declining in Malaysia?" *Journal of Contemporary Asia* 50, no. 1: 14–35.

Lee, Hwok-Aun and Lumkile Mondi. 2018. "Affirmative Action and Corporate Development in Malaysia and South Africa." In *Handbook of the International Political Economy of the Corporation*, edited by Christian May and Andreas Nölke, 229–243. Cheltenham and Northampton: Edward Elgar.

Lee, Kiong Hock. 1994. "Human Resources and Skill Development." In *Malaysian Development Experience: Changes and Challenges*, 819–852. Kuala Lumpur: INTAN.

Lee, Molly N. N. 2004a. "Malaysian Universities: Toward Equality, Accessibility, and Quality." In *Asian Universities: Historical Perspectives and Contemporary Challenges*, edited by Philip G Altbach and Tōru Umakoshi, 221–248. Baltimore: Johns Hopkins University Press.

Lee, Molly N. N. 2004b. "Global Trends, National Policies and Institutional Responses: Restructuring Higher Education in Malaysia." *Educational Research for Policy and Practice* 3: 31–46.

Leepile, Kelebogile. 2018. *Life in South Africa: Reasons for Hope.* Johannesburg: SAIRR.

Leete, Richard. 2007. *From Kampung to Twin Towers: 50 Years of Economic and Social Development.* Petaling Jaya: Oxford Fajar.

Leibbrandt, Murray, James Levinsohn and Justin McCrary. 2005. *Incomes in South Africa Since the Fall of Apartheid.* NBER Working Paper 11384.

Leite, Phillipe G., Terry McKinley and Rafael Guerreiro Osorio. 2006. *The Post-Apartheid Evolution of Earnings Inequality in South Africa, 1995–2004.* UNDP International Poverty Centre, Working Paper No. 32.

Lim, Guan Eng. 2019. *The 2020 Budget Speech.* Putrajaya: Ministry of Finance.

Lim, Hong Hai. 2013. "Public Service and Ethnic Restructuring under the New Economic Policy." In *The New Economic Policy in Malaysia: Affirmative Action, Ethnic Inequalities and Social Justice*, edited by Edmund Terence Gomez and Johan Saravanamuttu, 175–203. Singapore and Petaling Jaya: NUS Press, ISEAS and SIRD.

Loo, Seng Piew. 2007. "Schooling in Malaysia." In *Going to School in East Asia*, edited by Gerald A. Postigliane and Jason Tan, 201–232. Westport, CT: Greenwood.

Loury, Glenn. 2002. *The Anatomy of Racial Inequality.* Cambridge: Harvard University Press.

Lucas, Robert E. B. and Donald Verry. 1999. *Restructuring the Malaysian Economy: Development and Human Resources.* London: Macmillan.

MacDonald, Michael. 2006. *Why Race Matters in South Africa.* Cambridge: Harvard University Press.

Macroeconomic Research Group (MERG). 1993. *Making Democracy Work: A Framework for Macroeconomic Policy in South Africa.* Bellville: Centre for Development Studies.

Maharaj, Mac and Sidwell Medupi. 2015. "President Zuma Stands by Assertion that Black Ownership Stands at Three Percent." The Presidency press release, 1 March.

Malaysia. 1971. *The Second Malaysia Plan, 1971–75.* Kuala Lumpur: Government of Malaysia.

Malaysia. 1973. *Mid-Term Review of the Second Malaysia Plan, 1971–75.* Kuala Lumpur: Government of Malaysia.

Malaysia. 1976. *The Third Malaysia Plan, 1976–80.* Kuala Lumpur: Government of Malaysia.

Malaysia. 1981. *The Fourth Malaysia Plan, 1981–85.* Kuala Lumpur: Government of Malaysia.

Malaysia. 1986. *The Fifth Malaysia Plan, 1986–90.* Kuala Lumpur: Government of Malaysia.

Malaysia. 1991. *The Sixth Malaysia Plan, 1991–1995.* Kuala Lumpur: Government of Malaysia.

Malaysia. 1996. *The Seventh Malaysia Plan, 1996–2000.* Kuala Lumpur: Government of Malaysia.

Malaysia. 2001. *The Eighth Malaysia Plan, 2001–2005.* Kuala Lumpur: Government of Malaysia.

Malaysia. 2003. *Mid-Term Review of the Eighth Malaysia Plan, 2001–2005.* Kuala Lumpur: Government of Malaysia.

Malaysia. 2006a. *The Ninth Malaysia Plan, 2006–2010.* Kuala Lumpur: Government of Malaysia.

Malaysia. 2006b. *Universiti Teknologi MARA Act 1976.* Kuala Lumpur: Commissioner of Law Revision, Malaysia.

Malaysia. 2010a. *Federal Constitution.* Kuala Lumpur: Commissioner of Law Revision, Malaysia.

Malaysia. 2010b. *The Tenth Malaysia Plan, 2011–2015.* Kuala Lumpur: Government of Malaysia.

Malaysia. 2013. *Punca Kuasa, Prinsip dan Dasar Perolehan Kerajaan* (Public Procurement Authorization, Principles and Policies). Putrajaya: Government of Malaysia.

Malaysia. 2015. *The Eleventh Malaysia Plan, 2016–2020.* Kuala Lumpur: Government of Malaysia.

Malaysia. 2018. *Mid-Term Review of the Eleventh Malaysia Plan.* Kuala Lumpur: Government of Malaysia.

Malaysia. Various Years. *Personnel List of Government Ministries and Departments in the Federal Budget Estimate.* Kuala Lumpur: Government of Malaysia.

Malaysian Chinese Association (MCA). 2006. "Malaysian Civil Service: A Call for Diversity Towards National Unity." *The Guardian*, October, 3–5.

Mandaza, Ibbo. 1996. "The National Question and Affirmative Action in Africa: Some Reflections in Relation to South Africa." In *Affirmative Action and Transformation in South Africa*, edited by Blade Nzimande and Mpumelelo Sikhosana, 25–40. Durban: Indicator Press.

Manning, Claudia and Nokuzola Jennes. 2014. "Origins, Trends and Debates in Black Economic Empowerment." In *Oxford Companion to the Economics of South*

Africa, edited by Haroon Bhorat, Alan Hirsch, Ravi Kanbur and Mthuli Ncube, 313–321. Oxford: Oxford University Press.

Maphai, Vincent. 1989. "Affirmative Action in South Africa – A Genuine Option?" *Social Dynamics* 15, no. 2: 1–24.

MARA. 2014. *Annual Report 2014*. Kuala Lumpur: Majlis Amanah Rakyat (MARA).

MARA. 2015. *Annual Report 2015*. Kuala Lumpur: Majlis Amanah Rakyat (MARA).

Marais, Hein. 2001. *South Africa Limits to Change: The Political Economy of Transition*. London and New York: Zed Books.

Marais, Hein. 2011. *South Africa Pushed to the Limit: The Political Economy of Change*. London and New York: Zed Books.

Maré, Gerhard. 2011. " 'Broken Down by Race . . .': Questioning Social Categories in Redress Policies." *Transformation: Critical Perspectives on Southern Africa* 77: 52–69.

Matambo, Emmanuel and Ndubuisi Christian Ani. 2015. "Endorsing Intellectual Development in South Africa's Affirmative Action." *Journal of Third World Studies* 32, no. 1 (Spring): 273–291.

Mat Zin, Ragayah. 2008. "Income Inequality in Malaysia." *Asian Economic Policy Review* 3, no. 1: 114–132.

Mazibuko, Gezani Phineas. 2018. "Analysis of the Administration of Procurement Practices in the South African Public Sector." PhD thesis, University of Pretoria.

Maznah, Mohamad. 2012. "Ethnicity and Inequality in Malaysia: A Retrospect and a Rethinking." In *Affirmative Action in Plural Societies: International Comparisons*, edited by Graham K. Brown, Frances Stewart and Arnim Langer, 151–181. Basingstoke: Palgrave Macmillan.

McCrudden, Christopher and Stuart G. Gross. 2006. "WTO Government Procurement Rules and the Local Dynamics of Procurement Policies: A Malaysian Case Study." *The European Journal of International Law* 17, no. 1: 151–185.

Meerman, Jacob. 2008. "The Malaysian Success Story, the Public Sector, and Interethnic Inequality." In *Globalization and National Autonomy: The Experience of Malaysia*, edited by Joan M. Nelson, Jacob Meerman and Abdul Rahman Embong, pp. 76–115. Singapore: ISEAS.

Mehmet, Ozay and Yip Yat Hoong. 1985. "An Empirical Evaluation of Government Scholarship Policy in Malaysia." *Higher Education* 14 (2): 197–210.

Menon, Jayant and Thiam Hee Ng. 2013. *Are Government-Linked Corporations Crowding out Private Investment in Malaysia?* ADB Economics Working Paper Series No. 345, April.

Merdeka Center. 2010. *A Summary of the 2010 Political Values Survey Findings*. Bangi: Merdeka Center for Opinion Research.

Merdeka Center. 2015. *National Unity Survey*. Bangi: Merdeka Center for Opinion Research.

Michie, Jonathan and Vishnu Padayachee. 1998. "Three Years After Apartheid: Growth, Employment and Distribution?" *Cambridge Journal of Economics* 22: 623–635.

Milanovic, Branko. 2006. "Inequality and Determinants of Earnings in Malaysia, 1984–97." *Asian Economic Journal* 20, no. 2: 191–216.

Mincer, Jacob. 1958. "Investment in Human Capital and Personal Income Distribution." *The Journal of Political Economy* 66, no. 4: 281–302.

Mincer, Jacob. 1970. "The Distribution of Labor Incomes: A Survey." *Journal of Economic Literature* 8, no. 1: 1–26.

Ministry in the Office of the President. 1994. *White Paper on Reconstruction and Development*. Notice 1954 of 1994, Parliament of the Republic of South Africa, Cape Town, 15 November.

Ministry of Economic Affairs. 2019. *Shared Prosperity Vision 2030*. Putrajaya: Ministry of Economic Affairs.

Ministry of Education. 2001. *National Plan for Higher Education*. Pretoria: Ministry of Education.

Ministry of Education. 2013. *Malaysia Education Blueprint, 2013–2025 (Preschool to Post-secondary Education)*. Putrajaya: Ministry of Education.

Ministry of Education. 2019. *Higher Education Statistics, Chapter 7 – Graduate Tracer Study*. Putrajaya: Ministry of Education.

Mkongi, Bongani. 2013. "The Meaning of a Cadre." *Umrabulo* No. 38, 1st Quarter. www.anc.org.za/docs/umrabulo/2013/umrabulo38.pdf (accessed 7 August 2014).

Modisha, Geoffrey. 2008. "Affirmative Action and Cosmopolitan Citizenship in South Africa." In *Racial Redress and Citizenship in South Africa*, edited by Adam Habib and Christina Bentley, 153–178. Cape Town: HSRC Press.

Mohamed, Grace and Simon Roberts. 2008. "Weak Links in the BEE Chain? Procurement, Skills and Employment Equity in the Metals and Engineering Industries." *Journal of Contemporary Africa* 26, no. 1: 27–50.

Moleke, Percy. 2005. *Finding Work: Employment Experiences of South African Graduates*. Cape Town: HSRC Press.

Mondi, Lumkile. 2017. *Black Business and the State in South Africa*. Paper presented at the Biennial Conference of the Economic Society of South Africa, Grahamstown, 31 August.

Morrow, Sean. 2008. "Race, Redress and Historically Black Universities." In *Racial Redress and Citizenship in South Africa*, edited by Adam Habib and Christina Bentley, 263–288. Cape Town: HSRC Press.

Motala, Shireen, Veerle Dieltens, Nazir Carrim, Paul Kgobe, George Moyo and Symphorosa Rembe. 2007. *Educational Access in South Africa: Country Analytic Review*. CREATE, University of Sussex and Education Policy Unit, University of the Witwatersrand.

Muhamad Salleh, Ismail and Saha Dhevan Meyanathan. 1993. *The Lesson of East Asia – Malaysia: Growth, Equity and Structural Transformation*. Washington, DC: World Bank.

Mukherjee, Hena, Jasbir S. Singh, Rozilini M. Fernandez-Chung and T. Marimuthu. 2017. "Access and Equity Issues in Malaysian Higher Education." In *Policy Discourses in Malaysian Education: A Nation in the Making*, edited by Suseela Malakolunthu and Nagappan C. Rengasamy, 45–70. London: Routledge.

Nagaraj, Shyamala, Kiong-Hock Lee, Nai-Peng Tey, Chiu-Wan Ng and Jean Pala. 2009. "Counting Ethnicity in Malaysia: The Complexity of Measuring Diversity." *Malaysian Journal of Economic Studies* 46, no. 1: 5–32.

Naidoo, Vinothan. 2008. "Assessing Racial Redress in the Public Service." In *Racial Redress and Citizenship in South Africa*, edited by Adam Habib and Christina Bentley, 99–128. Cape Town: HSRC Press.

National Commission on Higher Education. 1996. "An Overview of a New Policy Framework for Higher Education Transformation." 22 August.

National Economic Advisory Council (NEAC). 2010. *New Economic Model – Part 1*. Putrajaya: NEAC.

National Planning Commission. 2012. *National Development Plan 2030: Our Future – Make it Work*. Pretoria: National Planning Commission.

National SME Development Council (NSDC). 2012. *Summary SME Master Plan 2012–2020: Catalysing Growth and Income*. Kuala Lumpur: National SME Development Council.

National Treasury. 2011. *Implementation Guide: Preferential Procurement Regulations, 2011, Pertaining to the Preferential Procurement Policy Framework Act, 2000*. Pretoria: National Treasury.

National Treasury. 2017. *Preferential Procurement Policy Framework Act, 2000: Preferential Procurement Regulations, 2017*. Cape Town: Government Gazette.

Ndletyana, Mcebisi. 2015. "African National Congress: From an Emancipatory to a Rent-Seeking Instrument." *Transformation: Critical Perspectives on Southern Africa* 87: 95–116.

Netshitenzhe, Joel. 1996. "The National Democratic Revolution – Is It Still on Track?" *Umrabulo* No. 1, 4th Quarter. www.anc.org.za/show.php?id=2968 (accessed 8 June 2014).

Nkomo, Stella. 2011. "Moving from the Letter of the Law to the Spirit of the Law: The Challenges of Realising the Intent of Employment Equity and Affirmative Action." *Transformation: Critical Perspectives on Southern Africa* 77: 122–135.

Nussbaum, Martha and Zoya Hasan, eds. 2012. *Equalizing Access: Affirmative Action in Higher Education in India, United States, and South Africa*. New Delhi: Oxford University Press.

Nzimande, Blade. 1996. " 'Black Advancement', White Resistance and the Politics of Upward Mobility in South Africa's Industrial Corporations." In *Affirmative Action and Transformation in South Africa*, edited by Blade Nzimande and Mpumelelo Sikhosana, 187–204. Durban: Indicator Press.

Nzimande, Blade and Mpumelelo Sikhosana, eds. 1996. *Affirmative Action and Transformation in South Africa*. Durban: Indicator Press.

Nzukuma, Khanyile C. C. and Mark Bussin. 2011. "Job-hopping amongst African Black senior management in South Africa." *SA Journal of Human Resource Management* 9, no. 1: 1–12.

Ooi, Kee Beng. 2013. "The New Economic Policy and the Centralisation of Power." In *The New Economic Policy in Malaysia: Affirmative Action, Ethnic Inequalities and Social Justice*, edited by Edmund Terence Gomez and Johan Saravanamuttu, 317–334. Singapore and Petaling Jaya: NUS Press, ISEAS and SIRD.

Oosthuizen, Rudolf M. and Vasantha Naidoo. 2010. "Attitudes Towards and Experience of Employment Equity." *South African Journal of Industrial Psychology* 36, no. 1: 1–9.

Othman, Haliza, Zulkifli Mohd Nopiah, Izamarlina Asshaari, Noorhelyna Razali, Mohd Haniff Osman and Norhana Ramli. 2009. "A Comparative Study of Engineering Students on their Pre-university Results with their First-Year Performance at FKAB, UKM." Paper presented at the 2009 Teaching and Learning Congress, National University of Malaysia, Bangi.

PARI. 2017. *Betrayal of the Promise: How South Africa is Being Stolen*. State Capacity Research Project report, May. Park Town: Public Affairs Research Institute (PARI).

Patel, Leila and Lauren Graham. 2012. "How Broad-based is Broad-based Black Economic Empowerment?" *Development Southern Africa* 29, no. 2: 193–207.

PCG. 2015. *GLC Transformation Graduation Report*. Putrajaya: Putrajaya Committee on GLC High Performance.

Pemandu. 2010. *Government Transformation Programme: The Roadmap.* Putrajaya: Performance Management and Delivery Unit (Pemandu).

Pemandu. 2011–2015. *Economic Transformation Programme Annual Report.* Putrajaya: Pemandu.

Pike, Angela, Juliet Puchert and Willie T. Chinyamurindi. 2018. "Analysing the Future of Broad-Based Black Economic Empowerment through the Lens of Small and Medium Enterprises." *Acta Commercii* 18, no. 1: a566.

Pollin, Robert, Gerald Epstein, James Heintz and Leonce Ndikumana. 2006. *Employment-Targeted Macroeconomic Program for South Africa.* Amherst, MA: Political Economy Research Institute.

Pong, Suet-ling. 1993. "Preferential Policies and Secondary School Attainment in Peninsular Malaysia." *Sociology of Education* 66, no. 4: 245–261.

Ponte, Stefano, Simon Roberts and Lance van Sittert. 2007. "Black Economic Empowerment', Business and the State in South Africa." *Development and Change* 38, no. 5: 933–955.

PRC-SOE. 2013. *Growing the Economy – Bridging the Gap: Final Report.* Pretoria: Presidential Review Committee on State-Owned Entities.

Price, Max. 2014. "Why UCT is Modifying its Undergraduate Admissions Policy." *Politicsweb,* 23 May.

Pricewaterhouse Coopers (PwC). 2015. *Economic Impact of the Trans-Pacific Partnership Agreement.* Kuala Lumpur: Pricewaterhouse Coopers.

Pricewaterhouse Coopers (PwC). 2019. *Executive Directors Practices and Remuneration Trends Report.* Johannesburg: Pricewaterhouse Coopers.

Puthucheary, James. 1960. *Ownership and Control in the Malayan Economy.* Singapore: Eastern Universities Press.

Quah, Chun Ho *et al.* 2009. "Employers' Preference for Foreign-Trained Graduates – Myth of Reality?" *European Journal of Scientific Research* 34, no. 3: 372–383.

Randall, Duncan James. 1996. "Prospects for the Development of a Black Business Class in South Africa." *The Journal of Modern African Studies* 34, no. 4: 661–686.

Rasiah, Rajah and Ishak Shari. 2001. "Market, Government and Malaysia's New Economic Policy." *Cambridge Journal of Economics* 25: 57–78.

REFSA. 2011. "Open Tender Policy in Penang – Nurturing Capable Malay Contractors." Focus Paper 2011/11/29. Kuala Lumpur: Research for Social Advancement (REFSA).

Ritchie, Bryan K. 2005. "Coalitional Politics, Economic Reform, and Technological Upgrading in Malaysia." *World Development* 33, no. 5: 745–761.

Roberts, Benjamin. 2006. "The Happy Transition? Attitudes to Poverty and Inequality After a Decade of Democracy." In *South African Social Attitudes: Changing Times, Diverse Voices,* edited by Udesh Pillay, Benjamin Roberts, and Stephen Rule, 101–130. Cape Town: HSRC Press.

Roberts, Benjamin, Gina Weir-Smith and Vasu Reddy. 2011. "Minding the Gap: Attitudes Towards Affirmative Action in South Africa." *Transformation: Critical Perspectives on Southern Africa* 77: 1–30.

Rogan, Michael and John Reynolds. 2016. "Schooling Inequality, Higher Education and the Labour Market: Evidence from a Graduate Tracer Study in the Eastern Cape, South Africa." *Development Southern Africa* 33, no. 3: 343–360.

Rogerson, Christian. 2012. "Supplier Diversity: A New Phenomenon in Private Sector Procurement in South Africa." *Urban Forum* 23: 279–297.

Rospabé, Sandrine. 2002. "How Did Labour Market Racial Discrimination Evolve After The End Of Apartheid?" *The South African Journal of Economics* 70, no. 1: 185–217.

Ruggunan, Shaun and Gerhard Maré. 2012. "Race Classification at the University of KwaZulu-Natal: Purposes, Sites and Practices." *Transformation: Critical Perspectives on Southern Africa* 79: 47–68.

Russayani, I., Haim, H.A., Yusnidah, I., Lim, H.E., Nor Azam, A.R., Roslan, A.H., *et al.* 2013. "A Review, Investigation and Recommendations Towards the Transformation of Higher Education Funding." Unpublished manuscript. Sintok: Universiti Utara Malaysia.

Sabbagh Daniel. 2004. *Affirmative Action Policies: An International Perspective.* Human Development Report Office Occasional Paper 2004/12. Geneva: UNDP.

Sabbagh, Daniel. 2012. "Affirmative Action." In *The Oxford Handbook of Comparative Constitutional Law,* edited by Michel Rosenfeld and András Sajó, 1124–1141. Oxford: Oxford University Press.

Sachs, Albie. 2007. "The Constitutional Principles Underpinning Black Economic Empowerment." In *Visions of Black Economic Empowerment,* edited by Xolela Mangcu, 9–17. Auckland Park: Jacana.

SAIRR. 2007. "Drivers of and Obstacles to the Growth of the Black Middle Class." *Fast Facts, September 2007.* Johannesburg: South Africa Institute of Race Relations (SAIRR).

SAIRR. 2017. *Reasons for Hope 2017: Sound but Fraying at the Edges.* Johannesburg: SAIRR.

SAIRR. 2018. *Reasons for Hope 2018: Holding the Line.* Johannesburg: SAIRR.

SAIRR. 2019. *Reasons for Hope 2019: Unite the Middle.* Johannesburg: SAIRR.

Salih, Kamal and Zainal Aznam Yusof. 1989. "Overview of the NEP and Framework for a Post-1990 Economic Policy." *Malaysian Management Review* 24: 13–61.

Sanchez, Diana. 2008. "Transformation in Small, Medium and Micro Enterprises." In *Racial Redress and Citizenship in South Africa,* edited by Adam Habib and Christina Bentley, 209–229. Cape Town: HSRC Press.

Santhiram, R. and Tan Yao Sua. 2017. "Education of Ethnic Minorities: Contesting Issues in a Multiethnic Society." In *Policy Discourses in Malaysian Education: A Nation in the Making,* edited by Suseela Malakolunthu and Nagappan Rengasamy, 29–44. London and New York: Routledge.

Sartorius, Kurt and Gerhard Botha. 2008. "Black Economic Empowerment Ownership Initiatives: A Johannesburg Stock Exchange Perspective." *Development Southern Africa* 25, no. 4: 437–453.

Sato, Machi. 2005. "Education, Ethnicity and Economics: Higher Education Reforms in Malaysia, 1957–2003." *Nagoya University of Commerce and Business Journal of Language Culture and Communication* 7, no. 1: 73–88.

Schreuder, Adré, Pieter van Heerden and Mzwandile Khanya. 2007. *The Progress of Broad-based Black Economic Empowerment in South Africa – Executive Report.* Consulta Research, University of Pretoria.

Scott, Ian. 2010. "Who is 'Getting Through' in South Africa? Graduate Output and the Reconstruction of the Formal Curriculum." In *The Next Twenty-five Years: Affirmative Action in Higher Education in the United States and South Africa,* edited by David Featherman, Martin Hall Martin and Marvin Krislov, 229–243. Ann Arbor, MI: University of Michigan Press.

Securities Commission. 2017. *Bumiputera Equity Requirements for Public Listed Companies. Securities Commission Malaysia.* Kuala Lumpur: Securities Commission.

Seekings, Jeremy. 2008. "The Continuing Salience of Race: Discrimination and Diversity in South Africa." *Journal of Contemporary African Studies* 26, no. 1: 1–25.

Seekings, Jeremy and Nicoli Nattrass. 2005. *Class, Race, and Inequality in South Africa.* New Haven and London: Yale University Press.

Selvaratnam, Viswanathan. 1988. "Ethnicity, Inequality and Higher Education in Malaysia." *Comparative Education Review* 32, no. 2: 173–196.

Senekal, J. and M. Munro. 2019. "Lessons Learnt from Two Decades of Graduate Tracer Research: Recommendations for the South African Context." *South African Journal of Higher Education* 33, no. 2: 230–248.

Shai, Lerato, Comfort Molefinyana and Geo Quinot. 2019. "Public Procurement in the Context of Broad-Based Black Economic Empowerment (BBBEE) in South Africa – Lessons Learned for Sustainable Public Procurement." *Sustainability* 11: 7164.

Shari, Ishak. 2000. "Economic Growth and Income Inequality in Malaysia, 1971–95." *Journal of the Asia-Pacific Economy* 5, no. 1/2: 112–124.

Singh, Ratnamala. 1996. "The Uses and Abuses of Affirmative Action in South Africa." In *Affirmative Action and Transformation in South Africa,* edited by Blade Nzimande and Mpumelelo Sikhosana, 41–64. Durban: Indicator Press.

Sloane, Patricia Sloane. 1999. *Islam, Modernity and Entrepreneurship among the Malays.* London: Macmillan.

SME Corp. 2018. *SME Annual Report 2017/18.* Putrajaya: SME Corp.

Soudien, Crain. 2010. "Race and Class in the South African Higher Education Sector: A Focus on the Undergraduate Experience." In *The Next Twenty-five Years: Affirmative Action in Higher Education in the United States and South Africa,* edited by David Featherman, Martin Hall Martin, and Marvin Krislov, 187–195. Ann Arbor, MI: University of Michigan Press.

South Africa. 1996. *Constitution of the Republic of South Africa, Act 108 of 1996.* Pretoria: Government Printer.

South Africa. 1998a. *Employment Equity Act, Act 55 of 1998.* Cape Town: Government Gazette.

South Africa. 1998b. *Skills Development Act, Act 97 of 1998.* Cape Town: Government Gazette.

South Africa. 2000. *Preferential Public Procurement Framework Act, Act 5 of 2000.* Cape Town: Government Gazette.

South Africa. 2001. *Industrial Development Amendment Act, Act 49 of 2001.* Cape Town: Government Gazette.

South Africa. 2003. *Broad-based Black Economic Empowerment Act, Act 53 of 2003.* Cape Town: Government Gazette.

South Africa. 2010. *The New Growth Path: The Framework.* Pretoria: Economic Development Department.

South Africa. 2013a. *Employment Equity Amendment Act, Act 47 of 2013.* Cape Town: Government Gazette.

South Africa. 2013b. *Broad-based Black Economic Empowerment Amendment Act, Act 46 of 2013.* Cape Town: Government Gazette.

South Africa. 2018. *Employment Equity Amendment Bill.* Pretoria: Government Gazette.

Southall, Roger. 1997. "Party Dominance and Development: South Africa's Prospects in the Light of Malaysia's Experience." *Journal of Commonwealth and Comparative Politics* 35, no. 2: 1–27.

Southall, Roger. 2004. "The ANC and Black Capitalism in South Africa." *Review of African Political Economy* 100: 313–328.

Southall, Roger. 2005. "Black Empowerment and Corporate Capital." In *The State of the Nation: South Africa 2004–2005*, edited by John Daniel, Roger Southall and Jessica Lutchman, 455–478. Cape Town: HSRC Press.

Southall Roger. 2007. "Does South Africa have a Racial Bargain? A Comparative Perspective." *Transformation: Critical Perspectives on Southern Africa* 64: 66–90.

Southall, Roger. 2016. *The New Black Middle Class in South Africa*. Johannesburg: Jacana.

Sowell, Thomas. 2004. *Affirmative Action Around the World: An Empirical Study*. New Haven and London: Yale University Press.

Sparks, Alister. 2003. *Beyond the Miracle: Inside the New South Africa*. Chicago: University of Chicago Press.

Standing, Guy, John Sender and John Weeks. 1996. *Restructuring the Labour Market: The South African Challenge*. Geneva: ILO.

Subotzky, George. 2003. "Public Higher Education." In *Human Resources Development Review 2003*, edited by Andre Kraak and Helene Perold, 362–379. Cape Town: HSRC Press.

Tan, Jeff, 2008. *Privatization in Malaysia: Regulation, Rent-seeking and Policy Failure*. London and New York: Routledge.

Tan, Yao Sua and R. Santhiram. 2017. "Race-based Policies and Practices in Malaysia's Education System." In *Education in Malaysia: Developments and Challenges*, edited by Moses Samuel, Meng Yew Tee and Lorraine Symaco, 17–32. Singapore: Springer.

Teraju. 2012. *Hala Tuju Transformasi Ekonomi Bumiputera* (Bumiputera Economic Transformation Roadmap). Petaling Jaya: Teraju.

Teraju. 2017. *Bumiputera Economic Transformation Roadmap 2.0*. Petaling Jaya: Teraju.

Terreblanche, Sampie. 2002. *A History of Inequality in South Africa, 1652–2002*. Scottsville: University of Natal Press.

Thillainathan, R. 1976. "An Analysis of the Effects of Policies for the Redistribution of Income and Wealth in West Malaysia, 1957–1975." PhD thesis, London School of Economics.

Thomas, Adèle. 2002. "Employment Equity in South Africa: Lessons from the Global School." *International Journal of Manpower* 23, no. 3: 237–255.

Thomas, Adèle and Harish Jain. 2004. "Employment Equity in Canada and South Africa: Prospects and Propositions." *International Journal of Human Resource Management* 15, no. 1: 36–55.

Tierney, William. 1997. "The Parameters of Affirmative Action: Equity and Excellence in the Academy." *Review of Educational Research* 67, no. 2: 165–196.

Tierney, William. 2007. "Merit and Affirmative Action in Education: Promulgating a Democratic Public Culture." *Urban Education* 42: 385–402.

Torii, Takashi. 2003. "The Mechanism for State-Led Creation of Malaysia's Middle Classes." *The Developing Economies* 41, no. 2: 221–242.

Van der Berg, Servaas and Megan Louw. 2004. "Changing Patterns of South African Income Distribution: Towards Time Series Estimates of Distribution and Poverty." *The South African Journal of Economics* 72, no. 3: 546–572.

Van der Westhuizen, Janis. 2002. *Adapting to Globalization: Malaysia, South Africa and the Challenges of Ethnic Redistribution with Growth.* Westport, CT: Praeger.

Van Zyl, Elize. 2008. "Financial Services Professions." In *Human Resources Development Review 2008*, edited by Andre Kraak and Karen Press, 365–387. Cape Town: HSRC Press.

Wan, Chang Da. 2007. "Public and Private Higher Education Institutions in Malaysia: Competing, Complementary or Crossbreeds as Education Providers." *Kajian Malaysia* 25, no. 1: 1–14.

Wan, Chang-Da. 2010. *Public Scholarships in Malaysia: What are the Missing Points?* Kuala Lumpur: Centre for Public Policy Studies.

Wan, Chang Da and Roland K. Cheo. 2012. "Determinants of Malaysian and Singaporean Economics Undergraduates' Academic Performance." *International Review of Economic Education* 11, no. 2: 7–27.

Wan, Chang Da, Morshidi Sirat and Dzulkifli Abdul Razak, eds. 2018. *Higher Education in Malaysia: A Critical Review of the Past and Present for the Future.* Penang: USM Press.

Warikoo, Natasha and Utaukwa Allen. 2019. "A Solution to Multiple Problems: The Origins of Affirmative Action in Higher Education Around the World." *Studies in Higher Education*, 1–15 (published online 10 May).

Weber, Everard. 2002. "Shifting to the Right: The Evolution of Equity in the South African Government's Developmental and Education Policies, 1990–99." *Comparative Education Review* 46, no. 3: 261–290.

Weeks, John. 1999. "Stuck in Low GEAR? Macroeconomic Policy in South Africa, 1996–98." *Cambridge Journal of Economics* 23: 795–811.

Weisskopf, Thomas E. 2004. *Affirmative Action in the United States and India: A Comparative Perspective.* London: Routledge.

Weisskopf, Thomas E. 2006. "Is Positive Discrimination a Good Way to Aid Disadvantaged Ethnic Communities?" *Economic and Political Weekly* 41, no. 8: 717–726.

Whiteford, Andrew and Dirk Van Seventer. 2000. "Understanding Contemporary Household Inequality in South Africa." *Studies in Economics and Econometrics* 24, no. 3: 7–30.

Woo, Kuan Heong. 2015. "Recruitment Practices in the Malaysian Public Sector: Innovations or Political Responses?" *Journal of Public Affairs Education* 21, no. 2: 229–246.

Woo, Kuan Heong. 2016. "Working for the Government: A Logit Regression Analysis." *International Journal of Humanities and Management Sciences* 4, no. 3: 259–264.

World Bank. 2005. *Malaysia: Firm Competitiveness, Investment Climate, and Growth.* Poverty Reduction, Economic Management and Financial Sector Unit (PREM), East Asia and Pacific Region. Report No. 26841-MA.

World Bank. 2009. *Malaysia: Productivity and Investment Climate Assessment Update.* Poverty Reduction, Economic Management and Financial Sector Unit (PREM), East Asia and Pacific Region. Report No. 49137-MY.

Wu, Chia-Chao, Bongani Khoza and Lungi Ngcobo. 2002. *Ownership, Acquisition and Transformation: The Correlation between BEE Ownership and Control of Companies on the JSE.* Empowerdex, November.

Yahaya, Jahara, Nai-Peng Tey and Kok-Kheng Yeoh, eds. 2004. *Ethnic Interaction and Segregation on Campus and at the Workplace.* Kuala Lumpur: Centre for Economic Development and Ethnic Relations.

Yusof, Zainal Aznam. 1994. "Growth and Equity in Malaysia." In *Malaysian Development Experience: Changes and Challenges*, 591–616. Kuala Lumpur: INTAN.

Yusof, Zainal Aznam. 2012. "Affirmative Action in Malaysia: An Overview of Progress and Limitations." In *Affirmative Action in Plural Societies: International Experiences*, edited by Graham Brown, Francis Stewart and Arnim Langer, 128–150. Basingstoke: Palgrave Macmillan.

Zoch, Asmus. 2016. "Life Chances and Class: Estimating Inequality of Opportunity for Children and Adolescents in South Africa." In *South Africa's Emergent Middle Class*, edited by Grace Khunou, 57–75. London and New York: Routledge.

Zulu, Pascal S. and Sanjana B. Parumasur. 2009. "Employee Perceptions of the Management of Cultural Diversity and Workplace Transformation." *South African Journal of Industrial Psychology* 35, no. 1: 1–9.

Index

Printed in the United States
By Bookmasters